REAL ESTATE LORE

Modern Techniques and Everyday Tips for the Practitioner

HARRIS OMINSKY

AMERICAN BAR ASSOCIATION
Defending Liberty
Pursuing Justice

REAL PROPERTY · PROBATE AND TRUST

Cover design by ABA Publishing.

The materials contained herein represent the opinions and views of the authors and/or the editors, and should not be construed to be the views or opinions of the law firms or companies with whom such persons are in partnership with, associated with, or employed by, nor of the American Bar Association or the Section of Real Property, Probate and Trust Law, unless adopted pursuant to the bylaws of the Association.

Nothing contained in this book is to be considered as the rendering of legal advice, either generally or in connection with any specific issue or case; nor do these materials purport to explain or interpret any specific bond or policy, or any provisions thereof, issued by any particular franchise company, or to render franchise or other professional advice. Readers are responsible for obtaining advice from their own lawyers or other professionals. This book and any forms and agreements herein are intended for educational and informational purposes only.

Library of Congress Cataloging-in-Publication Data

Ominsky, Harris.
    Real estate lore : modern techniques and everyday tips for the real estate
practitioner / Harris Ominsky.
        p. cm.
    Includes index.
    ISBN 1-59031-345-3
    1. Real property—United States. 2. Real estate business—Law and legislation—United
States. 3. Vendors and purchasers—United States. I. Title.

KF570.0475   2005
346.7304'3—dc22

2005032863

DEDICATION

To my father, Joseph Ominsky

This book is dedicated in loving memory to my
mentor—my father, Joseph Ominsky, the oldest
practicing lawyer in Philadelphia. My Dad, who
died at the age of 99, may have been the only one in
the world who, at his age, was fortunate enough to
have the intellectual capacity, motivation, and
sense of humor to understand and enjoy this
book—and the experience and authority to tell me
what *must* be changed.

PREFACE

"Practice is the best of all instructors."
—Pultius Syrus, Maxim 439

Most of the book has been developed from practical matters that have come to me in the practice of law. Many have been inspired by current developments in case law and legislation.

The book grew out of articles I have written and lectures I have presented over the past few years, including ABA and PBI programs. Some of the chapters are updated versions of materials from an earlier book. In selecting which of my articles to use here, I omitted those that have appeared in law reviews because they were generally technical, theoretical, and burdened with citations; and the conventional law review format clashed with the style of this book.

We have selected sometimes disparate topics, based on their practicality and currency. The book is not intended to be a textbook or exhaustive analysis of all of the law on any particular topic. In fact, a good case may be made for the proposition that lawyers do not need another comprehensive real estate text.

Each chapter stands on its own. Unlike sections of some books, one part does not depend on others for definitions, history, or background. For this reason, these essays should be easy to use as a basis for future workshops or short presentations.

These selections are intended to question perceived occasional flaws in lawyers' and courts' legal reasoning. The book raises some ironies, plays some intellectual games, pokes fun at the conventional wisdom, and may even provide a few chuckles about the light side of real estate law.

Author's Caveat

This book should be used as a guide but not definitive legal advice on specific problems. Legal conclusions may change from state to state or because of subtle factual distinctions. Also, the law constantly changes and the book doesn't—until we produce a new version.

The chapters, at times, critique legislation, cases, and regulations. They express only the views of the author—not those of his law firm or of the American Bar Association. Our views should not be considered as a substitute for analysis of a specific case or as advice of counsel on any particular matter.

Thanks

I acknowledge with thanks my many colleagues who have stimulated me with ideas and issues, and at times have completely changed my analysis on certain topics. Our firm's Friday financial-services luncheon, which is like a graduate seminar on the law, provides me with a constant source of materials. Anywhere from 20 to 35 attorneys may meet for lunch to listen to presentations of recent developments and comment on them.

Many others have contributed their considerable talents as advisors and editors, particularly Harry T. Lamb on income tax issues; Sam Becker, Harvey Forman, Leon Forman, and Joel Shapiro on bankruptcy issues; and my real estate partners, Barry Friedman, Arn Heller, Jon Hillsberg, Peter Kelsen, Bill Kerr, David Lebor, Mike Pollack, Phil Rosenfeldt, and Peter Soloff. I also owe a special debt of gratitude to my editor from the Pennsylvania Bar Institute, David Hominik, Esquire.

Last, but not least, my wife, Rosalyn, a former English teacher, a marketing communications specialist, and writer, was always there to help me, inspire me, and to push me in the right direction.

* * * * * * * *

Look over the table of contents and choose what you are most interested in. Like a bottle of wine, the contents should be sipped, not guzzled.

We hope you enjoy the book. It is dedicated to the proposition that every once in a while, the law can be fun! Not loud, frolicking fun—but the quiet fun of intellectual games. Not the exhilaration of biking and hiking—but the excitement of exploring and discovering.

Harris Ominsky

ABOUT THE AUTHOR

Harris Ominsky is associated with the law firm of Blank Rome, LLP, which has offices in Philadelphia, Media, and Allentown, Pennsylvania; New York; Cherry Hill and Trenton, New Jersey; Wilmington, Delaware; Baltimore, Maryland; Washington, DC; Boca Raton, Florida; and Cincinnati, Ohio. Mr. Ominsky has concentrated his practice on real estate law for more than 30 years and has represented clients in just about every type of real estate transaction, ranging from acquisitions and financing to leasing and zoning.

For years, he was co-chair of his firm's Real Estate Department, consisting of approximately 40 attorneys. Before joining the firm, he spent five years in general practice with his father, Joseph Ominsky, where he developed experience in other areas, including litigating cases ranging from insurance claims to murder cases.

Mr. Ominsky is a past president of the Board of Directors of the Pennsylvania Bar Association, and a past chair of the Real Estate Section of the Philadelphia Bar Association. He has been a board member of the American College of Real Estate Lawyers, a past chair of the Professional Education Committee of the Philadelphia Bar Association, and a recipient of the ALI-ABA Harrison Tweed Special Merit Award (1988), the Philadelphia Bar Association's Leon J. Obermayer Education Award (1989), and the Philadelphia Bar Association's Real Property Section's first "Good Deed Award" for excellence in the practice of law and legal education (1999).

He is a former instructor of law at Temple University Law School and teaches real estate law at Temple's Real Estate Institute. He is listed in *Who's Who in America, Who's Who in American Law*, and *Best Lawyers in America* (Woodward/White Inc.). He received his B.S. in Economics with Distinction from the Wharton School of the University of Pennsylvania and his LL.B., cum laude, from the University of Pennsylvania Law School, where he was awarded the Henry Wolfe Bikle Prize for Constitutional Law and a Skelton Harrison Foundation Grant. He was an editor of the *Law Review* and elected to the order of the Coif.

A frequent lecturer and course planner at continuing legal education programs, Mr. Ominsky has authored over 800 articles in a variety of journals, including *Dickinson Law Review, University of Pennsylvania Law Review, Temple Law Quarterly,* and *Villanova Law Quarterly.* He presently writes a regular weekly column on real estate law for the *Philadelphia Legal Intelligencer.*

SUMMARY OF CONTENTS

TABLE OF CONTENTS

Part IA
Mortgages—Doing the Loan

Part IB
Mortgages—Enforcement

Part II
Landlords and Tenants

Part III
Buying and Selling

Part IV
Real Estate Brokers

Part V
Land Use and Title Issues

Part VI
Operations and Ownership

PART IA

Mortgages—Doing the Loan

1   PITFALLS FOR REAL ESTATE LENDERS

A cynic once said that it may cost thousands of lives to train a great general. Fortunately, training a loan officer or a real estate lawyer does not cost lives, but it may cost thousands of dollars, unless the lender knows the crucial facts beforehand and stays alert during the loan process.

This chapter will discuss the practical problems that lurk out there for real estate loan officers and lawyers, and it will suggest answers to many of them. Some of these mistakes are commonplace. They are often so obvious they are not even discussed in training workshops and seminars. They occur, not necessarily because of failure to understand the complex problems of bankruptcy, marshalling, deficiency judgments, or "clogging the equity," but because of failure to do the obvious.

Describe Your Collateral

Take the lender's most basic question: What is the security for the loan? What you see is not always "what you get." Without a review of the metes and bounds description, a lender may wind up with only part of the expected property.

Sometimes proper usage of a property depends on having access to a public street through another property. Such access may be by an easement or outright ownership. In either event, it is important that the mortgage properly include the access. An as-built survey will show the location of access easements, utility easements, buildings, improvements, required set-back lines, and whether any improvements encroach on a neighboring property.

Sometimes a description involves several different lots. A survey will show whether the lots have common title lines so that they fit together as one overall parcel without any gaps in title. For example, in one recent financing transaction, an industrial plant was located on a lot separate from the parking and driveway areas.

3

These areas were owned jointly with owners other than the borrower. The first description presented to the lender did not include these other areas, but they were important to the value of the mortgaged property.

In another situation, an office project required the use of a sewerage pumping station that was located on a separate parcel. Lender's counsel, after a little probing, discovered that the proposed mortgage did not include the pumping station and was able to include it before the loan closed. If the pumping station had not been added, the office building may have been useless after foreclosure.

If more than one survey exists, they may be inconsistent. Obviously, the borrower must see that the surveyors work out these discrepancies before the loan is made.

Without a survey it is difficult to detect defects such as encroachments of buildings on adjoining properties or missing parcels. One may not even be able to discern whether the described property lines will close when they are plotted. That problem is alleviated with the use of commercially available computer programs that will plot the boundaries after input of the verbal description of courses and distances.

Title Insurance

To insure that the lender is obtaining a binding mortgage lien, a title insurance company must satisfy itself about many issues. An obvious one is whether all necessary parties have signed the mortgage. Borrowers are sometimes mistaken as to whether relatives, partners, or other corporate officers must sign a mortgage to bind the borrower and encumber the applicable property. The title company insures that the proper owner has signed, and insures many other rights and encumbrances, such as those involving restrictions, easements, and rights of way.

If the real estate is being taken merely as additional collateral for a short-term commercial loan and the lender is familiar with the borrower, it may not insist on title insurance. Unless it receives the comfort of an unqualified legal opinion, this can be a fatal error.

Restrictions

Restrictions are limitations on the property described in a recorded deed or some other document that is in the line of title.

They may even appear in a 100-year-old deed given to a predecessor of the current owner. Restrictions should not be confused with zoning or governmental building requirements. A property may be zoned industrial but contain a deed restriction limiting its use to dwelling units. Although there are ways to avoid certain deed restrictions, they are frequently enforceable despite the fact that they are more limiting than current zoning uses.

Sometimes the restrictions require what are known as "setbacks." For example, there may be a restriction against buildings within 50 feet of any street or property line.

One extreme example involved a defaulted mortgage on several acres of shorefront property in the Florida Keys. The combined required setbacks, both due to governmental coastal requirements and deed restrictions, conspired to limit possible construction to a 25-foot strip in the middle of the parcel. That obviously impaired the value of the site for planned luxury highrise apartments.

Special Title Endorsements

A full analysis of available title insurance provisions and endorsements is beyond the scope of this chapter. However, standard lender's endorsements can be used, including those insuring against violations of restrictions, and against encroachments of the mortgaged buildings on any other property.

A standard endorsement will insure that separately described properties are contiguous, without any gaps in ownership between them. However, another way to avoid multi-parcel problems is to require that separate properties be described as one parcel and insured in that way. The lender can insist that the borrower prepare and deliver one description for the combined parcels instead of accepting a series of separate descriptions.

Servient Easements

A property subject to or "servient" to easements given to others may be worth less than it would have been without those easements. In one extreme case, a power line easement split the mortgaged property in half. The owner had previously been paid a substantial sum of money for this easement, and the power company even had the right to prohibit the owner from crossing the property under the power line. This resulted in land-locking part of the property. Unless the appraiser on the loan had fully considered the effect of this easement, the appraisal would have been completely misleading.

Frequently properties are subject to what might be called "floating easements." These are rights of utility companies or other owners to install lines or to maintain passageways across the servient property. Unless they are pinned down, they can create a problem with proposed construction on that property.

Dominant Easements

As previously discussed, occasionally an access easement may be necessary for a certain use. Loan officers should check whether the property has access to a public street and whether necessary easements are permanent and irrevocable.

Frequently, they use loan checklists of dozens of other requirements, including availability of sewerage disposal, storm water disbursement, and water and gas supply. However, sometimes a subtle, but important, issue is overlooked. Even if these easements are recorded and available, they may run across properties that are themselves mortgaged or encumbered with liens. If the adjoining property has a mortgage recorded against it before the date of the recording of the access easement, the access easement may be wiped out upon default by the adjoining owner. A foreclosure on the adjoining property can result in a termination of all easements that are junior to that mortgage. Therefore the owner of the dominant property may be forced to bid at a foreclosure on an adjoining property in order to protect its easement rights.

This is where proper use of mortgagee's title insurance can be particularly helpful. Title companies should insure that the easement rights are free and clear of any senior liens. One way to achieve this is to make sure that the easement is part of the property description in the insured mortgage.

Rights of Parties in Possession

Title insurance policies contain what appears to be a standard, innocent-looking exception that occasionally can cause a lender problems. This is the title exception of "rights of parties in possession."

To use an extreme case, suppose there is a party in possession under a rent-free, 10-year contract. How much is that property really worth?

Often occupants have "sweetheart deals" or special arrangements. In one case, a bank realized it had a mortgage subject to a lease in which the tenant had paid two years' advance rent. On foreclosure, a prospective buyer was stuck with that concession, which had a chilling effect on bidding.

In another transaction, a senior lease contained an option to purchase the property for a price less than the amount of a proposed mortgage loan. That option created a ceiling for the property's sale value during the option period.

Therefore, it is important that lenders carefully review all leases and occupancy agreements and attempt to obtain estoppel letters (which confirm options, the status of lease, and other key elements) from significant tenants. One solution is to require tenants to subordinate leases to the mortgage loan. Another is to make sure to clarify the title exception for "rights of parties in possession."

Proper Signatures

Even though the title company can protect the lender against failing to obtain the proper signatures on a mortgage, this protection does not necessarily extend to other documents signed at a closing. For example, one of the key documents may be the guarantee, which is intended to bind principals or others to the loan transaction, and is sometimes brought to the closing already signed and sealed.

There are dozens of cases in law books involving parties who claim that they did not sign the documents in question. Although forgeries may not be that common, people who do not want to be obligated sometimes have "convenient memories"; and in those cases, a bank may be put to the test of proving to a jury whose signature appeared on a guarantee years after the event.

Even if the parties appear to be present at the closing, this may not be sufficient evidence unless the loan officer knows the people involved. Things are not always as they seem. It is not unheard of to have a borrower bring his girlfriend to a closing to sign his estranged wife's name. A cynic has said that one way to spot this is to observe how the man is talking to his companion. If he is paying attention to her, she is probably not his wife.

The lesson to be learned from this is to be suspicious. Important documents should be notarized, even where they do not appear to require it, and loan officers should ask questions at closings in an attempt to determine if they have the proper parties. Generally, guaranties and other key documents should be witnessed by third parties.

Insurance Limits and Direct Access

Even when title insurance is understood and required, another issue is frequently overlooked. Does the lender have a rule about how much title insurance may be accepted from a given title company? A title company with a $5 million net worth cannot afford to pay a $100 million loan claim. Some lenders maintain a schedule of acceptable title insurance limits for each title company. Other lenders apply a rule of thumb to help set limits, such as one-third of the net worth of the title company after deducting the stated value of the title plant. Each lender should establish a policy on this issue.

Lenders may decide to use more than one title insurance company on a large loan. In these cases, the lender can insist on either co-insurance or re-insurance with the various companies. As a general rule, lenders should require joint and several liability (as contrasted with proportionate liability). The coverage should provide what is called "direct access" to any of the insurance companies for recovery of the full amount of the loss. This would permit claims to be made against any of the participating companies without requiring the first action against the lead company.

Zoning and Use Regulation

Sometimes when loans go bad, loan officers look back at the appraisal and second-guess what went wrong. The answer may lie in false assumptions the appraiser made about the highest and best possible use for the property. Therefore, it may be helpful for lenders to be guided by five somewhat sardonic land-use axioms that are derived from hard-earned experience.

The first axiom: NEVER RELY ON THE FACT THAT A PERMIT WILL BE GRANTED UNTIL IT IS IN HAND; EVEN THEN, IT MAY SLIP THROUGH YOUR FINGERS.

Neighbors have a right to appeal permits within designated time periods. It is important to make sure not only that a final subdivision and site plan has been approved and the permit is available, but also that appeal periods have expired. One approach will require an opinion from reliable counsel that the property is zoned for the intended purpose and that final unappealable permits have been obtained, but one should beware the qualifications contained in the opinion.

In one case, a loan of approximately $2 million was made based on the borrower's assurance that a farm would be rezoned to apartments within a few months. Two years later, the farm was still a farm and worth only a fraction of the outstanding loan.

The second axiom: A PERMITTED USE MAY NOT INCLUDE THE LOGICAL, NATURAL EXTENSION OF THAT USE.

Zoning laws must be examined very carefully to determine whether they will permit expansions of a planned use when the borrower's business expands or when the property has to be sold on a foreclosure. Under many zoning laws, for instance, permitted repairs of automobiles do not include body and fender work; assembly and distribution of products do not include manufacturing; retail sales do not include wholesale sales; and abandoned warehouses cannot necessarily be converted to homes. In addition, many ordinances limit the amount of space that may be devoted to certain uses, and required parking ratios may be violated on expansion.

The third axiom: NOT ALL USES ARE CREATED EQUAL.

A use that is permitted by a variance or nonconforming use is not as valuable as the very same use included under the applicable zoning category. A nonconforming use is one in existence before passage of a zoning law prohibiting that use. Under those circumstances the owner has vested rights to the existing use that can continue.

A variance is approval by a zoning board or other governmental body of a use that is not permitted as a matter of right. Generally, variances can be obtained when the applicant proves that there will be an undue hardship if the property cannot be used for the requested purpose. One fear is that if the property is destroyed by fire or other casualty, the variance will be lost, and the owner may have to reapply for approvals. This may not be a practical disadvantage, where local ordinances require reissuance of permits upon timely reapplication.

In one case, a negotiation for the acquisition of a business that manufactures sausages and cheeses fell through because of zoning issues. The targeted plant was in an area zoned "residential" and was functioning legally under a nonconforming use. One of the reasons the purchaser withdrew was that he was concerned about the limited potential use. One fear was that any attempt to expand the use, or to sell the property in the future for a different type of manufacturing, might meet with opposition from neighbors or zoning officials.

The fourth axiom: BEWARE SEWER MORATORIUMS: THEY MAY MEAN THE DEATH OF A DEAL.

In some cases, a property cannot be developed because there is inadequate township sewerage capacity. This is not always easy to correct. Perhaps the township cannot accept more discharge than its present capacity until it builds another sewer plant. A sewer plant may not be built until certain environmental requirements are met and until necessary funds are raised by virtue of bonds or other methods. Sometimes political issues arise. Meanwhile, interest charges and real estate taxes may accumulate on an unused property.

The fifth axiom: THE POWER TO MORTGAGE IS NOT THE POWER TO DIVIDE.

One of the issues frequently missed when a mortgage is placed on a portion of a larger parcel is what might be called "de facto subdivision." If a subdivision is required for a sale, it can usually be assumed that a subdivision is required for mortgaging the property. Otherwise, when a lender attempts to foreclose on the smaller parcel, it will have created an illegal subdivision. The smaller mortgaged property may not conform to the existing requirements and therefore the new owner may not be able to obtain a permit to use it for anything (and the lender may incur other penalties).

If a mortgage must be granted without subdivision approval, one solution is to take the total property as mortgage security and agree to release the uncommitted portion whenever the borrower finally obtains subdivision approval.

The Super Lien

It is important to obtain proper engineering and legal advice so that the mortgaged property conforms to all applicable environmental laws. However, in certain states, even expert advice cannot insulate the lender from the priority of what is known as the "super lien." For example, New Jersey has the Spill Compensation and Control Act of 1980 (N.J. Stat. Ann. § 58: 10-23.11 (West 1992 and 1985 Supp.)) ("Spill Act"), which permits a state to clean up properties where toxic wastes have been stored or spilled and to charge the discharger for these costs. If these costs are not paid, they may become a lien against the property; to make matters worse, that lien may become a "super lien," which is an encumbrance against the property that can take priority even over existing mortgages.

Massachusetts and New Hampshire have similar laws, and several other states have superlien laws of one kind or another.

In the case of *Kessler v. Tarrats*, 476 A.2d 326 (N.J. Super. 1984), New Jersey paid $275,000 in cleanup costs and filed a super lien that had priority against the holder of a mortgage that was recorded several years earlier, even before passage of the Spill Act. Under this act, the mortgage security can be wiped out by a super lien even if wastes were dumped long after recording the mortgage, and even if the lender never dealt with the wrongdoer.

The *Kessler* case should be a lesson to lenders. First, loans should be made with great caution to any business likely to generate toxic wastes. It is important that the lender investigate this issue and obtain applicable affidavits from the borrower or a qualified engineer. Wherever possible, lenders should insist on guaranties and indemnification agreements from both the borrower and any creditworthy principals connected with the borrower. In addition, the commonly used due-on-sale provision can become important because it will give the lender some control over a proposed sale to a potential polluter. Unfortunately, because of exceptions and exclusions, title insurance or environmental impairment liability insurance won't provide much protection against super liens.

On the other hand, the adverse effects of the superlien priority may be overrated. The exposure to liability is triggered by the obligations to pay for the cleanup rather than with the super lien. Even without a super lien, the foreclosing lender or a prospective purchaser at sheriff's sale would be responsible for cleanup costs. This will affect the value of a property even without that lien. In either case, if the value of the property is not adequate to cover both the mortgage balance and the cleanup costs, the lender will be forced to take a loss.

Equal Credit Opportunity Act

Under the Equal Credit Opportunity Act, a lender cannot ask a borrower to obtain the guarantee of the borrower's spouse. 15 U.S.C. § 1691 *et seq.* The theory is that a spouse should not be required to sign when an additional signature would not be required from an unmarried borrower. Violation of these laws can result in penalties and may adversely affect the validity of the improper guarantee. See *Silverman v. Eastrich Multiple Investor Fund, L.P.,* 51 F.3d 28 (3d Cir. 1995).

Punitive civil damages may be assessed under the act for up to $10,000 a violation. However, the act draws a fine line between permissible and illegal conduct. If the borrower has married an independently wealthy person, the lender cannot require the spouse to guarantee or join in the loan except under limited circumstances. However, suppose the bank tells the borrower to find a guarantor with a good credit rating. This request is proper, but the lender may not require that the spouse be that person.

Unfortunately, in the real world, where borrowers raise whatever defenses they can years after the original loan discussions, the bank is vulnerable to the spouse's defense that the request improperly originated with the lender. Therefore, in any loan involving a spouse's signature, the lender should make and retain a record of how it was offered. In addition, a lender's policy on joinder of spouses, backed by written instructions, should be established and circulated to all personnel.

Flood Damage

In Biblical times, Noah's only flood remedy was to build an ark and ride it out. Modern day Noahs may resort to remedies from their insurance companies—or their banks!

In *Small v. South Norwalk Savings Bank,* 535 A.2d 1292 (Conn. 1988), a homeowner suffered serious flood damage. Although a flood is the classic "act-of-God" hazard, the Connecticut Supreme Court focused the blame a little lower. It blamed the lender for failing to advise the homeowner that the property was located in a special flood hazard area. The court based this on a federal statute requiring banks to notify purchasers of that hazard before making a loan on the property. It held the bank responsible for the damage, even though the homeowner had engaged an inspector who had reported there were no signs of major flooding at the property, and even though the loss may not have been insurable.

Under the National Flood Program, insurance coverage is available for properties located in flood hazard areas. That insurance must be obtained on the mortgage balance for the entire term of the loan to the extent of the maximum limit of available coverage under the program.

Federal regulations require Federal Reserve Banks and FDIC insured banks not only to notify borrowers of flood hazards and whether insurance is available, but they also require the bank to obtain the borrower's acknowledgment that the mortgaged property is in a flood hazard area. Although the regulations may require the insurance as a condition of making the loan, they do not require the bank to obtain the insurance for the borrower, or to pay for it.

The South Norwalk Savings Bank admittedly failed to comply with those regulations because its appraiser relied on outdated maps. One of the lessons learned from the case is that lenders and their advisors should make sure that they are using up-to-date information. Generally, Federal Emergency Management Agency community maps are available for public inspection in each local community.

While the federal statute sets up loan-compliance requirements for banks, it does not specifically give a homeowner a private right to sue if the bank fails to comply. However, the court had little problem with this because it invoked state common law to imply that right.

It is not clear whether other courts will follow this precedent, but if they do, some modern-day Noahs may have now found a new deep pocket to help them start over after the flood subsides and the dove has landed.

Documents: Frequently Overlooked Issues

Often, lenders will overlook issues that require careful documentation. In most states a bare mortgage will be inadequate if the lender intends to include certain types of equipment, machinery, furnishings, and other personal property as collateral.

The lender must be sure that standard financing statements are properly completed and filed in order to perfect its security interests in these types of collateral under the Uniform Commercial Code (UCC).

Books have been written on how to perfect and preserve these interests under the UCC. However, this article will focus on only three of the more common pitfalls in this area, which will be referred to as "the disappearing exhibit," "lost grace," and "the forgotten loan."

The Disappearing Exhibit. The National UCC Financing Statement (Form UCC-1) provides statutory notice that the lender has encumbered the borrower's personal property.

Very often loan officers or attorneys prepare the financing statement, fill in all the appropriate blanks, and then add an exhibit with a detailed description of the property covered. They do this because the blank space for describing property is too small to accommodate the detailed description they have zealously prepared. They then fill in "See Exhibit A" in the applicable space. See U.C.C. Revised § 9-521. In some cases, filing clerks receive the multi-carbon printed form, separate the exhibit, file the form, and file the exhibit in the wastepaper basket. The net result is no security at all.

The moral of this story is that if you want to use an exhibit, make sure the language in the printed form provides sufficient details about the security and that it can also stand on its own, if necessary, without an exhibit.

Lost Grace. The UCC provides a lender with a 20-day grace period in which to file the financing statement if the loan proceeds purchased the described property. If the lender files within this period, the lien dates back to the date of the financing statement, and the security interest in the property enjoys priority over any intervening lienholders. If the filing takes place after the 20-day grace period, other lienholders who have filed earlier will have priority. See U.C.C. Revised § 9-315 and compare with U.C.C. (not Revised) § 9-306.

Some lenders treat this filing casually, but it is important that the statements be submitted in time and promptly accepted for filing. Otherwise a lender will lose the advantage of the purchase-money grace period.

The Forgotten Loan. The UCC permits a lender to preserve its lien priority if it files continuation statements within five years of the original filing. See U.C.C. Revised § 9-515. If it fails to do this, the lender will lose its priority, and when it finally does file, its lien will date only from the filing. If this happens, the lender will lose out to all creditors who have filed liens since the original filing.

How many times are financing statements filed in connection with a real estate loan closing, returned with filing information, and promptly filed away and forgotten? Under the UCC, the continuation statement may be filed after a lapse of four and one-half years. A tickler system should be used to keep track of these deadlines.

Franchises and Liquor Licenses

If a lender finances a restaurant, hotel, or bar, the use of the franchise name and privileges or the liquor license can be a key element in carrying on the business. Careful thought should be given to structuring these loans. With franchises, special arrangements may have to be completed with the franchisor before making the loan. The lender may need to obtain prior consent from the franchisor in anticipation of a loan default. This means that if there is a foreclosure, the lender or a purchaser would be able to use the franchise rights in connection with the property.

State laws should be examined to determine the requirements for transferring liquor licenses. Since the licenses are often owned by corporations, the lender may have to protect itself by obtaining an assignment of the stock of the applicable corporation as additional security.

Estoppel Letters

As previously discussed, it is important that a lender not be stuck with either a dollar-a-year tenant or one who has an option to purchase the property at a price lower than the mortgage balance. One way this can be prevented is to require the borrower to deliver an estoppel letter from all commercial tenants in the mortgaged building. Among other things, this tenant's letter should describe:

- the terms of its lease
- the fact that there are no amendments other than those described
- that there are no defenses, claims, or offsets against the obligation to pay rent

15

- that the advance rent is paid
- that the lease is in full force and effect

Another type of estoppel letter can prevent an unexpected problem from a senior mortgage holder. That lender should confirm information about the senior mortgage to either a prospective junior lender or to a prospective purchaser of the property. For example, the senior lender should be asked to confirm:

- the balance of the mortgage
- the required payments
- whether the mortgage is in default

Although many senior lenders will not do it, it is a good idea to try to obtain their consent to giving a junior lender notice and a chance to cure any default.

Prime Rate Definitions

Much litigation has been started against banks that made loans based on the prime rate that they had defined as that rate charged to the banks' most creditworthy borrowers. Borrowers are claiming that they were charged interest based on a prime rate higher than that charged to some of the bank's most creditworthy customers. Although this issue has not been fully resolved by the courts, litigious borrowers have had some success. To make matters worse, some of these cases involve actions under the RICO Act (Racketeer Influenced and Corrupt Organizations Act), 18 U.S.C. § 1961 *et seq.*, for "treble" (triple) damages. Lenders should consult counsel and thoroughly discuss their definition of the prime rate or other applicable standard. In some cases, lenders have avoided the use of the term "prime rate." Others have attempted to solve this problem by referring to the prime rate as the rate that is announced by the bank from time to time as its prime commercial money rate, specifically providing that this may not be the bank's lowest lending rate.

Exclusive Jurisdiction and Waiver of Jury Trial

The lender should consider mortgage clauses requiring the borrower to acknowledge that the bank's home county should be the exclusive jurisdiction in the event of any litigation. If this is enforced by a court, a Texas lender will thus discourage a trial taking place in northern Alaska, where bank employees may have to travel thousands of miles some winter to defend the bank in a hostile judicial environment.

It is important that borrowers and guarantors waive their right to a jury trial. Institutional lenders have traditionally been better off having a judge decide the facts.

Deficiency Judgments—Running the Gauntlet

If a lender intends to place a mortgage on several properties located in different states or even different counties, it should be aware that upon default it may have to deal with a deficiency judgment act. In Pennsylvania for example, the Deficiency Judgment Act provides that once a lender has taken over a property on foreclosure, the underlying debt is automatically satisfied unless the lender follows the deficiency procedure. There the lender must petition for a deficiency judgment within six months of the foreclosure and prove that the first property it took over was worth less than the debt owed. If it succeeds, it can then proceed against other property to the extent of the deficiency.

Each time an additional mortgaged property is acquired, this procedure has to be repeated. Obviously this can be a burden in effort and expense and may cause considerable delay in the takeover of a series of properties in different counties.

One way to avoid the impact of these acts is to divide a proposed loan into separate loans. A lender can then place a separate mortgage on each property and foreclose on each one without affecting the others.

Implementing Documents

In making loans, lenders heed all kinds of caveats, rules, and procedures on important and sometimes subtle issues. Eventually, however, someone will step into one of the many obvious pitfalls that await the unwary.

Blanks and Exhibits

In many cases, detailed forms are used by lenders to describe the loan transaction, but often somebody forgets to fill in all of the blanks or adds an exhibit that incorrectly describes the mortgaged property. A practical solution to reduce the likelihood of error is to use standardized forms with a minimum of blanks, all on one page.

Equity Requirements, Plans, and Specifications

Sometimes errors are made in the way the carefully negotiated terms are implemented. In one major construction project, the loan documents required the borrower to invest a certain amount of equity before the loan would be advanced. For some reason, the construction sums were advanced, but nobody required the borrower to invest the committed equity. In addition, the project was to be built in accordance with approved plans and specifications that were submitted at various dates and discussed. However, even though millions of dollars had been advanced toward construction of the building, it became obvious in ensuing litigation that there had never been a clear agreement on what the final approved plans and specifications were.

Oral Promises

In the leading case of *K.M.C. Co. v. Irving Trust Co.*, 757 F.2d 752 (6th Cir. 1985), the appeals court decided that a provision for waiver of jury trial in the loan documents was unenforceable. Although the financing agreement contained that clause, the borrower succeeded in proving to the court's satisfaction that, during the course of negotiations, a loan officer told the borrower not to worry about the waiver clause.

The officer allegedly said that the clause would not be enforced unless the borrower was guilty of fraud. In this case, even rules of evidence, which were intended to discourage oral evidence contradicting a written contract, did not save the bank. One of the lessons to be learned from this is that loan officers must be careful about making any statements or promises that may be used against the bank in any future litigation.

Satisfying the Mortgage

In another matter, a bank seemed to have made all of the proper decisions in granting a loan. It received appraisals, issued a form commitment, prepared and filed appropriate mortgage documents, filled in the blanks, and obtained lenders' title insurance. Later, the borrower sought a release of a portion of the mortgaged

18

property from the bank. The borrower brought the loan officer a standard document that would satisfy the mortgage (instead of releasing it), and the officer inadvertently signed it. The borrower then satisfied the mortgage without paying the debt. This is a little like the sentry who arms himself with a high-powered rifle, infra-red sensors, and grenades, and then promptly falls asleep on the job.

In addition to incorrect satisfactions, there are many other ways that lenders get into trouble after closing the loan. For example, there seems to be a current trend for borrowers to sue institutional lenders for failing to make advances under certain circumstances. Lenders should anticipate these potential problems by making sure that advances are not cut off until they have satisfied themselves that there has been a significant default and proper notice given. Various buzzwords are being used by borrowers to describe what is perceived by them as improper conduct. These range from "inequitable conduct," "lack of good faith," and "breach of fiduciary duty" to "fraud" and "economic duress." Sometimes these issues become difficult. However, as previously discussed, there are many more-obvious mistakes that simply stem from a failure to understand the documents that are delivered for signature.

Conclusion

This chapter has discussed just a few of a potentially limitless number of loan pitfalls. It has not covered many of the more complex issues such as construction lending, equity kickers, secondary financing, or loan administration. However, knowing even a few of the pitfalls may alert the lender to others. With proper caution, the lending institution may make it across the rutted fields without a dangerous fall.

2   NINE ADVANCED LENDERS' CLAUSES (PLUS ONE)

Mortgage lenders generally use well-tested and one-sided mortgage forms to evidence and secure their loans. However, certain legal issues are not anticipated in most mortgages.

Volumes have been written about drafting and improving mortgages, and mortgage form books proliferate. This chapter will not join in that chorus or even attempt to play major recognizable themes. It will not repeat the more traditional terms discussed in the last chapter. Rather, it will attempt to deal with new tunes by discussing practical provisions that are rarely discussed and frequently omitted from mortgages.

Each of these clauses is forged from practical experiences in mortgage disputes. They may never be called into play, but when the battle starts, they may make the difference between winning and losing. The recommended clauses will give lenders improved weapons to:

- sustain supremacy of the defaulted mortgage after judgment is taken
- file tax appeals
- anticipate future mortgage modifications
- resolve disputes near home—without a jury trial
- cut off delayed defenses and punitive counterclaims
- limit damages
- inspect and test the property even without a default
- confess judgment and execute on it

Mortgage Survival Clause

Judicial decisions have impaired a mortgage lender's rights to recover interest and other costs after a judgment is entered against the borrower. In one case, a bankruptcy court limited the interest rate after judgment to the legal rate of 6 percent, rather than the agreed rate of over 10 percent. *In re Herbert*, 86 B.R. 433 (Bankr. E.D. Pa. 1988). In that case, the court held that a Pennsylvania statute providing for post-judgment interest at 6 percent trumped the contract rate in the mortgage even though the mortgage note called for payment of the contract rate "from the date of the note until paid."

Similar reasoning was followed in a Third Circuit case that held that the lender, FNMA, could not recover real estate taxes and insurance premiums it paid after judgment while foreclosing against a bankrupt debtor's property. *Stendardo v. Federal Nat'l Mortgage Ass'n*, 991 F.2d 1089 (3d Cir. 1993). The mortgage required the borrower to pay insurance premiums and real estate taxes, and when the borrower failed to do that, FNMA paid the premiums and taxes and tried to recover them in the foreclosure. In deciding against the lender, the court held that the mortgage merged into the judgment, and, therefore, the mortgage terms requiring reimbursement for those expenses were not applicable after the mortgage became ineffective:

> ... [I]t is elementary that judgment settles everything involved in the right to recover, not only all matters that were raised, but those which might have been raised. The cause of action is merged in the judgment which then evidences a new obligation.

Id. at 1094.

In each of these cases, the courts held that the lender's rights to collect interest, taxes, or premiums after entry of a judgment are matters of the parties' intent. Therefore, all is not lost for lenders. In light of these cases, lenders should specify that the mortgage *shall not merge* into the judgment, and also that the borrower must reimburse lenders for these payments and continue to pay the agreed interest rate *even after judgment is entered against the borrower.*

If a mortgage does not contain this "magic" language, a lender may not only lose out on regular interest, default interest, insurance premiums, and real estate taxes, but it also may not be able to collect other post-judgment expenses that appear in most mortgage documents, including collection fees, attorneys' fees, late fees, and other costs. Remember, standard mortgage language calling for payment of the contract rate "until paid" did not pass muster in the *Herbert* case. The "magic" language may have. (See chapter 19.)

These additional charges may become important, not only when dealing with the borrower, but also in a battle against junior lienholders who may be challenging the senior lender's right to proceeds.

Battles for Late Charges

Other cases have challenged the right of a lender to collect specified late charges when the mortgage note has been accelerated because of default. Courts have rejected such late charges because once the lender formally accelerates payment of the debt, it repudiates the right of the borrower to make installment payments, and since those installment payments are no longer due, there is no basis for compensation for administrative expenses in connection with specified late payments. Instead, the lender is relegated to its rights in the foreclosure action, including any rights to collect other fees and costs.

The case of *Security Mutual Life Insurance Co. v. Contemporary Real Estate Assocs.*, 979 F.2d 329 (3d Cir. 1992), noted that the issue appears to be one of first impression under Pennsylvania law, and the court based its finding for the borrower on precedent in other states: *In re Tavern Motor Inn , Inc.*, 69 B.R. 138 (Bankr. D. Vt. 1986); *Crest Sav. & Loan Ass'n v. Mason*, 581 A.2d 120 (N.J. Super. 1990); and *Reis v. Decker*, 516 N.Y.S.2d 851 (N.Y. County Ct. 1987). The *Security Mutual* court may have permitted the collection of late charges as an element of damages after default if the mortgage specifically provided for that right. In finding for the borrower, the court distinguished an earlier case that allowed late charges after acceleration on the basis that the agreements specifically provided for those late charges. See *Orix Credit Alliance, Inc. v. Pappas*, 946 F.2d 1258 (7th Cir. 1991). On the other hand, some courts will not permit collection of late charges after acceleration no matter how clear the language. The case of *Centerbank v. D'Assaro*, 600 N.Y.S.2d 1015 (N.Y. App. Div. 1993), held against the lender despite language in the late charge provision that permitted the charge whether before or after maturity, "including accelerated maturity."

In light of these cases, mortgage lenders who wish to continue to collect late fees after default and acceleration would be well advised to spell that out in their mortgage documents.

Tax Appeal Rights

One of the results of a real estate recession is that more borrowers fail to pay their mortgages. Another is that reductions of real estate tax assessments lag behind plunging values. Therefore, lenders frequently foreclose on properties that are overassessed. In these cases, the borrower may have no interest or incentive to appeal from the unduly high assessment, and the appeal deadline may be near.

Unless the lenders anticipate this problem, they will have no legal standing to file tax appeals without the owner's cooperation. Some courts will not recognize the right of anyone to file an assessment appeal other than the "real owner" or certain tenants. See *Filbern Manor Apts. v. Board of Assessment Appeals*, 589 A.2d 279 (Pa.Cmwlth. 1991), and *Marcus Hook Dev. Park v. Board of Assessment Appeals*, 449 A.2d 70 (Pa.Cmwlth. 1982).

The lender may realize the anticipated sheriff's sale is months away, and the appeal date is slowly slipping away. What is the lender to do? That's where a tax appeal clause is crucial. The mortgage can give a lender the right to take such appeals in its own name or the name of the mortgagor, and, generally, tax appeal boards will recognize that authority. While many mortgage forms protect borrowers against default if they are contesting a tax assessment in good faith, very few permit lenders to contest taxes until they have completed foreclosure.

An assessment reduction can not only save real estate taxes but also realty transfer taxes when the property is foreclosed. When transfer taxes are due, they are based on the applicable tax assessment at the time of the sheriff's sale. Therefore, a successful assessment appeal can decrease the lender's cost of foreclosure.

Anticipation of Mortgage Modification

Mortgage lenders must be cautious about modifying a mortgage to help a troubled borrower. Unfortunately, like the Good Samaritan who attempts to save an accident victim, a lender may be blamed when the "patient" gets worse. Senior lenders are sometimes surprised to find that a junior lienholder will later contend that the modification has impaired their lien priority. For example, a junior lienholder has sometimes succeeded in leapfrogging its lien (and priority for payment) ahead of a senior mortgage when the interest rate on the senior debt is increased in exchange for an extension of the maturity date of the senior loan. Courts have occasionally sided with junior lienholders on the theory that the change in the terms of the senior mortgage has prejudiced junior lienholders and increased the likelihood of a default by the mortgagor. Some courts have found prejudice in shortening the term of the mortgage—some even in extending it. The argument against shortening it is that the borrower may default because it has less time to pay off the mortgage. The argument against extending it is that the extension has permitted the borrower to run down the value of the property.

While most courts will not support these arguments, senior lenders must be cautious about agreeing to any mortgage modifications without consent from junior lienholders. Also, lenders usually will insist on title insurance to assure the priority after modification. (See Harris Ominsky, *When Lender Benevolence Backfires*, 14 Pa. L.J. Rep. 4 (1991)).

On occasion, lenders will want to modify mortgages even when they cannot obtain junior lienholders' consent. In these cases, a lender may benefit from a mortgage provision that anticipates a mortgage modification. That provision could permit mortgage modifications, including extending or accelerating the time of the payment, or other designated changes, without notice to or consent from a junior lienholder.

While it is not clear that this, in itself, will protect a mortgagee who enters into a modification agreement, it will provide mortgagees with an argument that the mortgage anticipated a mortgage modification and that the objecting junior lienholder had record notice of that possibility and should have known about it before making its loan and recording its lien.

In some states, the senior lender will receive comfort from legislation that facilitates modifications. For example, a New Jersey statute provides that the priority does not change by modifying the interest rate, the due date, or other terms, other than advancing new principal or substitution of collateral. N.J. Stat. Ann. § 46:9-8.1.

Waiver of Jury Trial

As demonstrated earlier, mortgage lenders occasionally engage in legal disputes with borrowers. When that happens, most financial institutions prefer that the disputed facts be resolved by a judge rather than a jury. Traditionally, railroads and mortgage lenders do not fare well with juries—particularly when they are battling widows, orphans, or one of the good ol' boys. That's why mortgage lenders should require borrowers to waive their right to a jury trial.

These waivers will be strictly construed by courts; therefore, when they are used, they should be comprehensive and set out in bold letters. They should be drafted broadly enough to cover any litigation related to the mortgage or the loan, including lender-liability claims by the borrower. See *Avenue Assocs., Inc. v. Buxbaum*, 373 N.Y.S.2d 814 (N.Y. Sup. Ct. 1975), and *Analytical Systems Inc. v. ITT Commercial Finance Corp.*, 696 F. Supp. 1469 (N.D. Ga. 1986) (waiver of jury trial contained in security agreement was applicable to borrower's tort claims of abusive litigation and intentional interference with contractual relationships).

The right to a jury trial is both provided and protected by various constitutional provisions. Courts generally do not favor jury waivers, and therefore they will be interpreted strictly against lenders, although customarily the right to jury trial may be waived under the right circumstances, at least in commercial loan transactions.

Absent a statute, jury waivers are normally permitted under basic contract law, although in some states advance waivers of jury are probably unenforceable unless they are in a document signed by all parties after they become aware of the causes of action to the litigation. See Sidney A. Keyles, *Commercial Real Estate Finance* 314 (1993); *Anderson v. Carnegie Steel Co.*, 99 A. 215, 217 (Pa. 1916); *Rodney v. Wise*, 500 A.2d 1187, 1189 (Pa. Super. 1985); *Seligson v. Plum Tree, Inc.*, 361 F. Supp. 748, 758 (E.D. Pa. 1973); and *Shulman v. Continental Bank*, 513 F. Supp. 979 (E.D. Pa. 1981). At least 15 states recognize the right to waive trial by jury and provide by statute a manner for such waiver; but in many of these states, the statute sets forth specific methods of waiver, and none of those includes waiver by contract. See Keyles, *Commercial Real Estate Finance,* at 314.

Lessons from Case Law. Courts frequently hold that jury waivers in agreements must be mutual, unequivocal, voluntary, and informed. See, e.g., *David v. Manufacturers Hanover Trust Co.*, 287 N.Y.S.2d 503 (N.Y. Civ. Ct. 1968) (fine-print jury waiver on back of bank deposit agreement is unconscionable); *National Equipment Rental, Ltd. v. Hendrix*, 565 F.2d 255 (2d Cir. 1977) (jury waiver provision in equipment lease struck down, allowing lessee to get to the jury on usury issue); *Gaylord Department Stores, Inc. v. Stephens*, 404 So.2d 586 (Ala. 1981) (contract between pharmacist and department store included jury waiver, which was buried in fine print); *In re Heartland Chemicals, Inc.*, 103 B.R. 1018 (Bankr. C.D. Ill. 1989) (court refused to enforce express jury waiver provision in loan agreement because of lack of mutuality and lack of any indication that parties bargained for waiver or even mentioned it in loan negotiations); *Leasing Service Corp. v. Crane*, 804 F.2d 828, 833 (4th Cir. 1986) (party seeking to enforce waiver of jury trial has burden of proof of proving waiver was knowing and voluntary); *K.M.C. v. Irving Trust Co.*, 757 F.2d 752 (6th Cir. 1985) (burden of proof on party opposing enforcement of waiver); *Bonfield v. AAMCO Transmissions, Inc.*, 717 F. Supp. 589 (N.D. Ill. 1989) (waiver of jury trial contained in franchise agreement was made knowingly and intelligently; waiver was in boldface type, was expressly discussed, and franchisee was experienced businessman); *N. Feldman & Son, Ltd. v. Checker Motors Corp.*, 572 F. Supp. 310 (S.D.N.Y. 1983) (court upheld jury waiver provision in contract upon showing agreement was result of years of negotiations and that parties had previously executed similar agreement containing same provision; provision was clearly visible and located directly above parties' signatures); *National Westminster Bank v. Ross*, 130 B.R. 656, 666–67 (S.D.N.Y. 1991), *aff'd*, 960 F.2d 1 (2d Cir. 1992) (jury trial waiver in loan guaranty was upheld where it was set off in its own paragraph, was signed by a sophisticated CEO of borrower with assistance of counsel); *Chase Commercial Corp. v. Owen*, 588 N.E.2d 705 (Mass. App. Ct. 1992) (jury trial waiver in a guaranty was enforceable when it was mutually binding on both parties and the guarantor was sophisticated).

See also *Secured Lend Law Alert*, Vol. 3, No. 8 (October 1987), Warren, Gorham & Lamont, Inc.; Annot., *Validity and Effect of Contractual Waiver of Trial by Jury*, 73 A.L.R.2d 1332 (1976). Sidney A. Keyles, *Commercial Real Estate Finance* (1993), at 315.

Conspicuous Waivers. In addition, generally, the jury waiver should be conspicuously set forth in the loan documents, or even in a separate document, and preferably should be prominently located in the mortgage in bold print and in capital letters. If feasible, it should even be placed on a separate page of the mortgage, which is signed by the borrower; or in the alternative, placed in a prominent location in the mortgage and initialed by the borrower. See *Commonwealth v. Carter*, 546 A.2d 1173, 1181 (Pa. Super. 1988);

Leasing Serv. Corp. v. Crane, 804 F.2d 828, 832 (4th Cir. 1986); *K.M.C. Co. v. Irving Trust Co.*, 757 F.2d 752, 755 (6th Cir. 1985); *National Equip. Rental, Ltd. v. Hendrix*, 565 F.2d 255, 258 (2d Cir. 1977); *In re Reggie Packing Co.*, 671 F. Supp. 571 (N.D. Ill. 1987); *ARH Distribs., Inc. v. ITT Commercial Finance Corp.*, No. 87 C 511 (N.D. Ill. Feb. 19, 1988) at 311; and *Standard Wire & Cable Co. v. Ameritrust Corp.*, 697 F. Supp. 368 (C.D. Cal. 1988).

Having counsel present in preparing the documents is a factor in determining that the waiver was knowing, voluntary, and intentional. Courts occasionally mention this as an important factor in upholding the waiver. In light of that, it may be a good idea to request the borrower's attorney to opine on the validity of the jury-waiver provision.

Risks to Lenders. These waivers are not without risk to the lender. For one thing, if the documents provide for mutual waivers, the mortgage lenders are then waiving their constitutional right to a jury trial. Under certain circumstances, it is possible to conceive of a situation where the lender would want a jury trial. However, generally, the lender will not be sacrificing much with that waiver.

Another risk of such waivers is that if the waiver is voided by a court, that provision may in itself be evidence of bad faith. See *K.M.C. Co. v. Irving Trust Co.,* cited above. Imagine trying a lender liability case to a jury with documents that include an unenforceable jury trial waiver. That waiver can create the impression with the jury that the loan documents are overreaching, that the lender did not want the dispute to be decided by the very jury that is hearing the case, and that the lender was afraid that its loan documents and practices would not withstand the scrutiny of a jury.

This impression may be offset somewhat if the waiver clause (as in the recommended clauses in the appendix to this chapter) states another rationale for the waiver other than that the lender does not want to be judged by a jury, e.g., streamlining the process and minimizing the cost of dispute resolution.

Limitations on Damages

For the same reason that lenders do not want to take a chance on jury trials, they want to limit their potential liability in counterclaims brought by borrowers. For example, in the *K.M.C.* case mentioned above, the lender's failure to make an $800,000 advance under a line of credit was found to be a breach of the lender's duty of good faith and precipitated a $7.5 million damage award against the lender. In another highly criticized case, *State National Bank v. Farah Manufacturing Co.*, 678 S.W.2d 661 (Tex. Ct. App. 1984), the lenders' alleged interference with the borrower's business relations resulted in a jury verdict of $19 million. While the trend toward lender liability cases has shifted lately in favor of lenders, it is easy to understand why lenders would attempt to protect themselves against tort-based consequential and punitive damages.

In most jurisdictions, the courts have upheld contract provisions that eliminate liability for special, indirect, or consequential damages. (See, for example, *National Cash Register v. Modern Transfer Co.*, 302 A.2d 486 (Pa. Super. 1973), and *Earl Brace & Sons v. Ciba-Geigy Corp.*, 708 F. Supp. 708 (W.D. Pa. 1989).)

While it is not clear that damage-limitation provisions would have saved the lenders in *K.M.C.* and *Farah*, their enforceability will be enhanced if they contain clear and descriptive headings, use large type, and are specifically initialed or signed by the borrowers. In addition, if both borrowers and lenders agree to be bound by these provisions, the courts are more likely to accept them as negotiated arrangements. These provisions may be inserted in mortgages either as part of a jury-trial waiver or as a separate provision similar to the ones suggested in the appendix to this chapter.

Lenders should not be surprised to find that some courts will hesitate to enforce exculpatory provisions against borrowers. In one case a construction loan agreement gave the bank the right to make advances "without liability" for actions "taken in good faith." It also gave the bank discretion to alter the basis of construction loan payments without incurring "liability of any kind."

Inspection Clause

We live in an age when federal and state environmental laws have a tremendous impact on mortgage lenders. Borrowers and, under certain circumstances, lenders, may be responsible for environmental damage to the mortgaged property. Therefore, most commercial mortgages spell out environmental compliance standards and saddle borrowers with broadly worded prevention and cleanup responsibilities, as well as default provisions, when they fail to comply. In addition, lenders look for environmental indemnification from the borrower, and sometimes, even the borrower's principals and affiliates.

In light of this, lenders will want the right to make sure that the owners are complying with these provisions. But how many mortgages make it clear that the lender may have access to the property to do the required inspections when there is no clear default under the mortgage? How many mortgages give owners the right to access remote parts of the building or to take core samples of the land or the foundation when the lender merely suspects a problem?

Owners will sometimes resist what they perceive to be lender's meddling, but if the lender has no way of checking suspected problems, the owner may be violating environmental laws and exposing the lender's security to millions of dollars of potential cleanup costs. Decisions have highlighted the importance to lenders of properly-worded inspection clauses in their mortgages. The case of *First Capital Life Insurance Co. v. Schneider, Inc.*, 608 A.2d 1082 (Pa. Super. 1992), presents a scenario that is unfortunately not much different from what many mortgage lenders encounter from time to time. In that case, the Pennsylvania Superior Court enjoined a borrower from interfering with the lender's attempts to conduct environmental tests on the mortgaged property. The lender held a $7,300,000 mortgage on the property, and the borrower had failed to make mortgage payments for several months. The borrower had consented to a Phase I inspection that showed that paint and other toxic materials might be leaking into the ground soil and potentially contaminating subsurface groundwater at the site. The environmental consultant recommended a Phase II investigation consisting of drilling approximately 12 holes into the ground and installing groundwater monitoring wells in some of these holes. However, the borrower denied the lender's request for access to the property and notified it that a Phase II investigation would be a trespass by the lender and its representatives. In the case, the parties stipulated that the intrusive investigation sought by the lender was not without risks and that under current governmental regulations, the borrower had no obligation to conduct that investigation. It was also stipulated that if substantial quantities of hazardous materials were found on the site, cleanup costs might well exceed $1 million.

The borrower argued against the proposed injunction because the lender would have an adequate remedy of law in the form of a foreclosure, and, therefore, it should not have to resort to the equitable remedy of an injunction.

On appeal, the Pennsylvania Superior Court analyzed the Environmental Compensation Liability Act and the various cases and regulations that recognize the potential for lender liability under this statute. It then concluded that foreclosure is not a complete and adequate remedy because that might merely result in the lender taking title to environmentally damaged or contaminated real estate.

However, the court had to deal with the language in the mortgage before it could grant the requested equitable remedy. On analysis, the mortgage inspection clause proved inadequate. It provided:

> 15. Inspections. Mortgagor shall allow Mortgagee and its representatives to enter upon the Subject Property during normal business hours and upon reasonable advance notice to inspect the condition of the same and to examine, copy and audit the books, records, accounting data and other documents of the Mortgagor or the party for whose benefit Mortgagor is acting relative to the Subject Property. . . .

608 A.2d at 1083.

After reviewing the definition of the term "inspection" in *Black's Law Dictionary*, the court concluded that the word "inspect" does not include the ability to dig holes and conduct the desired "intrusive environmental tests."

The court then examined the provisions that gave the lender various rights after the mortgagor's default and concluded that they were sufficiently broad to justify granting the requested injunction. Those provisions, among other things, permitted the lender to enter the mortgaged property to "make repairs, alterations and improvements to the Subject Property necessary, in Mortgagee's judgment, to protect or enhance the security thereof."

It should be emphasized that in this case, after much litigation, the lender was given the right to carry out the Phase II analysis, but this occurred only because the borrower had failed to make mortgage payments and was in default under the mortgage. The lesson is that lenders need to have adequate inspection clauses that are applicable whether or not the mortgage is in default.

Death Sentences

Borrowers frequently raise defenses or counterclaims against foreclosures and other remedies by charging lenders with acts of misconduct that occurred months or years before the start of the foreclosure action. Frequently, these defenses are created not out of the lender's alleged actions, but out of more subtle inactions or failures of the lender to do one thing or the other. Many times, the lender has no notice or previous knowledge of the allegations and therefore has not preserved key information or evidence that would be helpful in responding.

In light of this, a lender should require advance notice before a borrower may assert a lender liability claim. In addition, lenders may want to impose a contractual statute of limitations on such claim. For example, the lender could require that any such action or claim be brought within a designated period after that cause of action arises. If the borrower fails to do so, it loses its rights. In one article, this type of provision has been referred to as a "death sentence." See Robert A. Feldman, 3 *Corporate Legal Times* 10 (Oct. 1993).

One of the practical advantages of these provisions is that whether or not they are enforceable, the borrower would be more likely to notify the lender of a potential claim promptly after its occurrence and thereby enable the lender to react in a way that would either preclude the filing of the action or allow it to preserve the evidence necessary to defend itself. See Sidney A. Keyles, *Commercial Real Estate Finance*, at 232.

Frequently, these types of actions are controlled by state statutes of limitations. However, in the absence of a controlling statute, a contract provision limiting the time for bringing an action is valid if the stipulated period of time is reasonable. Annot., *Validity of Contractual Time Period, Shorter Than Statute of Limitations, for Bringing Action*, 6 A.L.R.3d 1197 (2000).

There may be statutory or other circumstances that will excuse compliance with a notice provision or a death sentence, particularly circumstances involving waivers or estoppels. However, as set forth in the cited A.L.R. annotation, it is generally recognized that contractual statutes of limitations are enforceable. But the time allowed must be sufficient to permit the plaintiff to investigate and file its case within the limitation period; and periods may not be so short that they effectively nullify the right of action, or require the claimant to bring its action before loss or damage can be ascertained. The annotation discusses various court decisions throughout the United States that uphold stipulations requiring the commencement of suit in as few as 30 to 60 days after the accrual of the cause of action. While the cited cases do not involve lender liability claims, there is no reason to think that courts would treat those claims differently than claims under other contracts. A quick survey of commonly used commercial mortgage forms reveals that very few contain the provisions recommended in this article. Mortgage lenders would be well-advised to review their own mortgage forms. Some of these clauses, such as the anticipation of mortgage modification, may not be enforceable or may not achieve their objectives for other reasons. However, there is no good reason not to use them, and under the right circumstances, they may prove to be the most significant weapon in the lender's arsenal.

Home Court Advantage

If there is a mortgage dispute, lenders would like to know that they can play the game, if you will excuse the expression, on their "home court." A mortgage may contain a governing law–selection clause that provides that a particular state's law will govern any disputes that arise under the loan documents. Also, litigating in your home state can make a considerable difference in the costs of litigation and in the availability of witnesses. Lenders will generally include these provisions in their mortgages, but frequently they will fail to include a provision that will expedite the service of process on a corporate borrower that is not qualified to do business in the lender's home state.

A forum-selection clause will be enforceable in the absence of a compelling, countervailing reason. *Instrumentation Assocs., Inc. v. Madsen Electronics (Canada) Ltd.*, 859 F.2d 4, 5 (3d Cir. 1988); see *Churchill Corp. v. Third Century Inc.*, 578 A.2d 532, 536 (Pa. Super. 1990). (If the designated forum can do substantial justice to the case, then the parties are bound by the agreed choice.)

While a forum-selection clause will be enforceable under certain circumstances, lenders should be aware that courts will not always enforce these provisions, particularly when the connections with the forum state are tenuous. Once a suit is started in federal court, a party may overcome the effect of the forum-selection clause by relying on a federal statute that governs the decision about whether to give effect to that clause (28 U.S.C. § 1404). Under various cases, a federal court now has significant discretion to reject

32

forum-selection clauses as part of its multi-factor transfer analysis. See Gregory B. Jordan and Mary J. Hackett, *Drafter Beware: Forum Selection Clauses May Not Achieve Their Goal*, 65 PA. BAR ASS'N Q. 101 (July 1994). Some states have refused to honor choice-of-forum clauses. See, for example, *Dileo v. Americorp Financial Inc.*, 18 Pa. D.&C.4th 449 (C.P. Fayette 1992).

Appointing Service Agent. A clause that is more rarely used will deal with borrowers who are not otherwise qualified to do business in the home state and have not otherwise appointed a local agent. In those cases, the mortgage should provide that the lender can serve process within the home state and that the borrower recognizes a designated party as its agent for service of process.

Generally, the Federal Rules of Civil Procedure provide that a corporation or partnership or other unincorporated association may be served in any judicial district of the United States "by delivering a copy of the summons and of the complaint to an officer, a managing or general agent, *or to any other agent authorized by appointment* or by law to receive service of process. . . ." Fed. R. Civ. P. 4(h)(i) (emphasis added). See *Davis-Wilson v. Hilton Hotels Corp.*, 106 F.R.D. 505, 508 (E.D. La. 1985), and *United States v. Marple Community Record, Inc.*, 335 F. Supp. 95, 101–02 (E.D. Pa. 1971).

Similar rules are generally recognized under state law. For example, leases that specified jurisdiction and venue in New York and named a New York agent to accept service of process of behalf of a defendant have been upheld. *Leasing Serv. Corp. v. Graham*, 646 F. Supp. 1410, 1415 (S.D.N.Y. 1986).

Confession of Judgment Waivers

The leading case of *Jordan v. Fox, Rothschild, O'Brien & Frankel*, 20 F.3d 1250 (3d Cir. 1994), held that a creditor (and its lawyer) can be liable for executing on a confessed judgment by garnishing the debtor's bank account simultaneously with the confession. While that case involved a confession of judgment under a lease and not a mortgage loan, future courts may apply the same rule to actions under mortgage notes.

The Third Circuit Court of Appeals invoked the Federal Civil Rights Law (42 U.S.C.A. § 1983), which permits civil damages for violation of constitutional right to due process.

In *Jordan*, the landlord had confessed judgment, as permitted in the lease, after becoming embroiled in a rent dispute, and then used a writ of execution to garnish the tenant's bank account. When the sheriff served the garnishment order on the bank, that froze the tenant's account and caused six of the tenant's checks to be returned unpaid.

While the entry of judgment by confession in itself is not the basis of liability, the execution on that judgment may give rise to that liability absent an effective waiver by the judgment debtor of the debtor's constitutional rights of due process.

The court reasoned:

> Because Pennsylvania permits writs of execution to be enforced on confessed judgments without providing any means for securing a pre-deprivation hearing or obtaining prompt post-seizure relief, the district court correctly concluded the acts of [the judgment creditors] and their Attorneys, absent pre-judgment waiver, deprived [the judgment debtor] of due process once they culminated in the sheriff's seizure of [the judgment debtor's] bank account.

20 F.3d at 1271. In coming to the conclusion that the debtor did not adequately waive its rights, the court stated that a waiver is possible if it is "an understanding and voluntary consent of the debtor." *Id.* at 1272.

On this issue, the court stated:

> ... a reasonably well-informed debtor need only be aware that he has given away an important right to notice and hearing before his creditor, acting under color of law, can enlist the state's power of legal compulsion to seize the debtor's property in order to satisfy or secure its debt. We think, rather, the debtor need only know that if he does not comply with the terms he has agreed to for payment of the debt, the creditor may confess judgment against him and forthwith seize his property to satisfy the debt it says is owed.

Id. at 1273.

In light of *Jordan* and other similar cases, lenders and their counsel may want to play it safe and either not use confessions of judgment at all, or use confessions and then give the borrower a chance either to challenge that confession or to request a hearing before execution on the judgment. The problem with that strategy is that a delay of that sort would give a borrower a chance to draw down on its bank accounts and take other measures to make collection more difficult.

Another alternative would be to require the loan documents to include clear waiver language that meets the requirements set forth in *Jordan*. The objective of the waiver, which is set forth in the appendix that follows, is to make it clear that the borrower surrenders its due process rights to any prejudgment or pregarnishment notice and hearing. In addition, it would be prudent to provide that waiver in a separate document, which is acknowledged by the attorney for the borrower in order to enhance the lender's position that the waiver was given knowingly.

APPENDIX
Special Mortgage Provisions

Non-Merger, Interest, and Late Fees

Non-Merger. Mortgagor intends and agrees that this Mortgage shall **NOT** merge into any judgment entered or recovered by Mortgagee against the Mortgagor under the [Mortgage Note] or under or pursuant to any other note, document, or instrument. Notwithstanding the recovery or entry of any such judgment against Mortgagor, all of the terms, provisions, covenants, undertakings, and agreements of the Mortgagor whether under the Mortgage or under the [Mortgage Note] or any other note, instrument, document, or undertaking of the Mortgagor, whether relating thereto or not, shall remain in full force and effect and shall be enforceable strictly in accordance with their terms as fully as though no such judgment had been entered or recovered against the Mortgagor.

Interest. Interest, to be computed at the rate set forth in this [Note], and late fees and all other fees and charges payable under the [Note], shall continue to be due and payable so long as any balance remains outstanding. This provision shall survive and apply even after default, maturity, acceleration, recovery of judgment, judgment of foreclosure, bankruptcy, insolvency proceedings of any kind, or the happening of any other event or occurrence, similar or dissimilar.

Late Fees After Default. Whether or not the loan evidenced or secured hereby has matured or been accelerated, all late charges related to delinquent installment payments or otherwise, shall continue to accrue and be due as though such maturity or acceleration had not occurred, and shall be included as an element of damages in calculating and assessing amounts due by the borrower hereunder.

Tax Assessment Appeals

Mortgagee shall have the right to institute and to prosecute to final determination or settlement an appeal of any real estate tax assessment or other lien or assessment on the Mortgaged Property, or take any other appropriate proceedings in the name of Mortgagee or Mortgagor in connection therewith. Mortgagee is hereby appointed as attorney-in-fact for Mortgagor, for such purposes, which appointment is irrevocable (said appointment being coupled with an interest). If such an appeal or other proceeding is taken, the expenses thereof, including counsel fees, shall be payable by Mortgagor to Mortgagee upon demand and such sums shall be secured by this Mortgage.

Mortgagee shall have the right to take such action whether or not Mortgagor is in default under the terms of the Mortgage and regardless of whether Mortgagor has instituted its own actions. In the event both Mortgagor and Mortgagee have instituted actions, the Mortgagee shall have the sole right to determine which action shall proceed; and if Mortgagee elects to proceed with its action, Mortgagor shall withdraw and terminate any procedures Mortgagor has commenced.

Mortgagee shall have no liability related to any such actions, including liability for any increase of taxes that may result therefrom, and Mortgagor waives any claims, actions, or other rights that it may have against Mortgagee in such connection.

Actions of Mortgagee

Mortgagee may, at any time and from time to time, without notice to, and without the consent of, any other person or entity (except for Mortgagor in the case of a modification of the terms of the [Note] or this Mortgage), (1) extend or accelerate the time of payment of the indebtedness secured hereby, (2) agree to modify the terms of the [Note] or this Mortgage, including increasing payments of interest and principal, (3) release any person liable for payment of any indebtedness secured hereby or for performance of any obligation, (4) release all or any part of the security held for the indebtedness secured hereby, or (5) exercise or refrain from exercising or waive any right Mortgagee may have.

Mortgagee shall have such rights and may exercise them without affecting the lien or priority of this Mortgage upon the Mortgaged Property or any part thereof, and without affecting the liability of any guarantor or surety, notwithstanding the fact that guarantors, sureties, junior mortgages, judgments, or other claims or encumbrances may be impaired, prejudiced, or otherwise adversely affected thereby.

Waiver of Right to Jury Trial

Lender and Borrower acknowledge that disputes arising under this Mortgage are likely to be complex and they desire to streamline and minimize the cost of resolving such disputes. Therefore, Lender and Borrower irrevocably waive all rights to a trial by jury in any action, counterclaim, dispute, or proceeding based upon, or related to the subject matter of this Mortgage. This waiver applies to all claims against all parties to such actions and proceedings including those involving Lender or Lender's parent, affiliates, or related entities, or any officer, director, shareholder, attorney, or partner of any of them. It also applies whether such dispute or proceeding arises under this Mortgage, any other agreement, note, paper, instrument, or document heretofore or hereafter executed, or any other contract, whether similar or dissimilar; and whether or not it arises from intentional or unintentional conduct, from fraud, other improper action or failure to act, or from other reasons. This shall be deemed a covenant and enforceable independently of all other provisions of this Mortgage.

This waiver is knowingly, intentionally, and voluntarily made by Borrower, and Borrower acknowledges that neither the Lender, nor any person acting on behalf of the Lender, has made any representations to induce this waiver of trial by jury or in any way to modify or nullify its effect. Borrower further acknowledges that it has been represented (or has had the opportunity to be represented) in the signing of this Mortgage and in the making of this waiver by independent legal counsel, selected of its own free will, and that it has had the opportunity to discuss this waiver with counsel. Borrower further acknowledges that it has read and understands the meaning and ramifications of this waiver provision and as evidence of this fact signs below.

_____

[signature of Borrower]

Waiver of Consequential, Punitive, and Special Damages

Borrower and Lender agree that in any action, suit, or proceeding related to or arising out of this Mortgage, the Notes, or any other document related to the Loan, each mutually waives to the fullest extent permitted by law, any claim for consequential, punitive, or special damages. [Add modified version of second paragraph in the paragraph set forth above for Waiver of Right to Jury Trial (with signature of borrower added).]

Inspection Clause

Strong Lender Clause.   From time to time, Lender and its representatives may [at Borrower's expense] enter the Mortgaged Property to investigate, inspect, and examine the Property and to make such repairs, alterations, and improvements (collectively, "Improvements") as it deems proper in its sole discretion to protect or enhance its security. Borrower shall fully cooperate in allowing, from time to time, Improvements and such examinations, tests, inspections, and reviews of the Property ("Examinations and Tests") that Lender, in its sole and absolute discretion, shall determine to be advisable in order to evaluate any potential environmental problems. Lender expressly reserves the right to conduct Examinations and Tests, including but not limited to, a geohydrologic survey of soil and subsurface conditions, and such other Inspections and reviews of the Property as Lender in its sole and absolute discretion may determine to be desirable.

Examinations and Tests shall be for Lender's protection only and shall not constitute any assumption of responsibility for the condition, construction, maintenance, or operation of the Mortgaged Property, nor approval by the Lender of any certification given to the Lender, nor relieve Borrower of any of its obligations. Lender shall have no obligation to notify Borrower of the results of any Examinations and Tests, and Lender's failure to notify Borrower of any default after Examinations and Tests shall not constitute a waiver of any Default then existing.

Compromise Inspection Clause.   (May be added at the request of Borrower.) Lender's rights of inspection shall be exercised in a reasonable manner, which includes Borrower's right to limit environmental testing which might interfere with Borrower's operations to Borrower's normal business hours. Lender shall take all reasonable steps to restore the Property to the condition in which it existed before the tests, and shall take reasonable steps to ensure that no such testing shall create an unreasonable risk or unreasonable hazard.

Required Notice and Period of Limitation on Borrower's Claims

Borrower's right to take action against Lender or Lender's parent, affiliates, or related entities, or any officer, director, shareholder, attorney, or partner of any of them in any action, claim, counterclaim, dispute, or proceeding based upon or related to the subject matter of this Mortgage (hereinafter referred to as Borrower's "Claim" or "Claims") shall be limited and conditioned upon the requirements set forth below:

- Borrower must give Lender written notice setting forth the nature of any such Claims within 30 days of the date that Borrower knew or had reason to know of the facts that establish the Claims, and such notice must specify with particularity the facts that establish the Claims; and

- Any Claim must be filed in a court having jurisdiction over such Claims within six months after the cause of action for such Claim accrues.

- If Borrower fails to meet these requirements, Borrower shall be irrevocably and irrebuttably deemed to have waived its rights to such Claims.

- This limitation and waiver applies whether such dispute or proceeding arises under this Mortgage, any other agreement, note, paper, instrument, or document heretofore or hereafter executed, or any other contract, whether similar or dissimilar; and whether or not it arises from intentional or unintentional conduct, from fraud, improper action, or failure to act, or from other reasons. This provision shall be deemed a covenant, shall be enforceable independently of all other provisions of this Mortgage, and shall survive payment of the note or any satisfaction or release of this Mortgage.

Forum-Selection and Service of Agent

Borrower agrees that _____ County, [*state*], presents the most convenient forum for both parties because applicable documents and witnesses are located in or near that County, and any other forum will pose an inconvenience to the parties in the event of litigation.

Borrower therefore has consented to the exclusive jurisdiction and venue of the Federal and State Courts located in _____ County, [state], in any action on, relating to or mentioning this Mortgage, the Notes, or any other loan documents ("Loan Documents") and to the extent permitted by law, the Borrower irrevocably appoints _____ having an office at _____, as its agent for the service of process in any action or proceeding undertaken or started in connection with the Loan Documents. To the extent permitted by law, Borrower waives any objection that it may have based on lack of jurisdiction or improper venue or *forum non conveniens* to the conduct of any such proceeding.

Nothing in this section shall affect the Lender's right to serve legal process in any other manner permitted by law or affect the Lender's right to bring any action or proceeding against the Borrower or its property or assets in the courts of any other appropriate jurisdiction.

Waiver of Defenses to Confession of Judgment and Execution

Borrower acknowledges that under the terms of the loan documents, it has empowered any attorney to appear for Borrower in any actions that Lender may bring for sums due under the loan documents and to confess judgment against Borrower for those sums.

Borrower has reviewed those provisions and this provision with Borrower's attorney and acknowledges that Lender is authorized to take that action without any advance notice to Borrower, both to confess judgment and immediately thereafter to take any additional action to enforce the judgment, such as attaching, executing upon, seizing, taking possession of, and selling any of Borrower's real estate, other tangible or intangible property, including bank accounts and receivables.

Therefore, Borrower is aware that it has given up any rights it might have to a hearing to contest the validity of any such judgment or other claims that Lender may assert thereunder.

Borrower specifically and voluntarily waives and relinquishes any rights that it may have to any notice or hearing or other due process in connection with Lender's implementation of its rights to take judgment, or to execute upon or take any additional action to enforce such judgment. Borrower also specifically releases any rights it may have to challenge such action by Lender or to claim or recover any damages against Lender in connection with such actions.

_____

[signature of Borrower]

SPECIAL CONDITIONS

Here's a tenth provision lenders may try! It may not help the bank much in a pinch, but it will sure test who's reading your drafts.

Death

Upon the death of any individual Borrower, the lien of this Mortgage will extend to, and include, any cemetery plot, crypt, or other place of final interment of such deceased Borrower, together with any and all rents, issues, incomes, profits, flowers, and crops arising therefrom; and any and all renewals, replacements, accessions, improvements, and substitutions, and a prior perfected security interest in and to any and all effects, articles of personal adornment, gold fillings, and other things of value severed or capable of severance without undue material injury to the corpse of the deceased Borrower. The foregoing lien and security may be enforced by any lawful procedure and will continue until whichever of the following occurs first: (i) full payment of the indebtedness; or (ii) Bank is furnished with a substitute hostage for the deceased Borrower of equal or better class, quality, usefulness, and value.

End of the World

Upon the occurrence of the end of the world before full payment of the Indebtedness, the Indebtedness, at Bank's option, will become immediately due and payable in full, and may be enforced against Borrower by any available procedure in law, equity, or otherwise. For remedial purposes, Bank will be deemed aligned with the forces of light, and Borrower with the forces of darkness, regardless of the parties' actual ultimate destinations, unless and until Bank elects otherwise in writing.

3   MODIFIED MORTGAGE MAY NOT STAND UP AGAINST A JUNIOR MORTGAGE

When a first mortgage holder modifies the terms of its mortgage loan, it may impair its lien priority over a second mortgage. This issue arose in *Burney v. McLaughlin,* 63 S.W.3d 223 (Mo. Ct. App. 2001), a case decided by the Missouri Court of Appeals. In that case, the court struggled with the general rule that any modification of a first mortgage that increases the risk or decreases the security of a second mortgage may cause the first mortgage to lose its priority and be reduced to a subordinate position.

The Subordination

The Burneys owned two adjacent parcels of land in Missouri, and in 1992 they built a 77-unit hotel on the front parcel, financing the work with a $1.1 million loan from the Ozark Mountain Bank. They then sold the hotel to a purchaser for $3.3 million, which was paid by $1 million in cash, the assumption of the Ozark loan, and by giving a purchase money second mortgage of $1.2 million to the Burneys. One year later, the purchaser (which meanwhile had purchased the second parcel) borrowed approximately $3.2 million from Bank of America in order to pay off the existing Ozark loan and construct an additional 101 units on the back parcel. The Burneys then agreed to subordinate their existing mortgage so that Bank of America could record a first mortgage of $1.077 million on the front parcel.

The Modification

When the purchaser began having financial problems, it negotiated eight modification agreements with the Bank of America over a six-year period. That resulted in increasing the interest rate from 7 percent to 10.75 percent and extending the maturity

44

date from six months to over six years. The modifications also imposed new fees and added cross-default and cross-collateralization terms to the mortgage. The purchaser finally defaulted in 1999, and the bank started foreclosure.

Right before the foreclosure, the Burneys, who had been unaware of the mortgage modifications, filed a petition for equitable relief. They asserted that their second mortgage should be declared superior because the modifications materially impaired their collateral and so "destroyed the original economics of the subject property so as to render the Subordination Agreement ... null and void." *Id.* at 228. The trial court then entered a temporary restraining order enjoining the foreclosure sale, and the bank appealed.

Matter of First Impression

The appeals court said that the reordering of mortgage priorities was a matter of first impression in Missouri. It agreed with the general doctrine that a junior lender is entitled to protection from loan modifications to which it has not agreed. However, elevating the junior mortgage to a full priority above the first mortgage should rarely be employed. According to the court, this should be done only when the impairment of the junior loan is so substantial as to be "materially prejudicial."

The court first held that the various extensions of the loan term do not rise to the level of materially prejudicing the Burneys' interest in its collateral. The law regards a junior lender as necessarily taking the risk of a postponement of the date of repayment (which frequently will be to its advantage). In this case, the principal amount of the loan was reduced by approximately $145,000 during the six years of extension (all of which benefited the Burneys). On the other hand, the appellate court said that the increase in the interest rate on the extended note resulted in additional interest payments amounting to $166,000. Furthermore, the cross-collateralization and cross-default provisions that tie together unrelated properties "materially impaired the value of [Burney's] interest" in the front parcel that secured their loan. The court said that without these provisions the purchaser could have paid off one loan and not the other, thus possibly avoiding the risk of foreclosure on both properties:

> ... The cross-collateralization clauses meant that the front parcel, as well as the back parcel, were pledged as collateral for two of Bank's loans, and in a similar vein, cross-default provisions contained in the modification agreements meant that a default by C&J under either of Bank's loans acted as a default under both. Without these cross-collateralization and cross-default provisions, C&J would have been better posed to pay on one Bank note and not the other. While speculative, C&J might have been better positioned to have avoided the risk of a foreclosure on the entire property.

Id. at 233 [citation omitted].

Despite that, the appellate court reversed the trial court's ruling that the Burney's mortgage became a first lien because the "equities in this case" do not require such an extreme result. However, their mortgage was deemed to hold a senior position only as to those terms of the bank's modified mortgage executed without their consent. For example, presumably the increased interest rate would not maintain priority over the Burneys' mortgage. Therefore, the court remanded the case to the trial court to determine the balance due under the original terms of the loan, as to which the bank retained its first lien position.

Other Cases

These types of cases occasionally pop up around the country, and generally, courts are reluctant to reverse priorities of mortgage lenders. However, in extreme cases where the junior lender has been prejudiced by the senior lender's modification, the court may take the rare step of reversing priorities. It is unlikely that this will happen unless the maturity date on the senior mortgage is substantially accelerated, and the interest or principal payments are increased in a way that would make it difficult to even calculate the prejudice to the junior's position. Courts are most likely to reverse priorities in cases like *Burney* where the junior lender had subordinated its lien to a later mortgage (which otherwise would have had no priority over the subordinated loan). In these cases, the courts must deal with an element that the subordinated party has relied to some extent on the implicit promise that the former junior lender will do nothing to prejudice or impair the security of the subordinated lender.

In siding with the junior lienholder, one court stated:

> ... Such prejudice is compounded to the extent that the agreement increased the likelihood of a second default by the mortgagor and thus increased the possibility that (the mortgagor) would indeed have to cure at the higher rate of interest. We think it a fair inference from the record that the agreement placed a greater burden on the mortgagor who, having already suffered default due to delinquency, was now forced to meet a significantly larger monthly payment, and that this strain on the mortgagor's financial capacity contributed at least in part to the second default.

Shane v. Winter Hill Fed. Sav. & Loan Ass'n, 492 N.E.2d 92 (Mass. 1986).

Since courts focus on how the junior lender has been prejudiced, one would think that increasing the interest rate in a first mortgage would only affect the junior lienholder to the extent of the unauthorized increase. Given that, the junior lender should receive a priority that only applies to the extra interest.

However, when it comes to other mortgage modifications, some courts go further. They maintain that a modification may taint the whole mortgage relationship. Under this rationale, the tainted first mortgage—principal, interest, and all—may lose priority to the junior lender.

Therefore, as in *Shane,* courts may reverse the normal mortgage priorities, which is a decision that could completely nullify the senior lender's security. See *Gluskin v. Atlantic Sav. & Loan Ass'n,* 108 Cal. Rptr. 318 (Cal. Ct. App. 1973); Giesen, *Routine Mortgage Modifications: Lenders Beware,* 17 REAL ESTATE L.J. 22 (1989).

Courts justify such decisions on the grounds that a modification that increases the mortgage payments deprives the borrower of needed funds and leads to a default. Also, a modification that shortens the mortgage term could precipitate a foreclosure at a time when the property value is at rock bottom.

A corollary argument has been made when, instead of shortening the term, the senior lender extends it. See *Citizens & Southern Nat'l Bank v. Smith,* 284 S.E.2d 770 (S.C. 1981). But see *Guleserian v. Fields,* 218 N.E.2d 397 (Mass. 1966). In such a case, the junior lienholder then may argue that the extension permitted the value to deteriorate until it was below the existing mortgage balances. It may contend that if the senior lender had taken action against the borrower on the unmodified due date, everybody might have been paid. Normally, a court should reject such attacks, because a lender has no duty to take legal action on default or exercise any other remedies under its mortgage. However, the expense and delay needed to defend against them are troublesome.

Tainting Factors

Some arguments for reversing mortgage priorities are somewhat spurious, but lenders would be wise to consider them before they rush into modification agreements. The arguments make even less sense when the lender modifies a mortgage after default. Suppose the lender holds a defaulted mortgage with a remaining 10-year term. The lender could accelerate the full balance of the mortgage and foreclose. However, if the lender gives the borrower another chance and modifies the mortgage so that it becomes due in a year or two, the junior lender may argue that its security was impaired because of the accelerated maturity date. That argument should not carry water because the lender's security probably would not have been impaired any less than if the senior lender merely foreclosed upon default.

Sometimes the position of the junior lender and its ability to reverse priorities depend on subtle factual nuances surrounding the modification agreement. For example, the junior lender's argument is substantially weakened if the first mortgage holder shortens the stated mortgage term after the first mortgage holder has given formal notice of default to the borrower and has demanded payment in full.

Senior lenders have been helped by another case that has limited a junior lender's rights to reverse priorities. In *Friery v. Sutter Buttes Savings Bank,* 72 Cal. Rptr.2d 32 (Cal. App. 4th 1998), the court clarified California's position on one of the leading cases in the country on reversal of liens. See *Gluskin v. Atlantic Sav. & Loan Ass'n,* 108 Cal. Rptr. 318 (Cal. App. 3d 1973). *Gluskin* had handed a potent weapon to a subordinating seller who held a junior lien by deciding that a senior could not substantially impair a junior's security without the junior's consent.

In *Friery,* a case that limited the scope of *Gluskin,* Ms. Friery bought a property, then sold it without consent of the bank holding the first mortgage. She took back a junior mortgage from the buyer for part of the sale price. Friery not only refused to assume the bank's first mortgage that became due at the time she acquired the property, but she also knew, or should have known, that when she sold the property without the bank's consent, it would trigger a due-on-sale clause in the first mortgage.

When the bank learned of the sale, it declared its mortgage in default and demanded payment in full. This led to a workout agreement between the bank and Friery's buyer, who assumed the first mortgage and agreed to modify it by advancing the maturity date from May 1, 2001, to October 1, 1996, which was 15 days after the Friery junior mortgage was due.

When the bank foreclosed, Friery sought to have the court declare her lien superior to the bank's because the bank had modified its first mortgage. She argued that any modification of a senior loan without the consent of the junior lender that materially prejudices the security of the junior loan should cause the senior loan to lose its priority.

Subordinated Lien

The court rejected that broad approach and held that the basic rationale for the "loss-of-priority" doctrine is contractual. For example, when a party holding a first lien voluntarily subordinates it to a subsequent lien (that would otherwise have no priority over the existing loan), that party is entitled to rely on the former junior lender and the borrower to do nothing to reduce the security of the subordinated lender. The typical case is when the seller of land takes back a purchase money first mortgage and then subordinates it to a construction loan that is expected to result in an enhancement of the value of the property (hence the security of the original seller).

In the *Friery* case, however, Mrs. Friery had never been senior. She took a calculated investment risk. She originally bought a distressed property, and should have known that even this purchase violated a due-on-sale clause in the first mortgage held by the bank. The bank undertook no expressed or implied duty toward Friery and stood in no special relationship to her. One of the hazards that Friery accepted when she sold the property without the bank's consent and took back a second mortgage was the likelihood that the defaulted bank mortgage would have to be renegotiated by her buyer.

Prejudice to Junior Lien

One of the issues that comes up in modification cases is whether the change to the first mortgage is even material to the second lender. It is easy to see that accelerating the maturity date of the mortgage and increasing the interest or principal payments could prejudice a junior's position in a way that would be difficult to calculate. In extreme cases, particularly where the junior has become junior by subordinating its mortgage lien, courts may reverse the priorities because the senior lender did not obtain consent of the junior.

In *Friery,* the trial court had said that merely accelerating the maturity date was not material. While the appellate court did not rule on that issue, it cited one treatise writer, who has taken the position that post-lien additions to the original principal of the senior loan should lose their priority to a junior lien because they have worsened the junior's security. However, modifications that merely alter the time period in which to pay off the senior loan should not result in a loss of priority. 4 POWELL, REAL PROPERTY 37-219, § 37.31.

In many other states that do not have court decisions on these issues, the courts are likely to follow the principles set forth in these cases. They are also likely to rely on the applicable sections of the Restatement of the Law of Property, which was cited in the *Burney* case. In that case, the court stated:

> (b) If a senior mortgage or the obligation it secures is modified by the parties, the mortgage as modified retains priority as against junior interests in the real estate, except to the extent that the modification is materially prejudicial to the holders of such interests and is not within the scope of a reservation of right to modify as provided in Subsection (c).
>
> RESTATEMENT (THIRD) OF THE LAW OF PROPERTY, Mortgages, § 7.3(b) (1997) (emphasis added). The term "materially prejudicial" cannot be precisely defined. It is similar to the term "substantially impaired." See Shultis, 594 N.Y.S.2d at 892. Necessarily a determination when material prejudice occurs is fact-driven by the circumstances of each case. In this connection, Comment b, to

§ 7.3 RESTATEMENT (THIRD) OF THE LAW OF PROP-
ERTY, Mortgages, (1997) supra, sets out:

There is a strong presumption under this section that a
time extension on a senior mortgage or obligation, standing alone, is not materially prejudicial to intervening interests. A finding of material prejudice is justified only in
the rare situation where the time extension can fairly be
said to place the junior interest in substantially weaker
position. The typical junior lienholder is normally grateful
to have a time extension forestall the destruction of its lien
by a senior foreclosure.

63 S.W.3d at 231–32.

Practice Tips

Lenders who wish to accommodate their borrowers by modifying mortgages in the face of junior liens should be alerted to taking certain precautions. Wherever there is any possibility that a
court may view the proposed mortgage change as too prejudicial,
the lender should make sure that it has received the consent of all
junior lienholders before agreeing to the change. Also, it should
require a title search to confirm that it knows about all junior liens
on the property. A lender should take these precautions even
though a consent may not be required to modifications in any of the
loan documents. Otherwise it might have to face future litigation
by a disgruntled junior looking to improve its position. The senior
lender should insist on a title insurance endorsement that confirms
its existing priority in light of the proposed modification.

Another suggestion might help. Lenders could insert so-
called "savings clauses" in modification agreements. Such clauses
would provide that although the modification is binding between
the lender and the borrower, it is not intended to affect the lien priority of the mortgage or to impair the security of another lienholder. These clauses should also provide that, to the extent a court
finds an adverse effect on another security interest or lien, the
offending provision shall be invalid.

In addition, lenders should anticipate that they may want
to modify their mortgages at some future time, even in the face of
a second mortgage holder that is unwilling to cooperate. Therefore,
mortgage lenders should consider using a mortgage form that specifically permits mortgage modifications, including extending or

accelerating the time of the payment, increasing interest or other designated changes, without notice to or consent from a junior lien holder.

While it is not clear that this, in itself, will protect a mortgagee who enters into a modification agreement, it will provide mortgagees with an argument that they anticipated a mortgage modification, and that the objecting junior lien holder had record notice of that possibility and should have known about it before making its loan and recording its lien.

The following is a suggested clause:

SUGGESTED MORTGAGE CLAUSE TO ANTICIPATE MODIFICATIONS

Mortgagee may at any time and from time to time, without notice to, and without the consent of, any other person or entity (except for Mortgagor in the case of a modification of the terms of the [Note] or this Mortgage), (1) extend or accelerate the time of payment of the indebtedness secured hereby, (2) agree to modify the terms of the [Note] or this Mortgage, including increasing payments of interest and principal, (3) release any person liable for payment of any indebtedness secured hereby or for performance of any obligation, (4) release all or any part of the security held for the indebtedness secured hereby, or (5) exercise or refrain from exercising or waive any right Mortgagee may have.

Mortgagee shall have such rights and may exercise them without affecting the lien or priority of this Mortgage upon the Mortgaged Property or any part thereof, and without affecting the liability of any guarantor or surety, notwithstanding the fact that guarantors, sureties, junior mortgages, judgments, or other claims or encumbrances may be impaired, prejudiced, or otherwise adversely affected thereby.

4 WHY LENDERS SHOULD RESIST JUNIOR FINANCING

Mortgage lenders are frequently asked to consent to secondary financing. Lenders with clear legal rights to withhold consent under a due-on-encumbrance clause may automatically refuse a borrower's request. Yet lenders seldom articulate the reasons for their apparent intransigence on this subject.

A lending officer may simply explain to the borrower that it wants the loan to be paid off so the money can be lent out at higher interest rates. On the other hand, lenders may consent if the borrower agrees to increase the interest rate and pay a fee. However, this is not good public relations and, indeed, may not stand up in court in some states when a frustrated applicant challenges the lender.

A borrower will argue that a lender cannot be hurt by secondary financing because it does not disturb the lender's first lien position and, in fact, may improve the lender's position by bringing needed funds into the project. The borrower may accuse the lender of acting arbitrarily. On the other hand, an informed lender who receives proper legal advice should be able to state a number of reasons, each more compelling than the lender's desire to increase its profits, for refusing to permit secondary financing.

Overextended Borrowers

Perhaps the most obvious reason for a lender's refusal to permit secondary financing is to avoid permitting the borrower to overextend itself financially and thereby increase the likelihood of default, which in turn might result in bankruptcy or receivership. Although the senior lender preserves its priority in such a proceeding, it may find that its interest becomes subordinate to trustees' or receivers' fees and monthly mortgage payments are delayed.

Challenges by Junior Lenders

If a senior lender takes over a property after a borrower's failure to collect rents and pay bills, it may run into a problem with a junior lender that wants some of the income. The junior lender may challenge the senior's rent-collection policies and question whether the senior's expenditures were absolutely necessary to run the building. For example, the junior lender may claim that a boiler could have been repaired rather than replaced, thus saving money that should have been paid to the junior.

Foreclosures

Generally, a senior lender is required to notify all junior lenders of a pending foreclosure sale. This requirement could delay or impair a foreclosure action, particularly if the junior lender is difficult to reach or challenges the form or method of the notice. Also juniors may try to upset a foreclosure by arguing that the sale price was grossly inadequate, that the senior made an agreement that chilled the bidding, or by picking on flaws in descriptions of the real and personal property being sold.

Voluntary Transfers

A lender can sometimes avoid the formality of a foreclosure proceeding if the borrower agrees to transfer the property to the lender voluntarily, by a deed-in-lieu-of-foreclosure. As a practical matter, however, this option may not be available to a lender when a junior mortgage exists on the property without some agreement from the junior.

A deed-in-lieu-of-foreclosure does not discharge the junior mortgage as a foreclosure does, unless the junior mortgage holder consents. The junior lender may seize a request for approval and attempt to exact some payment from the senior.

For these reasons, the federal Department of Housing and Urban Development (HUD) is reluctant to permit a second mortgage. HUD regulations state specifically that if a junior mortgage is permitted, it must provide that it is automatically terminated when the senior lender is given a deed-in-lieu-of-foreclosure. While the legal impact of this provision is not completely clear, senior lenders should consider the provision before permitting a junior encumbrance.

54

Marshalling

If a second mortgage is permitted, the first lender's remedies may be delayed or restricted by the somewhat obscure and mysterious legal doctrine known as "marshalling."

When a lender holds a blanket mortgage and the second lender holds a mortgage on only one property, the second lender may be able to require the first lender to foreclose first against the property in which the second lender is not involved. To the extent that the first loan is paid from this sale, the second lender's position will improve because the senior mortgage has been reduced. In short, while the doctrine of marshalling helps a second lender, it complicates and restricts the remedies of the first lender.

Pursuing Other Assets

If the lender holding a first mortgage intends to pursue other assets of the borrower upon default, a second mortgage may present another problem. Since the borrower's other assets, e.g., bank accounts, automobiles, or other real estate, may not be encumbered by the first mortgage, the lender who executes and sells these assets first will have an advantage. Therefore, it is against the interest of the first mortgage holder to sanction the creation of a second mortgage holder, who may in the future succeed in a race to seize the borrower's assets upon a default.

Priority Problems

If a lender advances money to a borrower as construction progresses or as other events occur during the term of the mortgage, a junior mortgage could create priority problems.

In many states, certain loan advances not considered obligatory, i.e., not required to be made by the lender, are given priority only as of the date these advances are made. Therefore, if a second mortgage is placed on the property and the senior lender makes advances after that date, those advances may not have priority over the junior advances.

Also, under certain circumstances when the borrower goes bankrupt, a court may subordinate the senior lien for "equitable" reasons involving the senior's misconduct in dealing with the borrower of the collateral.

Obtaining the Junior Lender's Consent

Once a junior lender enters the picture, the borrower and the first lender may not be able to act in certain matters without first obtaining the junior lender's consent.

For example:

- increasing the amount of the first mortgage or the interest rate to refinance
- converting to condominiums and selling them
- attracting a major tenant who insists on having a nondisturbance agreement from all lenders
- granting easement rights or restrictions in a mutual pact with a neighbor
- purchasing equipment on credit

Sometimes the first lender will give the borrower permission to purchase equipment on credit so that the mortgaged property will be more valuable. The seller of the equipment or the company financing the purchase will often want a security interest and a disclaimer from all mortgage holders. A troublesome second lender may withhold its disclaimer and hold up the desired purchase.

Modifying Mortgages

Generally, senior lenders require junior lienholders to consent to modifications of their senior mortgages. Where they have failed to do this, scattered cases around the country have even reversed the normal priorities and given the junior lien holder a first lien over the senior mortgage, if the modifications substantially prejudiced the junior lender. This may be viewed as the lender's fulfillment of the Oedipal fantasy: Junior takes advantage of his father's changes to replace him.

California Cases

However, seniors have been propped up by a California appellate case that has made it clear that the junior lender's rights to reverse priorities are severely limited. In *Friery v. Sutter Buttes Savings Bank*, 72 Cal. Rptr.2d 32 (Cal. Ct. App. 1998), the court clarified the California position on one of the leading cases in the country on reversal of liens. See *Gluskin v. Atlantic Sav. & Loan Ass'n*, 108 Cal. Rptr. 318 (Cal. Ct. App. 1973). *Gluskin* had handed a potent weapon to a subordinating seller who held a junior lien. A senior could not substantially impair a junior's security without the junior's consent.

In the *Friery* case, Ms. Friery bought a property, then sold it to a third party without consent of the bank holding the first mortgage. She took back a note from the buyer secured by a junior mortgage. She not only refused to assume the bank's first mortgage due at the time she acquired the property, but also she knew, or should have known, that selling it to a third party without the bank's consent would trigger a due-on-sale clause in the first mortgage.

When the bank learned of the sale, it declared its mortgage in default and demanded payment in full. This led to a workout agreement between the bank and the buyer, who assumed the first mortgage and agreed to modify it by advancing the maturity date from 2001 to October 1, 1996, which was 15 days after the Friery note was due.

When the bank foreclosed, Friery sought to have the court declare her lien superior to the bank's because of the modification of the first mortgage. She argued that any modification of a senior loan without the consent of the junior lender and that materially prejudices the security of the junior loan, should cause a loss of priority to the senior loan.

Subordinated Lien

The court rejected that broad approach and held that the basic rationale for the "loss-of-priority" doctrine is contractual. For example, when a party holding a first lien voluntarily subordinates it to a subsequent lien (which would otherwise have no priority over the existing loan), that party is entitled to rely on the former junior lender and the borrower to do nothing to reduce the security of the subordinated lender. The typical case is when the seller of land takes back a purchase money first mortgage and then subordinates it to a construction loan that is expected to result in an enhancement of the value of the property (hence the security of the original seller).

In the *Friery* case, however, the second lender had never been senior. Friery took a calculated investment risk. She bought a distressed property, and should have known that this violated a due-on-sale clause in the first mortgage held by the bank. The bank undertook no expressed or implied duty towards Friery and stood in no special relationship to her. Renegotiation of the senior loan following a sale on the property without the lender's consent was one of the hazards that Friery accepted when she sold the property and took back a second mortgage.

Prejudice to Junior Lien

One of the issues that comes up in modification cases is whether the change to the first mortgage is even material to the second lender. It is easy to see that accelerating the maturity date of the mortgage and increasing the interest or principal payments could prejudice a junior's position in a way that would be difficult to calculate. In extreme cases, particularly where the junior has become junior by subordinating its mortgage lien, courts may reverse the priorities because the senior lender did not obtain consent of the junior.

In *Friery*, the trial court had said that merely accelerating the maturity date was not material. While the appellate court did not rule on that issue, it cited one treatise writer, who has taken the position that post-lien additions to the original principal of the senior loan should lose their priority to a junior lien since they have worsened the junior's security. However, modifications that merely alter the time period in which to pay off the senior loan should not result in a loss of priority. Richard R. Powell, 4 *Powell on Real Property* 37-219, § 37.31.

Despite the *Friery* case, certain precautions should be taken in Pennsylvania by a lender who wishes to accommodate its borrower in the face of junior liens. Because a court may view the change as too prejudicial, the lender should make sure that it has the consent of all junior lienholders before agreeing to the change. Even though such a consent may not be required in any of the documents, it should head off the potential of later litigation by a disgruntled junior who is looking to improve its position. Also, the senior should insist on a title insurance endorsement that confirms the existing priority in light of the proposed modification.

Another suggestion might help. Lenders could insert so-called "savings clauses" in modification agreements to provide that although the modification is binding between the lender and the borrower, it is not intended to affect the lien priority of the mortgage or to impair the security of any other lien holder. They should also provide that, to the extent a court finds an adverse effect on another security interest or lien, the offending provision shall be invalid.

The *Friery* case and these precautions will sustain seniors who are struggling to preserve their rightful position in life against aggressive and intrusive juniors striving to replace them.

Blanket Mortgages

When a second mortgage is to be placed on several properties at the same time, as in the case of a blanket mortgage on a tract of homes under construction, another problem may arise in connection with junior financing.

A senior lender that wants to complete the sale of a home to pay off its loan out of the sale proceeds may not be able to do so without the junior lender's cooperation, and the junior lender may exact a payment for that cooperation! Unless the senior lender forecloses and discharges the junior mortgage, the senior lender will not be able to clear title for the home buyer. This procedure may take too long to meet delivery dates on pending home sales.

Fire Insurance Claims

If a fire occurs on the mortgaged property, the senior lender will have less control of the fire insurance proceeds when a junior mortgagee is also named in the fire insurance policy.

Although a senior lender has first rights to the proceeds, unless special policy endorsements are obtained, the insurance company will insist on making the check payable to all the parties named in the policy, which, in the case of secondary financing, will include the junior lender. Obtaining the use of the proceeds may be complicated or delayed by a recalcitrant or litigious second lender.

Conclusion

The significance to the first lender of these potential pitfalls varies with the circumstances of each loan. If the borrower has a deep pocket and the potential second lender is a reputable institution, the senior lender should be less apprehensive about granting permission for a junior loan.

Also, many of the pitfalls can be alleviated with properly drawn subordination or intercreditor agreements. In any event, lenders cannot afford to ignore these potential problems whenever a borrower requests consent for junior financing.

5 ARE BORROWERS PAYING MORE INTEREST THAN THEY THINK?

How many days will we have in this year? The answer may depend on whether you're looking at a lunar calendar or a loan calendar.

Suppose you are dealing with a loan that states that interest is calculated based on a 360-day year, or comparable language. Is the effective interest rate more than the stated rate per year, or is that formulation only a convenient way of calculating interest for purposes of prepayment or other interim calculations?

These provisions are commonly used in institutional loans, and you should know the answer. According to many experts, the borrower will pay a "disguised" increase in the stated interest rate of approximately 1.4 percent of the stated interest rate. That means that if straight interest at 9 percent for one year on a $10,000 loan would be $900, the short-year computation would be $912.60. In effect the lender gets five days' extra interest each year.

That's not so bad if you're dealing with $10,000, but suppose you're dealing with $100,000,000. Then it would cost $126,000 extra a year.

Lenders' Language

Since 360-day interest is a practice that is followed by most institutional lenders, what can you do? For one thing, look at the commitment language and the language in the note. It may not be clear that the lender has a right to charge that extra interest.

On the other hand, lenders will want to use clear language such as: "interest on this note is computed on a 365/360 simple interest basis, i.e., by applying the ratio of the annual interest rate over a year of 360 days, multiplied by the outstanding principal balance, multiplied by the actual number of days the principal balance is outstanding." Or they may say: "interest shall be computed

based on the daily rate produced assuming a 360-day year multiplied by the actual number of days elapsed."

Those provisions make it pretty clear that lenders are getting a slightly greater rate from the 360-day method. But if the language is not clear in the commitment and the note, you may be able
to help yourself with the argument that the 360-day calculation is
only to cover interim payments and not to create a higher effective
interest rate. Based on current interest rates, you could save
approximately 11 basis points above the stated annual rate.

According to one commentator, imprecise lenders' language
that may be challenged by borrowers includes phrases like "360-
day annual rate of interest earned," and "360-day simple interest
basis." See Allan W. Vestal, *No Longer Bending to the Purposes of
the Money Lenders: Prohibiting the "Bank Method" of Interest Calculation,* 70 N.C. L. REV. 243, 267 n.105 (1991).

Negotiate

Is a stated interest rate somewhat misleading when the
lender comes out with a 360-day calculation? For most people the
word "year" means 365 days. However, institutional lenders will
take the position that the method of calculation cannot be deceptive
if it embodies "the custom of the trade" that most commercial borrowers and lenders understand. This may be true in commercial
settings, but it is not true in consumer loans. Most consumers,
including many lawyers, have no understanding that a stated
interest rate may only account for 360 days' interest and they will
also have to pay what amounts to an extra five days' interest (or six
days' in a leap year).

In that context, a New Jersey regulation specifically protects certain borrowers against these extra interest charges. It
applies to consumer lenders and licensed mortgage lenders. See
N.J.A.C. 3:15-10.1(c). But many states do not have a specific regulation on the subject.

You will ultimately get down to whether the lender can be
moved to change its standard way of doing business. The time to
deal with it is before the commitment is signed. Perhaps that issue
can be negotiated along with other loan costs, including points,
commitment fees, attorneys' fees, and interest to be paid on any
escrows and reserves. If the lender won't budge on that, at least you
can make sure that when you check alternative sources of

financing, you compare proverbial "apples to apples." There may be nontraditional lenders who will calculate interest differently.

A more interesting question arises if the commitment has been accepted without clear 360-day language and you then encounter for the first time a note and mortgage that contain that language. That's where you may have rights to object.

The 360-Day Year

It may be of some comfort to lenders to know that the use of a 360-day year is merely part of an ancient tradition of using the lunar calendar and has very little to do with greed. These traditions were no more than an attempt to make all months equal because contracts were often written for a period of months and not days. Ancients would take the 31st day from some months and add two days to February to accomplish this. Montesquieu in the *Spirit of Laws* stated: "The preservation of the ancient custom is a considerable point in respect to manners." See also Werner Sombart's *Die Juden und das Wirtschaftsleben*, page 285, which discusses the use of 360 days in Hellenistic Egypt in the second and first century B.C.

On the other hand, some authorities have not been sanguine about 360-day years. In one class action the U.S. Ninth Circuit Court of Appeals held that a national bank's method of computing interest on the basis of a 360-day year made the loan usurious under Oregon law. The borrower had the right to recover twice the amount of all interest paid. *American Timber & Trading Co. v. First Nat'l Bank*, 511 F.2d 980 (9th Cir. 1973). The court rejected the bank's contention that it relied upon industry custom. It questioned the existence of such a custom, "but even if it were industry practice, it is highly unlikely that this would be sufficient to justify nonretroactive application. Any claim by the banking industry that ease of calculation is justification for exacting higher interest is of dubious validity in this age of computer technology."

In a comprehensive article on the subject, Professor Vestal explores what he considers a "failure" of the American legal system. He concludes that "banks are diverting perhaps in excess of one billion dollars annually from their customers into their own coffers by simply redefining what constitutes a year." Vestal, cited above, at 243. Vestal argues, as has been stated in various court opinions, that the laws of nature do not have to bend "to the purposes of the money lender." Vestal concludes that the 360-day-year interest calculation ought to "offend our sense of fairness and propriety." In the debate over the calculation of interest, he finds "yet another frontier of the legal system's chronic abandonment of the less powerful."

In light of the long tradition of the 360-day lending year, this will seem to many to be a cynical assessment. That's particularly true with large commercial loans where many borrowers are represented by attorneys and other sophisticated advisors—and some are more "powerful" (!) than their lenders. It is also hard to fault those lenders for "unfairness" who have disclosed up front how they will be calculating interest.

6 PERCENTAGE LATE CHARGES ARE LEGAL

Courts around the country have been struggling with the problem of whether percentage late charges and default rates are enforceable in mortgage loans.

The New Jersey appellate courts became the battleground for this in 1999, and for the moment at least, lenders have won the battle. In the case of *MetLife Capital Financial Corp. v. Washington Avenue Assocs.*, 713 A.2d 527 (N.J. Super. Ct. App. Div. 1998), cert. granted, 719 A.2d 1025 (N.J. 1998), *aff'd in part, rev'd in part, rem'd*, 732 A.2d 493 (N.J. 1999), the New Jersey Supreme Court held that a 5 percent late charge and a 15 percent default rate are reasonable charges in a commercial loan.

The court stated that a 5 percent late charge was a valid measure of liquidated damages and "reasonableness" should be based on the following factors:

- The charge was customary, and fairly compensated the lender for administrative costs needed to service delinquent loans.
- Various New Jersey and federal statutes authorized late charges of 5 percent.
- Case law from other jurisdictions generally upholds these charges, which are a normal part of the costs of doing business.

The Supreme Court criticized the Superior Court decision and held that in a commercial contract between sophisticated parties, liquidated-damages provisions are presumed to be reasonable and the party challenging them should bear the burden of proving otherwise.

The logic of supporting a percentage measure of damages is that larger loans "command more attention than do smaller loans" and engender more costs than a delinquent payment on a smaller loan. Also, a lender suffers larger "opportunity-cost" damages when a borrower is late with a larger payment.

Default Interest Rates

When discussing whether a default interest rate is reasonable, the court adopted a presumption that these default interest rates, like late fees, are reasonable. In *MetLife* the court held that the 3 percent extra interest rate was a reasonable estimate of the potential cost of administering a defaulted loan, and "the potential difference between the contract rate and the rate that MetLife might pay to secure a commercial loan replacing the lost funds."

The court also discussed the difficulties faced by lenders in determining actual losses resulting in a loan default, in predicting the nature and term of a loan default or market conditions for future loans, in predicting their own borrowing costs in the future, and in estimating their collection costs.

The court acknowledged that the imposition of percentage late charges and default interest rates is "a practical solution to the problem of pricing loans according to anticipated rather than actual performance, and the difficulty in allocation and determining the costs and damages of late payments and default." It was concerned with the alternatives of trying to calculate actual damages in every default situation, which the court indicated would be "economically inefficient or judicially impractical."

The court made it clear that its holding applied only to commercial loan transactions and did not address the issue of liquidated damage clauses and penalties in consumer contracts or residential mortgages. However, much of the rationale of the court would seem to apply even to those type loans.

The case involved a mortgage loan of $1,500,000 secured by a commercial property leased to Walgreen's, and the borrower defaulted on making the final mortgage balloon payment of almost $1,400,000 at the end of the four-year term. MetLife claimed the default interest rate of 15 percent on the balance due and a late fee of 5 percent on various delinquent monthly mortgage payments, but on appeal withdrew its original claim to recover a 5 percent late fee on the defaulted balloon payment.

Because these issues are still alive in other states, it is helpful to review the earlier Superior Court decision that was reversed.

Are Charges a "Penalty"?

The Superior Court stated that, although there was no reported case in New Jersey dealing directly with the question of the penal nature of a fixed percent late charge, the requested fees and interest rate were uncollectible penalties because they were not related to any damages suffered by MetLife in connection with the delinquencies. That court adopted the Restatement (Second) of Contracts § 356(1) (1981), which provides: "Damages for breach by either party may be liquidated in the agreement but only at an amount that is reasonable in light of the anticipated or actual loss caused by the breach and the difficulties of proof of loss. A term fixing unreasonably large liquidated damages is unenforceable on grounds of public policy as a penalty."

In reaching the conclusion that the reclaimed charges were not "reasonable," the court found that MetLife's testimony was inadequate to show that actual default costs approached the agreed percentages. In addition, the court found that the 5 percent late fee is probably usurious because that same 5 percent is charged whether the installment is one day late or 30 days late. Also, if the purpose of the late fee were to compensate the lender for loss of the use of money for the period of the delinquency, the element of damage to the lender is ascertainable and it would not be merely a flat 5 percent charge applicable to all circumstances.

The Superior Court was persuaded that MetLife had been unable to show that a fixed percentage fee was "reasonably related to the anticipated or actual internal costs" of MetLife. It went on to explain that it was convinced that one of the purposes of the late charge was "coercive," and intended to provide an incentive to the borrower to make timely payments "on pain of incurring the late charge." According to the court, that was a penalty by definition.

The Twofold Test

It is instructive to review the court's analysis of the 5 percent late fee in light of the language of the Restatement that was quoted earlier. The Superior Court viewed the question as "twofold." First, whether the 5 percent was "reasonably related to the anticipated or actual damage likely to be suffered by the lender," and second, whether those damages were "unascertainable or difficult to prove, resulting in the inconvenience or nonfeasibility of otherwise obtaining a remedy." *MetLife*, 713 A.2d at 534. In the court's analysis, MetLife failed on both these counts.

On the first count, it determined that a fixed percentage without consideration of the duration of the breach or the amount of the late installment could not be "reasonably" related to the anticipated damages. "Thus, the same five percent applies whether the late installment was $1,000 or $10,000 or $100,000, and whether it was one day late or thirty or sixty." *Id.* Therefore, the court concluded that a reasonable liquidated provision would have to be in the nature of a flat fee that would be the same for all borrowers.

On the second count, the court determined that "at least some" of the legitimate elements of damage to which MetLife testified are neither unascertainable nor difficult to calculate. Therefore, the court implies that the lender does not need a liquidated damage provision because it might be feasible to calculate the actual damages.

It is not clear about how much of the court's conclusion was based on the limited evidence presented in *MetLife* and whether the court might decide cases differently where lenders present more persuasive evidence on the actual damages. For example, suppose evidence were introduced showing some relationship between the amount of a mortgage default and a loss. After a declared default, regulated lenders such as commercial banks, thrifts, and insurance companies are required to place money in reserves based on the amount of a defaulted loan in order to meet regulatory standards. Since that reserve does not bear interest, the lender immediately starts losing income in an amount that is difficult to calculate. See, e.g., "Accounting by Creditors for Impairment of a Loan," *Statement of Financial Accounting Standards No. 118* (Financial Accounting Standards Bd. 1994); *1997 NAIC Life Risk-Base Capital Report Including Overview and Instructions for Companies* (National Association of Insurance Commissioners, Nov. 18, 1997); "Allowance for Loan and Lease Losses," *Commercial Bank Examination Manual*, § 2070 (Bd. of Governors of the Fed. Reserve Sys., Div. of Banking Supervision and Regulation, 1998); "The greater the reserves, the greater the cost to the bank of maintaining the loan," Patricia T. Habicht, "Commercial Banks' Perspectives on Real Estate Financing in the 1990s," in 5 *The American College of Real Estate Lawyers Papers* 5, 7 (1992).

Car Wreck Factor

Also, there is another factor that is arguably related to the amount of the loan. One might call it the "car wreck factor." When an automobile is wrecked in an accident, the car is worth less in the market than it was before the accident—even though it appears to be fully repaired. The frame may be bent in some way that does not affect the appearance of the car. A depreciation factor may be estimated in determining the calculation of damages because that car is forever blemished in the marketplace.

In the same way, defaulted loans may be blemished. Even if the borrower brings itself current after a declared default, the loan may be worth less on resale because the borrower has demonstrated its unreliability. That loss factor arguably relates to the amount of the default and the amount of the loan, and is difficult to calculate. Why shouldn't the reduced market value be covered by an agreed liquidated damage provision such as a late fee? In fact, several courts that have upheld late fee provisions have pointed to this market loss factor as an element of a lender's damages when the borrower misses a payment. In addition, as stated above, a loan that has suffered a default often suffers a loss in its market value. Enabling a lender to increase the rate through the use of a late charge enables the lender to recover some of the value it has lost by virtue of the default.

Many loans are being serviced in securitized pools and defaulted loans become special cases. "At some point the loan goes to a special servicer, with a different fee structure. The fee servicer often receives a percentage of the proceeds, even out of a corrected loan." Michael S. Gambro and James P. Carroll, "What You Need to Know About Real Estate Securitization," 14 *The Practical Real Estate Lawyer* 9, 14 (ALI-ABA, Sept. 1998).

In addition to these issues, other evidence might bear on the second count, which relates to whether the damages are "unascertainable or difficult to prove." Suppose the lender proved that once a default is declared, regulatory agencies such as the Comptroller of the Currency and State Banking Departments frequently require an updated analysis of the loan and delinquency reports. Suppose evidence is introduced about all of the extra time required by loan officers, workout officers, in-house inspectors and appraisers, and others after a default in order to complete that analysis and to assess whether to sell the delinquent mortgage or proceed with foreclosure. A proper estimate would have to include an appropriate allocation of staff and officers' compensation, and overhead office costs for factors such as rent or occupancy expenses. Since these are internal costs, it can be shown that calculation of these costs will be "difficult to prove." Will that be enough for future courts to approve similar late fees?

Also, institutional lenders frequently establish special departments or "workout groups" to deal with delinquent loans. They never know which loans will go into default but can usually estimate that a certain percentage of the dollar volume of loans will need special attention. Compensation for these officers and staff is a continuing overhead cost and it is appropriate for lenders to allocate these costs among loans that go into default. How can this be calculated unless borrowers are required to pay delinquent fees and increased interest rates on default? Should lenders be required to allocate these costs among all loans or only the delinquent ones?

Applicable Statutes

Numerous federal and state statutes authorize a lender to charge a fixed late fee. Under federal law 12 U.S.C. § 85, national banks, which are governed by the office of the Comptroller of the Currency, may charge late fees and default interest rates up to that allowed under their home state's laws, irrespective of the limits imposed on such charges by the home state of the borrower. See *Smiley v. Citibank*, 517 U.S. 735 (1996); *Bank One v. Mazaika (In re Citibank Credit Card Litig.)*, 680 A.2d 845 (Pa. 1996) (12 U.S.C. § 85 encompasses both flat and percentage late fees). Similarly, under 12 C.F.R. § 560.2 and 12 C.F.R. § 701.21, particular institutions, such as federal savings and loan associations and federal credit unions, are exempt from state laws that regulate loan-related fees, including late charges.

In addition, various provisions in federal law authorize lenders to impose fixed late fees. The Department of Veterans Affairs authorizes a VA-guaranteed mortgage lender to charge up to 4 percent of any installment that is delinquent more than 15 days, 38 C.F.R. § 36.4212. See *Moore v. Lomas Mortgage USA*, 796 F. Supp. 300 (N.D. Ill. 1992) (lender entitled to impose 4 percent late charge under standard VA mortgage forms). Furthermore, the Department of Housing and Urban Development provides that a HUD guaranteed mortgage may include a 4 percent late charge for installments that are more than 15 days in arrears. 24 C.F.R. § 235.1216.

Additional federal statutes and regulations authorize late charges. For example, the Federal Housing Administration authorizes a lender to assess a late fee for a loan installment more than 15 days overdue of up to 2 percent of the late installment in connection with an FHA guaranteed mortgage loan. 24 C.F.R. § 241.1105.

The Superior Court was correct that it was presented with a question of first impression about the validity of late fees in commercial mortgages under New Jersey law. But the court failed to mention that in 1996, the New Jersey legislature enacted a statute authorizing the collection of late charges on junior mortgage loans made to non-corporations in connection with two to six dwelling units, as long as that charge does not exceed 5 percent of the defaulted payment. N.J. Stat. 17:11C-28(c).

Fixed percentage late charges are permissible under several different New Jersey statutes, all in furtherance of the clearly stated policy of the legislature that New Jersey should be as equally attractive to banks as other states "which have the least restrictive laws regarding interest and related charges." N.J. Stat. 17:3B-29. Therefore, in various statutes dealing with home repair contracts (N.J. Stat. 17:16C-71), credit union loans (N.J. Stat. 17:13-104), revolving credit loans (N.J. Stat. 17:3B-29), and savings and loan association loans (N.J. Stat. 17:12B-48(13)), the New Jersey legislature has reinforced the notion that late charges based on a fixed percentage of the amount due do not violate New Jersey public policy.

Late Fees—Traveling the Route of Other States

Outside of New Jersey, a variety of courts have evaluated loan late fees. In general, two different types of analyses have been done. First, some courts have viewed the imposition of late fees as a means of providing additional interest and have evaluated whether such additional interest violates the state's usury laws.

Second, some courts have viewed the imposition of late fees as a means of providing for liquidated damages, and have evaluated whether the liquidated damage provision is reasonable under the circumstances. See, generally, annot., *Validity and Construction of Provision Imposing "Late Charge" or Similar Exaction for Delay in Making Periodic Payments on Note, Mortgage or Installment Sale Contract,* 63 A.L.R.3d 50.

Given the number of decisions and the variety of their outcomes concerning various types of late fees in mortgages, loans, and other consumer transactions, it is difficult to predict how a particular late fee will be viewed by a court. However, a few generalizations are supported by the case law.

Usury

First, late fees may be considered interest, and subject the loan or mortgage to usury violations, under particular state statutes that employ a broad definition of "interest" in determining usury or that exempt only certain lenders or type of loans from usury review. For example, several Louisiana cases have interpreted that state's usury law to include late fees as interest, based on a statutory provision that damages paid because of the delay in making a loan payment constitute interest. *Gordon Finance Co. v. Chambliss*, 236 So.2d 533 (La. Ct. App. 1970), cert. denied, 239 So.2d 364 (La. 1970); *Thrift Funds of Baton Rouge v. Jones*, 274 So.2d 150 (La. 1973), cert. denied, 414 U.S. 820 (1973); *Wright Ins. Agency, Inc. v. Scott*, 371 So.2d 1207 (La. Ct. App. 1979); *Ganus v. Jopes*, 470 So.2d 237 (La. App. 1985).

Additionally, in *Begelfer v. Najarian*, 409 N.E.2d 167 (Mass. 1980), the Supreme Judicial Court of Massachusetts held a 5 percent late-fee provision in a mortgage note invalid under that state's usury laws, which calculate usury by including both interest and expenses paid by borrowers. Furthermore, a 10 percent late charge imposed by the seller of a home under a mortgage taken back from the buyer constituted interest under Texas's usury law because the seller did not fall into one of those classes of lenders exempt from the state's usury law, such as savings and loan associations. *Dixon v. Brooks*, 604 S.W.2d 330 (Tex. Ct. App. 1980).

However, as Nelson and Whitman state, the precedential value of these cases is limited because of the varying nature of states' usury statutes. Grant S. Nelson and Dale A. Whitman, *Real Estate Finance Law* § 6.9, p. 518. The treatment of late-payment charges and default interest rates varies considerably from state to state, and at least 15 states have adopted individual statutes regulating late fees. Most of these laws impose a minimum grace period, ranging from seven to fifteen days, and restrict the fee to an amount between 2 percent to 6 percent of the delinquent installment, with 5 percent designated as the most common figure. See Nelson and Whitman, above, § 6.8–6.10, pp. 514–523.

Unconscionable Fees

A second generalization is that a late-fee provision may be held invalid if the amount of the late fee is deemed to be "unconscionable" by the court. *Garrett v. Coast & Southern Federal Savings & Loan Ass'n*, 511 P.2d 1197 (Cal. 1973), is often cited as one of the leading cases holding a late-fee clause unenforceable as an invalid liquidated damage provision. However, a distinguishing factor in that case was that the late-fee provision required the borrower to pay a late fee equal to 2 percent of the unpaid principal balance, as opposed to one based solely on the unpaid installment. See also *Bank of Crockett v. Cullipher*, 752 S.W.2d 84 (Tenn. Ct. App. 1988) (late charge of one-tenth of one percent per day, annualized at 36 percent, of the outstanding principal balance was unconscionable).

Finally, a few courts have upheld late fees but limited their use in conjunction with other remedies the documents provided the lender. For example, in *Centerbank v. D'Assaro*, 600 N.Y.S.2d 1015 (N.Y. Sup. Ct. 1993), and *FDIC v. Napert-Boyer Partnership*, 671 A.2d 1303 (Conn. App. Ct. 1996), the courts held that the lender could not recover late fees once the lender had accelerated the loan. These courts reasoned that the late installments were no longer due, and hence subject to a late charge, once acceleration occurs.

In addition, the court in *In re Holliday Mart, Inc.*, 9 B.R. 99 (Bankr. D. Hawaii 1981), held invalid a 5 percent late fee that was used in conjunction with the lender's FIFO (first in, first out) policy regarding payments. The court reasoned that such a policy left the borrower in a position where the failure to pay one installment when due had the effect of causing all future installments to be late, and hence subject to the late charge.

Liquidated Damages

Outside of a handful of statutory provisions and the limited exceptions described above, courts have generally upheld late-fee percentage clauses in mortgages or other loan documents as valid liquidated damage provisions. See, e.g., *Fowler v. First Fed. Savs. & Loan Ass'n*, 643 So.2d 30 (Fla. Dist. Ct. App. 1994), *rev. denied*, 658 So.2d 990 (Fla. 1995) (5 percent late fee); *TMG Life Ins. Co. v. Ashner*, 898 P.2d 1145 (Kan. Ct. App. 1995) (5 percent late fee); *Mattvidi Assocs. Ltd. Partnership v. Nationsbank*, 639 A.2d 228 (Md. Ct. Spec. App.), cert. denied, 647 A.2d 1216 (Md. 1994) (5 percent late fee); *Travelers Ins. Co. v. Corporex Properties, Inc.*, 798

F. Supp. 423 (E.D. Ky. 1992) (4 percent late fee). But see *Garcia v. Canan*, 851 F. Supp. 327 (N.D. Ill. 1994) (10 percent late charge was unenforceable penalty under Illinois law, though lender did not seek recovery of late charge until loan has been accelerated upon borrower's default).

Late-fee provisions are generally upheld under the theory that "agreements for penalties to induce prompt payment are free from usury, because the buyer has it in his power to avoid the penalty by discharging the debt when it is due." *Hayes v. First Nat'l Bank*, 507 S.W.2d 701, 703 (Ark. 1974).

Default Interest Rates—Traveling Route One

Aside from upholding late-fee percentage clauses, many courts throughout the country have upheld default interest rates. For example, in the case of *In re Route One West Windsor Limited Partnership*, 225 B.R. 76 (Bankr. D.N.J. 1998), the United States Bankruptcy Court for the District of New Jersey, applying New York law, sustained a default-interest rate that was 8 percent greater than the non-default rate. Therefore, the lender in that case was able to enforce a default rate of 15 $1/_8$ percent and the borrower was hit with an additional sum of approximately $900,000 because of the default.

That court, in a well-researched opinion, stated:

> One factor which the courts have considered is the difference between the non-default and the default rates. Not surprisingly, courts have declined to enforce very high default rates. See, e.g., *In re Kalian*, 178 B.R. at 316–17 (refusing to enforce a default rate of 36%); *In re Consolidated Properties*, 152 B.R. at 458 (refusing to enforce interest rate which was 36% higher than base); *In re Hollstrom*, 133 B.R. 535, 539–40 (refusing to enforce default rate of 36% where pre-default rate was 12%); *DWS Investments, Inc.*, 121 B.R. 845, 850 (Bankr. C.D. Cal. 1990) (refusing to enforce default rate of 25% where non-default rates were 14% and 15%); *In re White*, 88 B.R. 498, 511 (Bankr. D. Mass. 1988) (default rate of interest of 48% was unenforceable where pre-default rate was 16.5%). Courts have, however, permitted lower default interest rates. *In re Terry*, 27 F.3d at 244 (holding increase in pre-default rate of $14^1/_4$% to default rate of $17^1/_4$% was not unreasonable); *In re Lib-*

erty Warehouse, 220 B.R. 546, 552 (enforcing 22.8% default rate where non-default rate was 14%); *In re Courtland Estates*, 144 B.R. at 9 (enforcing default rate of 18% where the pre-default rate was 15%); *In re Skyler Ridge*, 80 B.R. 500, 511 (Bankr. C.D. Cal. 1987) (stating the 14.75% default interest rate fell "well within the range of interest rates that the Court has seen frequently in recent years"). While the 8% difference between the non-default and default rates is large, it is not unprecedented. It is in fact slightly less than the default rate which was enforced in *Liberty Warehouse.*

As noted in *In re Liberty Warehouse*, the spread between the non-default and default rates of interest (i.e. 8.8%) is smaller than the differential present in most cases where courts have found the default rate to constitute a penalty. See, e.g., *Kalian*, 178 B.R. at 309 (18% spread); *Boardwalk Partners*, 171 B.R. 87, 92 (14.5% differential); *Hollstrom*, 133 B.R. at 537 n. 3–4 (24% spread); *DWS Investments*, 121 B.R. at 849 (9–10% differential); *White*, 88 B.R. at 499 (35% spread). 220 B.R. at 552. The court finds that the default rate is not so high as to be inherently unacceptable.

Id. at 90.

Life After *MetLife*

After the New Jersey Superior Court decision in *MetLife,* two federal cases took a completely different route regarding default interest rates. *In re Route One West Windsor Limited Partnership*, discussed above, sustained a default rate 8 percent higher than the regular rate; and *Florida Asset Financing Corp. v. Dixon (In re Dixon)*, 228 B.R. 166 (Bankr. W.D. Va. 1998), sustained a 36 percent default interest rate!

In the *Route One* case, the court decided to apply New York law instead of New Jersey law. Therefore, it did not have to apply the *MetLife* rule. Even though the case involved a New Jersey debtor and a New Jersey property, the court honored the choice-of-law provision in the loan agreement, which stated that New York law governs. The court concluded that New York courts have upheld default rates of up to 25 percent and that default interest rates are not penalties because they are compensation for the increased costs of collection.

The court held that the purpose of the bankruptcy petition in that case was to avoid paying interest to the lender at the default rate and that there was nothing in the record that would justify relieving the "sophisticated" debtor from the burdens of the contract it had made on default interest. As quoted above, the court concluded that the spread of 8 percent between the non-default and default rates of interest is smaller than the differential present in most cases where the courts have found the default rate to be a penalty. The court cited several cases where default interest rates were not considered penalties because they were "compensation for the increased cost of collection."

In the *Dixon* case, the U.S. District Court for the Western District of Virginia reversed a bankruptcy court decision and held that an oversecured creditor could recover a default interest rate of 36 percent. The bankruptcy court had held that such a rate was "in the nature of a penalty and punitive." The district court cited the applicable Bankruptcy Code section (11 U.S.C. § 506(b)) and various federal cases. It concluded that "default rates are also necessarily higher than basic interest rates in order to compensate creditors for both the predictable and unpredictable costs of monitoring the value of lateral in default situations." *Dixon,* above, at 172. It based its decision on an analysis of both federal and state law and concluded that it was sufficient for the lender to represent that the default rate was proportionate to the reasonably anticipated damage from default, and therefore not a penalty.

In contrast to the *MetLife* decision, it was not necessary for the lender to introduce evidence in support of the default rate if 36 percent interest, although acknowledged as high, was considered to be a lawful business transaction between sophisticated parties. The court held:

> In turn, I find that the *bankruptcy court below erred by resting part of its holding on Florida Asset's failure to justify the reasonableness of the default rate.* An affirmative showing of reasonableness would only reinforce the clear conclusion in this case, while unnecessarily burdening the statutory rights of Florida Asset as an oversecured creditor under Section 506(b). Consequently, I find that the bankruptcy court's reliance on Florida Asset's failure to introduce evidence in support of the default rate, through a showing of demonstrated need, commercial reasonableness, or otherwise, was erroneous.

While a thirty-six percent interest rate is high, the courts do not have plenary power to alter commercial contracts or to substitute their judgment for that of the parties. This was a lawful business transaction between sophisticated parties. Despite the generous default interest rate, there are no third parties hurt by recognition of the contract term, and no evidence exists that Dixon will be thwarted in his efforts to reorganize. To relieve Dixon from his contractual obligation, therefore, would be unjustified.

Dixon, above, at 176 (emphasis added) (footnote deleted). The court went on to say that:

Furthermore, a per se rule which requires justification for the use of a particular default rate seems to go against the purpose behind the use of default rates in the first place. Default interest rates are used as a means of compensating a lender for the unpredictable and hard-to-quantify administrative expenses and inconvenience in monitoring untimely payments. See *In re Terry Ltd. Partnership*, 27 F.3d at 244. "The costs incurred in performing this task vary from case to case and simply cannot be provided for beforehand." *Id*.

Id. at 174, n.8.

It is noteworthy that in both *In re Route One West Windsor Limited Partnership* and *Dixon*, the lender had attempted to enforce not only the default interest rate, but also late fees based on a percentage of the late payment. In each of those cases, the court held that an oversecured creditor may receive payment of either default interest or late charges, but not both.

Was the Superior Court Legislating?

The policy on commercial-loan late-payment charges should not be considered in the abstract. Legal precedent on those loans may have an impact on similar charges for other loans and other contracts. Also, that policy may have broad economic implications for interest rates and availability of loans. In that light it seems that legislatures are in a better position to deal with these charges than courts.

Given that New Jersey already allows 5 percent late fees on junior residential mortgages, the Superior Court was out of line. If a

5 percent charge is not "against public policy" when a loan is made to individuals who are financing their residential properties, it should not be against public policy to charge that amount to sophisticated corporations borrowing money for commercial purposes.

Frequently, commercial loans like the one in *MetLife* are many times the magnitude of the consumer-type loans, and those commercial borrowers are generally represented by attorneys and in a better position to protect themselves than consumers. Courts should be reluctant to reverse customary business practices, particularly when they sometimes result from agreements entered by sophisticated partners represented by counsel. As explained by one court in rejecting a borrower's argument that a 5 percent late-fee provision was invalid, "If appellants truly believed that this provision was not reasonable, they could have negotiated different terms, as they did with regard to other portions of the loan documents." *Mattvidi*, 639 A.2d at 239.

Similar percentage provisions for a penalty interest rate and a late fee are provided in literally hundreds of thousands of mortgage loans throughout the United States. Over the years many delinquent borrowers have paid those fees in full or in part without protest.

The *MetLife* case carries enormous implications for both lenders and borrowers. The Superior Court acknowledged that the validity of the percentage late charge has been sustained in other jurisdictions primarily on the basis of industry custom and standards, without analysis of its nature or relationship to anticipated or actual damages. So the issue is whether *MetLife* will be applied to non-mortgage loans, installment sales, construction contracts, and other agreements.

If courts will require evidence of a lender's costs after default in order to show that the percentage charges are related to those costs, the effect will be to bar most of these charges. Borrowers will argue that the costs of servicing a late payment consist only of employee and computer time involved in adjusting the borrower's file plus the cost of an envelope, stamp, and notice form.

In *MetLife* the Supreme Court pointed out that it did not address the issue of liquidated damages in consumer contracts or residential mortgages. Also, it didn't base its decision on whether the borrower and lender had negotiated at length with competent attorneys to agree on the late fees and default interest rates, or how sophisticated the borrowers were. The Supreme Court merely accepted percentage charges, similar to those that have been customarily used in commercial loan documents and enforced in many states for some time.

Testing the Decision

As other courts deal with these issues, the wisdom of the *MetLife* decision may be tested against additional analysis.

Commitment Fees

Suppose in *MetLife* the loan documents had provided for a 5 percent "commitment fee" when the loan became due, instead of a 5 percent delinquency payment. The loan documents could have provided that if the mortgage was not paid in full when due, the loan would automatically extend for another two or three months, or more. Suppose the documents called for a 5 percent commitment fee if that extension were triggered. Generally, an agreement to pay a loan-commitment fee may be enforced even if based on a percentage of the loan. See Charles B. Katzenstein, *The Law of Mortgage Commitments* § 16.02 (1992, 1998 supp.). Would that have been a less difficult case to decide?

Suppose a similar arrangement was made about each monthly installment? If a payment was not made on time, the mortgage could require a 5 percent fee for a 10-day extension. Wouldn't that clearly be enforceable?

Discounting the Interest Rate

Suppose the original loan documents in *MetLife* had provided that the interest rate on the loan was 15 percent, but that the borrower would have a right to pay only 9.55 percent (which was the regular interest rate under the *MetLife* loan before default) as long as the borrower were not in default. Suppose during that period MetLife was willing to waive the excess interest as long as there was no default, and that was all spelled out in the loan documents. Suppose the document provided for a "discount" to the lower rate for any month that payment was made on time. This would have the same economic effect as a default interest rate, but it would be clear to the borrower from the beginning that the agreed rate without a discount was 15 percent.

Fifteen percent interest is clearly within the range of commercial legal interest rates and cannot be considered "usurious."

Would this discounting system make decisions for other courts easier once borrowers go into default and lenders claim the original 15 percent contract rate?

In re Route One West Windsor Limited Partnership, above, at 89, suggests a rationale for supporting that approach. There, the court quotes with approval a statement from the Second Circuit Court of Appeals:

> A variable interest provision in event of a stated default such as we have here is not a penalty, nor should it be considered unconscionable. It can be beneficial to a debtor in that it may enable him to obtain money at a lower rate of interest than he could otherwise obtain it, for if a creditor had to anticipate a possible loss in the value of the loan due to his debtor's bankruptcy or reorganization, *he would need to exact a higher uniform interest rate for the full life of the loan. The debtor has the benefit of the lower rate until the crucial event occurs; he need not pay a higher rate throughout the life of the loan.*

Route One, above, at 89, quoting *Ruskin v. Griffiths*, 269 F.2d at 827 (2d Cir. 1959) (emphasis added, citations omitted).

The waiver provision or the discount still might be considered a disguised penalty, but consider a different scenario.

Increased Rate at End of Loan

Suppose the documents provided for a 9.55 percent interest rate up to the beginning of the last month of the loan. After that, interest would increase to 15 percent. The increased rate would not even depend on a default. A court would then have no reason to invalidate the 15 percent as a penalty on nonpayment.

These hypotheticals are just a few of the examples that courts may have to struggle with once they intervene in arm's-length agreements between sophisticated parties who have agreed on what results should follow when a borrower defaults on a commercial loan. If they start finding that percentage late fees are penalties, future courts will no longer have the luxury of applying agreed percentages to calculate liquidated damages. And lawyers on both sides will introduce complex and detailed evidence concerning such issues as internal costs, interest factors, and the allocation of the time that officers and committees of the lender work in connection with the default after it occurs. This could precipitate a proliferation of litigation whenever defaults occur.

Refund Claims

Also, what will courts do about all of those borrowers who in past years have paid late fees and default interest rates under loans that have been satisfied? Many of those payments have been discounted by settlement agreements with lenders and work-out agreements involving numerous properties. Would any of those borrowers then be able to sue for refunds? If so, how will those refunds be calculated?

Other Contracts

In addition, once courts invalidate late charges in mortgages, how will it affect late charges in leases, sales agreements, and other contracts? How will it affect collection of attorneys' fees that are often set as a percentage of the balance of a defaulted loan? See, e.g., *Citicorp Mortgage v. Morrisville Hampton Village Realty, Ltd.*, 662 A.2d 1120 (Pa. Super. 1995) (10 percent attorney's fee is reasonable).

As discussed earlier, an inability to charge percentage late fees may encourage loan defaults and either discourage lending in the applicable state or cause interest rates to rise to compensate for certain intangible losses that will not otherwise be recovered. For example, the overhead costs of maintaining work-out groups may have to be spread over all loans and not just defaulted loans.

As recognized by some courts:

> A variable interest provision in event of a stated default such as we have here is not a penalty, nor should it be considered unconscionable.... It can be beneficial to a debtor in that it may enable him to obtain money at a lower rate of interest than he could otherwise obtain it, for if a creditor had to anticipate a possible loss in the value of the loan due to his debtor's bankruptcy or reorganization, he would need to exact a higher uniform interest rate for the full life of the loan. The debtor has the benefit of the lower rate until the crucial event occurs; he need not pay a higher rate throughout the life of the loan.

... [I]t seems to us the opposite of equity to allow the debtor to escape the expressly-bargained-for result of its act.

Ruskin v. Griffiths, 269 F.2d 827, 832 (2d Cir. 1959), cert. denied, 361 U.S. 947 (1960) (citations omitted).

"Good Faith and Fair Dealing"

Other courts that consider these issues should not ignore special circumstances that may have influenced the Superior Court decision in the *MetLife* case. MetLife had collected the Walgreen's rent during a 10-month period after default, and had never accounted for those rents other than making a notation on the proof of the amount due that the borrowers were entitled to a credit. In dealing with this issue, that court mentioned twice how that treatment demonstrated a failure by MetLife of "good faith and fair dealing" and also how that conduct illustrated "essential unfairness."

The court stated:

> ... What Metlife did was to accord itself the interest-free use of the money it had collected on the mortgagor's account at the same time that it was charging the mortgagor the enhanced default interest rate on the entire principal balance on a daily basis.... Illustrative of what we perceive to be the essential unfairness of Metlife's conduct was the manner in which it addressed the advances for taxes. It treated the direct tax payments it made after the default as further advances to the mortgagor on the loan. Although it had collected rents sufficient to pay the taxes, it chose not to apply the rents to that obligation of the mortgagor but instead, while retaining the interest-free use of the rents, advanced the taxes against the loan and charged the mortgagor the post-default rate of 12.55 percent on those advances. The point, of course, is that while Metlife was free to apply the rents in any order it chose, it was not applying them at all, but was, rather, continuing to charge the mortgagor interest on the entire debt while at the same time making interest-free use of the collected rents.

MetLife, 713 A.2d at 532.

Perhaps there is some wisdom in the old expression: "Hard cases make bad law."

Chaos and "Saddam Hussein Strategy"

It is difficult to assess the impact of barring penalty-type late fees on loan defaults. However, one critic has predicted that one of the most dramatic consequences of outlawing percentage late charges will be that the incentive to pay on time will be lost, "as every borrower will be better off by delaying payment as long as possible, knowing that the charges will be the same in the event of default as they will be in the event of prompt payment. Indeed, if interest rates have risen the borrower would be foolish in the extreme to pay his loan, rather than investing his/her money elsewhere. . . . In light of the default crisis already plaguing the lending industry, this encouragement to borrowers to ignore their obligations will yield chaos." Clark Alpert, *Voice of the Bar—Late Fee Ban Will Make Defaults Mushroom*, 153 N.J.L.J. 1245 (Sept. 21, 1998).

The *MetLife* case may be the best example of this attitude. Evidence showed that the borrower was late for 40 of 48 required installments. To make things worse, no evidence was presented that the borrower could not have paid on time. Since the tenant's monthly rent exceeded the borrower's required mortgage payment, it is conceivable that the borrower was taking advantage of the financial float each month.

Without the threat of a default fee, borrowers might be tempted to follow what might be called a "Saddam Hussein Strategy." The borrower could keep the rent payments as long as possible, build up a "war chest," and pay up on the brink of foreclosure when the lender sent in its troops of lawyers. The temptation to do this will be particularly great if interest rates rise or the stock market shoots up, so that the float becomes more valuable.

In addition, commercial mortgage lenders have stated that the loss of late fees and default interest payments will decrease the availability and increase the cost of commercial mortgage loans in New Jersey. *Amici Curiae Brief on Behalf of the Mortgage Bankers Association of America and the Commercial Real Estate Secondary Market and Securitization Association*, September 3, 1998. The growth of the capital-markets-mortgage industry has resulted in an enormous secondary market where commercial mortgages are sold and money is raised from investors in mortgage-backed securities. This program generally decreases the cost of financing mortgage loans.

However, that market requires predictability and when a commercial mortgage lacks or varies loan terms that the capital-market investors expect, or a provision like default charges becomes unenforceable, the loan loses predictability. The loan then becomes what is sometimes called a "story loan," which means that it has to be explained because it is different. That "story loan" can become more costly and must be dealt with as an exception because its differences must be disclosed to the capital-market investors and the national credit agencies if the loan is to be deposited in a pool with other mortgages for securitization. See Michael S. Gambro and James P. Carroll, "What You Need to Know About Real Estate Securitization," 14 *The Practical Lawyer* 9, 14 (ALI-ABA, Sept. 1998). In fact that is what has happened with loans from California and Louisiana that also ban certain percentage-default charges.

Summary

If the New Jersey Supreme Court had not reversed the Superior Court's decision in *MetLife*, New Jersey commercial loans could have become "story loans," with the loss of fixed percentage late fees and default interest rates viewed as causing a greater risk of default. Some lenders continuing to do business in New Jersey would simply have increased interest rates for commercial borrowers. Other lenders may have completely avoided making certain loans in New Jersey.

That's what could happen in other states that are seduced by debtors to outlaw percentage late fees and default interest rates in commercial mortgage loans.

7   PROFIT-MAKING PREPAYMENT PREMIUMS

In the classic children's tale about greed, the fisherman's wife asks the magic fish for one wish too many and loses everything. A California bankruptcy court decision places lenders on the same beach as the fisherman when they insist on overly punitive prepayment premiums in their loan agreements.

Mortgage lenders use various devices in their attempts to ensure that income flows generated by their loan agreements will not erode if market interest rates subsequently decline. To discourage borrowers from prepaying their loans and refinancing at lower rates, lenders use lock-in provisions, prohibitions of prepayment, and steep prepayment premiums. These prepayment premiums can be computed in various ways. They may be specified as a percentage of the amount prepaid, and sometimes, that percentage is reduced as the mortgage term approaches maturity. Some prepayment formulas relate the amount of premium to the level of market interest rates at the time of prepayment.

Mortgage lenders use prepayment premiums to protect legitimate economic interests. For example, insurance companies and investment funds often commit to maintain returns to their investors at certain levels based on anticipation of long-term cash flow from mortgage investments. If high-yielding mortgages are prepaid because market interest rates have fallen, these lenders will not be able to maintain the yield commitments made to their investors.

A "Fair" Prepayment Formula

Lenders often base a prepayment formula upon the interest rates of U.S. Treasury notes at the time of prepayment. This formula uses the difference between the stated mortgage rate and the Treasury rate at the time of prepayment to calculate the interest income the lender will lose during the normal term of the mortgage as the result of prepayment. The borrower must pay this amount as a premium. The Treasury rate is asserted to be an appropriate rate because (1) it is easy to ascertain, and (2) it is the rate of a safe investment—presumably, at least as safe as the mortgage being prepaid. These prepayment formulas are sometimes called "yield maintenance formulas."

Are these fair formulas? Will the courts enforce them? Two cases decided that these answers depend on details of the formula. If the formula is reasonably related to the loss the lender will suffer from prepayment, it may be enforceable. If it overcompensates the lender, it may not.

Fair Is Not Always Fair

In a leading case, *In re Skyler Ridge*, 80 B.R. 500 (Bankr. C.D. Cal. 1987), the bankruptcy court was asked to consider the legitimacy of a prepayment premium based upon the yield of U.S. Treasury notes at the time of prepayment. The premium was calculated by deducting the interest rate on designated Treasury notes from the mortgage rate, multiplying that difference by the number of years remaining on the loan, and multiplying the product by the principal being prepaid.

The borrower argued that this formula did not merely compensate for losses suffered by the prepayment, and therefore, it was an unenforceable penalty. That argument was two-pronged.

First, the loan was a construction loan on an apartment building. Because of the elements of risk in such activity, the interest rate on U.S. Treasury notes is systematically lower than the interest on this type of loan.

The court agreed and held that the market interest rate on U.S. Treasury notes was systematically and approximately 1.3 to 2 percentage points below the market for first mortgages. The court, therefore, held that if a lender chooses an index rate, such as a U.S. Treasury note index, "some appropriate adjustment" is required to make this rate comparable to the first mortgage rate. Presumably, a rate of 1.3 to 2 percent above the Treasury rate would be an acceptable benchmark.

The court found a second deficiency in the lender's formula. It contained no discount for present value. Therefore, application of the formula would permit the lender to recover the entire amount of lost interest at the time of prepayment; whereas, absent prepayment, this sum would accrue to the lender over the life of the loan. The court found that since the formula did not consider the time value of money, it was unreasonable and could not stand. In 1988, another bankruptcy court adopted the rationale of *Skyler Ridge* on a similar prepayment formula. *In re Kroh Bros. Dev. Co.*, 88 B.R. 997 (Bankr. W.D. Mo. 1988).

Legal Implications

The *Skyler Ridge* court's factual analysis led to its legal conclusions. Because the apartment project was located in Kansas, the court applied Kansas law to conclude that the unreasonable calculation of prepayment charges was an illegal penalty and void. Kansas law is harsh. If the court does not find that a liquidated damages formula results in a reasonable estimate of lender's damages (i.e., that it is "unreasonable"), the formula must be condemned as a penalty and struck down.

A second legal attack was based upon Section 506(b) of the Bankruptcy Code. (This section was applicable because the debtor had filed a voluntary bankruptcy petition under Chapter 11 of the Bankruptcy Code.) The code provides that "[t]o the extent that an allowed secured claim is secured by property the value of which ... is greater than the amount of such claim, there shall be allowed to the holder of such claim, interest on such claim, and any *reasonable* fees, costs, or charges provided for under the agreement under which such claim arose." 11 U.S.C. § 506(b) (emphasis added).

The court pointed out that the Bankruptcy Code may be more permissive than the common law on liquidated damages. Under the Bankruptcy Code, the court may award a reasonable portion of the premium even if the lender originally sought an amount that is unreasonable. However, because the court had already found that the total premium should be disallowed under Kansas law, the court did not have to reach the issue of whether, or to what extent, a "reasonable" liquidated damage award may have been allowable.

Skyler Ridge also invalidated an alternate prepayment premium, even less onerous than the Treasury note formula. The mortgage also included a provision that if that formula resulted in a premium of less than 1 percent of the prepaid balance, the premium would not, under any circumstances, go lower than 1 percent. The 1 percent, which would have been $150,000, was also held not "reasonably related" to the lender's anticipated loss. The court rejected the lender's (Travelers Insurance Company's) argument that it "could not relend $15,000,000 immediately upon its repayment, and that it would suffer additional lost interest from premature repayment." On this point, the court reasoned:

> ... First, the prepayment penalty provision requires thirty days notice to Travelers, which would give it a substantial amount of time to find a new home for the funds. While thirty days may not be entirely sufficient for this purpose, it would substantially attenuate any lost interest. Second, Travelers would certainly place the funds temporarily in the commercial paper or short term loan market, and thereby reduce any loss to one or two percent per annum for the gap. Thus any lost interest before the funds are placed in a new long-term loan would be limited to approximately $10,000 to $20,000. Cf. *Teachers [Ins. & Annuity Ass'n v. Butler]*, 626 F. Supp. [1229] at 1236 (disallowing claim for difference between short-term interest rate and contract rate for a period of six months). If this sum (or a formula to calculate it) had been included in the liquidated damages provision, it may have been upheld under Kansas law (if the provision as a whole were otherwise reasonable), either as a floor or as additional damages.

Skyler Ridge, 80 B.R. at 506.

This rationale would knock out most prepayment premiums in use today.

Prepayment on Default

A 1988 case, *Ridgley v. Topa Thrift & Loan Ass'n*, 953 P.2d 484 (Cal. 1998), highlights another facet of prepayment penalties. In that case, Ridgley, an architect and developer, bought a parcel of land in order to build a custom home for sale. When he sought a bridge loan to pay off the construction loan until a buyer could arrange permanent financing, he received a two-year mortgage loan for $2.3 million.

The printed form of note provided for monthly payments of interest with the right to prepay at any time upon payment of a fee equal to six months' interest. When Ridgley objected to this, the lender inserted a typewritten amendment that no prepayment would be required, provided all scheduled payments were made not more than 15 days after the due date.

Ridgley later defaulted on a payment and the bank billed him for a prepayment fee of $114,000, which Ridgley disputed as an unenforceable penalty. The Supreme Court of California held that a charge for a late payment measured against the unpaid balance of the loan must be deemed punitive in character. It is an attempt to coerce timely payments by forfeiture, which is not reasonably calculated to merely compensate the injured lender.

On the other hand, the court explained that a prepayment charge for a voluntary prepayment is generally considered a proper provision for alternative performance (i.e., prepayment), rather than a penalty. The *Ridgley* case was complicated by the fact that the charge was contingent both on prepayment and the late payment of an interest installment. Therefore, the charge could be characterized as both a prepayment charge and a late payment penalty. The court looked to the substance rather than the form of the provision, and agreed with the borrower that the charge operated as a penalty for late payment. It was therefore unenforceable.

Late-Payment Penalty

It is noteworthy that if the prepayment had been designed in the usual way, that is, it would be payable upon any prepayment regardless of default, it probably would have stood up. However, because the lender had yielded to the borrower's request that the prepayment should only be charged upon a default, the court characterized that fee as a late-payment penalty.

One great irony of the case is that if the bank had been less accommodating and insisted on a prepayment premium under all circumstances, it might have been better off. Some will seek a lesson in all of this as another little illustration of the cynical aphorism that "good guys finish last."

Conclusion

Research has revealed a scarcity of court decisions that invalidate prepayment premiums in commercial mortgages. The courts are reluctant to overturn negotiated provisions arrived at between two business entities that negotiate at arm's length, frequently with the advice and consent of attorneys and other advisors.

For a more detailed analysis see John C. Murray, *Enforceability of Prepayment-Premium Provisions in Mortgage Loan Documents* (http://www.firstam.com/faf/html/cust/jm-articles.html)

(2000), and Grant S. Nelson and Dale A. Whitman, *Real Estate Finance Law,* §§ 6.1–6.5 (3d ed. 1994).

Because *Skyler Ridge* and *Kroh Brothers* involved bankruptcy proceedings, these cases may not apply to a nonbankruptcy attempt by a borrower to make a voluntary prepayment. It seems likely that courts throughout the country will still enforce these premiums when a solvent borrower merely wants to refinance. However, some courts may scrutinize the financial impact of these formulas. Premiums that reasonably reimburse a lender for loss undoubtedly will withstand attack. And those lenders who try to measure their loss by formulas with the obvious defects of the *Skyler Ridge* formula may find themselves in the position of the fisherman's wife and lose it all.

8   MOST COURTS WILL NOT IMPLY PREPAYMENT RIGHTS

A 2001 case decided by the District of Columbia Court of Appeals emphasizes how important it is to spell out prepayment rights in a mortgage. Frequently, borrowers are careful about delineating the term of the loan, the interest rates, the principal payments, and default provisions; but they ignore their rights to prepay the loan. Prepayment rights are particularly important these days when interest rates have decreased and many borrowers would like to refinance and pay off their existing high-interest-rate mortgages. Sometimes millions of dollars of potential savings are at stake.

Perfect Tender in Time

In *Trilon Plaza, Inc. v. Comptroller of the State of New York*, 788 A.2d 146 (D.C. Ct. App. 2001), the District of Columbia Court of Appeals adopted the common-law rule that when loan documents are silent on the issue of prepayment, the borrower may not be permitted to make prepayments of the loan. This rule, known as the "perfect tender in time" rule, is contrary to the civil law rule that is set forth in the Restatement (Third) of Property (Mortgages) § 6.1 (1996).

The "perfect tender in time" rule is followed in a majority of jurisdictions in this country and applies to borrowers who promise to repay loans in installments at specified times or at a specified date. The rule acknowledges that understanding, and in an unregulated transaction would not give borrowers the right to compel a creditor to accept prepayment, because they are assumed to be bound by the payment dates set forth in the document.

Prepayment Language

In the *Trilon Plaza* case, the New York state comptroller made a loan of $12.45 million that was memorialized in a deed of trust (a form of mortgage), a promissory note, and two letters related to the mortgage commitment. The first letter was unsigned and stated the loan terms, including a provision that a repayment may be "prepaid in whole, but not in part," on 30 days' notice following the tenth anniversary of the note at a premium that was 5 percent of the outstanding principal balance to be prepaid. A later letter from the comptroller spelled out in detail various "phases" of the loan and referred to the earlier commitment letter.

The deed of trust also referred to the commitment letter, but the note did not. The note further stated that Trilon had the option "to prepay the entire outstanding principal amount of this Note" after a certain date. The note did not mention "partial prepayment" at all; and otherwise, the prepayment terms of the note were identical to those in the commitment letter.

When Trilon tendered partial prepayment of the principal, the comptroller rejected this payment because the loan documents prohibited such prepayments. Trilon argued that the applicable letter contained no limits on prepayment except in the default provision, which Trilon argued was inapplicable because it had not defaulted. In addition, the loan documents entered into after the unsigned commitment letter deliberately omitted any limitations on partial prepayment, thereby giving Trilon a right to make partial prepayments.

The court of appeals rejected Trilon's arguments and accepted the comptroller's argument that all the loan documents cross-referenced each other and, when read as a whole, precluded partial prepayment. The court ruled that the absence of any limitation on partial prepayment in the note, when read together with the commitment letter, had to be construed as manifesting an intent to adhere to the prepayment restrictions in the commitment letter.

That discussion involved the specific language in the documents and the interplay between the commitment and the note and deed of trust. However, a more significant part of the decision involved the court's view that even if the documents could be read as being silent on the issue of partial prepayment, Trilon would be bound by the common-law rule that prohibits prepayment of the debt secured by a mortgage unless there is an agreement between the parties (or a statute) specifically permitting such a prepayment. That is what the court approved as the "perfect tender in time" rule. It specifically rejected the Restatement rule, which it identified as the minority rule in the United States. See *Mahoney v. Furches,* 468 A.2d 458 (Pa. 1983).

In most states, commercial mortgage documents that do not spell out prepayment rights will generally impair borrowers' ability to refinance their loans. In those cases, silence is golden only for lenders. For borrowers, silence can cost gold.

9　NONRECOURSE LOANS MAY NOT BE WHAT THEY SEEM

A 2002 Illinois case illustrates how a borrower can be misled by so-called "nonrecourse loans." "Nonrecourse" generally means that if a borrower defaults, the lender has rights to sell or repossess the mortgaged real estate or other collateral in order to recover on the loan, but not other unrelated assets of the borrower.

Carve-Outs

It's rare when these types of loans are available to residential borrowers; however, they are frequently available in commercial deals—often with strings attached. These conditions make the borrower personally liable for certain "bad acts," such as improper transfers, unauthorized encumbrances, misappropriation of funds, tolerance of environmental problems, and a variety of other defalcations. Lenders that provide nonrecourse loans need these types of carve-outs from nonrecourse liability to discourage borrowers from committing these "bad acts."

In *Heller Financial, Inc. v. Lee,* No. 01 C 6798 (N.D. Ill., August 12, 2002) (unpublished opinion), the borrower (Lee) found himself liable for the full balance of what he viewed as a nonrecourse loan. In that case, Lee, along with other parties, co-signed an equity loan agreement and a promissory note in connection with a $10 million loan that was needed to purchase a hotel in Orlando, Florida. The note contained a nonrecourse provision that on its face purported to exculpate all makers from personal liability, and left the lender to look solely to the collateral pledged to secure the loan.

Lee's downfall proved to be the carve-out provision in the note, which stated that despite the nonrecourse language, each maker would be personally liable for repayment of the loan upon a breach of certain covenants in the loan agreement concerning "transfers, assignments and pledges of interests and additional encumbrances in the Property, the Partnership and the Corporation." *Id.* at 3. The note specifically stated that each of the makers would not permit the filing of any lien or encumbrance on the collateral.

After Lee's partnership purchased the hotel, several tax liens and mechanic's liens were filed against the partnership, and as a result, Heller Financial declared a default under the loan, sold the hotel, and then came after Lee for the deficiency between the loan balance and the amount received. Lee defended his position on the grounds that he had no knowledge of the offending liens that were placed against the hotel because it had been managed "with the knowledge and agreement of Heller" by a separate management company unrelated to the borrower. The court rejected this defense, stating that it was the borrower who had contracted with Heller for the loan, not the manager. Also, ignorance of the liens was not considered a defense because they were a matter of public record.

Unenforceable Penalty

Lee then raised an issue that will attract the attention of borrowers and lenders around the country. He argued that the carve-out was a liquidated damages provision that was unenforceable as a penalty. In Illinois and many other states, the courts tend to permit parties to recover only damages that are actually sustained.

The court stated:

> ... The common law principle is that a liquidated damages provision is enforceable when it appears in advance that it would be difficult at the time of breach to compute actual damages and the liquidated damages provision is a good faith attempt to estimate what actual damages would be.
> ... However, in interpreting provisions which affix the amount of damages in the event of a breach, courts lean toward a construction that excludes the idea of liquidated damages and permits the parties to recover only damages actually sustained.

Id. at 14 [citations omitted].

Under the *Heller* case carve-out, the maker could become fully liable for the balance of the $10,000,000 loan, merely for permitting liens to be placed against the property. In this case, the aggregate amount of the liens was approximately $820,000, and apparently that was significantly less than the outstanding balance due on the loan after application of the sale proceeds. Therefore, the borrower argued that the personal liability was a "penalty" because it could be substantially more than the damages triggered by the prohibited liens.

The U.S. district court rejected the borrower's arguments and sustained the carve-outs that had been negotiated and agreed to by the parties. It pointed out that one of the makers of the note had exempted himself from any personal liability for violation of the carve-outs, but Lee had not done so. The court agreed with Heller's arguments that because the loan was secured only by the equity interests of the entities that had purchased the hotel and not the hotel itself, Heller was especially concerned about liens. Those liens could affect the operation of the hotel and directly impair its security for the loan. While the court didn't spell this out, a judgment creditor with a loan against the real estate could exercise a priority right against hotel income and interrupt the cash flow needed to pay the Heller loan.

The court also rejected the penalty argument because the carve-out provided for only the recovery of Heller's actual damages, that is, the amount of the unpaid loan indebtedness at the time of default. Therefore, according to the court, "[t]his amount is the actual damage to Heller based on Lee and VanWhy's breach. Since [the carve-out section of the note] involves actual damages it cannot be a liquidated damages provision." *Id.* at 16.

On the other hand, the borrower's position has some merit. If the borrower could have cured the problem by putting up $820,000 and satisfying the liens, or by paying that to Heller to pay the liens, why isn't that the proper measure of "actual damages"?

Nonrecourse Loans Are Suspect

The decision is not surprising based on the facts of the case. In *Heller,* the loan was only secured by equity interests in the entities that purchased the hotel, and not even by the hotel itself. Heller had agreed to nonrecourse liability only because the borrower had agreed to personal liability if any of the listed "bad acts" occurred that could diminish the value of the property or divert cash flow from it. In addition, if one views the so-called penalty as merely an obligation to pay back a loan that benefited Lee and his corporation, the result does not seem harsh.

Many people who are not steeped in the custom of nonrecourse loans, including some judges, are suspicious of them anyway. There is a general feeling that a borrower must have taken advantage of some special relationship with a lender when it makes a deal to borrow money and is excused from any personal responsibility to pay that money back. A judge I know once asked me how favored borrowers are able to make these special deals with lending officers. He queried, "How come they can get that kind of deal, but when I borrow money on my house, I can't?"

All of this should serve as a lesson to borrowers who are promised nonrecourse loans in mortgage commitments. They should read the carve-outs very critically before they accept these loans, and compare them to other nonrecourse loans that are being offered. Most of all, they should try to avoid springing liability that makes them liable for the full loan, even though the defaults may trigger damages that amount to only a small fraction of the loan balance.

10 DISADVANTAGES TO BORROWERS OF LIMITING LOAN LIABILITY

When the gods wish to punish us
they answer our prayers
—Oscar Wilde

Can a borrower ever lose by limiting its loan liability? This is a sophisticated trick question for lawyers. It is also a practical one.

Often lawyers and experienced borrowers seek limited liability on commercial loans. They bargain vigorously with banks and other lenders to limit potential liability. They refuse to enter into guaranties or surety agreements and attempt to provide exculpation clauses or other provisions limiting their liability to the real estate collateral. Frequently, they succeed, particularly with longer-term loans.

However, success is fleeting. A borrower may discover that sometimes personal ("recourse") liability is better.

Recourse Liability and Negative Basis

One obvious advantage of personal liability occurs when a borrower tries to reduce taxes by taking deductions in excess of its investment in real estate. A taxpayer who borrows substantial sums would like to include the borrowed sums in its tax basis. It may not need personal liability to achieve this, but generally, if the borrower is a partnership and only some of the partners are liable, those partners who have limited their liability cannot include any part of the borrowed amount in their basis.

An even more subtle advantage of personal liability applies to a troubled borrower. This may be of special importance in the present economic and real estate climate. The tax impact of a foreclosure may be reduced if the borrower is personally liable, and that will not happen with limited liability.

Here's how it works. Many borrowers hold property where the current tax basis is less than the mortgage balance. That could occur because the borrower reduced the basis by deducting depreciation and other losses over a period of time. Generally, when property is sold for the amount of the mortgage, or foreclosed by the lender, the borrower is deemed to have sold the property for the mortgage balance and interest to the same extent as though that sum had been paid to the borrower. However, the borrower, in fact, received no money from that event. Economic disaster now strikes the taxpayer. It loses the property and receives no cash but must pay an income tax on the difference between the mortgage balance and its tax basis, i.e., the so-called "negative" basis.

When troubled developers with negative basis lose their properties, some seek the protection of the bankruptcy laws to relieve themselves of continuing liability to creditors. They willingly turn everything over to their creditors, move away from a life of managing unpaid bills, and attempt to enter a more productive phase of life. Bankruptcy laws help them do that.

However, what about unpaid income taxes? Generally, they will not be discharged by bankruptcy unless income tax payments were due more than three years before the bankruptcy filing. Therefore, current tax liabilities, including those incurred from transferring properties with a negative basis, could follow the taxpayer to the grave.

Ironically, this is where personal liability on a loan could help. With personal liability, the tax code and its interpretations provide an exception to taxing a negative basis on foreclosure. In effect, the full amount of the mortgage balance is not deemed income to the taxpayer. Income subject to the tax will still be recognized but only to the extent the value of the property exceeds its tax basis (Rev. Rul. 90-16, 1990-1 C.B. 12). However, the excess of the loan over the market value of the transferred property will be considered as a "discharge of indebtedness," which is not taxable to the bankrupt taxpayer. This exclusion may also apply to certain insolvent taxpayers not in bankruptcy. When the market value declines as low as the basis, the taxpayer could be off the hook entirely.

Why should that be an exception? Apparently, if a taxpayer is insolvent, the tax rationale is that it cannot pay its debts and will be discharged from personal liability anyway. Therefore, the release of that portion of the mortgage liability that exceeds the market value will not benefit the taxpayer and should not be considered income. On analysis, it is difficult to understand why IRS does not apply this same rationale to relief from non-recourse debt.

IRS exacts a price for this nonrecognition. The taxpayer must first offset the discharged indebtedness against loss carry-overs or against the basis of other properties owned by the tax-payer. To that extent, the taxpayer will be using potential offsets against future gains. But if the taxpayer has no such offsets, it pays no price for the discharge.

The tax code does not require booking the offset until the tax year following the year of the discharge. This suggests tax strategies the troubled taxpayer may employ.

Trumping One's Own Trick

When some properties are subject to recourse debt and others are not, which should the owner give up to the lender first? The answer is that it makes no difference if the owner transfers them all in the same tax year. Then the taxpayer retains no properties, the offset will be properly used, and the discharge will not affect the next tax year. However, if they are not transferred in the same year, generally, the taxpayer should first give up the one with non-recourse debt. Since that property will not qualify for the discharge exception, the taxpayer should attempt to "match" the gain on that transaction against the loss carryover, and not "waste" the carry-over on the recourse debt.

Assume an insolvent taxpayer has two shopping centers about to be foreclosed, each with a tax basis of $1 million and a market value of $1 million. Each has a $2 million mortgage, but only the mortgage on the first center provides for personal liability. Assume that each center must be transferred to the lender, either by foreclosure or deed in lieu of foreclosure. If the taxpayer has a net loss carryover of $1 million available to offset against these gains, the taxpayer will benefit from transferring the non-recourse property either in the same year or in the year before the property with the recourse mortgage is transferred. The $1 million loss car-ryover will then offset the $1 million of recognized gain on that property. The second property, subject to recourse indebtedness, would qualify for non-recognition of gain, so the taxpayer may walk away with no tax liability!

If the taxpayer reverses the timing of the transfers so that the recourse indebtedness is triggered a year earlier, the taxpayer suffers a taxable gain of $1 million on the very same transactions.

That occurs because the loss carryover will be used up on the transfer of the recourse property; and when the non-recourse property is transferred, that $1 million gain will not qualify for nonrecognition.

Wasting the loss carryover in that way may be compared to trumping one's own trick in bridge or pinochle! While a taxpayer cannot always control the order in which it loses troubled properties, it can transfer a defaulted property to the lender at will and avoid the timing trap.

Once a taxpayer is in deep financial trouble, there may not be much recourse to these strategies if its liability has been limited. Then it is probably too late to volunteer personal liability. However, insolvent taxpayers "lucky enough" to be personally liable on their loans should take note of this little-known tax advantage and thank the gods for not granting their wish when they originally negotiated the loan documents.

11 MORTGAGE MAY BE LOST FOR LACK OF NOTARY SEAL

For want of a nail, a shoe was lost
For want of a shoe, a horse was lost
For want of a horse, a battle was lost
For want of a battle, a war was lost.
—*Anonymous*

This anonymous poem reminds me of what may happen when a lender neglects to check whether a notary's seal has been affixed to a mortgage. Under the recording statutes in most states, a mortgage must be recorded with a notary's acknowledgment with the notary's seal affixed.

Sometimes mortgages are signed and acknowledged without a notary's seal and inadvertently recorded. The question then arises about whether these slightly flawed mortgages can still do the trick. They have been recorded and properly indexed, and, therefore, should be notice to the world that the property is encumbered. However, they do not conform to the statutory requirement. A bankruptcy trustee may file adversary actions challenging such mortgages and thereby attempt to invalidate the security of the lenders. The loan will still be valid between the borrower and the lender, but the lender's lien may be lost.

A Missing Witness

A 2001 case in the U.S. Court of Appeals for the Sixth Circuit held that a bankruptcy trustee could avoid a mortgage because it was not properly executed under Ohio law. *In re Zaptocky v. Chase Manhattan Bank*, 250 F.3d 1020 (6th Cir. 2001). In that case the borrowers refinanced their home with Chase Manhattan Bank and signed a second mortgage to Chase. The mortgage bears the signatures of two witnesses, "Gary Williams" and "Taylor Lloyd."

When the borrowers filed for Chapter 7 bankruptcy, the bankruptcy trustee filed an adversary proceeding against Chase. He asserted the so-called "strong-arm power" under the bankruptcy code (11 U.S.C. § 544(a)), which allowed the estate to avoid the Chase mortgage because it was not validly executed under Ohio law. Specifically, the trustee claimed that the mortgage violated the Ohio code that required that it be signed in the presence of two witnesses.

At the trial, the debtors testified that they signed the mortgage at their dining room table in the presence of Gary Williams. However, they both insisted that Williams was the only witness present at the signing and that they did not know any person by the name of Taylor Lloyd. In response, Chase offered the testimony of Williams, who testified that he had no specific recollection of the signing and that he did not know of any person by the name of Taylor Lloyd. However, he also stated that the title agency that employed him at the time maintained a policy of not closing loans unless two witnesses were present, and that he would not have signed and notarized the mortgage in contravention of that policy.

Invalid Mortgage

Based on that evidence, the court found that the Ohio law was violated because there was insufficient evidence that two witnesses were present at the signing. Therefore, the bankruptcy trustee had the right to assert the same rights as a bona fide purchaser to invalidate the improperly executed mortgage. The court ruled against Chase's argument that under Ohio law a facially valid mortgage bears a presumption of validity and those who contest such a mortgage must prove the instrument is defective by clear and convincing evidence.

Chase argued that the presumption of validity is so strong that Ohio courts have established a per se rule that the mortgagor's testimony standing alone is not sufficient to invalidate a facially valid mortgage.

The court disagreed with Chase and held:

> In this case, the per se rule is not applicable because the mortgagors' testimony was not rebutted by the certificate of acknowledgment. As noted above, the mortgagors alleged that the mortgage was not properly executed because only one witness attested to the signing of the mortgage.

Given that the notary's certificate of acknowledgment does not purport to certify that two witnesses were present when the Zaptockys signed the mortgage, the certification is irrelevant to the factual dispute in this case.

The court went on to say:

We agree that the evidence introduced at trial creates a serious doubt as to the validity of Taylor Lloyd's signature. If Williams had brought Lloyd with him to the house to act as a witness, it seems that Williams would at least recognize the name. On the other hand, if Lloyd had been a friend or neighbor of the Zaptockys, it seems likely that they would know who he was. The fact that both the Zaptockys and Williams testified that they do not know who Taylor Lloyd is suggests that a second witness was not present at the closing of the Zaptockys' mortgage.

Mortgage "Frittered Away"

In a vigorous dissent, Judge Alice M. Batchelder disagreed with the majority's interpretation of Ohio law. According to her, Ohio law provides that the testimony of mortgagors is insufficient to overcome a certificate of acknowledgment by a notary, and, the positive statement of an inflexible rule always adhered to by a notary or witness "must carry great weight" in the consideration of their evidence. Otherwise she was concerned that the security of a mortgage will be "frittered away," and it will be left "to all the uncertainty incident to the imperfect and slippery memory of witnesses."

Batchelder emphasized that this is not a case where the mortgagors denied signing the mortgage or borrowing the money. She pointed out that Ohio has enacted new legislation that was not in effect in time for this case, but makes it clear that mortgages are irrefutably presumed to be properly executed, regardless of the actual or alleged defect in witnessing or acknowledging, unless the mortgagor, under oath, denies signing the mortgage.

Because the mortgage in question had been signed and recorded, it should have served as notice to subsequent purchasers and creditors. The *Zaptocky* case is a dangerous precedent for lenders and title companies. Title companies that insure these mortgages will frequently wind up holding the bag.

Pennsylvania Precedent

An earlier case in Pennsylvania by Bankruptcy Judge David A. Scholl had created a similar stir. In the case of *In re Rice,* 133 B.R. 722 (Bankr. E.D. Pa. 1991), Scholl held that even though a home improvement mortgage had been signed by the bankrupt borrower and recorded a month earlier, it was invalid because the notary public was not present at the time the borrower signed. This raises questions about procedures followed at a closing that could be challenged months or years after the closing, after everything had been recorded in the proper public records.

To some observers the invalidation of a mortgage on these grounds is shocking because the mortgages had been signed and routinely recorded, and all later lienholders and mortgage holders could have searched the record and seen the outstanding mortgage loans. The decisions seem to fly in the face of traditional doctrines of constructive notice.

Significant Formality

The court in *Rice* reasoned, however, that the statutory requirement for acknowledgment is significant because it brings home to a borrower that a mortgage is being executed. "This formality would have tended to guard against a situation such as occurred in the Debtor's fact pattern, where she in fact executed a mortgage, but was unaware of doing so." *Id.* at 727.

This decision should focus mortgage lenders and title companies on the significance of making sure the notary is present when a mortgage is signed. It is not unheard of for a borrower to mail a signed mortgage to the lender's office or to the title company without an acknowledgment. The borrower then expects that the recipient will simply find a notary to take the acknowledgment.

Sometimes the mortgage is even accompanied by a letter that spells out the borrower's request. It does not take much imagination to envision how that evidence may be used in a future challenge to the mortgage.

Questions Remain

The *Rice* decision seems somewhat off the track from earlier Pennsylvania case law that held that latent or hidden defects related to an acknowledgment do not affect the validity of a document. For example, in *Scott v. Penn Title Insurance Co.,* 10

Pa. D.&C.2d 129 (C.P. Berks 1956), the court explained that "Where the acknowledgment is regular on its face so that it becomes the duty of the recording officer to admit the instrument to record, its record will afford constructive notice, although there are latent or hidden defects in the acknowledgment...." In that case, the borrower, a notary public, signed a fictitious name to the loan documents and took his own acknowledgment. The court found that even though the acknowledgment was improperly taken by an interested party, on its face the mortgage was properly notarized and accepted for recordation. Therefore, it constituted constructive notice to future lienholders.

Under this rule the *Rice* mortgage should have held up because it would appear that the absence of a notary officer at the time of signing is a latent defect. How would recording officers or later lienholders know that the mortgage was signed outside the presence of a notary?

The older cases have not been overruled; therefore, future courts will have to choose between the general rule and the *Rice* decision. If the Pennsylvania courts adopt the *Rice* decision, they will be faced with certain questions that the *Rice* court left open.

Since recording statutes in many states provide that a notary must be present during the signing, what will happen in those states when the borrower signs and later delivers the mortgage to the notary's office for acknowledgment?

What will courts decide when the notary has returned to the settlement table from the next room at the title company to acknowledge a signing that has taken place outside the notary's presence? Technically, that also violates the rule in the *Rice* case.

Once the courts open the door to this kind of challenge, what chance does a mortgage lender have before a jury? If the facts are disputed, the decision may come down to the word of the bank officer (and possibly the notary) against the borrower and an array of his or her friends and associates, who all remember that the notary was not present when the vinyl siding salesman was there.

Decision Carries Over

The *Rice* case was a bankruptcy matter but it applied Pennsylvania state law. Other cases may raise the same issues, even when the borrower is not bankrupt, in the context of mortgage lenders battling over priorities. Also, the case may be used as precedent in other states that have similar recording statutes.

Rice involved a somewhat sympathetic, apparently vulnerable homeowner, who was solicited to buy vinyl siding and was unrepresented by legal counsel. But the same statutory provisions and logic would seem to apply to multi-million-dollar commercial loans where the parties are sophisticated and fully represented. Once courts sustain a challenge to the validity of an acknowledgment in a recorded document, how far will they go in seizing on technicalities to upset commercial mortgage priorities?

In *Rice*, Judge David A. Scholl emphasized the ceremonial significance of having a notary present while the borrower signs. He distinguished this from other more technical violations of the recording statute that do not carry the same ceremonial implications. These could include defective forms of acknowledgment, notaries from the wrong county, or acknowledgments dated before the date of the mortgage. If these errors slip through the recorder's office and the mortgage is accepted for recording, will future courts use them to invalidate the mortgage months or even years later?

A Small Comfort

One small comfort to lenders may be received from a statute of repose that validates all mortgages recorded before a date certain, regardless of certain specified technical flaws in the acknowledgment. For example, a Pennsylvania statute provides in part:

Defective acknowledgments prior to 1996.

No ... mortgage ... bearing date prior to the year one thousand nine hundred ninety-six ... shall be ... invalid or defective ... by reason of any informality or defect in such acknowledgment as not being made according to law, or because the date of the acknowledgment predates the date of the instrument, or by reason of the acknowledgment thereto having been made by any trustee or attorney in fact in his individual capacity instead of as such trustee or attorney in fact; but all and every ... mortgage ... acknowledged, as aforesaid, shall be as good, valid and effectual ... as if all the requisites and particulars of such acknowledgment had been made according to law, ..."

21 P.S. § 281.1.

While such statutes should put to rest certain defects, many lenders are still left holding the bag. For example, under *Rice,* the Pennsylvania statute of repose does not lay to rest that cardinal sin of the absentee notary.

Other Implications

Furthermore, what about flawed acknowledgments taken after 1987? The quoted statute implies that without the saving provision, the designated technical flaws could invalidate a mortgage.

The *Rice* decision raises even more subtle issues. If the mortgage is invalid, what happens to the regular monthly mortgage payments that had been made by the borrower? Can it be argued that those payments were made on an unperfected loan? If so, under certain circumstances, those payments made within 90 days before bankruptcy may be recoverable as a voidable preference by the borrower or a trustee in bankruptcy. That preference period may even extend to one year with an "insider."

While *Rice* covers a somewhat technical and limited issue, it has major implications to the real estate industry because every recorded document contains an acknowledgment governed by the applicable statutes. That case makes it clear that the sins of the notary may not be absolved merely by recording the mortgage.

It should be noted, however, that although the *Rice* acknowledgment was defective, the court concluded that the mortgage was not totally void, like a forged instrument. Therefore, the notary defect would not affect the validity of the mortgage between the debtor and the lender.

Unless acknowledgments are treated more carefully, mortgage lenders and their title insurers may wind up losing some expensive battles against bankrupt debtors and their creditors during the next few years. In addition, *Zaptocky* and *Rice* may have now focused junior lienholders on another negotiating issue to use as leverage against senior lenders who may find themselves defending the validity of their mortgages.

PART IB

Mortgages—Enforcement

12   BANKS WIN THE TUG OF WAR OVER RENTS

Troubled real estate companies may not be aware that even a borrower's bankruptcy may not wrest away a lender's rights to rents. *First Fidelity Bank, N.A. v. Jason Realty L.P. (In re Jason Realty, L.P.)*, 59 F.3d 423 (3d Cir. 1995), *reh'g denied*, 3d Cir. N.J., August 4, 1995. In that case Judge Aldisert resolved a dispute of long standing under New Jersey law about the effectiveness of assignments of rents.

"Absolute Assignment"

First Fidelity Bank held a note, a mortgage, and an assignment of rents on a single asset New Jersey limited partnership that owned and operated a two-story retail and office building. The assignment gave all rents, income, and profits to the bank but granted Jason Realty rights to collect the rents until a default occurred.

After default, the bank notified the tenants to pay their rent directly to the bank and then started foreclosure and petitioned for a receiver. Within one week, Jason filed a voluntary Chapter 11 petition and stayed the foreclosure. The parties battled over the right to the rents, which amounted to approximately $12,500 per month. Were those rents "cash collateral" that could be used by the bankrupt estate—or did they belong to the bank?

The court stated the "major question" was whether the assignment was "an absolute assignment" or merely a "collateral pledge." The assignment had granted Fidelity an immediate right to rents, even though the borrower could collect and use the rents until default and the assignment would expire when the loan was repaid.

The court held that since the assignment was "absolute," rents were not available as cash collateral or as a funding source for the debtor's reorganization plan. It reasoned that a rent assignment "may be independent of the mortgage security," and was "impressed that the instant assignment was contained in an agreement separate from the mortgage."

As Judge Aldisert acknowledged, in many cases, debtors will not be able to reorganize without using cash collateral, especially in single-asset cases involving commercial real estate. Therefore, this decision should discourage certain types of bankruptcy filings and delight those mortgage lenders who feel that borrowers tend to overuse the bankruptcy courts to impair their collateral and stall an inevitable foreclosure.

Race to the Courthouse

In light of the *Jason* decision, lenders may prefer a separate assignment of rents rather than relying on assignment language in a mortgage. However, one may question whether courts should reach different results merely because the operative language appears in two documents rather than one.

In addition, lenders may want the rents to be assigned "absolutely," without use of conditional phrases such as "for collateral" or "as security for the loan." Obviously, some courts are reaching different results for absolute and conditional assignment language, even though in each case the debtor retains the right to collect rents until there is a default, and the assignment ends when the loan is paid.

The *Jason* decision mentions that the lender had notified the tenants to pay rent to it and had filed an application for appointment of a receiver before the bankruptcy was filed. While that action may not have made a difference in the decision, future decisions may be influenced by the lender's conduct before bankruptcy. If that action nails down lenders' claims to rent, some may be inspired to move quickly before borrowers beat them to the punch with a bankruptcy filing.

In some ways this "race to the courthouse" may have switched tracks. Before the Bankruptcy Reform Act of 1994, the stakes were whether lenders could retain a security interest in rents accruing after the debtor's filing. This depended on whether they had "perfected" this interest under state law. The new Section 552(b)(2) of the Bankruptcy Code gives lenders valid security interests in assigned rents, even though they may not have taken other action under state law. That perfection no longer depends on whether the mortgagee activated its security interest in rents by some form of self-help or judicial action before bankruptcy.

Now the issue in some states will be whether the lender owns these rents (as contrasted with retaining a mere security interest in them). Under the *Jason* case, the lender's conduct after default may be relevant to that issue.

Apples, Oranges, and the Golden Fleece

Just as the *Jason* decision applied New Jersey law to analyze the parties' interests in rent, future cases will apply the law of the situs of the mortgaged property. In reaching its decision, the court cited with approval an earlier circuit court case (*Commerce Bank v. Mountain View Village*, 5 F.3d 34 (3d Cir. 1993)), which came to a similar conclusion under Pennsylvania law. The *Jason* court criticized the bankruptcy judge who had declined to follow the teachings of the *Commerce Bank* case because of that judge's analysis that mortgages are treated differently in New Jersey than in Pennsylvania. The lower court had distinguished that case because "Pennsylvania is a 'title state and not a lien state.'"

Judge Aldisert found that a lender's rights to rents as an assignee are different from those as a mere mortgagee. Therefore, he did not see the relevancy of the bankruptcy court's distinction between a title state and a lien state; and he charged the bankruptcy judge with confusing "assignee apples with mortgagee oranges."

In its quest for income, *Jason Realty* could not overcome the obstacle of an absolute assignment of rents. Classic mythology tells us that Jason of the Argonauts overcame difficult obstacles in ancient Greece, and outwitted formidable adversaries to finally recover the golden fleece. In the United States Third Circuit, *Jason Realty* did not fare as well as its namesake in its quest for "gold" because of legal obstacles and a formidable adversary named Fidelity.

13 FRAUDULENT CONVEYANCES: CASE SUGGESTS DEBTORS' LOOPHOLE

A 2001 federal circuit court case gave the debtor a break on pre-bankruptcy payments that seemed, to some observers, to be fraudulent conveyances. In *Shaia v. Meyer (In re Meyer),* 244 F.3d 352 (4th Cir. 2001), the U.S. Court of Appeals for the Fourth Circuit was faced with the validity of prepayment of mortgages secured by a residential property held by the debtor and his wife as tenants by the entireties. By February 1994, the debtor was indebted to various unsecured creditors in connection with certain business ventures and also owed $168,000 on his home mortgages.

In 1993, the debtor's father had died and bequeathed to him a "sum equal to the remaining principal balances, if any, of all mortgages" on the debtor's residence. The debtor then deposited that bequest into a joint checking account with his wife and paid off the mortgages on their residence.

Valuable Consideration

Almost sixteen months later, the debtor filed a petition under Chapter 7 of the Bankruptcy Code and claimed that the residence was exempt from the claims of creditors because it was held by the entireties. The bankruptcy trustee argued that debtor's actions had converted his nonexempt cash bequest into an exempt interest in the residence, and therefore was voidable as a "voluntary conveyance" and a fraudulent conveyance under the applicable Virginia code and Section 544(b) of the Bankruptcy Code.

Both the bankruptcy court and the district court had supported the trustee's position that the mortgage prepayment was a voluntary conveyance under Virginia fraudulent conveyance law, and was not supported by consideration "deemed valuable in law." The court of appeals reversed the district court and held that the mortgage prepayment was supported by valuable consideration

114

because in return for that prepayment, the mortgages were released.

The court of appeals also rejected the trustee's argument that the prepayment was a fraudulent conveyance because it increased the equity in the residence held by the entireties. The court was concerned that any decision to the contrary would give creditors a right to upset every payment under a mortgage on a home held by the entireties that was made when the filing spouse was insolvent, or rendered insolvent by the payment. The court of appeals stated that it reversed the district court because otherwise the result of the holding would be "chaotic at best."

Inconsistent Cases

In the case of *United States v. Green,* 201 F.3d 251 (3d Cir. 2000), the U.S. Court of Appeals for the Third Circuit dealt with a transfer by a bankrupt debtor who had conveyed his home to himself and a new wife to hold as a tenancy by the entireties. In that case the court invoked the Pennsylvania Uniform Fraudulent Conveyance Act and invalidated the transfer even though the debtor may have been solvent on the date of the transfer.

That court invoked a line of cases holding that actual fraud may be presumed where a husband transfers property to a wife for "inadequate consideration," and that even solvency may not be relevant to the actual fraud inquiries involving property transfers between husbands and wives for nominal consideration. The reason for that presumption is that family collusion by a debtor is so easy to execute and so difficult to prove. That rule applies not only to the earlier Pennsylvania Uniform Fraudulent Conveyances Act, but also to the new Pennsylvania Fraudulent Transfer Law that replaced that act. See Harris Ominsky, "Fraudulent Conveyance Laws Can Reach Property After Transfer," *The Legal Intelligencer* (July 5, 2000).

In *Green,* the Third Circuit was dealing with intent to defraud, but the Fourth Circuit merely had to find a transfer while insolvent for inadequate consideration. In any event, it is not clear whether the *Green* case would have been decided the same way if the court were only dealing with a prepayment of a mortgage as in *Shaia,* instead of a transfer of the residence to the debtor and his wife.

Some will argue that the two cases have spawned inconsistent results. Unsecured creditors will say that removing assets from creditors' reach should be treated the same, whether a debtor transfers his real estate to himself and his wife or prepays a mortgage on their home. The *Shaia* court does not agree with that, and it specifically distinguished earlier cases that treated transfers by husbands to joint tenancies with their wives as fraudulent conveyances.

Avoiding Creditors

Suppose a financially troubled debtor wants to avoid creditors. If he then arranges for his spouse to share the down payment on a house that they then purchase in joint names, that purchase would not seem to be a fraudulent conveyance because each party has put up an equal amount of the down payment and they have each received consideration "deemed valuable at law." Suppose the husband then takes his own cash and prepays the mortgage while he has creditors who he is unable to pay. Does that then remove that cash from the reach of his creditors? It would seem that his actual fraudulent intent should render that transaction invalid against creditors, whether the court applies bankruptcy doctrines or state fraudulent conveyance concepts.

In *Shaia* the debtor may have been helped by the fact that he used sums that had been bequeathed to him for the specific purpose of paying off the mortgages. While the opinion didn't discuss that factor, it would seem that the "earmarked" bequest should help to mitigate the argument that the debtor acted with actual intent to defraud creditors or in exchange for inadequate consideration.

Also, *Shaia* may not be followed in jurisdictions that have fraudulent conveyance laws different from Virginia's. The debtor was aided by statutory language that permitted transfers supported by "consideration deemed valuable in law." That articulates a different standard than "fair consideration" or "reasonably equivalent value" (12 Pa. C.S. § 5104(a)(2)) as set forth in some statutes, although the legislative purpose was substantially the same. The debtor also benefitted from the fact that the court ignored the real transfer, which converted the cash into equity in the home and placed it beyond the reach of creditors.

If the *Shaia* decision is followed by other courts, it is not hard to see how troubled debtors may be able to use a mortgage-prepayment strategy as a loophole to avoid fraudulent conveyance laws.

14   MORTGAGES: HARDBALL STRATEGIES PROVE EXPENSIVE

In a California case, which drew a lot of attention among real estate lawyers, a defaulting borrower made a tactical error in trying to negotiate a settlement with its lender. The resulting lesson was that in negotiating a business deal, a hardball player can easily wind up striking out.

The case held the mortgagor liable for tortious waste for deliberate nonpayment of taxes, and for punitive damages when the tactic of withholding taxes was used as a weapon against the lender in attempting to revise a defaulted loan. *Nippon Credit Bank, Ltd. v. 1333 North California Blvd.,* 86 Cal. App. 4th 486 (1st Dist. 2001). There are relatively few cases making nonpayment of taxes a tort, but the *Nippon Credit* case stands as a warning light for real estate borrowers throughout the country.

In that case, a limited partnership had borrowed $73 million secured by office buildings in California and when the real estate market deteriorated, the borrower asked to postpone an interest payment for six months. The bank refused.

Borrower's Tactics

In response to this, the borrower refused to pay $350,000 in property taxes owed on the property although it had received the cash to do so. Instead, the partnership paid over $600,000 to one of the partners to reduce its equity position in the partnership.

In the restructuring negotiations with the bank, one of the principals stated that the bank was not cooperating in restructuring and that he wanted it to "share the pain" of the problems with the buildings. He also stated that he thought the bank was squeezing as much money as it could from him and other outside investors, and that it would ultimately take the property at foreclosure.

117

He admitted, however, that the bank had no legal obligation to defer the payment of interest, as he requested.

Later the bank paid the taxes and added that claim to the debt. It then sued the limited partnership, and the principal for committing tortious waste to the bank's security interest by acting in bad faith. According to the court, the property was then worth millions of dollars less than the loan.

A jury did not take kindly to the borrower's tactic. It found that withholding the tax payment constituted waste that was perpetuated maliciously and in bad faith. It awarded compensatory damages to the lender of $394,000 and punitive damages of $8.3 million! The court granted a remittitur of the punitive damages and reduced them to $1.2 million, and on appeal the California appeals court upheld the verdict.

The court pointed out that there was a split in jurisdictions about whether nonpayment of taxes could constitute waste, but it agreed with the Restatement on Mortgages that the best policy was to recognize that type of claim. The court rejected the borrower's argument that a tort action should not be recognized where a contract action would lie for a breach of mortgage. It noted that the relationship between a mortgagor and mortgagee is that the mortgagee is a holder of a present interest and a contingent future interest in land that is entitled to protection against torts.

It is significant that *Nippon Credit* involved a mortgage loan in which the lender had agreed that the borrower's liability for the loan was limited to its interest in the mortgaged real estate. That is, by the terms of the mortgage documents, no personal liability could be incurred under the mortgage. Despite that provision, the court permitted the tort of waste to open up the borrower's exposure, not only to repayment of the unpaid real estate taxes, but also to substantial punitive damages.

Bad Faith

In this case, the jury and the court obviously reacted to the bad-faith conduct of the borrower. However, some observers have expressed concern that the decision may be used in future cases to find the tort of waste even when the borrower is not acting in bad faith.

It is not clear whether this court would have imposed that affirmative duty to pay taxes if the property were not generating revenue. It would be surprising to see future decisions that impose torts on borrowers where they do not pay taxes because they have used the cash flow not merely to pay themselves, but to pay other costs or expenses of operating the property. Also, it is unlikely that the court would have gone the same way if the borrower had not made statements about its vengeful motivations. Ordinarily, a court would be expected to honor the contractual provisions that protect the borrower against personal liability on the loan.

In summary, *Nippon Credit* is unusual because it permitted a tort action for nonpayment of real estate taxes even though the loan was non-recourse. It may be the first case ever to award punitive damages under those circumstances.

Carve-Outs

Frequently, in non-recourse loans the lender demands recourse for certain types of borrowers' misconduct, including paying money to partners after default, creating hazardous waste liabilities and failing to pay real estate taxes. Apparently, these non-recourse carve-outs were not part of the *Nippon Credit* documents.

In arriving at its conclusion, the court cited and quoted from a New York case, *Travelers Insurance Co. v. 633 Third Associates,* 14 F.3d 114 (2d Cir. 1994), which also held partners liable for making a partnership distribution out of sums that could otherwise have paid a delinquent real estate tax bill. That decision also held that the borrower had committed waste by making that payment, even though the loan was secured by a traditional non-recourse commercial mortgage.

It seems that the borrower in *Nippon Credit* would have fared better even if it had been stuck with a non-recourse carve-out that provided personal liability for failing to pay real estate taxes. Under those circumstances, most borrowers would know that they should not take a chance of risking personal liability, and they might then be alerted to using the money to pay the real estate taxes, even in preference to making a required mortgage payment.

On the other hand, because of the way that the court viewed the borrower's hardball tactics, the lender may have come out better with a punitive damage recovery in *Nippon Credit* than it would have, even if the borrower had used the money to pay the real estate taxes as Nippon Credit requested. At the end of the day, the lender succeeded in establishing its claim against the borrower, not only for the taxes it laid out, but also for personal liability of almost $2 million in punitive damages.

One issue that the court doesn't discuss involves whether the claim for waste would have stood up if the lender had been able to receive a full recovery on its mortgage balance, including all interest due. The question is whether a borrower has committed waste against a lender if the lender has been able to recover in full on its loan, either because of a foreclosure or because of a sale of its mortgage.

15   MORTGAGES: WHEN IS A LOAN IN DEFAULT?

A U.S. circuit court of appeals has helped define when a mortgage is considered in default.

The first lesson is whether a payment occurs when the check is sent or when it is received. The second lesson has to do with whether a loan default is erased once a foreclosure action is ended by a stipulation and order where the parties arrange to cure the default.

Defamation

These issues arose in a somewhat untraditional context. They presented themselves in a suit for defamation that was brought against a lender by a borrower who had defaulted under a mortgage loan. *Ciuffetelli v. Apple Bank for Savings,* No. 99-7741 (2d Cir. March 30, 2000).

The case involved a failure by the borrower to pay required mortgage payments and water and sewerage charges on time. After Apple Bank started foreclosure, the parties worked out a stipulation disposing of the foreclosure action in which the borrower acknowledged it owed an agreed sum of money, including an amount that Apple advanced to cover the disputed water and sewer charges.

After the borrower failed in its attempt to refinance Apple's mortgage, it blamed that failure on Apple's defamatory statements to the potential lenders. The alleged false statements were about the borrower's conduct both before and after the stipulation.

Acknowledged Default

Apple was apparently saved in the defamation case by the language in the stipulation where the borrower acknowledged that it was in default and that the borrower agreed to repay Apple for sums it had advanced for water and sewerage rents. That brings us back to one of the lessons raised earlier. For defamation purposes the default was not automatically erased by the settlement of the dispute.

The court held:

> Plaintiffs argue that the District Court erred in holding that in this case truth was a defense to their claim for defamation; defendants' statements, they claim, were indeed false. ... Upon a review of the record, we agree with the District Court that the record supports the conclusion that defendants' allegedly defamatory statements made to third parties were substantially correct. Accordingly, plaintiffs' claim for defamation was properly dismissed.

While the decision does not say exactly what the so-called defamatory language was, it appears that the borrower complained about statements made to prospective lenders about defaults and late payments. In supporting the lender, the court obviously confirmed the lender's characterization of the borrower's defaults.

One issue involved alleged defaults in making timely payments under the workout arrangement. Apple claimed it received late payments that were required in the stipulation, and that the issue centered on whether the "mailbox" rule applied to make payments timely that were mailed within the grace period but were not received until after the stated deadline. On that issue, the court held that the language in the stipulation and order that required payments to be "delivered" to Apple within a five-day grace period meant the payments had to be received, and not just mailed, as of the deadline. That payment standard contrasts with the original mortgage, which stated:

> . . . if any portion of the Debt is not paid within ten (10) days after the date on which it is due, Mortgagor shall pay to Mortgagee [certain late charges].

That requires only timely payment and not receipt.

Lessons

Borrowers may learn certain lessons from this case. First, when a dispute is settled, the borrower should give careful attention to the characterization of the disputed claims. Because the borrower admitted that it was in default when the mortgage was reinstated, it enabled the lender to tell other lenders with impunity that the borrower had defaulted on the loan.

In hindsight, the borrower must have regretted these admissions, which may not have been necessary in documenting the foreclosure settlement. Sometimes borrowers are able to protect themselves in workout agreements by insisting on confidentiality provisions that inhibit disclosure of cured defaults.

The second lesson relates to the operative time for determining defaults. If in fact it is intended that a properly addressed, mailed payment should be adequate to overcome a late receipt, the loan documents should spell that out. On the other hand, if the document requires receipt by a certain date, merely mailing the check by the date will not do the trick.

16   MORTGAGE FORECLOSURES AND COUNTERCLAIMS

Courts will generally not permit counterclaims to be filed by borrowers when mortgage foreclosures are started against them. In the Pennsylvania case of *DiGiovanni v. 835 County Line Assoc., L.P.*, 69 Bucks Co. L. Rep. 242 (1996), the borrowers who had purchased a commercial property from the mortgage holder defended a foreclosure action by filing a counterclaim against the lender. The borrowers alleged that after taking possession of the property they discovered environmental hazards in the septic system and that they had to spend $51,000 to fix the problem. Therefore, instead of paying their monthly mortgage payments, they paid them into an escrow account.

The borrowers argued that fraud by the lender in connection with the agreement of sale cannot be distinguished from the fraud in connection with the purchase money mortgage and therefore the borrowers' counterclaim is proper because it "arises from the same transaction or occurrence ... from which plaintiff's cause of action arose" under rule 1148 of the Pennsylvania Rules of Civil Procedure. The Bucks County court rejected the borrowers' argument and held that the cited rule permits "only those counterclaims that are part of or incident to the creation of the mortgage itself...."

The court cited the case of *Overly v. Kass*, 554 A.2d 970 (Pa. Super. 1989), to support its decision. In that case the court granted summary judgment in favor of the lender on a purchase money mortgage and rejected the borrowers' argument that the lender's misrepresentations had induced them into purchasing a farm. According to the borrowers, the seller-mortgagee made numerous misrepresentations regarding the condition of the mortgage premises. They argued that the misrepresentations formed part of the consideration for the agreement of sale. The sellers had promised that they would remove from the property a rusted trailer

124

and certain other items. They had also allegedly made other misrepresentations that cost the borrower money. The Superior Court in *Overly* found that the alleged representations about the agreement of sale were not part of, or incident to, the creation of the mortgage.

The Bucks County court held that the only types of claims that the Superior Court has permitted as counterclaims are "a claim of a defect in title, a claim that the mortgagee had promised a greater percentage of financing than it provided and a claim that the mortgagee promised lenient treatment in the event of a default." Also it cited one case where a counterclaim was sustained because consideration was lacking for the mortgage and the bank had fraudulently induced the borrowers into executing the mortgage to finance a nonexistent debt.

In contrast to these cases the court held that in *DiGiovanni* the claim of fraudulent misrepresentation about the septic system related not to the creation of the mortgage, but to the sales agreement.

This case is a lesson for borrowers' attorneys about what kinds of issues they can use to defend against a mortgage foreclosure. It also highlights an issue that buyers may be able to raise in negotiations under an agreement of sale. If there is to be a purchase money mortgage taken back by a seller, the buyer should try to specifically negotiate a right to offset or counterclaim for any damages incurred from fraud, misrepresentations, or breach of warranties by the seller under the agreement of sale. If the purchase money mortgage in *DiGiovanni* had provided for such offsets, the fraudulent misrepresentation would appear to be a "part of or incident to the creation of the mortgage itself," and the borrower could have counterclaimed and protected itself against the foreclosure.

17   BAD-FAITH BANKRUPTCIES BANNED

Borrowers may have a difficult time using bankruptcy as a device to stall foreclosures. The U.S. District Court for the Eastern District of Pennsylvania has sent a message to the bankruptcy courts that they should start to honor the Bankruptcy Code's prohibitions against "abuse or misuse of bankruptcy jurisdiction." *In re Lippolis*, 228 B.R. 106 (Bankr. E.D. Pa. 1998). In *Lippolis*, Judge Kelly held that the bankruptcy court abused its discretion by failing to lift an automatic stay "for cause" under Section 362(d)(1) of the Bankruptcy Code because it failed to determine the debtors' motive for filing the bankruptcy and to dismiss the debtor's Chapter 13 petition for cause under Section 1307(c).

Borrower's Default

The borrowers' conduct in dealing with the mortgage had not been exemplary. Marie Truitt, mother of Joseph Lippolis, one of the debtors, took out a mortgage loan of about $118,000 from the lender to acquire the residence. Truitt lived on the property with her son (the debtor), his wife, and others until shortly after the purchase. Then Truitt moved out. The debtors were supposed to continue making the mortgage payments, but within six months after the purchase, they failed to make payments and the lender started foreclosure. Two weeks after that, Truitt filed her own Chapter 13 bankruptcy proceeding in the District of New Jersey where she had moved, and ultimately obtained confirmation of the Chapter 13 plan. However, the borrowers did not make mortgage payments and in May of 1997, the lender was granted relief from the automatic stay and continued its foreclosure proceedings in Pennsylvania.

Two days before the scheduled sheriff's sale, Truitt voluntarily dismissed her Chapter 13 case and sold the property to the debtors for $1.00. According to the court, that was also a mortgage

126

default. The following day, the debtors started their own Chapter 13 bankruptcy proceeding in the Eastern District of Pennsylvania and the sheriff's sale was postponed by that proceeding.

The lender immediately moved for relief from the automatic stay, arguing that the debtors' Chapter 13 filing was an abuse of the bankruptcy process and constituted a "cause" to lift the automatic stay and dismiss the case. The lender also argued that the debtors had no equity in the property.

At a hearing on the lender's motion, the lender proved that the loan was delinquent by 21 payments, for a total of more than $23,000. Also, since the loan was made, the lender had only received 12 of 28 required payments and only 7 of these payments were good, while 5 checks were returned for insufficient funds. To make matters worse for the borrowers, one of the debtors testified that the property was worth less than the balance of the mortgage and that the sole purpose of the transfer from Truitt to the debtors was to prevent the sale of the property at the scheduled sheriff's sale.

Despite all of this evidence, the bankruptcy court postponed the sheriff's sale and ultimately denied the lender's motion for relief from the stay and to dismiss the Chapter 13 case. It held that the debtors were entitled to cure the mortgage defaults.

Reprimand of Bankruptcy Judges

Judge Kelly reversed the decision and agreed with the lender on two grounds. First, the stay had to be lifted because the petition was filed in "bad faith." Second, under Section 362(d)(2) of the code, the stay had to be lifted because there was no equity in the property and the property was not necessary for reorganization. On the second issue, the debtors had failed to provide evidence that retention of the residence was necessary either because no comparable housing was available or because the home was necessary to the debtors' business.

The judge cited several cases that held that bad faith establishes sufficient cause for relief from an automatic stay. In what appeared to be a reprimand of the bankruptcy courts in the Eastern District, Kelly stated: "Although the weight of authority is in favor of lifting the automatic stay for 'cause' consisting of 'bad faith' in filing a Chapter 13 petition, the Bankruptcy Court for the Eastern District of Pennsylvania has steadfastly refused to accept that there is any 'good faith' requirement as a condition of filing a Chapter 13 case. E.g., *Taylor*, 96 B.R. at 591." 228 B.R. at 112.

Undoubtedly, one decision like this will not end this abuse of the bankruptcy system, but the *Lippolis* case has taken a step in the right direction. The decision involved a Chapter 13 proceeding. However, it also may serve as a warning to commercial borrowers in Chapter 11 proceedings that bankruptcy courts may not permit themselves to be used by borrowers who seek to prolong foreclosure proceedings by frivolous actions. Whether the decision will be applied to Chapter 11 cases remains to be seen, although the ruling is broad enough to apply to all bankruptcy filings.

18   BORROWER'S BANKRUPTCY DEFEATS DEFAULT INTEREST

Despite bans on bad faith bankruptcies, a 2002 California case shows how a delinquent borrower can use the Bankruptcy Code to avoid default interest. In *Platinum Capital, Inc. v. Sylmar Plaza, L.P.*, 314 F.3d 1070 (9th Cir. 2002), *cert. denied*, 123 S. Ct. 2097 (2003), the Ninth Circuit Court of Appeals upheld the confirmation of Sylmar Plaza's Chapter 11 reorganization plan that had been filed for the sole purpose of avoiding approximately $1 million of default interest due on the debtor's mortgage.

The dispute arose over an $8 million mortgage loan secured by the Sylmar Plaza Shopping Center that carried an interest rate of 8.87 percent and a default interest rate of 5 percent more (13.87 percent). When the borrower encountered cash flow problems, it stopped making payments on the loan, allowed taxes to become delinquent, and then, in violation of the loan, transferred the shopping center to a new limited partnership. The lender then foreclosed in state court; the day after that court issued its statement of intended decision in favor of the lender, the borrower filed for bankruptcy.

$1 Million Saved

The bankruptcy court permitted the Sylmar Plaza to be sold for approximately $7 million free and clear of the mortgage lien, even though the lender claimed that its lien then exceeded $10 million. Because the lender did not appeal the sale order, the lender's claim was bifurcated into a secured claim measured by the net proceeds of the sale and an unsecured claim for the balance.

The confirmed plan of reorganization provided for payment of both the lender's secured claim and its unsecured claim in full (at

8.87 percent interest) on the effective date of the plan. The court explained how this plan cured the default:

> The procedural significance of this treatment was that Platinum's claims would not be "impaired" under the plan and it would, therefore, not be entitled to reject the plan or receive "cram down" protections, including protection against "unfair discrimination" under 11 U.S.C. Section 1129(b). The financial significance was to effect a "cure" of the default so that all interest, including post-petition interest, would be calculated at the 8.87% non-default rate, rather than the 13.87% default rate. The difference in accrued interest calculated between the two rates amounts to approximately $1 million. All other unsecured claims were to be paid 10% interest retroactive to the filing date of the bankruptcy case.

314 F.3d at 1073.

Plan in Good Faith

As expected, the lender objected to the confirmation contending that the plan had not been "proposed in good faith" as required under the Bankruptcy Code. The lender contended that the various classes of claims proposed under the entire plan was a "sham" conceived to deprive the mortgage lender of $1 million in default interest. The lender also argued that paying all other unsecured classes 10 percent post-petition interest, while it would receive only 8.87 percent post-petition interest, was so unfairly discriminatory as to cast doubt on the plan's good faith.

According to the court, the original borrowers on the loan, the Hornwoods, had a diverse real estate portfolio worth more than $55 million with a net equity value exceeding $15 million. In support of its argument that the plan lacks good faith, the lender argued that the plan leaves the Hornwoods solvent while permitting them to avoid paying post-petition interest at the default interest rate.

The circuit court pointed out that the Bankruptcy Code does not define "good faith," and that even insolvency is not a prerequisite to a finding of good faith under Section 1129(a). It held that an adverse effect on a creditor's contractual rights "does not by itself warrant a bad faith finding." Also, in enacting the Bankruptcy Code, Congress determined that debtors should have the opportunity to avail themselves of numerous code provisions that adversely alter creditors' contractual and nonbankruptcy rights. Therefore, to take advantage of a particular provision of the code for the purpose of capping the amount of a creditor's claim is not bad faith. The court cited precedents that one power to cure defaults under the Bankruptcy Code is the power to avoid default penalties such as higher interest.

The circuit court also determined that the bankruptcy courts should determine a debtor's good faith on a "case-by-case basis," taking into account the particular features of each plan. Therefore, it rejected the lender's argument that the court should apply a "per se rule" that would automatically find bad faith under these circumstances. The court also rejected the lender's argument that it would receive only 8.87 percent on its mortgage, while other unsecured creditors would receive 10 percent. It held that as an "unimpaired creditor," the lender had no standing to complain of discrimination, because under Section 1126(f), the lender is "conclusively presumed to have accepted the plan." Apparently, the failure of the plan to include $1 million of default interest was not considered an "impairment" of the lender.

Deference to Bankruptcy Court

The decision is not surprising based on the cited precedent that grants bankruptcy courts wide discretion to decide whether a particular reorganization plan meets the good faith standard. The circuit court showed its deference to the bankruptcy court on this issue.

Some will be disturbed by the appearance that the borrower in *Platinum Capital* "got away" with something. The case highlights a legal system that allows a wealthy business entity, presumably represented and advised by lawyers and financial consultants, which borrowed millions of dollars under specific payback terms, to disregard the agreement terms. Under this case, a borrower can violate a due-on-transfer clause in a mortgage and transfer the property to another entity, which then files for bankruptcy. In that way, the original borrower also can avoid some of the negative publicity and the stigma of entering into bankruptcy itself.

Also, by this tactic, the borrower used bankruptcy as a tool solely to avoid $1 million in default interest that it would have been obligated to pay under a state court foreclosure proceeding. And all of this was done pursuant to a bankruptcy petition filed only one day after the state court had acted. Moreover, the unsecured creditors are entitled to receive interest at the rate of 10 percent, more than the mortgage lender.

19 DOES POSTJUDGMENT INTEREST HAVE LIFE AFTER DEBT?

In an improbable TV tale, an embezzler discharged from prison finally returns the concealed $10 million loot in full to the tenacious insurance investigator. When asked by a friend what he accomplished, the thief replies, "Do you realize what $10 million at compounded interest earns over 10 years?"

Curtailed Interest Rate

The tale seems improbable, because traditional legal systems recognize the value of interest, and courts would probably require the embezzler to pay back principal and interest. But the value of interest will not always be recognized.

In a bankruptcy case, *In re Herbert,* 86 B.R. 433 (Bankr. E.D. Pa. 1988), the court found that an agreed mortgage interest rate would not have to be paid by the debtor after judgment was entered against him. This wasn't a case involving an embezzler, only a defaulting borrower; and the decision didn't bar interest. The court merely curtailed the amount of interest that could be collected. However, as in the embezzlement story, the culprit retained interest he didn't deserve.

In the *Herbert* case, the parties had agreed on an interest rate of 10.125 percent, and after default the lender took judgment against the borrower and attempted to collect that interest on the unpaid balance. The note, which was then a standard Pennsylvania Federal National Mortgage Association (FNMA) form, provided for payment of 10.125 percent interest "from the date of this note until paid." This is still standard language in many notes and mortgages.

Despite the contractually stated rate, the borrower argued that after judgment the interest rate should be limited to 6 percent, which is the legal rate as defined in a Pennsylvania statute. Judge

133

Scholl accepted that argument based on his interpretation of an old Pennsylvania statute that establishes the legal rate of interest on a judgment. The applicable provision states:

> Except as otherwise provided by another statute, a judgment for a specific sum of money shall bear interest at the lawful rate from the date of the verdict or award, or from the date of the judgment, if the judgment is not entered upon a verdict or award.

42 Pa. C.S. § 8101.

The judge's decision jolted many attorneys because the parties apparently had agreed on the interest rate, and most observers thought that the Pennsylvania courts would enforce an agreed rate even after judgment, if the documents provided for that. The decision is even more startling in light of other cases. For example, another bankruptcy court (*In re Skyler Ridge*, 80 B.R. 500 (Bankr. C.D. Cal. 1987)) decided that a contract interest rate as well as a higher agreed default rate should be enforced after judgment.

Furthermore, the *Herbert* decision may not be limited to consumer or residential cases. It seems to apply as a general rule. Also, it flies in the face of an earlier Pennsylvania decision that considered the same issue. In *Secari v. Barua*, 45 SOM. LEG. J. 390, 392 (1986), the court held that

> ... The 6% legal rate of interest, we believe, is a gap-filler to be used when parties either have not contracted for a specific rate of interest, or when parties have agreed to interest "at the legal rate." The legal rate of 6%, was not, in this court's opinion, enacted by the legislature as an absolute mandate that would inhibit freedom of contract, and as a result, complicate settlement negotiations.

Lowest Legal Rate

What's wrong with applying a legal rate of interest to a loan? For one thing, Pennsylvania's legal rate was established in 1723 at 6 percent, and has not changed since. See Act of March 2, 1723, ch. 262. That occurred 64 years before our forefathers signed the U.S. Constitution in Pennsylvania.

Six percent may now be the lowest fixed legal interest rate in the United States. John M. Giunta, *The Postjudgment Interest Rate in Pennsylvania: Ignoring Reality for Too Long*, 23 DUQ. L.

REV. 1083, 1084 (1985). Today, interest rates are approximately four percentage points higher than that, and at 6 percent, the defaulting borrower will receive an unnecessary windfall.

In addition, the statutory policy behind establishing a legal rate for judgments seems to be to encourage settling disputes when the parties have not agreed on a rate. Therefore, the statute provides a rate in those cases where parties have agreed on interest at the "legal" rate. It does not seem appropriate to apply a 1723 rate when the parties have in fact agreed on a higher rate.

Why should the law reward a defaulting borrower with a lower rate than the borrower was paying before default? The law should attempt to discourage defaults by permitting the lender to collect at least the agreed rate. Otherwise, slippery debtors who can delay collection may profit from the *Herbert* rule. If they have hidden assets that earn more than 6 percent, they may be tempted to keep one step ahead of the sheriff as long as they can. Then a modified version of the TV embezzlement tale may be a reality in Pennsylvania.

Furthermore, the *Herbert* rule will give borrowers an economic incentive to crowd court dockets by dragging out postjudgment litigation as long as possible.

Agreed Default Rates

If the parties have specifically agreed to an increased default rate, why shouldn't the courts permit that increased rate to be enforced? (See *Skyler Ridge*, above.) Lenders' attorneys are hoping that other courts will not adopt the *Herbert* decision when the issue arises again.

Judge Scholl apparently downplayed the provision in the note that the contract rate of interest was to be applicable "until paid." The judge stated:

> ... [The] mortgage merged with the foreclosure judgment ... thus allowing the mortgagee to collect interest measured only at the Pennsylvania legal rate of six (6%) percent per annum thereafter. [86 B.R. at 434.]

> ... A judgment creditor is entitled to interest on the judgment at the legal rate only, *even if the rate of interest on the obligation on which the judgment is entered was greater.* [86 B.R. at 436, emphasis added.]

> We believe that FNMA's claim arises under the judgment, not the mortgage agreement ... [86 B.R. at 438.]

However, in *Herbert*, the judge was not confronted with a note that specifically called for payment of the contract rate after judgment was entered. It is possible that specific language establishing postjudgment interest may have made a difference.

Regardless of what the judge intended, he has clearly struck a blow against lenders who try to recover on a defaulted loan. In light of this, they would be well advised to make it clear that the contract rate (or a greater default rate) should apply, even after judgment.

Perhaps the best system would follow the federal model, which bases postjudgment interest on a variable standard such as treasury bill rates.

20   BANK'S CONDUCT MAY FORFEIT RIGHTS AGAINST GUARANTORS

A bank's conduct may bar it from collecting against guarantors—even when they sign a standard waiver of defenses.

In *National Westminster Bank v. Lomker*, 649 A.2d 1328 (N.J. Super. Ct. App. Div. 1994), the bank sued the borrower's partners under guaranties of a defaulted mortgage loan that had been secured by the borrower's 35-acre industrial site. However, the guarantors struck back and counterclaimed, primarily alleging bad faith, fraud, and conspiracy with the mortgaged parcel.

Guarantors' Waivers

In an attempt to knock out those defenses, the bank trotted out the guaranty waivers, which, as in many similar forms, gave the bank "virtually unlimited power" to dispose of and deal with the collateral, and specifically provided that the guarantors would not have any rights against the bank even if it failed:

> ... to preserve any rights in the Collateral or take any action whatsoever in regard to the Collateral ... nor by reason of the fact that any of the Collateral may be subject to equities or defenses or claims in favor of others ... nor by reason of any deterioration, waste ... [or] ... release, in whole or in part, with or without consideration, of the Collateral ....

Westminster, 649 A.2d at 1332.

The guaranties also provided that the guarantors "waive[s] the right to interpose counterclaims or setoffs of any kind and description in any litigation arising hereunder...." *Id.*

Despite that language, the New Jersey Superior Court reversed the lower court's summary judgment for the bank and permitted the guarantors to raise various defenses related to the bank's handling of the collateral. In coming to that conclusion, the court held that if the guarantors' allegations were correct, the bank's conduct would be enough to provide the guarantors with a defense.

Bank's Conduct

How were the guarantors able to get around their own waivers? They did it by alleging that the bank used bad faith, fraud, and inside dealing in responding to the potential sale of the mortgaged property. They argued that the bank engaged in a conspiracy with a prospective buyer to deprive the debtor of the property by interfering with the debtor's attempts to market it.

The guarantors alleged that the borrower, in an attempt to pay off the $1.2 million debt, obtained a contract to sell the property for $1.8 million to a buyer who became a client of the bank. That deal fell through. The same buyer then entered into another contract for $1,350,000. That deal also fell through. The guarantors also alleged that the buyer became aware of the borrower's precarious position through the bank and then used that information to obtain a contract for the property through the bank for only $700,000, and that the buyer was able to do this because the bank divulged to it "significant confidential data" that enabled it to avoid its contract at the higher price. They alleged that another buyer was discouraged because it was informed by the bank's counsel that the bank would shortly take over the project and that the bank was having active discussions with the first buyer.

The court cited other cases where a debtor defended on similar grounds. In *Ramapo Bank v. Bechtel*, 539 A.2d 1276 (N.J. Super. Ct. App. Div. 1988), a bank allegedly engaged in a concealed pre-transaction agreement not to pursue a co-guarantor in the event of default. In *Lenape State Bank v. Winslow Corp.*, 523 A.2d 223 (N.J. Super. Ct. App. Div. 1987), a bank allegedly intentionally obstructed the sale of the collateral by improperly administrating the loan and allowing tenants to remain in default for over a year without notifying the debtor so that he could remedy the situation.

"Magic" Words

The *National Westminster Bank* decision overcame the guarantors' waiver by accepting the guarantors' arguments that the language in the guaranty was not completely clear and must be strictly construed against the bank that prepared the form. The waivers were not "unequivocal" because they did not specifically "waive the defenses of bad faith, fraud or conspiracy." Since the guaranty provides that guarantors do not escape liability even if the bank "wastes" or completely "releases" the property from the mortgage, this decision will surprise many lenders. Obstructing a sale of the collateral would seem to be a lesser offense to a guarantor than completely releasing it from the mortgage!

This case could create problems for banks trying to enforce not only guaranties, but also mortgages, notes, and other loan documents. Frequently those documents provide for waivers that are similar to the National Westminster Bank waivers.

Under the rule of this case, allegations by borrowers about the bank's conduct could easily give rise to delays in foreclosures and other enforcement proceedings, even if the borrowers are not later able to prove anything with specificity. For example, in *National Westminster Bank*, the guarantors claimed that the bank disclosed to a prospective buyer that the borrower was in a "precarious position" and that the borrower was already dealing with another prospect. While that by itself should not be enough to create a defense against the foreclosing lender, it is not hard to see how a desperate borrower could put those allegations together with other allegations of how the bank had dealt with prospective buyers in order to create a factual issue that would delay proceedings for months or even years.

The court left one ray of hope for lenders. It seemed to say that if the waiver had contained certain "magic words," the bank would have won, i.e., if the guarantors had specifically and expressly waived defenses of "bad faith, fraud and conspiracy." The court's view on that is not completely clear because the court raised in a footnote (footnote 3) the possibility that "as a matter of public policy" a party may not even be bound by a specific waiver of defenses for bad faith, fraud, or conspiracy. Lenders should not be surprised by that point of view. Future courts may have difficulty barring borrowers from pursuing banks for intentional misconduct like fraud or conspiracy.

In any event, it would be well for lenders to take the *National Westminster Bank* decision to heart and use the magic language in their loan waivers.

PART II

Landlords and Tenants

21 TIPS FOR FINDING THE BEST BARGAIN RENTALS

To successfully conduct comparative shopping, conventional wisdom dictates you must first find the per-unit price. For example, to compare prices of sodas or detergents in differently sized containers, find the price per ounce. Informed businesspeople try to do this when shopping for office space.

Generally, commercial and office space are offered at so many dollars "per square foot." Unfortunately, pricing rental space is more complex than pricing soda or detergent. Also, bargains cannot always be found this way. Therefore, prospective tenants may not easily recognize the biggest and best bargains.

Net, Gross, and Stops

Does the landlord quote a net figure or a gross figure? If rent is $20 per square foot net, that generally means building expenses such as real estate taxes and operating expenses will be included. In newer buildings in center city Philadelphia, for example, those costs could amount to $6 or more per square foot. To prudently compare with gross quotes, add those projected costs to the net rental figure.

Frequently with buildings under construction, a landlord will quote a gross rent with a tax stop and an operating expense stop. For example, the stop might be for $4 per square foot in operating expense, and $2 per square foot for real estate taxes. That means tenants pay for any excess over those figures.

A quoted rental of $26 per square foot with a $2 tax stop and a $4 operating expense stop is equivalent to a $20 per square foot net rental. If taxes for that building do not exceed $2 per square foot and the operating expenses do not exceed $4, tenants will not have to pay any of those charges. But what happens when taxes go beyond $2 per square foot, say to $2.50, and the operating expenses are only $3.50? That is within the tax stop for operating expenses but $.50 over the real estate tax stop.

Can the combined two stops of $6 shield against the combined taxes of $2.50 and operating expenses of $3.50? The answer to that depends on negotiated terms in the lease.

Tenants also should be aware of real estate tax abatements. Owners may receive a three-year tax moratorium on improvements. This saving may be passed along to the tenant in one building and not in another.

Measuring Space

A more subtle issue is how a landlord measures space. Does the tenant pay for an allocated share of the core area of the building, elevators, atriums, and corridors on floors occupied with other tenants? If a tenant must pay for this space, how much of each floor is devoted to these areas? It may vary considerably from building to building.

Does the owner measure the rentable space from the outside walls or from inside the convectors? The difference could be as much as three feet, possibly translating to thousands of dollars per year.

The difference between "usable space" and what an owner designates as "rentable space" is not always easy to pin down. The loss factor could easily amount to 20 percent or more on some buildings. One common standard of measurement is published by the Building Owners and Managers Associations International (BOMA), but not all landlords use this standard.

Allowances

In addition to this rental analysis, it is important to calculate "work-letter costs" by estimating the cost per square foot of conforming the offered space to the tenant's needs, setting off the credit offered by the landlord against this cost, and adding the excess over this credit to the basis rent per square foot. On some buildings, the landlord may be willing to offer free rent and other allowances at the beginning of the lease. One way to evaluate these items is to deduct them from work-letter cost before adding anything to basic rent.

All of this may become very confusing and complicated. So what should a prospective tenant do? Seek an expert. An expert's fees may be more than made up by the savings in selecting the right space. For example, an architect or space planner can obtain the building plans of each targeted building and draw layouts of projected office space.

Calculations of the loss factors between rentable and usable space will help determine whether the offered rent really constitutes a bargain.

22   FOUR MOST COMMONLY MISSED TENANT NEEDS IN THE COMMERCIAL LEASE

Certain lease clauses are analogous to the spare tire in your car. If you have it, you may drive around for years without ever needing it. If you don't have it, you may find yourself stranded on an abandoned road with a flat tire in the middle of a blizzard.

Tenants who are eager to get going with their new ventures sometimes sign a form lease without taking precautions and may run into certain problems. This chapter discusses four issues that tenants frequently miss.

The Delayed Start

If a tenant is planning to move into a new office by a certain date, it may be frustrated by an existing tenant who stays on beyond its lease. Your client may have terminated its old lease and made arrangements to move, only to find that the old tenant is not planning to move out.

This may not be the landlord's fault. It may not even be the old tenant's fault. Its plan to vacate may have been delayed by a holdover tenant somewhere else.

There is very little your client can do to solve this problem after the lease is signed. However, if it is aware that this may occur and if timing is crucial, other comparable space should be considered before signing a lease.

Even if the space is occupied, careful questioning may give you some assurance that the existing tenant will move on time. If it signed a new lease for vacant space, chances are it will move on time.

Most printed leases buck the problem of the holdover tenant to the new tenant. They provide that if a tenant stays beyond its term, the new lease will be binding, but the start of the term is simply postponed. This open-ended feature is completely unsatisfactory to most clients. No obligation is imposed on the landlord to take action against the culprit, no compensation is available to your client for damages it will suffer, and theoretically, its move could be postponed for months or years. Unless you negotiate a change in this clause, your client may not be able to take other space because the new lease is not terminated by the delay. It is merely postponed—indefinitely.

The Premature Start

Like a premature baby, a new retail store should not be taken out in public until it is ready. And the tenant should not start paying for it either.

This is the other side of the coin from the holdover tenant problem. In this situation, the landlord wants the tenant to take over the space and start to pay rent before it can use the space. This arises when tenant fix-up work runs behind schedule, and the lease provides for rent to start anyway.

This is bad enough if the work is the tenant's responsibility. It will begin paying rent for space it can't start using. But it is worse if the landlord caused the delay.

Many leases do not focus on this issue, and frequently it is not clear who was supposed to do what or who caused the delay. The tenant may claim that the landlord's contractors didn't start early enough. The landlord may claim that they were ready to work, but the tenant's architect didn't give them enough detail early enough. How could the electrician and the carpenters proceed when they weren't told where the tenant wanted the outlets for its computers and printing equipment?

These problems can be reduced if a proper schedule assigning responsibility is set out in detail in the lease. Also, the tenant may want to specify that rent does not begin until a specified number of days after the landlord has completed all of the described work in accordance with designated standards.

The "Middle Game"

In addition to the unanticipated issues that arise at the start of a lease, there are some that may be encountered after the lease term has begun.

One recurring and common problem is what a landlord will do about inadequate heating, ventilating, and air-conditioning (HVAC). If the air-conditioning or circulation system is inadequate to meet extreme conditions, the landlord may be running it full time, but the tenant may still be sweltering. The environment can become so uncomfortable that the tenant may lose employees and customers.

Another issue in this age of information technology is the need for continual access to telecommunications conduit, such as wiring, cable, fiberoptics, satellite dishes, and to other special equipment. Failure of this access can put the tenant out of business.

The printed form lease doesn't help the tenant. It usually provides that the property is being rented "as is." Moreover, it usually prohibits the tenant from making any alterations or installations without the consent of the landlord. Therefore, even if the tenant were willing to install additional air-conditioning or heating equipment at its own expense, it may be unable to do so. Also, even if the system is good, the landlord may be tempted to save energy costs by running it at less than full capacity, particularly at certain hours.

Tenants are best able to protect themselves by hiring reliable experts to check out all these systems before they sign leases. This will at least assure that the systems are adequate.

Since the tenant and his or her expert are usually not visiting the prospective space on both the hottest and coldest days of the year, they will not be observing the HVAC under the most extreme conditions. If you are negotiating the lease in the winter, it is difficult to test how the air-conditioning system will work during the dog days of summer. You can ask other tenants, but their standards may be different from your client's. And you may be dealing with a new building or one undergoing major renovations with systems still untried. Therefore, you should deal with this issue in the lease. You should try to obtain warranties "with teeth." Require the landlord to warrant its claims about the system.

Tenants should push for performance standards. For example, the landlord should warrant that the temperature inside (except for certain remote locations) will be maintained to at least 75 degrees when the temperature outside reaches 96 degrees. And if the landlord breaches this warranty, perhaps the tenant should be given the right to install supplemental equipment at the landlord's expense, or to take other action.

148

Tenants will also want to write in protections of certain levels of telecommunications capacity, speed, and continuing performance. While "redundancy" is not good in an English essay, it may be a requirement for operating systems in a lease.

Nondisturbance

Once a tenant is settled in and happy, it will want to remain there as long as it's paying rent. However, for technical reasons, the lease could be terminated by the landlord's lender.

If your client has a low-rent, long-term lease, has spent several hundred thousand dollars fixing up its restaurant or office, and is doing great business, a mortgage lender could put it out of business merely because the landlord failed to pay its mortgage payments. If the mortgage was in existence before the lease, the lender is not bound by the lease, so on default of the mortgage, the lender can foreclose, and your client will be forced to renegotiate its lease or leave.

Many form leases make it worse. They provide that the lease is subordinate not only to existing mortgages on the property but also to future mortgages.

Keep in mind that your client may occupy only part of a large complex, and its rent may constitute only a small part of the massive mortgage payment in default. Even if it is doing everything it is supposed to under its lease, there may be nothing it can do to save itself.

What you should have is a nondisturbance agreement with the lender. If you are a subtenant, you need a similar agreement with the over-landlord to protect against your immediate landlord's default.

Also you should not accept a subordination clause in the lease. A nondisturbance agreement provides that as long as a tenant is not in default under its lease, the lender will recognize the lease, even if the landlord is in default on its mortgage. The tenant simply pays rent directly to the lender should a default occur.

The specific terms of this agreement may be difficult to work out, and frequently the landlord or the lender will be unwilling to accommodate the tenant. The owner or the lender may refuse to give a nondisturbance agreement at all, or it may impose unacceptable conditions to that agreement. For example, a lender may not be willing to honor lease-construction obligations or allowances incurred by your landlord before the lender forecloses.

149

Moreover, if you are dealing with a financially solid landlord and the tenant is investing very little in fixing up the space, it may not be worth fighting over. The landlord may never default, and if it does, the tenant may be able to work something out with the lender at that time.

The Printed Form

Even if you can't get a nondisturbance, there may be another solution. One compromise is an indemnity agreement from your landlord backed by adequate security, or a letter of credit that covers anticipated damages if the lease is terminated. If you can arrange that, you should make sure the indemnity covers all fees and expenses that you may have in completing a new lease and in planning, renovating, and moving into new space. This solution is only a compromise because it will be different to calculate charges for the intangibles, such as lost good will, and the time, trouble, and aggravation of moving.

While only four important issues have been selected for discussion here, counsel for the prospective tenant should focus on many other commonly missed issues. These will vary with the nature of the transaction. Restaurants have different needs than offices, and a service business and a factory present different problems. It is not within the scope of this chapter to solve all of these problems. The intent is merely to alert attorneys to some of the less obvious dangers that lurk within the printed form.

23   TENANTS MAY PAY THE COST OF
          TERRORISM

The fallout from terrorism has created unintended victims. While political analysts focus on legislation and election results, real estate analysts focus on commercial tenants.

After 9/11, the cost of insurance and building security has increased substantially. Who will pay those costs in commercial buildings? The simple answer is tenants—unless they do something to prevent it.

This issue arises under customary lease provisions that pass on operating cost increases to tenants. We see this in shopping centers and office leases—even in your own law firm leases.

Insurance Premiums

We now live in a world where insurance premiums have skyrocketed. For one thing, much of the real estate community believes that insurance companies have taken advantage of the threat of terrorism to play catch-up with the low insurance premiums that had been charged on casualty and liability policies before 9/11. Owners have reported that their renewal premiums have increased by 50 to 100 percent with no additional coverage. At a meeting of the American College of Real Estate Lawyers, one insurance expert reported that throughout the country, insurance companies had been paying losses estimated at 110 percent of the premiums they received. Before downtrends in the stock market and in interest rates, insurance companies were able to make up these deficits from their investments. All of that changed when investment returns collapsed.

Also, consider the cost of terrorism insurance. After the World Trade Center disaster, owners and lenders started focusing on covering themselves against future terrorism attacks. Often, this coverage isn't even available, but when it is, the cost of this insurance alone could easily exceed the premium for all other building insurance. In one notable New York case, the terrorism insurance premium required by the lender for Four Times Square in Manhattan was reportedly $3.2 million. When the owner refused to pay it, the lender paid the premium out of lockbox income that the owner controlled under the mortgage documents.

Where does all of this leave the tenants of those buildings? The answer is that increases in insurance costs are passed on to the tenants, generally on a pro rata basis under traditional pass-through provisions.

Additional Security

Another fallout from terrorism is the increased cost of building security. Essentially, cost pass-through clauses will include the cost of increased security in buildings. What happens if the landlord decides to post security guards around the clock in a building that never had them before? You guessed it. These costs will generally be passed on to the tenants.

A more subtle issue can arise when the landlord decides to upgrade its security systems by doing things such as installing more-advanced alarm systems, automated identity checkers, state-of-the-art video surveillance systems, security gates, better locks, or even exterior barriers against motorized bomb threats. Many leases distinguish between "operating expenses," which may be passed through, and "capital improvements," which may not. If that distinction is not carefully defined, a tenant may even find itself paying for those costs.

Negotiating Pass-Throughs

Tenants who are stuck with existing pass-through provisions in their leases should carefully examine these bills in light of their leases. It is possible that some of the charges may not be appropriate. For example, under some circumstances, it may be argued that the cost of terrorism insurance is not a "commercially reasonable" operating expense. If that type of insurance is not customary in comparable buildings, but is a peculiar requirement of the lender who happens to hold the loan on the landlord's building, tenants may argue that this is not a "normal or customary operating expense," as that term may be defined in the lease. The argument can be made that the cost of an exorbitant insurance premium for this purpose stems from unreasonable demands of a lender selected by the landlord—and not from building operations.

Similar arguments may be made about increased costs of building security. Are these extra costs customary in comparable buildings? Are they justified by incidents that are likely to occur, or, to put it in legal terms, that are "foreseeable"? Can these expenses be reasonably expected to prevent terrorism attacks on this building?

There may not be much that tenants can do with existing leases negotiated in more peaceful times. However, tenants who are negotiating new leases may have options.

For one thing, they can try to negotiate provisions that place limits, or caps, on these types of increases. The issue can be complicated because some landlords will require tenants to pay even for capital improvements, if those improvements can be demonstrated to save other operating expenses. For example, if in computing a base year for determining increases, a landlord includes elevator operators, and in later years is willing to upgrade the elevators so that those employees are no longer needed, the landlord will want the tenants to pay for that type of capital improvement. That same rationale could apply to capital improvements like a video monitoring system or an ID scanner that could reduce the cost of security guards.

However, the tenant may still be able to negotiate limits. For example, tenants should resist having to pay for the entire capital improvement in only one year. They might be able to negotiate a provision to amortize the capital improvement over the expected life of the improvement so that the payment is spread out over many years. If the lease term is shorter than that expected life, the tenant may wind up paying for only part of those costs.

In the same way, a prospective tenant may try to negotiate insurance pass-throughs. There are many ways to go with this negotiation. One way is to try to negotiate a cap on increases of insurance costs, or other costs, either each year or during the term of the lease. The tenant may be able to justify percentage limits.

Compare Buildings

Landlords will resist these efforts by tenants, particularly with those costs that are not under their control, such as insurance premiums. But it doesn't hurt to ask. At least by focusing on these issues, tenants who have alternatives may be able to factor in these potential costs in making comparisons with other buildings. For example, if one building already has improved security systems and around-the-clock guards, those costs will be built into the base year that is used for computing cost increases. It is therefore less likely that the total cost of occupancy will be jacked up for these reasons, than it would be in a building that does not have those items built into the operating-cost base.

Similarly, if the prospective tenant will look into insurance costs of various buildings, it may find that one building has already built the increased insurance rates into its base year, while another has not. Low base-year costs lead to what is sometimes called "hidden rent."

Also, one building may not require terrorism coverage or, in the alternative, that coverage will not be part of the computation of increased costs. That, too, should be considered when a tenant compares buildings in projecting its total occupancy costs.

Tenants may also want to compare each building's policies for access in this new atmosphere of fear. If the tight security and limited access of one building is different from another, the prospective tenant should weigh the effect of these policies on its own needs. Some tenants will see that as merely expensive "window dressing" for which they have to pay extra operating costs. Others will be willing to pay the price.

Some tenants will not want to see their customers or clients delayed, photographed, questioned, or searched in the lobby of their building. What about a psychiatrist who specializes in addictions, or a law firm that concentrates in corporate bankruptcy consulting, securities fraud, or highly confidential domestic relations disputes?

Other tenants may value the extra security. In any event, if building-access policies are important to the tenant, the tenant should spell them out in the negotiated lease.

None of these issues may be important enough to worry some tenants or to affect their decision of where they will spend their working life during the next 5 to 20 years, but tenants should pay attention to them. As we know, it is difficult to prepare for a terrorist attack, which can visit death and devastation on a building and its occupants. But, with proper advice, the tenant can at least prepare itself for the terror of escalating occupancy costs.

A 2003 New York case emphasizes the importance of carefully defining "gross sales" in a lease that bases additional rent on a percentage of these sales. The issue arose in *Bombay Realty Corp. v. Magna Carta, Inc.,* 790 N.E.2d 1163 (N.Y. 2003). In *Bombay,* the New York Court of Appeals reversed the lower courts and held that the tenant had to pay a percentage based only on the commissions generated from telephone service plans sold at the leased property, not from the total value of the service plans generated there. This decision emphasizes how special care must be given to the drafting of the term "gross sales."

Changed Use

The original landlord had leased the property to Magna Carta, Inc., which operated a restaurant at the site until it closed. Magna Carta then sublet the property to Cellular 2000 and Beyond, LLC. Cellular, a retail-communications store that sells cellular telephones, pagers, chargers, and related accessories, agreed to pay Magna Carta a monthly sublease rent plus pay Bombay a "percentage rent in the amount of 5% of any gross sales as defined in the original lease above $480,000." The original lease between Bombay and Magna Carta defined "gross sales" as "income generated by the business conducted by the lessee on the demised premises including income derived from the sale of all services and all products whether for cash or for credit."

The problem arose because of the way that Cellular derives its income. When purchasing a cellular telephone, a customer can sign a contract with Southwestern Bell Mobile Services for a variety of cellular phone-service plans. Southwestern bills the customer directly, receives all of the revenues generated from the customers for phone service, and pays Cellular based upon a commission schedule as well as a residual fee.

Gross or Net?

In calculating its gross sales for the percentage-rent calculation, Cellular included only its earned commissions, and not the full amount received by Southwestern under its various phone service plans. Bombay maintained that the percentage rent should be based on all sales of Southwestern services to customers signed by Cellular and not merely the commissions. Bombay argued that using only the commissions for the percentage rent would be like converting the rent calculation to a percentage of net rather than gross proceeds.

The court of appeals rejected Bombay's arguments and reversed the lower court. It held:

> Reading the lease as whole, the contractual term "gross sales" must be tied to the gross income actually received by the lessee, Cellular. The sublease provides that the additional rent is 5% of the lessee's annual gross sales. It is clear, however, that Cellular's customers directly pay Southwestern—not Cellular—for the service contracts. Cellular's income in relation to service contracts comes from Southwestern only. Thus, the gross income Cellular derives from the sales of goods and services consists of the commissions received from Southwestern, not the total value of the contracts paid by customers to Southwestern.

The court of appeals reasoned that the lease required the lessee to report the gross sales as attested to by an officer of the lessee's company to the lessor. The lease permits the lessor access to the lessee's records at all reasonable times in order to verify the lessee's reported information. Thus, the provision shows that the contracting parties must have intended to use only the tenant's gross income as a base for the percentage rent, and not third-party income.

The court stated:

> Only the outside third party, Southwestern, which administers the cellular telephone plans, would have access to the "income" earned on a particular account. This information would not be maintained within Cellular's books.

The "reasonable expectation and purpose of the ordinary business [person] where making an ordinary business contract" would not require an outside third party such as Southwestern to voluntarily open up its books to Cellular.

Sublease Strategies

One issue illustrated by this case is that subleases can be anything but routine, particularly when the subtenant will be in a different business than the original tenant. In this case, the definition of "gross sales" would not have been a problem if the property were still operated as a restaurant. However, the new use raised different issues.

Sublessors and subtenants who think that they are merely making a simple deal obligating the new subtenant to terms in the master lease should carefully evaluate all of the lease issues. Aside from misunderstandings involving the definition of gross sales, other issues overlooked include different operating needs for the space, use restrictions on the space, different insurance needs, and subtenant protections in case the sublessor defaults. In addition, another issue sometimes overlooked is the subtenant's ability to implement lease renewals and other options included in the prime lease.

25   HOLDOVER TENANTS

Another important issue for tenants is what happens if the tenant stays beyond the agreed term of the lease?

Holdover rent clauses are used by landlords to deal with the tenant that stays on after the lease has expired. Like *The Man Who Came to Dinner,* the holdover tenant has outstayed his or her welcome and can wreak havoc with a landlord who has a prospect for the space and needs to move them in immediately—or lose them.

Extra Rent

That's why landlords want to make it costly for a tenant to hold over. A typical landlord's form lease will provide holdover rent at twice the normal rent. Some forms even provide for triple rent.

Tenants should review and negotiate these provisions before signing the lease. Sometimes landlords will agree to holdover provisions at a lower premium, for example, at 125 percent of the last month's rent. Also, the tenant should try to negotiate that the premium will serve as liquidated damages. Then, the landlord may be barred from other remedies if the tenant holds over.

Automatic Renewals

Holdover rent is not the worst provision that tenants may have to deal with if they overstay their welcome. Some leases provide that the lease is then renewed on the "same terms" as the original lease, except that rent may be escalated on some basis.

Think of what that does to the tenants. A tenant may be delayed in getting into its new space, or otherwise fail to move out its equipment and furnishings in time for reasons beyond its control. If that happens, a delay of just a few days could cost the tenant a whole additional year's rent—or more.

Sometimes, if the lease provides for a renewal on the same terms as the original lease, the tenant may be inadvertently stuck with a renewal for a term that is as long as the original term. After all, that is one of the original "terms" of the lease. Therefore if that was five years, a holdover tenant could be stuck with another five years, even when it has moved to another place. That penalty is even worse than being stuck with three times the rent for another few days—or even another month.

We recently encountered such a claim by a landlord when we represented a tenant who held over. That's when we looked at the state's law to see if that kind of a clause could really be sustained by the landlord. The lesson is that courts will sometimes enforce this language and that tenants had better be very careful about agreeing to it.

In the case of *Cusamano v. Anthony M. DiLucia, Inc.*, 421 A.2d 1120 (Pa. Super. 1980), the holdover tenant was held responsible for a full one year extension of a two-year lease term. The lease had provided that at expiration of the original term the tenant could renew for an additional term of one year. The tenant never sent out any renewal notice, but the court held that the tenant's unauthorized holdover constituted "an election by the tenant" to extend the lease—even though the tenant intended to terminate earlier.

On the other hand, a case in the U.S. District Court rejected the landlord's argument that the tenant's holdover automatically triggered renewal. In *Morelli v. Huffman Koos, Inc.*, No. 97-1807 (E.D. Pa. January 28, 1998), the lease provided a five-year extended term if written notice were given by the tenant at least four months in advance of the end of the initial one-year term. The tenant had not given such notice, and when the tenant held over, the landlord elected to collect double rent during the holdover period. That option of doubling rent was provided for in the lease—in a clause that covered month-to-month holdovers.

The court held that the landlord was precluded from taking what it viewed as an inconsistent position, that the tenant had renewed for five years. It is noteworthy that the district court did not seem to have any problem about requiring the holdover tenant to pay double rent.

The problem is exacerbated when a tenant has to face a holdover claim because of a subtenant who is unwilling to move out in time. The tenant could be charged for a holdover on the whole lease, even when the subtenant occupying only a small portion of the space refuses to move. While that subtenant might be liable for damages under its sublease, it may not be creditworthy. Therefore, under the circumstances of *Cusamano* or *Morelli*, the main tenant could be stuck for another year, or more, of rent on the total space— at premium rates.

Also, the subtenant on one floor of five may be liable for five floors' rent if it holds over on the one floor. See *1133 Bldg. Corp. v. Ketchum Communications, Inc.*, 638 N.Y.S.2d 450 (N.Y. App. Div. 1996).

Guarantor Not Liable

Even though the tenant may be liable for its holdover, a case has held that its guarantor may not. *Wilmington & Northern R.R. Co. v. Delaware Valley Ry. Co.*, No. 97C-09-297-WTQ (Del. Super. Ct. March 30, 1999). In that case the Superior Court of Delaware held that while a lease provided that the parent would guarantee rent, it did not say that the parent would continue to act as a guarantor if the subsidiary held over. Even though the guarantor guaranteed "all obligations of Lessee," the court ruled that the guarantor did not expressly agree to assume liability during a holdover tenancy. Guarantors should not count on this case being followed by other courts.

While holdover clauses are frequently overlooked in negotiating leases, these terms should be carefully negotiated. In those situations where a tenant unexpectedly finds itself in a holdover pattern, that clause may become the most important and costly provision in the whole lease.

26 THE HAZARDS OF LEASE RENEWAL NOTICES

When a tenant misses a lease renewal deadline, it may be out of luck—and out on the street. That bad news was delivered to a commercial tenant by the Utah Supreme Court in *Utah Coal & Lumber Restaurant, Inc. v. Outdoor Endeavors Unlimited,* 40 P.3d 581 (Utah 2001).

Missed Window

In that case, the tenant had entered into a lease in Park City, Utah for a five-year term with three five-year options to extend. It contained a "window" of time during which the tenant was required to notify the landlord of its option to renew. The property originally needed substantial work and the tenant spent $105,000, over three times the annual rent, to make repairs during the first few months. The tenant had invested this sum because it intended to remain on the lease for the full 20 years of the initial term and the renewals—and the landlord was aware of this.

The tenant was supposed to give notice of intent to renew between May 13th and July 11th but it missed the date by 11 days. The tenant claimed that during that time, she was overwhelmed with the intense negotiations with Park City because the tenant's cross-country skiing license was in jeopardy. Also, she was coping with the loss of a critical employee, restructuring the business's management, and was having various family problems.

On July 15th the landlord sent notice that the lease would expire at the end of the present term, and the tenant promptly attempted to renew the lease. When the landlord opposed the late renewal notice, the parties found themselves in court. The sympathetic trial court found that the tenant's failure was an "honest and justifiable mistake" and because the delay was so short, it would permit the renewal. The court reasoned that the few days' delay would not injure the landlord, but on the other hand, would significantly injure the tenant in light of its substantial investment in the property and the business.

Supreme Court Reverses

On appeal, the Utah Supreme Court was less sympathetic. It acknowledged that while in the past it had recognized an equitable exception to the usual rule that required prompt renewal of options, earlier precedent had not set forth any standards about which circumstances would justify invoking the exception. The court refused to use equitable relief "to assist one in extricating himself from circumstances which he has created...." It cited earlier precedents that permitted the use of equity where there was "fraud, misrepresentation, duress, undue influence, mistake and waiver." None of those reasons was present here.

Although the court recognized that some jurisdictions have been more generous to tenants who miss option dates, it was not ready to revise the bargained-for deadlines that the parties had set. It was concerned that if it changed the strict rule, the equitable exception would swallow the basic principle of strict compliance and "apply equitable excuse in almost all cases." They will hold that "time is of the essence" when it comes to the exercise of options. See *Western Savs. Fund Soc'y v. SEPTA*, 427 A.2d 175 (Pa. Super. 1981). But see *Bantam Four Cinemas, Inc. v. Zamias*, 544 A.2d 487 (Pa. Super. 1988). However, the court acknowledged that cases in many other states reject Utah's strict rule and permit late renewals where inequitable results are likely to occur.

Written Notices

In *Bantam Four*, above, the tenant, a movie theater operator, admitted that he did not give formal notice, and after the deadline, sent a mailgram to the landlord confirming the earlier oral notice. The tenant said this was equivalent to the written notice required in the lease because it was the practice established by him and the landlord.

The landlord denied he had been given either the oral notice or the mailgram. Despite the denial, the court found that the tenant's allegations were sufficient to resist a request by the landlord for an automatic judgment in his favor.

The decision is significant because once a summary judgment is denied, evidence may be presented at trial, and the case may be decided on a factual issue that could provide relief from the literal language of the lease.

When tenants miss a notice and stand to lose a valuable renewal option, they may find a sympathetic judge or jury who will side with their version of the case. Therefore, if tenants can get past a summary judgment, they have a chance.

The time-of-essence rule on tenant renewal notices in Pennsylvania has been a difficult rule for tenants to overcome. See *Western Savs. Fund Soc'y v. SEPTA*, 427 A.2d 175 (Pa. Super. 1981). Some other states have been more flexible. In New Jersey, courts will consider whether the tenant's tardiness was an inadvertent mistake and whether the landlord was injured by the tenant's failure to give timely notice. While that is not the law in Pennsylvania, the case of *Bantam Four Cinemas* will ease the burden of Pennsylvania tenants who fail to toe the mark in giving notice. See also *Aickin v. Ocean View Investments, Inc.*, 935 P.2d 992 (Haw. 1997) (four-month delay forgiven); and *Investment Builders of Florida, Inc. v. S.U.S. Food Mkt. Investments, Inc.*, 753 So.2d 759 (Fla. Dist. Ct. App. 4th Dist. 2000) (eight-day delay forgiven).

A Tennessee case indicates how some courts will give no sympathy to tenants who are perceived as giving late notice. It also illustrates the importance of preciseness in setting forth when a lease must be renewed. In *Norton v. McCaskill*, 12 S.W.3d 789 (Tenn. 2000), the Tennessee Supreme Court held that the tenant lost its option to renew a lease because its notice was sent too late. In that case, the tenant entered into a 10-year lease and had an option to renew that stated: "City Sign Company reserves an option to renew this lease at the end of ten years for a like period."

When the lease terminated, the owner notified the tenant that the lease had expired and leased the property to another party. Ten days later the tenant attempted to exercise the option by notice and delivery of a check for the next month's rent.

The tenant argued that the phrase "at the end of ten years" does not mean before the end of the 10 years. Instead, a "reasonable time" should be implied. On the other hand, the owner asserted that the language of the option required an exercise before the end of the term.

The court ruled that the quoted language requires the option to be exercised before the term ends. To make matters worse for the tenant, the court refused to give any equitable relief for the late notice based on the tenant's argument that it had made a mistake because of the unclear language, and that the late notice was not the tenant's fault. A reading of the decision indicates that the tenant may have fared better if the owner had not already entered into another lease before the tenant gave its notice of renewal.

Negotiate a Deadline "Safety Valve"

One way for a tenant to avoid missing renewal deadlines is to establish a tickler system with a backup mechanism to highlight the deadline so that the tenant is not dependent on mere memory. This is relatively easy to do on a computer.

In addition, the tenant could employ a more sophisticated approach in its negotiation of a lease. For example, if the tenant has a five-year option that must be exercised six months before the end of the lease term, the tenant should try to reverse the burden of sending notice and shift it to the landlord. The tenant could add a clause to the lease that says that if it fails to exercise the option by the deadline, its right to the option is extended for a specified period, and the exercise period begins only after the landlord has notified the tenant that the option deadline has passed—see the suggested clause at the end of this chapter.

Landlords may be concerned that postponing the exercise of a renewal option may not give them enough time to find another tenant, if the tenant doesn't renew. However, the provision could include an automatic extension of the lease term equal to the extended exercise period, or for some other designated period.

While some landlords will resist any renewal "safety valve," they should be reminded that a missed deadline could cost the tenant its whole business, but if the landlord misses the date for the reminder notice, it would merely postpone the date on which it finds out whether the tenant wishes to renew. That postponement will rarely have significant consequences to the landlord because occupancy and rent continue during the extended period.

Also, it is noteworthy that in *Utah Coal & Lumber* the lease provided for a window of two months in which the tenant had to exercise the option. It's easy to understand why a landlord would want a tenant to give it enough notice of its decision to renew or terminate the term. But why is it important to bar the tenant's exercise before a designated date?

A tenant may have made a decision to renew years before the deadline. Why shouldn't it be able to act on that decision while it is fresh in mind? That right would also reduce the tenant's odds of missing the deadline.

Other Hazards

In one case, a Chicago bank tenant had a valuable option to lease additional space throughout a large office building. The option called for advance notification of upcoming vacancies and allowed the tenant 30 days to exercise the option. When the owner notified the tenant about available additional space, the tenant exercised the option for the space "subject to inspection." The owner then refused to honor this qualified exercise of the option and rented the space to a new tenant.

The court supported the landlord and found that the acceptance "subject to inspection" was an acceptance to take the space *only if* the inspection proved satisfactory. Since the lease option did not include an inspection right, the court held the exercised option invalid.

In another case, a tenant claimed it gave timely lease renewal notice by telling the owner of the renewal and also by depositing a notice in the owner's mailbox. The owner claimed he never received the renewal letter, and under the lease, notices had to be sent by registered or certified mail. A New York court held that the notice was ineffective since oral notice was inadequate and the tenant could not prove the owner received the delivered notice. See *Court Decisions,* "Exercise of Renewal Option Must Be In Strict Compliance with Lease: *LaMana v. King Tut Restaurant, Inc.,*" N.Y.L.J. (Sept. 26, 1990), at 21.

Generally, there is no reason why tenants should take the chance of having a court hold that they have not complied with specific notice requirements. If a notice must be sent by registered mail, they should spend the few extra cents it costs to do it.

Although a renewal provision seems like a technical detail that hardly requires attention among the myriad of issues that arise under a lease, it must not be ignored. If the number of cases on defective notices is any indication, it appears tenants are not paying enough attention to these important provisions.

Tenant's Renewal Clause
With "Reminder" Notice

The tenant shall have the right and option to extend the term of this lease for two (2) successive five-year terms after the expiration of the original term. Each renewal extension shall be under the same terms, conditions, and covenants as set forth in this lease for the original term. If the tenant elects to exercise any of the renewal options, the tenant shall as to each such renewal, give written notice to that effect to the landlord at least six (6) months before the expiration of the then current term. However, if tenant shall fail to give such notice in the time period specified above, such rights to renew shall automatically be extended for a period of 30 days commencing from the date tenant receives written notice from landlord that such option will expire unless exercised.

What is wrong with this language?

"TERM. The Term of this Agreement shall begin on 2nd day of January, 1988 and shall run continuously for 1 (one) year and shall have 1 (one) full ten years option to lease again."

Don't worry about the poor sentence structure or the grammar. Those defects jump out at you. Instead, think about what business concepts are missing.

That clause became the focus of litigation in *Troutman Oil Co. v. Lone,* 57 S.W.3d 240 (Ark. Ct. App. 2001), that involved the lease of a service station. In that case, the landlord (Troutman Oil) tried to deny the renewal option because it did not provide for the amount of rent to be paid during the 10-year option period. It argued that the contract was "void for vagueness" and could not be renewed "on uncertain terms." In addition, the landlord challenged the fact that the tenant (Lone) had never specifically notified the landlord that he had exercised the option to renew.

No Ambiguity

The Arkansas Court of Appeals ruled against the landlord on both counts. However, two judges dissented because they took the position that the quoted lease clause neglected to specify the renewal rent.

While the majority held that the language meant that the rent for the 10-year option should be the same $500 a month specified for the first year, the whole dispute could have been avoided with very little effort on the part of the drafters. Since the tenant had subleased the service station for $1,500, an apparent profit of $1,000 a month, the decision helped Mr. Lone preserve a profitable lease.

The court held that while it will not supply missing terms in a lease, in this case it did not have to do so because the lease was not ambiguous. Also, since the option language did not require a specific notice of intent to renew, the holding over of the tenant after the one-year period, coupled with the acceptance of rent by the landlord, was enough to constitute a renewal of the lease for 10 years.

Dissent

On the other hand, on the issue of whether the rental was ambiguous, the dissenting judges read the language differently. They stated:

> To construe the lease renewal clause as a general covenant to renew would contradict the contract's express terms. The second paragraph of the contract provides that the monthly rent shall be $500 per month "for the term of the lease." The third paragraph states that "the term of this agreement shall begin on the 2nd day [of January], 1998, and shall run continuously for 1 (ONE) year and shall have one full ten years option to lease again." The term of the agreement provides only for a one-year term; thereafter, there is an option for an additional term.

> ... To read the renewal clause as integrating the $500 rental rate for the ten-year renewal period would contradict the express provision that the $500 rental rate applied to the expressed one-year term of the lease. These different clauses are harmonized by recognizing that the contract explicitly provides the rental rate for the one-year lease and explicitly remains silent as to the rent for the renewal period. Otherwise, construing the clauses would contradict the contract's express terms.

Id. at 247 [citation omitted].

In essence, the dissent concluded that the lease failed to set rent for the renewal period and, therefore, the contract was void for indefiniteness. This reasoning is in line with other cited cases in which options were not recognized for similar reasons.

In one case, the option was deemed defective because it provided that the renewal terms were to be "compatible to similar facilities" and the other because the option was to contain terms and conditions "to be negotiable, but not to exceed the annual cost-of-living index." These cases support the proposition that courts will not supply missing terms in a lease when the parties have not stated in the agreement a definite basis to guide the court's efforts to effectuate the parties' agreement.

All of this illustrates how easy it is for parties to create unnecessary litigation when drafting option terms. With a little thought it would have been simple for the drafting parties in this case to add a few words to clarify their intention. It also shows how easy it is for one judge to be clear on language that another reads as ambiguous.

28   WHO IS BEING REASONABLE?

If a lease prohibits assignment or subleasing without the landlord's approval, the courts in some states will require the landlord to act reasonably in granting this approval whether or not the lease sets forth that obligation.

In one California case, for example, it was determined that the landlord could not object to a sublease of a gasoline station unless the landlord had a good-faith, reasonable objection to the new tenant. *Prestin v. Mobil Oil Corp.*, 741 F.2d 268 (9th Cir. 1984); but see *Kendall v. Ernest Pestana, Inc.*, 709 P.2d 837 (Cal. 1985). The court held that an implied covenant of good faith and fair dealing militates against the arbitrary and unreasonable withholding of consent to an assignment.

While courts vary on this issue most states do not impose this obligation on the landlord. Therefore, it is up to the tenant to request in the lease that the landlord's consent not be unreasonably withheld. See *Consent to Assignment Subleasing: Must the Landlord be Reasonable?* 7 COMM'L LEAS. LAW & STRAT. 4 (September 1994).

Magic Clause

The magic clause is: "Whenever landlord's consent or approval is required herein, it shall not be unreasonably withheld or delayed." It can transform the whole lease.

By adding this innocent-sounding phrase to the landlord's well-structured, otherwise one-sided lease form, a lessee may saddle the owner of an office building with a competing tenant or an impecunious corporation, and an owner that is a religious institution may be stuck with dreaded abortion advocates.

Several court decisions have looked favorably at the tenant's position on these issues. In one case involving a five-and-dime store, the lease provided that the landlord's consent to subleasing was not to be "unreasonably withheld." The landlord objected to the subtenant on the grounds that such subtenant's business would compete with the landlord, and the court held that an objection for that reason is not "unreasonable."

In another case, a landlord refused to consent to a sublet on the grounds that the proposed subtenant was a tenant in another office building owned by the landlord. The court held that the potential loss of a tenant in another building is not sufficient reason to withhold consent. Presumably, if the prospect were in the same building, this would have made a difference to the court.

A third case, involving the Yeshiva University Foundation in New York, objected to a proposed assignment to the Planned Parenthood Federation of America. The university objected on the grounds that the assignee's support of birth control conflicted with basic religious principles of the university. The court held this was not a "reasonable" objection to a right to assign a lease.

A landlord's vulnerability is illustrated by a case where an anchor tenant in a suburban tenant wanted to assign its lease to a thrift store, Value Village, which sold second-hand clothing, *Ernst Home Center v. Sato*, 910 P.2d 486 (Wash. Ct. App. 1996). The lease provided that the landlord's consent must be obtained but would not be "unreasonably withheld."

The objecting landlord proved that other shopping mall owners would not lease to Value Village because of its effect on customer traffic, percentage rents, and lease rates. Despite that, the court ruled that it was unreasonable for the landlord to refuse the consent to the assignment.

The *Ernst* court emphasized how important it would have been for the landlord to provide objective evidence to support its position. For example, it would have helped to have appraisals that showed an adverse effect on the value of the center if the assignment were allowed, and to produce evidence from lenders showing that the assignment would have adversely affected the ability to finance the center. See *Newman v. Hinky Dinky Omaha-Lincoln*, 512 N.W.2d 410 (Neb. Ct. App. 1994).

For a thoughtful analysis of some of these assignment cases, see Brent C. Shaffer, *Counseling the Client on the Reasonable Consent Standard to Assignments,* THE PRACTICAL REAL ESTATE LAWYER, 7–14 (July 2003, ALI-ABA).

Rub-A-Dub Car Wash

With appropriate evidence, landlords can win these cases. The case of *Wright v. Rub-A-Dub Car Wash, Inc.*, 740 So.2d 891 (Miss. 1999), held that it was reasonable for the landlord to withhold his consent to the assignment of a lease by a car-wash business.

The landlord had concerns about leaking from underground gasoline tanks that had been installed by a previous tenant and used to dispense gasoline in connection with its car wash. The landlord would not agree to the assignment unless Rub-A-Dub or the prospective buyers assumed liability for the condition of the tanks and satisfied the state and federal EPA about the tanks, including removing them if required. Neither party was willing to agree to those conditions and the sale was never completed. As a result, after suit Rub-A-Dub was awarded $50,000 in damages from the landlord.

After much discussion about who owned the tanks and the earlier history of assignments of the lease, the Supreme Court of Mississippi reversed the lower court and held that the case should be remanded to determine who owned the tanks. If it is shown that the tenant owned the tanks, it would be reasonable for the landlord to impose that responsibility on the tenants as a condition of the requested approval.

The court stated:

> ... The owner of the property can not be required to stand idly by and suffer the continuation of, and possible aggravation of, a condition that damages his property when that condition is brought on by the activities of the lessee. That is a classic example of a lessee committing waste, for which the law provides the owner a remedy.

Wright v. Rub-A-Dub Car Wash, Inc., No. 97-CA-00113 COA (Miss. Ct. App. September 15, 1998) (unpublished).

Several dissenting judges vigorously argued that the landlord's conditions to consent were "unreasonable." Essentially they maintained that a landlord should not be allowed to use a request for consent to an assignment as an opportunity to rewrite the lease and reallocate his or her responsibilities. They cited other cases that held that landlords had no commercially reasonable basis to refuse consent where there would be no change in the financial risks and the landlord was merely using this as an opportunity to increase profit or obtain an increase in economic benefit.

The name of the tenant, "Rub-A-Dub Car Wash," seems to be borrowed from the children's nursery rhyme, "Rub-a-Dub-Dub, Three Men in a Tub." With a name like that, it may be said that the plaintiff was starting off with a slight psychological handicap when it was trying to persuade a court about who was acting reasonably. After all, who can take seriously a plaintiff that conjures up a vision of three grown men scrunched into a small tub as they float out to sea.

Right to Be Arbitrary

A landlord may also have difficulty denying other tenant demands, such as permission to alter the property or to change its use. Moreover, if a landlord rejects a "reasonable" request, such as one for approval of a proposed subtenant, the tenant may claim the landlord breached the lease and may abandon the property. And if a future jury disagrees with the landlord's judgment in this rejection, the landlord may find itself with no tenant, no subtenant, and no right to collect rent for the vacated property. See *Associates Commercial Corp. v. Bayou Mgmt. Inc.*, 426 So.2d 672 (La. Ct. App. 1982); *Ringwood Assoc. Ltd. v. Jack's of Route 23, Inc.*, 379 A.2d 508 (N.J. Super. Ct. Law Div. 1977); and *Halper v. Demeter*, 610 N.E.2d 332 (Mass. App. Ct. 1993).

One compromise solution to assignment or sublease requests is to define in the lease those grounds for rejection that are considered reasonable. For example, as starters, the landlord will want to make it clear that both the old and new tenants are fully liable on the lease. Also, the landlord may want to set standards for the amount of space, the location, the rent, and the term of any proposed sublease. Generally, it will want to limit the use of the space to defined operations, the type of alterations, and possibly, the character and financial status of the new tenant.

It may also want to prohibit subleasing or assignment while the landlord is attempting to lease comparable vacant space in the building. Some landlords even seek the right to terminate the lease that is offered for assignment or sublease, so they can retake the offered space.

These solutions may require negotiations, and undoubtedly do not give the landlord complete or arbitrary control. In an egalitarian society where we pride ourselves on conducting our affairs with rationality, it is never easy to advocate the right to be arbitrary. However, when the landlord is negotiating its rights to have input about proposed new occupants in its building, it may not be unreasonable to demand the right to be unreasonable.

Damages

A recent case shows how agreeing to be reasonable can expose the landlord to substantial damages. In *Parr v. Triple L&J Corp.*, 107 P.3d 1104 (Colo. App. 2004), the Colorado Court of Appeals held that a landlord breached a lease by unreasonably withholding consent to an assignment, thereby subjecting it to liability for intentional interference with a prospective business advantage. In that case, the landlord had agreed not to unreasonably withhold consent to an assignment. When the tenants attempted to sell their restaurant business and assign the lease, they provided detailed information about the prospective buyer, as requested by the landlord, but the landlord asked for more information. After receiving that information, the landlord deferred making a decision and the prospective sale was delayed so long that the buyer withdrew his offer.

As a result of that, the tenant was awarded $20,000 for the landlord's breach of contract, and an additional $1,500 for "emotional distress" plus $5,000 for "exemplary damages." The court held that damages for emotional distress can be based on either physical or mental illness, such as chronic nausea, headaches, or hysterical attacks. It also held that the record supported a finding that the landlord had acted "in a malicious manner" toward one of the tenants because of a prior lawsuit between the parties.

The court rejected the landlord's defense that it never refused consent, but merely delayed giving an answer to the tenant. The court noted that the lease language stated that consent was not to be unreasonably "withheld."

This type of case makes it even more risky for landlords to accept the vague concept of being "reasonable." If a landlord must agree to that in order to make a deal, in addition to setting forth specific standards, the landlord should attempt to spell out that the tenant's remedy should be limited to specific performance, or at most, actual out-of-pocket expenses incurred by the tenant as a result of any default.

29 LANDLORD UNREASONABLY WITHHOLDS CONSENT TO BELOW–MARKET-RATE SUBLEASE

A Massachusetts case highlights how important it is to define standards for a landlord to approve assignments or subleasing by a tenant. In *National Union Fire Insurance Co. v. Rose,* 760 N.E.2d 791 (Mass. App. Ct. 2002), a tenant with an 11-year lease of office space in downtown Boston requested the landlord's consent to a sublease, and the landlord refused on grounds that the sublease rent was inadequate. The lease provided that the landlord's consent could not be "unreasonably withheld." It also gave the landlord 75 percent of any subleasing profits made by the tenant. Essentially, that percentage was to be based on the amount of rent received from a sublease to the extent it exceeded the amount paid by the tenant under the prime lease. That sum was to be calculated after allowing for certain defined costs associated with facilitating the subtenancy.

The tenant in this case had decided to sublease to one of its major customers at the same square foot rental rate as in the prime lease, but in the period since that lease had been signed, market rates had increased. Therefore, the landlord withheld its consent on the theory that the tenant had an obligation to sublease only at market rents, and if it did not do so, it would be denying the landlord its share of excess rent as set forth in the prime lease.

Appeals Court

The Massachusetts appeals court found that the landlord had improperly withheld its consent and that the rental-sharing provision in the lease did not obligate the tenant to sublease at market rates. It agreed with the lower court's conclusion that

175

"profit sharing is operative only *'if'* sublease rent exceeds tenants' rent, which it does not." *Id.* at 793.

Obviously, the landlord could have protected itself in the prime lease by specifically stating that it did not have to consent to a sublease at less than market rental. Because it did not do so, the court refused to imply such a provision.

Some landlords insist on setting the sublease rent at the contract rental, as it may increase by a Consumer Price Index (CPI) formula. They may spell out terms stating that if the tenant should sublease at less than a fair market rate, it would still have to share the profit with the landlord in the same way as if it had received a fair market rate. In effect, the tenant would have to share an "imputed profit" during the sublease. Of course, if the lease had provided for that, since the landlord would not be losing profit from the less-than-market rent, the landlord would have even less of a reason to justify turning down the sublease.

Sweetheart Rent

Unless these types of provisions are buttoned down, it would be easy to imagine a scenario where the tenant could take advantage of the landlord. For example, in *National Union Fire Insurance Co.,* the tenant was subleasing to a major customer at below-market rates. It would be difficult for the landlord to figure out whether the customer made up for the "sweetheart rent" by benefiting the tenant in some other subtle way.

Under different circumstances, landlords might object to subleasing space at less than the market rent because they are concerned about vacancies in other parts of the building, and the competition with its own tenant for leasing prospects. The landlord could then lose a potential tenant to the subtenant because of a lower rent than the landlord itself had been offering, and in addition, that lower rent could affect the ability of the landlord to receive the prevailing rental rate in other space that becomes vacant. Also, some landlords will reserve the right to withhold consent to subleasing at any rent when they are attempting to rent other space either in the same building or a nearby building. These are some of the reasons why landlords will want to spell out that they will not have to consent to subleasing or assignment under such conditions.

30 TENANTS MUST PROTECT THEMSELVES AGAINST LANDLORDS' MORTGAGES

When doing a commercial lease, tenants will negotiate the rent, their construction allowances, the term of the lease, options to renew, and many other visible issues. Unfortunately, they frequently miss one issue that can prove to be their downfall. They fail to protect themselves against the possibility that their lease could be wiped out when the landlord defaults on its mortgage. That mortgage can either be an existing or a future mortgage, but if the landlord fails to make payments and the lender forecloses, the lender may be able to terminate the lease, even if the tenant is making all of its payments and doing everything else it is required to do under that lease.

Paying Double Rent

These issues are highlighted in a leading New York appellate case in which the tenant occupied a property under a 10-year lease made in 1983. Four years later, the landlord mortgaged the property to the Dime Savings Bank and the mortgage prohibited the landlord from collecting any advance rent from the tenants. That provision is normally included in a mortgage in order to prevent a landlord from pocketing a large rent prepayment right before the mortgage goes into default.

The Dime Savings mortgage was then recorded and therefore had priority over future leases, and even existing leases that contained provisions that are commonly called "subordination clauses." In 1992 the tenant and the landlord signed an amendment to the original lease that required the tenant to prepay $160,000 in rent.

After that the landlord defaulted on the mortgage and when a receiver was appointed for the property, he demanded that rent be continued during the receivership even for the months that had been prepaid. The tenant argued that it was not bound by the mortgage prepayment ban because the 1992 amendment merely extended the original 1983 lease and, therefore, the lease had priority to the 1987 mortgage.

The New York Court of Appeals ruled against the tenant, and held that the 1992 amendment must be considered a new lease between the parties, which was entered years after the Dime Savings mortgage. *Dime Sav. Bank FSB v. Montague St. Realty Assocs.*, 686 N.E.2d 1340 (N.Y. 1997). The court said that the tenant was "deemed" to be on notice against prepaying the rent after the Dime Savings mortgage was recorded in 1987. Consequently, the prepayment of rent violated the mortgage prohibition and the tenant must again pay for the same months that it had already prepaid to the landlord.

Subordination Clause

In addition the court suggested that even if it assumed, as the tenant argued, that the 1992 lease amendment did not create a new lease, the tenant would still be required to pay the rent again because the original lease had provided that it was subordinate to all mortgages that might later encumber the property.

This decision delivers several important messages to tenants in New York and in many other states. First, tenants should not passively agree to subordinate their leases to future mortgages. That type of subordination provision is included routinely in standard form leases used by landlords.

A subordination provision means that when mortgages are placed on the property by the landlord that contain prohibitions that conflict with the tenants' obligations under a lease, the tenant may face the choice of violating either the mortgage or the lease at some future date. The tenant can protect itself by providing in the lease that if there is a conflict, the lease will take priority to the mortgage unless the lender agrees to a so-called "nondisturbance" provision that requires the lender to accept the lease as long as the tenant is not in default. Second, if the lease enjoys priority to an existing mortgage, no amendments should be made without the consent of the lender. The tenant will then avoid a risk that the amendment will be deemed so material that it amounts to a new lease.

Malpractice Concerns

It is also important that the tenant negotiate for a provision that requires the landlord's lender to enter a nondisturbance agreement in favor of any parties to whom the tenant may seek to assign an interest under its lease or sublet. In the alternative, the tenant should make sure that the nondisturbance agreement it enters with the lender will protect those other parties.

The importance of these agreements is highlighted by malpractice suits that have been started by tenants against the lawyers who represented them in connection with their leases. Although the lawyers won in two of those cases, each of the cases illustrates the frustration of tenants who don't have the protection of nondisturbance agreements. In *Wittich v. Wallach*, 607 N.Y.S.2d 725 (N.Y. App. Div. 1994), tenants sued their lawyers for negligence in negotiation of a real estate lease, claiming that their lawyers' failure to include a nondisturbance provision in their lease effectively prevented them from subletting their space.

The New York appellate court held that the attorneys could not have the case dismissed on summary judgment proceedings, and gave the tenants the opportunity of proving that the attorney's alleged negligence was the proximate cause of the loss incurred by the tenants. The trial court then had to determine whether the landlord, and presumably the lender, would have agreed to that provision if the lawyers had properly represented them.

In *Hazel & Thomas, P.C. v. Yavari*, 465 S.E.2d 812 (Va. 1996), the Supreme Court of Virginia reversed a jury's finding that the tenants' lawyers committed malpractice by failing to include a nondisturbance provision in the lease, thereby preventing the tenant from entering into certain sublease agreements. Although the jury had concluded that the lawyers were negligent, the Virginia Supreme Court disagreed. It held that the tenant must prove that the landlord would have agreed to include the nondisturbance provision in the lease if the attorneys had raised that issue in the negotiations; or, in the alternative, that the tenant would not have signed the lease if the landlord had refused to include that provision.

While these cases indicate that tenants may have a difficult burden to carry in suing their attorneys, the mere fact that these cases were brought emphasizes the importance of seeking appropriate nondisturbance provisions in a lease.

31   DUTIES TO MITIGATE VARY STATE BY STATE

Different courts disagree about the extent of landlords' duties to mitigate damages (i.e., attempt to re-rent) after commercial tenants have breached their leases. A review of appellate decisions from New York, Pennsylvania, Texas, and Iowa highlight the differences.

New York Law

In *Holy Properties, Ltd., L.P. v. Kenneth Cole Productions, Inc.*, 661 N.E.2d 694 (N.Y. 1995), a tenant vacated space in a commercial office building, stopped paying rent, and was sued for back rent and damages. The tenant defended by arguing that the landlord had failed to mitigate damages when it did not offer the property to prospective replacement tenants. The lease expressly provided that the landlord was under no duty to mitigate and that if the tenant abandoned the property or was evicted, it would remain liable for rent. The New York Court of Appeals reaffirmed the settled law in New York that under these circumstances a landlord has no duty to mitigate damages and had the right "to do nothing and collect the full rent due under the lease."

Pennsylvania Law

Similarly, the Pennsylvania Superior Court has held that when a tenant vacated a video rental store in a shopping center, the landlord had no duty to mitigate damages and could recover all of the unpaid rent to the end of the lease term. *Stonehedge Square Ltd. Partnership v. Movie Merchants, Inc.*, 685 A.2d 1019 (Pa. Super. 1996), aff'd, 715 A.2d 1082 (Pa. 1998). The court pointed out that nothing in the lease called for the landlord to mitigate damages, and it was not persuaded by the tenant's arguments

180

that the landlord had taken possession of the space and used it for temporary storage after the tenant had abandoned it.

The two cases have obvious similarities. First, each decision recognizes that a general contract rule that requires mitigation does not apply to these types of lease defaults. Second, each specifically discusses and rejects earlier decisions that had imposed a duty to mitigate even in commercial leasing. Third, each court values the "stability" of maintaining this settled rule.

Holy Properties states, "Parties who engage in transactions based on prevailing law must be able to rely on the stability of such precedents." Also: "In business transactions, particularly, the certainty of settled rules is often more important than whether the established rule is better than another or even whether it is the 'correct' rule.... This is perhaps true in real property more than any other area of the law, where established precedents are not lightly to be set aside." In *Stonehedge*, the court quoted Judge Learned Hand, who once wrote that it is not "desirable for a lower court to embrace the exhilarating opportunity of anticipating a doctrine which may be in the womb of time but whose birth is distant."

Texas Law

In Texas, the state Supreme Court held that under certain circumstances a landlord does have a duty to mitigate. In that case, the landlord claimed that the tenant had breached a lease or an office by giving the landlord conflicting directives about completing the leasehold improvements. The landlord then sued the tenant for an anticipatory breach of the lease and the tenant argued that the landlord's damage award should be reduced by the amount that the landlord could have saved if it had exercised reasonable care in reletting the property. *Austin Hill Country Realty, Inc. v. Palisades Plaza, Inc.*, 948 S.W.2d 293 (Tex. 1997). In that case the Supreme Court of Texas made it clear that Texas law requires a landlord to mitigate damages under two circumstances: (1) when the landlord seeks a remedy that is contractual in nature, such as any anticipatory breach of a contract, and (2) when the landlord re-enters or takes control of the property. However, the decision seems limited to those two situations and would not apply to a case where the landlord intends merely to sue for rent (as contrasted with suing for damages) because of an "anticipatory breach." Also, the decision did not discuss whether the lease by its terms provided that the landlord does not have a duty to mitigate if the tenant defaults. If the court had been dealing with that kind of clause, which is common in many form leases, the court may have favored the landlord. Obviously, the landlord's duty to mitigate has been a troublesome issue and courts throughout the country have varied in their approach to it.

Pandora's Box

It then explained: "This is especially true for an issue as complex as the duty to mitigate damages in the commercial lease setting, which raises a myriad of troublesome questions: e.g., what constitutes 'reasonable efforts' to mitigate by the landlord; what happens when the demised premises are on the fifth floor but a new prospective tenant desires space on the twentieth floor; what responsibility does the landlord have in granting 'concessions' to a prospective tenant in order to mitigate the breaching tenant's damages? See Harris Ominsky, "Leasing: Landlord Must Mitigate Damages," 59 *Philadelphia Lawyer* 72 (Fall 1996).

The *Stonehedge* case adopted this writer's analysis, which raises many issues that "must be answered once courts impose this duty to mitigate." The cited article predicted a "Pandora's box of potential defenses" when the landlord tries to recover damages from the defaulting commercial tenant.

That includes issues about whether a landlord would have a right to hold out for a term of at least three or five years, or for a certain minimum rent. Also, how will a landlord know how much money to spend to promote and advertise a large block of office or retail space after the tenant vacates? Will the defaulting tenants be able to argue that competing landlords are receiving most of the prospects because they have better marketing programs? Does the landlord have to accept the tenants who have less-desirable credit ratings or business uses than the defaulting tenant? In addition, which party should bear the burden of proving that there was no reasonable attempt to mitigate?

States Split

It is obvious that the landlord's duty to mitigate has been a troublesome issue, and courts throughout the country have varied in their approach to it. See Milton R. Friedman, 2 *Friedman on Leases* 979 *et seq.* (3rd ed. 1990). In another example, the Iowa Supreme Court confirmed that landlords must use reasonable diligence to relet an abandoned property. However, it gave landlords a break by permitting claims for accelerated rent without offset when they do not succeed in their attempts to relet. *Aurora Business Park Assocs., L.P. v. Michael Albert, Inc.*, 548 N.W.2d 153 (Iowa 1996).

One survey charted the law in all states (including the District of Columbia) on the duty to mitigate when a tenant abandons the property. The score was 21 "Yes," 16 "No," and 14 "Uncertain" (Elizabeth H. Belkin, "Landlord's Duty to Mitigate Damages When Tenant Abandons Premises," 8 COMM'L LEAS. LAW & STRAT. 1, 6–7 (August 1995)).

The survey made no distinction between residential and commercial leases. While similar factors should apply, the courts in some states may favor mitigation only with residential tenants.

The *Austin Hill Country Realty* case analyzed the law in the other states and concluded that 42 states and the District of Columbia have recognized that a landlord "has a duty to mitigate damages in at least some situations when there is a breach of a residential lease, a commercial lease, or both." According to the court, only six states have explicitly held that a landlord has no duty to mitigate in any situation. The analysis for all these states is listed in footnotes 1 and 2 of the Supreme Court's opinion.

The count is different in the two surveys, and that only goes to emphasize the difficulty of trying to summarize the law on such a complex issue. Some states rely on statutes, some of which are unclear; others rely on the common law. Some of the decisions on mitigation depend on the nature of the breach, how the landlord reacted to that breach and what remedy is sought by the landlord. In addition, as discussed above, the decision may very well depend on what the lease provides about the landlord's duty to mitigate and whether the court is dealing with a residential or a commercial lease.

While the appellate cases discussed here help clarify the law in New York, Pennsylvania, Texas, and Iowa, we have not heard the end of disputes over these issues. As an example, the lease form in the New York and Pennsylvania cases did not specifically require the landlord to mitigate damages when the tenant defaulted. That is true of most leases. However, if the lease had specifically required the landlord to mitigate or take action to re-rent under certain circumstances, the tenants may have fared better.

Significantly, neither *Holy Properties* nor *Stonehedge Properties* involved landlords who clearly accepted the tenant's surrender and took over the property for their own account. If a court should decide that a landlord has done that or has otherwise terminated the lease, it might then apply the traditional contract rule requiring an injured party to mitigate its damages. Also, if the lease doesn't provide for continuing liability after termination, a court might release the tenant entirely. See Milton R. Friedman, 2 *Friedman On Leases* § 16.3 (3rd Ed. 1990); and *Restatement (Second) of Property (Landlord and Tenant)* § 12.1, comments g and i (1977).

As illustrated in this article, the law on landlords' duties to mitigate damages is still evolving throughout the United States. It is important for attorneys who must deal with these issues to understand the latest cases in their jurisdiction and the subtle issues that could affect these decisions. Lawyers would be well advised not to try to rely on surveys or charts that characterize the law of mitigation with "Yes," "No," or "Uncertain."

32 SHOPPING CENTERS: CALCULATING DAMAGES WHEN ANCHOR TENANT BREACHES

When an anchor tenant breaches its obligations to continually operate its store, can the landlord recover, not only for lost rent, but also for the loss of value to the shopping center?

First Impression

This issue could arise when an anchor tenant fails to open its doors for business, as required, or withdraws after opening. It will surprise some readers that the law is not well settled.

In the case of *BVT Lebanon Shopping Center, Ltd. v. Wal-Mart Stores, Inc.*, 48 S.W.3d 132 (Tenn. 2001), the Tennessee Supreme Court identified this as an issue of "first impression" in Tennessee. It held that diminution of value of the center is an appropriate measure of damages under circumstances where the Wal-Mart anchor store abandoned occupancy of a shopping center and breached its implied covenant of continuous operation under its lease. In that case, the court held that Wal-Mart replaced its occupancy with a Bud's Discount City Store, which did not qualify as a "permitted use" under the lease.

Wal-Mart had agreed to a percentage rent clause based on gross receipts and Bud's never generated sufficient gross receipts to permit the owner to collect any percentage rent. While the court did not analyze its finding of an implied covenant of continuous operation, many states and a number of commentators do not support that concept.

Diminution of Value

The trial court awarded the owner approximately $2.5 million in damages on the theory that the landlord could recover only the present value of lost future percentage rent and not for diminution in the fair value of the shopping center. On appeal to the intermediate appellate court, the landlord was awarded approximately $4.7 million by the Court of Appeals of Tennessee. The Tennessee Supreme Court agreed with the court of appeals, but remanded the case to the trial court to resolve certain conflicting evidence on the issue of diminution in value. The supreme court found that the trial court overlooked the testimony of Wal-Mart's expert, who estimated that the diminution in fair market amounted only to $55,000.

In reaching its conclusion, the supreme court held that its decision is in line with other Tennessee law about the general remedy for breach of contract. That court stated:

> The purpose of assessing damages in breach of contract cases is to place the plaintiff as nearly as possible in the same position she would have been in had the contract been performed, but the non-breaching party is not to be put in any better position by recovery of damages for the breach of the contract than he would have been if the contract had been fully performed.

The court explained that an award that is based solely on the value of lost future rents fails to consider other economic losses when an anchor tenant abandons occupancy. A loss of an anchor store affects not only the rental income, but also the stability of the center, attraction of customers and other tenants, and long-term financing. The court cited cases in Nevada and North Carolina to support the proposition that calculating damages based on the diminution in value would include all of these factors and, therefore, promote the objective of placing the parties in as good a position as they would have been if the contract had not been breached.

Wal-Mart had argued that factors other than loss of an anchor tenant may contribute toward loss in value, such as economic downturn, population shift, population decrease, or a store similar to the anchor store opening nearby. The court agreed that the parties should be allowed to present evidence in these types of cases regarding all of these factors. Judge Barker in a concurring opinion agreed with the majority that the plaintiffs in these cases should meet a heightened standard of proof to succeed in a claim of diminution-in-value damages, but wanted to make it clear that he thought that that degree of heightened proof should not have to apply to evidence of loss of future rent.

One of the dangers of the *BVT Lebanon Shopping Center* opinion is that when a tenant defaults, a jury may buy into a theory that the value of the center has been diminished even when that conclusion is somewhat speculative. When an anchor tenant is lost, unlike loss that occurs from a fire or condemnation, the loss of value may be only temporary. How can there be any certainty about whether the anchor tenant who replaces Wal-Mart will be worse for the shopping center, or when that replacement may occur?

Parties' Intent

In support of its decision, the court cited the Restatement (Second) of Contracts, Section 347 (1979), which permits recovery of damages based on the injured party's expectation as measured by stated standards, including whether the special damages were "within the contemplation of the parties at the time of the contract." This formulation should send a message to drafting parties of a shopping center lease. They should clarify whether their intent on default is to include specific damages for diminution-in-value.

If the landlords intend to include that measure of damages, it would be best to include specific recitals confirming the importance of their anchor tenants to the center's stability, and spell out that if the tenants don't continue to operate, they must pay for diminution in value of the center. On the other hand, if a Wal-Mart does not intend that kind of loss to be included in the calculation of damages, it would help to spell that out. Generally, tenants will resist any provision that requires them to continuously operate or to stay open. Obviously, if Wal-Mart had specified that it had a right to abandon occupancy, it would have solved the problem of having to defend against any damage claim when it closed shop.

33 LEASES: MUTUAL WAIVER OF CASUALTY CLAIMS MAY NOT PROTECT PARTIES

Many commercial leases provide for mutual waivers of subrogation in the event of a casualty loss. Essentially, both landlords and tenants agree to surrender certain rights their insurance companies might have to step into their shoes and sue each other for negligence or other misconduct. They accept these limitations on their right to sue because they believe they can rely on their own insurance policies to cover their property damages if there is a fire or other casualty.

In *The Gap Inc. v. Red Apple Cos.*, 725 N.Y.S.2d 312 (N.Y. App. Div. 2001), the lease waivers proved inadequate to protect the landlord against a suit by the tenants. In that case, Gap Inc. and Rite Aid Corporation leased first-floor space from the landlord and suffered a loss from a fire, which started in the space of another tenant. They alleged that the landlord negligently failed to provide adequate fire protection equipment—in particular, a sprinkler system.

The Landlord's Defense

The Gap and Rite Aid both suffered property as well as business interruption damages, and sued the landlord to recover damages that they didn't recover under their fire insurance policies. The landlord invoked the leases' waiver of subrogation clauses. It pointed out that the Gap's waiver of subrogation clause stated that each party waived all claims against the other party for any loss or damage caused by any risk insured against, or required to be carried, under the lease. Rite Aid's lease contained a slightly different clause, which stated that each party waives all rights of recovery against the other to the extent that fire or other casualty insurance is "in force and collectible."

Landlord's Downfall

The Supreme Court of New York rejected the landlord's defenses after concluding that neither clause prohibited the tenants from claiming those losses that they were unable to recover because of insurance deductibles or limited insurance coverage.

The leases did not require any party to maintain fire insurance, and that turned out to be the landlord's downfall. The court noted that a deductible is an "uninsured segment of loss [that] falls outside the ambit of 'risk insured against' for purposes of inclusion in the waiver of subrogation clause." Because there was no coverage or payment of an insured loss, there was no right to subrogation and the waiver clause did not apply.

Also, the court found that Rite Aid's claim for business interruption damages was not waived by a lease provision limiting the landlord's liability resulting from the landlord's failure to make repairs. Rite Aid based its damage claim on the negligence of the landlord, but not in connection with the "failure to make repairs." Therefore, the court concluded that Rite Aid's claims for business interruption damages should be allowed.

The court stated:

> ... While there are significant differences in the respective leases' waiver of subrogation clauses, neither clause includes within its embrace the uninsured loss that is encompassed by an insurance policy deductible. Accordingly, those claims should be reinstated. In addition, we disagree with the IAS court's dismissal of the claims for business interruption loss.

> In the waiver of subrogation clause in its lease, The Gap waived any claim against the owners for damage to its property "caused by any risk insured against." While The Gap did obtain insurance coverage for the specific risk in question, i.e., fire loss, it limited its coverage by its assumption of a $1 million deductible. As the courts have held, this uninsured segment of loss falls outside the ambit of "risk insured against" for purposes of inclusion in the waiver of subrogation clause. *(Federal Ins. Co. v. Honeywell, Inc.,* 243 A.D.2d 605; see *Kaf-Kaf, Inc. v. Rodless Dec-*

orations, 90 N.Y.2d 654.) Absent coverage and payment of an insured loss, there is no right to subrogation and, thus, the waiver clause has no application.

Rite Aid's lease is even clearer on the waiver of subrogation issue. It provides that "each party shall look first to any insurance in its favor before making any claim against the other party ... and to the extent that such insurance is in force and collectible and to the extent permitted by law, Landlord and Tenant each hereby releases and waives all right of recovery against the other or any one claiming through or under each of them by way of subrogation or otherwise." Clearly, Rite Aid's $10,000 deductible does not fall within the category of insurance that is "in force and collectible" and is therefore outside the ambit of the waiver of subrogation clause.

Under these waiver of subrogation clauses both tenants succeeded in their claims for losses that were not fully covered by their insurance policies. Gap had sued for recovery of its $1 million insurance deductible. Rite Aid had sued for its $10,000 insurance deductible, and also more than $500,000 in business interruption losses that were not covered by its policy.

Lessons

In summary, the court held that the respective waiver of subrogation clauses barred only "risks insured against" in the case of the Gap, and losses covered by insurance "in force" in the case of Rite Aid. In each case the landlord could have protected itself with proper drafting. According to the court, the landlord could have protected itself if it had used waiver of subrogation clauses that expressly included deductible amounts in the waivers. Also, it should have insisted on a commonly used provision that requires tenants to be fully insured.

In the same way as the subrogation clauses worked against the landlord in *Gap Inc.,* under other circumstances they could work against the tenants. Frequently, commercial leases contain mutual waivers of subrogation that are intended to protect both landlords and tenants, and the defects highlighted in this case could have easily exposed the tenants to liability. For example, since the rented space is often in the control of the tenants, when a fire occurs, the landlord occasionally charges the tenant with negligence and tries to recover its losses from the tenant.

The *Gap* case should serve as a drafting lesson for both landlords and tenants who are seeking to limit their exposure to liability.

34   NEGLIGENT TENANTS ARE RELIEVED FROM LIABILITY TO LANDLORDS' INSURANCE COMPANIES

When an insurance company pays a landlord for fire damage, can it then recover for that loss against a negligent tenant?

That question is easier to answer if a lease contains a waiver of subrogation clause. That is, the landlord waives any rights it (or its insurance company) may have to sue the tenant to the extent that the landlord has insurance coverage for the loss. Then, in most states, the insurance company can't recover.

But what happens if the lease is silent on that issue? If the landlord has arranged for the insurance policy to cover the tenant as a co-insured, that answer is also easy. In that case, the insurance company has no right to sue its own insured tenant, even though the tenant may have caused the fire.

Cases

In other instances, the answer to the question may depend on your state of residence, or even whether you are dealing with a residential or commercial use. If the lease is silent about subrogation, does an insurance company acquire a right of subrogation "by default"? Two 2002 cases have dealt with that issue. The Supreme Court of Connecticut decided that an insurance company does not have a right of subrogation, unless it is stated in the lease. *DiLullo v. Joseph,* 792 A.2d 819 (Conn. 2002). The Massachusetts Supreme Judicial Court followed that rule for residential tenancies but rejected it for commercial tenancies. *Seaco Ins. v. Barbosa,* 761 N.E.2d 946 (Mass. 2002). Apparently, in Massachusetts, insurance companies are subrogated to rights against commercial tenants even when the lease is silent on that issue.

In the *DiLullo* case, the Connecticut Supreme Court affirmed the trial court's decision to dismiss the plaintiff's claim on a motion for summary judgment by the tenant. The trial court had dismissed the claim based on a theory that a tenant is an "implied co-insured" under a landlord's insurance policy, and therefore the insurance company may not bring an action for subrogation against its own insured.

The Supreme Court reached the same conclusion but noted that it took a "different route." The court held that where parties do not make an agreement about subrogation rights, no right of subrogation exists because: "Our strong public policy against economic waste, and the likely lack of expectations regarding a tenant's obligation to subrogate his landlord's insurer, lead us to conclude that, as a default rule, no such right of subrogation exists." *DiLullo,* 792 A.2d at 821.

Further, the court stated that there was a split of authority on this question among other jurisdictions, and that the trial court had followed what is known as the "*Sutton* Rule." That is the majority rule, and is based on the concept that the tenant is presumed to be a co-insured party under the landlord's insurance policy even if not specifically named, because the tenant's rent presumably includes some calculation of the landlord's fire insurance premium.

The court pointed out that a minority of courts have declined to follow the *Sutton* Rule, and instead have adopted a case-by-case analysis based on the facts and the circumstances surrounding each particular case to determine what the parties might have intended. See, for example, *Remy v. Michael D's Carpet Outlets,* 571 A.2d 446 (Pa. Super. 1990).

Economic Waste

While the Connecticut Supreme Court disagreed with the *Sutton* rationale, it agreed with the result of that doctrine, holding that:

> Our decision is founded, in large part, upon the principle that subrogation, as an equitable doctrine, invokes matters of policy and fairness. ... One such policy implicated by the issue presently before us is that disfavoring economic waste. ... This strong public policy convinces us that it would be inappropriate to create a default rule that allocates to the tenant the responsibility of maintaining

sufficient insurance to cover a claim for subrogation by his landlord's insurer. Such a rule would create a strong incentive for every tenant to carry liability insurance in an amount necessary to compensate for the value, or perhaps even the replacement cost, of the entire building, irrespective of the portion of the building occupied by the tenant. That is precisely the same value or replacement cost insured by the landlord under his fire insurance policy. Thus, although the two forms of insurance would be different, the economic interest insured would be the same. This duplication of insurance would, in our view, constitute economic waste and, in a multiunit building, the waste would be compounded by the number of tenants. ... We think that our law would be better served by having the default rule of law embody this policy against economic waste, and by leaving it to the specific agreement of the parties if they wish a different rule to apply to their, or their insurers', relationship.

DiLullo, 792 A.2d at 822 [citations omitted].

Expectations

Another reason for the court's decision is that neither landlords nor tenants "ordinarily expect that the landlord's insurer would be proceeding against the tenant, unless expert counseling to that effect had forewarned them." *Id.* at 823. Therefore, barring subrogation in such a case would comport with the "equities of most situations."

The concept of an implied waiver of subrogation seems to make sense in light of the parties' expectations and the economics of insurance coverage. It seems that the insurer's risk is really not significantly increased by giving up a right of subrogation, and the evidence of that is that in most cases insurance policies permit parties to release or to waive subrogation rights without any change in premium.

Also, we should look to expectations of owners and tenants when it comes to fire coverage. It is a little dangerous to speculate here, but it would be safe to assume that most of them would not even know what the word "subrogation" means. In addition, most tenants probably assume that if the landlord has insurance, that insurance will cover fire loss, and will not precipitate suits against the tenant, even if the fire is caused by the tenant's negligence.

While the *DiLullo* case does not discuss this issue, some will have concerns that a negligent party will be let off the hook and will therefore not be accountable for its own negligence. If one looks at this from the perspective of a fire started either by the tenant's gross negligence, its failure to meet code requirements, or even possibly arson, it seems that the tenant may be getting off easy. That concern would also apply to a grossly negligent or willfully delinquent landlord when the implied waiver of subrogation works the other way.

It is noteworthy that insurance companies do not raise their premiums when leases contain waivers of subrogation. Therefore, it appears that these companies do not depend on recoveries of subrogation claims from lease parties in rating risks of loss. Under these circumstances, a forfeiture of those subrogation rights "by default," should not visit any unexpected economic impact on insurance companies.

35 LANDLORDS BLAMED FOR INTRUDERS' CRIMES

Traditionally, landlords were not responsible to their tenants for injuries inflicted by criminal intruders. Generally, courts held tenants responsible for providing their own security, particularly when we were an agrarian society. However, in recent times, courts have imposed liability on landlords when tenants become the victims of such crimes as assault, robbery, or rapes in and around their apartments.

While the law varies from state to state, tenants have relied on three basic theories of liability: breach of contract, breach of implied warranty or habitability, and negligence in providing security for the tenant. Legal obligations imposed on landlords for intruders' crimes are not always clear-cut, but Pennsylvania landlords seem to fare better than New Jersey landlords.

A Program of Security

A leading case in Pennsylvania, *Feld v. Merriam*, 485 A.2d 742 (Pa. 1984), involved tenants whom armed assailants abducted from a parking garage next to the Cedarbrook Apartments, despite the fact that Cedarbrook maintained a guarded gate security system. The assailants forced the wife-tenant at gunpoint to perform sexual acts, and the victims argued that the landlord was responsible for failing to provide proper security against potential criminal intruders.

A jury originally awarded $6 million in damages to the tenants based on instructions from the court that landlords are responsible to protect tenants from foreseeable criminal acts. However, this verdict was reversed on appeal when the Pennsylvania Supreme Court held that landlords have no general duty to protect tenants against even foreseeable criminal conduct unless the landlord has established or advertised a so-called "program of security"

196

that is "neglected and not fully implemented." Such a "program" is not merely the usual and normal precautions that a reasonable homeowner would employ to protect property. Rather, it must be "an extra precaution, such as personnel specifically charged to patrol and protect the premises."

This standard will let many landlords off the hook for intruders' crimes, because it appears that a landlord may choose to provide no security program at all. The articulated rule will impose liability only when a landlord chooses to adopt a program that is not properly implemented. Even though this now seems to be the rule in Pennsylvania, the court left the door open about whether a landlord had a duty to adopt usual and normal precautions that "a reasonable homeowner would employ to protect his property." The *Feld* case distinguished an injury caused by a physical defect on the property from one caused by a criminal act of the third person. Since the latter case rises from the conduct of an unpredictable, independent person, the duty of the landlord is much more limited in that case.

A later Pennsylvania case, *Reider v. Martin*, 535 A.2d 83 (Pa. 1987), focused on what the court meant by "a program of security." In that case, a tenant sued her landlord for damages sustained in the stairway outside her apartment when an intruder entered the building through the front door and raped, beat, and robbed her. There was evidence that the landlord had on several occasions promised to fix the door lock and that tenants had relied on that promise.

The *Reider* case held that even a promise to fix a lock rose to the standard of a "program of security" that the landlord was required to implement once he had offered it. Essentially, the Pennsylvania cases say that landlords may not have to provide security, but if they do or say they will, they had better do it right. This case delivers a loud warning to landlords. Once a landlord is responsible for a crime committed in the building, rapes, assaults, robberies, and murders may all be laid at the landlord's doorstep.

Johnson v. Goldstein, 864 F. Supp. 490 (E.D. Pa. 1994), followed these earlier cases in refusing to overturn a $550,000 verdict awarded to a rape victim in her case against apartment owners. *Johnson* held the defendants liable when they had "voluntarily" installed security bars on the windows of all the "relevant" apartments except for the victim's second floor apartment.

New Jersey Standards

In contrast, New Jersey imposes a higher standard on landlords. A leading New Jersey case, *Trentacost v. Brussel*, 412 A.2d 436 (N.J. 1980), found a landlord responsible for an intruder's assault against a tenant on the theory that the landlord breached an "implied warranty of habitability." The court reasoned that under state legislation and modern living conditions, an apartment is not habitable unless the landlord provides a "reasonable amount of security" from the risk of criminal intrusion. While that case seems to impose a difficult burden on the landlord, the court shed little or no light on how far landlords must go to protect under this rule.

In high-crime areas, is it "reasonable" to require landlords to install metal bars on first-floor windows? How about second-floor windows? What about bright lights? Suppose tenants prefer no bars and dim lights for aesthetic reasons. Must the landlord insist on them?

Should the landlord be required to install an electronic security alarm system? And if so, what type and at what expense? Is it enough to provide good locking mechanisms on doors, or must the landlord also provide internal security such as intercom systems in elevators and laundry rooms?

Should the security requirements be related to the quality of the apartments or the level of rent charged by the landlord? Is it reasonable to require a doorman when the expenses of the complex exceed the income? These are some of the questions that courts may have to sort out in future liability cases.

In any event, the increasing number of tenants' suits and the legal trends towards landlords' liability in New Jersey and other states should highlight the importance of providing adequate security in apartment buildings, particularly when there has been a history of break-ins.

Landlord's Response

The landlord's approach may vary, depending on the nature of the building and its location; and protection could range from simple deadbolt door locks to elaborate electronic systems, gates, and guards. Also, liability insurance should be carefully evaluated to determine if limits of coverage are adequate and punitive damages covered. In some policies, punitive damages are specifically excluded from insurance coverage; and even if they are not excluded, they may not be payable because, in some states, it is against "public policy" to obtain insurance for punitive damages.

In light of these cases and others throughout the country that are awarding victims compensation under similar circumstances, many believe that property owners should give serious consideration to holding title to all real estate in separate corporate names, or separate limited liability companies, which in many states protect the principals against personal liability.

Aside from protecting themselves against legal liability, landlords should also consider security programs because they may help rentals. A survey by the NAHB's National Council of the Multifamily Housing and the Economics and Housing Policy department found that tenants rank security as a higher priority than access to public transportation, having friends and relatives in the complex, and being able to keep pets. In addition, surveyed tenants included security improvements in a list of factors that would induce them to pay higher rent.

The real estate industry should be watching carefully how far the *Reider* case will be carried in Pennsylvania. Cases in other parts of the country have extended this doctrine to many other types of violent crimes.

A landlord has been held liable in one case for damages caused by arson in a building that had a history of suspicious fires, and in another for murder resulting from a landlord's failure to provide adequate security for a common area of an apartment complex. But see *Simmons v. Chicago Housing Auth.*, 641 N.E.2d 915 (Ill. App. Ct. 1994) (rape victim could not recover against Housing Authority for failure to properly select or train guards where there was no previous history of attacks); and *Ann M. v. Pacific Plaza Shopping Ctr.*, 863 P.2d 207 (Cal. 1993) (shopping center operator has no duty to provide security guards in common areas absent evidence of earlier criminal acts or other compelling basis to foresee criminal activity).

In the renowned case involving singer Connie Francis, a judgment of $2.5 million was awarded to Francis on the theory that the motel in which she was raped did not provide adequate security. A California case awarded a rape victim $1.2 million against an apartment owner and manager who ignored complaints about lack of light in the building's underground garage. *Pamela B. v. Hayden*, 30 Cal. App.4th 1063 (Cal. Ct. App. 1994). In some states, the doctrine has been extended to universities and governmental bodies for crimes committed on campus, and to homeowners' associations of condominium complexes.

No one knows how far the courts will go with these cases. One wonders, however, how long it will be before the courts hold homeowners liable to their own families and other guests injured during a burglary if owners fail to maintain burglar systems on their door locks.

Parking Lot

Several California appellate cases set standards that essentially let owners off the hook for parking-lot assaults unless there is an earlier history of assaults related to the property.

In *Nicole M. v. Sears, Roebuck & Co.*, 90 Cal. Rptr.2d 922 (Cal. Ct. App. 1999), a customer was attacked in a Sears parking lot by a "nicely dressed and clean cut" man who attempted to drag her into the bushes bordering the parking lot. Although she fought off the attack, she later sued Sears for failing to prevent it, and she alleged that the proximate cause for the attack was the untrimmed shrubbery. Evidence showed that homeless people had been "encamped" there, and that the store manager instructed his maintenance workers to trim back the shrubbery, but they hadn't done it. The victim alleged that the bushes had been in a dangerous, untrimmed condition for a year. Her expert testified:

> ... This danger is particularly high when the characteristics of the area create what are referred to as "rape corridors" or "rape areas" which can be described as dark passageways or burrowed out areas in bushes where a criminal act would be concealed from view. The nature and characteristics of the location where [plaintiff] was attacked facilitated the commission of the crime and increased its likelihood. I would characterize the area as a sexual assault waiting to happen ...

Id. at 923.

The court adopted earlier precedent and held that in order to show that a landlord has a duty to protect invitees from being attacked, a plaintiff must show evidence that an owner could anticipate that criminal attacks are especially likely to occur. Normally, this is shown by evidence of earlier attacks of a similar nature.

In adopting the reasoning of an earlier case, the court held:

Ann M. observed, "Unfortunately, random, violent crime is endemic in today's society. It is difficult, if not impossible to envision any locale open to the public where the occurrence of violent crime seems improbable." To hold a property owner legally liable for a crime occurring on his or her premises, the law requires that the owner should have "reasonably anticipated" the crime. *The requisite degree of foreseeability rarely, if ever, can be proven in the absence of prior similar incidents of violent crime on the landowner's premises.*" On the record before us, we conclude that the low lighting and overgrown bushes alone did not make the property inherently dangerous and further that these circumstances were not cause for the property owner to reasonably anticipate crime in the absence of prior similar incidents.

Id. at 928 (emphasis added).

Indoor Garage

The *Sears & Roebuck* decision was filed by the California Court of Appeals on December 13, 1999. Just three days later, the California Supreme Court decided another case involving a parking garage, and again blew off the plaintiff. In the case of *Sharon P. v. Arman*, 91 Cal. Rptr.2d 35 (Cal. 1999), the claimant sued the owner when she was attacked in an underground garage while going to her car. She argued that the owner had a duty to protect against such attacks because these facilities were "inherently dangerous." Also, that some "minimal level of security," short of security guards, should have been provided.

Again, the court held that because there was no evidence of earlier criminal attacks, it would be a very rare circumstance where any special measures would be required by the owner. The court suggested that there was a balance to be reached between the burden of the landowner to provide security measures and the degree of risk of injury from criminal attacks.

The claimant also argued that the garage was poorly lit, but the court noted that an expert for the defense testified that the garage was small, with no dark corners, and could be viewed in its entirety from almost anywhere inside. While the court found for the owner, it is still possible that future courts would find that there is a duty under certain circumstances to provide adequate lighting in a garage, even without evidence of earlier criminal attacks.

Social Policy

In these cases, the California courts purport to be applying the Restatement (Second) of Torts (Section 344), which is now, and will undoubtedly be followed in many other states. That rule gets down to whether the owner has "reason to believe" from what the owner has observed, or from past experience, that intentional attacks of third parties should be anticipated. If so, the owner must "exercise reasonable care to use such means of protection as are available."

These types of cases require courts to make difficult judgments about social policy. On the one hand, the court must consider whether to pass on the cost of criminal attacks to commercial owners. On the other hand, sometimes very little cost, such as trimming bushes or taking them down, could help prevent attacks.

One of the problems that courts face is that if they let the issue of foreseeability go to a jury, today's juries are likely to find against the owners, and the gruesome details of these types of attacks can result in verdicts of millions of dollars. Since owners (and their insurance companies), cannot take a chance on a verdict like that, many owners will be forced to settle for high figures before they even have their day in court.

Landscaping and Lights

Traditionally, townships and protesting neighbors battle developers who bring in shopping centers with their bright lights and traffic. Objectors generally push for low-keyed developments with green barriers and abundant foliage. If cases like *Sears* and *Arman* lead to large verdicts against owners, developers may fight even harder to resist plush landscaping areas and dark corridors that have been characterized as "assaults waiting to happen."

These are just some of the policies that must be balanced by courts in a crime-ridden and litigious society. Owners are damned if they do and damned if they don't. They might get sued for installing bright lights and bushes, and they might even get sued for not installing them.

When a party, other than the tenant, guarantees a lease, the parties frequently miss the significance of the form of guaranty that they use. The landlord should attempt to have the guarantor waive rights, defenses, and notices so that it does not get snagged on technicalities in trying to collect. Also, the landlord will want the guaranty to be unconditional so that the landlord can collect directly from the guarantor without having to proceed against the tenant. In addition, since leases are sometimes modified, and the terms are waived, landlords should specify that the guaranty is not impaired by those changes, and, in fact, embraces them automatically.

The guarantor, on the other hand, should try to narrow the scope of its guaranty. For example, it may want to place a cap on its total liability under the guaranty. It may want to try to use a dollar limit, or exclude liability for any obligations other than rent, such as judgments against the tenant resulting from negligence or obligations to rebuild the property. It may not want to guaranty percentage and escalation rents.

The guarantor may want even more subtle limits. If more than one guarantor is on the hook, each guarantor may want to limit its liability to its pro rata share of the entire obligation, and avoid what is known as "joint" liability. In addition, it may want to negotiate a "step-down guaranty" that will decline over the lease term as the remaining obligation of the tenant dwindles over time. Some guarantors are able to negotiate a reduction based on arguments that the landlord's investment in tenant improvements is amortized over the term of the lease, or by persuading the landlord that the guaranty is not needed once the tenant achieves a designated credit rating.

One of the frequently negotiated limits where the guarantor is a partnership, involves partners of the guarantor who retire or resign. Sometimes, particularly with a partnership of lawyers or doctors, the landlord will permit the retiring or resigning partner to be dropped from the guaranty.

Collateral Impairment

A landlord can easily lose the benefit of a lease guaranty. In *Shurlow v. Bonthuis*, 576 N.W.2d 159 (Mich. 1998), an office lease had granted the landlord the right to file a lien covering the tenant's personal property. Also, one of the officers of the tenant's predecessor had signed a personal guaranty of the tenant's performance under the lease.

After the landlord had included that right to lien in the lease, it made what later turned out to be a fatal error. It did not perfect this lien. While the lease and the court refer to a "lien" on the tenant's property, the court views the potential lien as a right to perfect a security interest by filing financing statements on that property under the Uniform Commercial Code (UCC).

When the tenant went bankrupt, the personal property was sold for approximately $35,000 and because the landlord had never perfected its lien against that property, the proceeds went to other creditors. Then the landlord looked to the guarantor for payment of the rent, and he was met with the defense that he had not perfected the landlord's lien. The guarantor argued that he was released from his obligations under the guaranty because the landlord had negligently impaired the collateral for the rent.

At the first appellate level, the Michigan Court of Appeals, 553 N.W.2d 366 (Mich. Ct. App. 1996), in what was viewed as a case of "first impression" in Michigan, agreed with the guarantor. It decided that under Section 9-207 of the UCC, a secured party must use reasonable care to ensure that a security interest is properly perfected. If it fails to do so, then the secured party is liable for any resultant damages.

Section 9-207 specifically provides:

> A secured party must use reasonable care in the custody and preservation of collateral in his possession. In the case of an instrument or chattel paper reasonable care includes taking necessary steps to preserve rights against prior parties unless otherwise agreed.

Even though that section of the code seems to refer only to collateral in the landlord's "possession" or "an instrument or chattel paper," the court found that this section applied because the UCC "considers a landlord's lien to be a form of chattel paper."

The UCC imposes some duties to preserve collateral on the theory that some guarantors would not have signed a guaranty unless there had been collateral security, and that they expect to have recourse against that collateral by subrogation to the landlord's rights, if they are called upon to pay. Therefore, their expectations are frustrated by the secured party's failure to perfect.

The court of appeals decision was reversed on appeal by the Supreme Court of Michigan in *Shurlow v. Bonthuis*, cited above, on the theory that article 9 of the UCC did not apply because the applicable collateral was not "chattel paper" and therefore was not intended to be covered by that section. However, the court raised an issue that might save the guarantor anyway. It suggested that it was not deciding the case one way or the other under the common law and that the common law might provide a defense for the guarantor based on the impairment-of-collateral defense.

Waiver Forms

Generally, lenders, as well as landlords, would be subject to this same defense if they impair collateral. That's why institutional lenders will use guaranty forms that protect themselves against these defenses. These detailed guaranties will generally provide that the guarantor waives any defenses based on impairment of collateral. Even then, the waiver may not save the lender unless the language specifically waives the defenses of the guarantor even when, for example, the lender failed to perfect its lien against collateral. See Richard L. Epling, *Waiver Clauses in Commercial Loan and Guaranty Agreements*, 15 U.C.C.L.J. 231 (1983); *Federal Deposit Ins. Corp. v. Nobles*, 901 F.2d 477 (5th Cir. 1990); *Federal Deposit Ins. Corp. v. Hardt*, 646 F. Supp. 209 (C.D. Ill. 1986); *National Acceptance Co. v. Demes*, 446 F. Supp. 388 (N.D. Ill. 1977); *Congress Financial Corp. v. Sterling-Coin Op Machinery Corp.*, 456 F.2d 451 (3d Cir. 1972).

Practical Issues

Since guarantors generally tend to waive all their defenses, what is the practical significance of issues raised by the *Shurlow* case? The answer to that lies in the way leases are sometimes handled.

First, sometimes landlords require guaranties from financially secure corporations or individuals, and do not bother to provide for the waivers that lenders customarily require. For example, one printed form lease that has been used in Pennsylvania has the following guaranty on the back:

> **IN CONSIDERATION** of the letting of the premises described in this lease _____ do hereby become sureties for the punctual payment of rent and performance of the covenants mentioned in said lease to be performed by _____, and if any default shall be made therein _____ do _____ hereby promise and agree to pay onto the said _____ such sum or sums of money as will be sufficient to make such deficiencies, and fully satisfy the conditions of such lease, without requiring any notice of non-payment, or proof of demand being made. _____ hand and sealed this _____ day of _____, 20___.
>
> _____
> (Signature)

That's it! No waivers of defenses. No permission for the landlord to fail to perfect its lien in the collateral.

Secondly, many commercial leases now provide what landlords and their lawyers perceive as an extra security device. That is, like *Shurlow*, they give the landlord the right to file UCC financing statements and otherwise perfect the landlord's rights to secure the payment of rent with the tenant's personal property. Unfortunately for the landlord, sometimes the landlord then merely files the lease away and never bothers to follow up with filing the UCC financing statements. In light of the *Shurlow* case, that failure to perfect could create an impairment-of-collateral defense by the guarantor, at least under the common law.

The Fisherman's Wife

When landlords attempt to reserve that right to perfect against personal property, tenants will often object to it as overreaching and try to negotiate it out of a lease. The irony of all this is that if the landlord succeeds in this negotiation, he or she may, as they say, "be hoisted on his (or her) own petard." If the landlord neglects to perfect, he or she may find that there is no enforceable guaranty.

The lesson to landlords from all of this is simple:

1. All guaranties should be prepared and approved by counsel and contain airtight waivers by the guarantor.

2. If the landlord reserves the right to secure himself with the tenant's personal property, he or she should be sure to perfect that interest and to renew the UCC finance statements within the required five-year periods.

3. If the landlord is not sure he will carry out this advice, he or she should delete that lease provision that permits the lien.

Otherwise, landlords may find out too late that their collateral and their guaranties disappear into thin air like the castles and jewels granted by a grateful fish to a fisherman in the classic children's fable. In that tale, the greedy wife asked for one wish too many, and the magic fish took it all away.

37 LEASE GUARANTOR LIABLE EVEN FOR AN IMPROPERLY EXTENDED TERM

An Illinois appellate decision illustrates the value to landlords of an airtight lease guarantee. When a tenant stopped paying rent on a five-year lease extension, the landlord sued the guarantor of the lease and was met with a defense that the extension had been improperly exercised. *T.C.T. Bldg. P'ship v. Tandy Corp.,* 751 N.E.2d 135 (Ill. App. Ct. 2001), app. denied, 763 N.E.2d 326 (Ill. 2001). The tenant in this case had exercised an option in its lease to extend the lease for an additional five years, but sent its renewal notice too late to exercise the option under the lease. Despite that, the landlord waived the later notice, and acknowledged that the lease had been extended. However, the landlord never obtained consent of the waiver from the guarantor.

Strict Limits on Liability

When the landlord sued the guarantor for the tenant's default, the guarantor defended on the grounds that a lease extended by a late notice will not be binding on guarantors. This is in accordance with the rule in Illinois and many other states that provides strict limits on the guarantor's liability.

While the decision does not spell out how the guarantor's argument might best be articulated, it might run something like this: "Since the date for renewal was missed, the consent by the landlord to the extra five years should be viewed as a 'novation' or new lease. The guarantor only guaranteed the existing lease, and, therefore, should not be bound by a new lease."

The trial court supported the guarantor on this issue and ruled in its favor. However, the Illinois appellate court reversed the trial court because the guarantor had waived this kind of a defense in the guaranty.

This rule does not seem unfair when the guarantor is the parent of the tenant or is otherwise associated with it. However, the result is more onerous when the guarantor is no longer associated with the tenant at the time the lease is extended. This sometimes occurs many years after the original lease was signed, and after the original tenant has assigned the lease.

Magic Words of Guaranty

The guaranty in *T.C.T. Building Partnership* provided that "[No] extensions of time granted to the [Lessee] for the payment of said rents or other sums, or for the performance of any of the obligations of the Lessee or forbearance or delay on the part of the Lessor to enforce any of provisions, covenants, agreements, conditions and stipulations of said Lease, or waiver by Lease [sic] of any of said provisions, covenants, agreements, conditions and stipulations, shall operate to release or discharge the Guarantor from its full liability under this instrument of guaranty or prejudice the rights of Lessor hereunder." 751 N.E.2d at 138.

The court analyzed that language and found that the guarantor's objection to the landlord's agreement to accept the late renewal of the lease was waived in the last phrase of the guaranty. That phrase made it clear that the guarantor was not released, even when a landlord waives "covenants" or "conditions" of the lease.

The guarantor argued that strict compliance with the notice provision for extending the lease term was not waived because the notice provision was not specifically mentioned in the guaranty's waiver provision. However, the court rejected that argument and stated:

> ... the fact that this provision of the guaranty does not specifically refer to the lessor's waiver of Color Tile's strict compliance with the lease terms relating to notice of its intent to exercise the option to extend the term of the lease is of no moment. We know of no rule which requires that a waiver-of-defense provision in a guaranty specifically itemize each defense which is waived. We believe that the defendant clearly and unambiguously agreed to be bound by its guaranty, notwithstanding the fact that the lessor waived a condition of the lease.

Id. at 141.

Landlord's Alert

This case highlights two important issues that landlords must pay attention to in connection with guaranties. First, landlords must be aware that if they alter the lease terms, even in some minor way, they may have impaired their ability to keep the guarantor on the hook. In this case, if it hadn't been for the waiver of defenses in the guaranty form that was used, the landlord could have lost its guaranty merely because it sympathetically permitted the tenant to exercise the lease extension two days late.

More importantly, without the language in the guaranty that made it clear that the guarantor would be liable even though the landlord did not strictly enforce provisions of the lease, or even though the landlord waived terms of the lease, the landlord would have lost its guaranty. Landlords should be aware that some of the standard printed leases being used around the country are accompanied by guaranties that do not include the magic words that saved the landlord in the *T.C.T. Building Partnership* case.

38   PARENT COMPANY LIABLE FOR JUDGMENT-PROOF SUBSIDIARY'S RENT

The New Jersey Superior Court held that a company that sets up an impecunious subsidiary to rent space may be held liable under the lease if its conduct deceives the landlord into thinking that the company, and not the subsidiary, is the tenant. *OTR Assocs. v. IBC Servs., Inc.*, 801 A.2d 407 (N.J. Super. Ct. App. Div. 2002). Blimpie International, Inc., a restaurant franchisor, set up a subsidiary, IBC Services, Inc., for the single purpose of acting as a tenant under its restaurant leases. When the tenant failed to pay the rent for space rented in a shopping center, the landlord (OTR) sued not only the named tenant, IBC, but also the parent corporation, "Blimpie," on the grounds that Blimpie used the subsidiary as "a conduit for the parent," and perpetuated a "fraud or injustice" on the landlord.

Puppeteer and Marionette

Under the circumstances of the case, the court held that the landlord could pierce the corporate veil and invoked the metaphor of a puppeteer being responsible for the marionette.

It stated:

> Thus, the basic finding that must be made to enable the court to pierce the corporate veil is "that the parent so dominated the subsidiary that it had no separate existence but was merely a conduit for the parent." ... But beyond domination, the court must also find that the "parent has abused the privilege of incorporation by using the subsidiary to perpetrate a fraud or injustice, or otherwise to circumvent the law." ... And the hallmarks of that abuse are typically the engagement of the subsidiary in no independent business of its own but exclusively the performance of

a service for the parent and, even more importantly, the undercapitalization of the subsidiary rendering it judgment-proof.

801 A.2d at 409–10 [citation omitted].

Blimpie conceded that it formed its subsidiaries for the sole purpose of holding leases and that the subsidiary in this case

... had virtually no assets other than the lease itself, which, in the circumstances, was not an asset at all but only a liability since [it] had no independent right to alienate its interest therein but was subject to Blimpie's exclusive control. It had no business premises of its own, sharing the New York address of Blimpie. It had no income other than the rent payments by the franchisee, which appear to have been made directly to [the landlord]. It does not appear that it had its own employees or office staff.

Id. at 410.

In addition, the court noted that Blimpie knowingly retained the right to approve the subsidiaries' leases and managed these leases from its corporate office. It was also noted that the individual subsidiaries didn't make a profit because the leases don't make any profits in this type of organization.

Deception

The court held that the control of the subsidiary was clear, and then went on to determine whether Blimpie abused the privilege of incorporation by using its subsidiary to commit a fraud or injustice, or other improper use. In that analysis, it concluded that OTR believed that it was dealing with a national and financially responsible franchising company, and never discovered that Blimpie was using separate corporate entities until after the eviction occurred under the lease.

The court concluded that the subsidiary "never apparently expressly claimed to be" the parent company, but it affirmatively, intentionally, and calculatedly led the landlord to believe that it was the actual franchisor company. The court cited OTR's example of IBC's deception. Before the lease for the space was signed, two men entered OTR's on-site office in the mall clothed in uniforms bearing the Blimpie logo. The men stated that they wanted to open a Blimpie sandwich shop. Because the name of the leasing subsidiary used the initials of the franchisor-parent, the court concluded that there was a reasonable inference that the initials of the subsidiary stood for the name of the parent. In addition, the correspondence from IBC to OTR was done on stationery headed only by a Blimpie's logo, and the address of the subsidiary was shown as in "care of" Blimpie.

Many cases around the country find injured parties trying to pierce a corporate veil, and sometimes succeeding. Based on the stated facts in this case, it is not too surprising that the court gave the landlord the benefit of the doubt.

Implications

However, this case raises serious legal issues for future cases in which parent companies are sued for the actions of their subsidiaries. For one thing, this is not a tort case, but a contract action. Generally, a parent/subsidiary case, or if you prefer, a puppeteer/marionette case, would be easier to sustain when dealing with a tort action. For example, in a negligence claim involving a straw owner of a commercial property, the injured party may be able to succeed in a case against the principal under the doctrine of respondeat superior.

In a contract action, whether the plaintiff is dealing with a straw company set up to deal with a plaintiff, or an impecunious subsidiary, the injured party can be said to be relying on the creditworthiness of the party it has dealt with, not the parent. Otherwise, it would be expected to ask for the parent's signature on the contract, or to require a guaranty. That was not done in the *OTR Associates* case.

In addition, the court admits that the subsidiary, IBC, never expressly claimed to be the Blimpie Company, nor did it observe all of the corporate proprieties. IBC had its own officers and directors, it filed annual reports, kept minutes, held meetings, and had a bank account.

Based on the facts, the landlord, OTR, was able to make a sufficient case to satisfy the court to pierce the corporate veil. However, in another case where some of the facts might not be as favorable to proving a fraud, a court may go the other way.

Parent companies who are trying to insulate themselves from subsidiaries' lease liability could learn a lesson from *OTR Associates*. For example, the landlord may not have succeeded if

Blimpie had made it clear that it was not responsible for lease payments, had set up a separate office for the subsidiary, used separate stationery, or even had a different corporate logo and corporate initials.

On the other hand, this case raises the broader issue of how much responsibility a sophisticated landlord and its advisors and lawyers should have to check out the creditworthiness and other information that is reasonably available about the party who has been named as a tenant on a proposed lease. Some would say that grownups should not find it difficult to distinguish between a marionette and the person pulling the strings.

A good tenant may be like gold, but who would have expected that a good tenant would have to pay in gold? Some courts have
required tenants to pay their rent in gold coin under long-dormant
lease clauses. These decisions are based on long-term leases that
originally provided an inflationary hedge by giving landlords the
right to collect rent in gold coin. For example, in the case of *Trostel
v. American Life & Casualty Insurance Co.*, 92 F.3d 736 (8th Cir.
1996); remanded, 133 F.3d 679 (8th Cir. 1998), *aff'd*, 168 F.3d 1105
(8th Cir. 1999), the lease stated, "at the option of the lessor, all payments under this lease shall be made in gold coin of the United
States of America, of or equal to the present standard of weight and
fineness." *Trostel*, 92 F.3d at 738.

The issue is not merely academic. We recently advised a
landlord about an old lease on Pennsylvania property that contained a gold clause.

In another case, *Wells Fargo Bank v. Bank of America*, 38
Cal. Rptr.2d 521 (Cal. Ct. App. 1995), a 1929, 95-year ground lease
provided for an unadjusted monthly base rent of only $2,000. A
clause required the rent to be paid in U.S. gold coin of a defined
quality that was the then-present standard of weight and fineness
of gold coin. According to the court, that would have brought the
$2,000 rent to over $47,000 based on the 1987 price of gold. In *Trostel*, the monthly rent would be $445,000 under the 1917 standard
as compared to $18,000 under the original lease.

Gold Clauses Not Buried

Here's the nugget of these cases. Most people assumed that
the gold clauses had been buried by Congress in 1933. That's when
Congress, in a joint resolution, declared gold clauses to be against
public policy and provided that "dollar for dollar" payments in U.S.
currency would discharge any obligation. Joint Resolution of June

5, 1933, 48 Stat. 112, 113, 1933, formally codified at 31 U.S.C. § 463 (codified as amended at 31 U.S.C. § 5118(d)(2)). This was one of a series of measures taken to stabilize the value of U.S. currency. During the same period, private ownership of gold was banned and the dollar was devalued.

In 1975 Congress repealed the ban on private ownership of gold, and in 1977 it passed an amendment to the 1933 gold-clause statute, which overrode the earlier statute for any obligations issued after October 27, 1977. Therefore, after that time it once again became legal to contract for payment in gold.

In the cited cases, the tenants could have continued to pay their rent in dollars, even after the 1977 amendment, but they each handed their landlord a golden opportunity. In each case, they assigned the lease to a new tenant who assumed the lease and all of the obligations under it. After that, the landlords demanded payments in gold coin as permitted in the original leases. As expected, tenants opposed those demands and argued that the 1933 act had in effect "melted down" the gold clauses in the original leases.

Each of the courts rejected that argument. Even though the original act rendered the clauses unenforceable, they held that the clauses did not disappear, but in fact were incorporated by reference into new lease obligations after the act was reversed in 1977. According to the *Trostel* court, after 1977, parties were free to enter into contracts that were payable in gold or gold coin, and an assignment and assumption agreement was such a contract. That assignment constituted more than a mere continuation of the lease. It became a "novation," or new contract between the assignor and the assignee.

As a result of 1996 congressional action intended to reverse these cases, the U.S. Supreme Court granted certiorari and remanded the case to the court of appeals. However, the following year Congress reversed itself and eliminated the 1996 change. Based on that action, the same court of appeals affirmed its earlier decision. *Trostel v. American Life & Cas. Ins. Co.*, 133 F.3d 679 (8th Cir. 1998), *aff'd*, 168 F.3d 1105 (8th Cir. 1999).

In both *Trostel* and *Wells Fargo Bank*, the tenants made the expected arguments to the courts, but they did not hit pay dirt. They argued that the assignment did not create a new obligation "as to the gold clause" because the parties did not intend to incorporate that clause into the assignment. Since that clause could escalate the rent to a large multiple of the existing rent, it would have been hard for the landlord to argue that the parties to the assignment had a different actual intent.

No Estoppel or Laches

In *Wells Fargo Bank*, the tenant also argued the defenses of estoppel and laches. The assignee/tenant argued that to purchase the leasehold interest, it paid over $4,000,000, plus over $840,000 in taxes and other charges based on certain assumptions about the rent. However, the court rejected the estoppel defense because the landlord did not know about the assignee's purchase of the lease until after the purchase had been completed, and also because the expenses were not incurred by the tenant in reliance on the landlord's conduct or delay in making a claim.

The court in *Wells Fargo Bank* also rejected the tenant's laches argument even though the tenant proved that it had paid rent in dollars at the rate of $2,000 per month after the lease was acquired in 1981. The landlord did not object to such payments until one of its principals became aware of the gold-clause issue in November 1986, and even then the landlord did not take legal action until October 1991. Despite the tenant's arguments, the court rejected the laches defense on the technical ground that laches is unavailable as a defense in a suit for damages, even when the damage claim has been combined with a request for declaratory relief.

A Treasure Hunt

It could be fairly said that these landlords have gone on a treasure hunt and hit a gold vein. On the other hand, the tenants apparently could have staked out their own claims merely by avoiding an assumption of the gold clause or any other agreements that might be considered a novation. It is possible they could have accomplished their goals either by drafting the assignments to reject the gold clause, or by using a sublease instead of an assignment. That way they would have continued to pay rent in dollars, and the gold clauses would have remained buried by the 1933 Congressional act.

That is the nugget of wisdom for tenants who are faced with a gold clause. The wisdom these cases bring to landlords is that you may be able to strike it rich if you can dig up one of those old leases with a gold clause in it, provided the tenant has made the mistake of assuming the lease after October of 1977. You may then be able to increase the rent by 2000 percent—or more!

40 DEBTOR-IN-POSSESSION MAY HAVE TO PAY ACCRUED REAL ESTATE TAXES AS CURRENT RENT

The U.S. Third Circuit Court of Appeals will help landlords collect so-called "pass-through" charges that have accrued against a bankrupt commercial tenant. *Centerpoint Properties v. Montgomery Ward Holding Corp. (In re Montgomery Ward Holding Corp.)*, 268 F.3d 205 (3d Cir. 2001). On October 10, 2001, the Third Circuit Court of Appeals filed a decision that supported the landlords' claim to treat accrued real estate taxes with the same bankruptcy priority as current rent. The decision reversed both the bankruptcy court and the district court, and created a split of authority among the federal courts of appeals.

Real Estate Taxes

In this case Montgomery Ward had filed for bankruptcy on July 7, 1997, under Chapter 11. Montgomery Ward continued to make use of the premises as a debtor-in-possession, but it neither assumed nor rejected the lease before the lease's expiration on September 1, 1997. On July 11th, four days after the bankruptcy filing, the landlord sent three invoices to Montgomery Ward. The first was for a first installment of 1996 taxes (payable in 1997) in the amount of $320,000, the second was for an estimated second installment of 1996 taxes in approximately the same amount, and the third was issued under a section of the lease permitting the landlord to bill for 1997 taxes in the amount of $427,000.

Instead of paying these invoices totaling over a million dollars, Montgomery Ward paid $96,000 as a partial payment on the third invoice. This amount represented the prorated portion of taxes attributable to the period after Montgomery Ward's petition for bankruptcy because it took the position that all the other taxes were attributable to the pre-petition period and they constituted unsecured claims.

"Obligations of Debtor"

The issue in this case arises under Section 365(d)(3) of the Bankruptcy Code, which reads:

> The trustee shall timely perform all the obligations of the debtor, except those specified in Section 365(b)(2), arising from and after the order for relief under any unexpired lease of nonresidential real property, until such lease is assumed or rejected, . . .

The landlord argued that all of the invoices were payable immediately as "obligations of [Montgomery Ward] . . . arising from . . . the lease" after the order for relief. Montgomery Ward argued that the bankruptcy statute was ambiguous, and that it should be obligated to pay only the taxes attributable to the period after the order.

The Third Circuit posed the question as what Congress meant when it referred to "obligations of the debtor arising under a lease after the order of relief." It queried:

> . . . In the factual context of this case, does it require payment by the trustee of all amounts that first become due and enforceable after the order under the terms of the lease? Or does it require the proration of such amounts based upon whether the landlord's obligation to pay the taxes accrued before or after the order?

Montgomery Ward argued for the proration approach by adopting the theory of other cases that maintained that an "obligation" can arise before the tenant is obliged to perform. This would lead to the conclusion that the obligation to pay back taxes arose before bankruptcy and that, therefore, the invoices sent to Montgomery Ward were not needed to trigger the obligation under the Bankruptcy Code.

The Third Circuit rejected that approach and cited an earlier case involving an obligation to pay advance rent, *Koenig Sporting Goods, Inc. v. Morse Road Co. (In re Koenig Sporting Goods, Inc.)*, 203 F.3d 986 (6th Cir. 2000). In that case the rent for the coming month was due under the lease on the first day of the month, and the debtor-in-bankruptcy rejected the lease on the second day.

There the court held that the debtor's rent obligation accrued on the first of the month, and that required payment of the full month's advance—even though the debtor rejected the lease the next day!

Also, that proration would be inconsistent with the Bankruptcy Code.

The *Montgomery Ward Holding Corp.* court acknowledges that its conclusion is different from the conclusion reached by one sister court of appeals and a number of other courts that have opted for a proration approach. It also acknowledges that its approach may "in some cases leave room for strategic behavior on the part of landlords and tenants." However, it concludes that "strategic behavior" can be "constrained by forethought and careful drafting."

It is not clear what the court means by its reference to "strategic behavior."

Dissenting Opinion

In a dissenting opinion, Judge Mansmann criticizes the majority for holding in effect that an obligation that accrues over time does not arise as it accrues, but instead "arises at whatever time the parties specify in the lease." She concludes that the majority's holding gives an "unwarranted preference to landlords for recovery of 'pre-petition' debts." Mansmann is disturbed by the majority's conclusion that because the billing took place within the eight-week administrative period between the bankruptcy and the expiration of the lease (before assumption or rejection of it), "the entire 20 months' worth of tax obligations *arose* during that eight-week period." She maintains that:

> In so holding, the majority elevates the accident or artifice of the billing date above the economic reality of the accrual, and thereby inappropriately burdens the administration of the bankrupt estate and unfairly favors landlords over similarly situated pre-petition creditors.

Under Mansmann's analysis, the obligations "attributable to a particular time should be said to 'arise' at that time, and an obligation that accrues over time may be said to 'arise' as it accrues." She points out that before a 1984 amendment to the Bankruptcy Code, the earlier practice was to prorate accrued obligations, and that there is no indication that Congress had a specific intent to displace this approach with what she calls the "billing date approach." Rather, she concludes that the statute was aimed at providing landlords with current pay for current services, and relieving them from the "actual and necessary" analysis that was required before that change.

Strategies

What is the "strategic behavior" that the court thinks may be opened up as a result of this decision?

If a lease provides that the obligation to pay real estate taxes is not due until the taxes are billed to the tenant, the landlord may be able to time its billing to create a result that it desires. For example, if a million dollars in taxes has accrued against a troubled tenant, a landlord may hold up the bill. This strategy is contrary to the normal instincts of the creditor. However, if a landlord sends out a bill before bankruptcy, the obligation may become due at that time, and if there is a later bankruptcy, that sum will be relegated to a pre-petition debt and a lower order of priority. If on the other hand, the bill is sent out after bankruptcy is filed and before the lease is rejected, under the third circuit case, that bill could be treated as an administrative expense, just like current rent.

That result occurred in *Montgomery Ward* because the lease provided that pass-through real estate taxes were not payable until they were billed by the landlord. Therefore, the "obligation" under the statute did not occur until after bankruptcy.

Drafting Tip

The result would probably have been different if the lease had provided that real estate taxes were payable when they were "accrued" or when they became due to the municipality. This may lead to a contrary-to-instinct drafting tip. The tendency of landlords is to make certain lease obligations, including advance rent, become automatically due under a lease, without a required notice to the tenant. For example, some leases provide that if a tenant defaults in its duty to make repairs to a property after a casualty or under other circumstances, the landlord will have a right to cure the default and charge the tenant for the advanced costs. After this case, landlords may want to draft leases so that the triggering event for a tenant's payment will not merely be the expenditure by the landlord, but will be a formal notice or a bill from the landlord to the tenant.

That drafting tip might also apply to obligations to pay real estate taxes or other pass-through expenses. Then the landlord could have the option of waiting until a troubled tenant goes into bankruptcy before making a request for payment. That strategy could elevate the claim from a lower order of priority to an administrative obligation of the bankrupt estate.

The Pendulum Swings

The issue of when an obligation arises is not an easy one for the courts. On the one hand, the Bankruptcy Code, taken literally, seems to militate against proration. It seems to stick the debtor with any obligation that becomes due during its possession. On the other hand, it obligates the debtor to pay accrued sums as an administrative expense, no matter how long they have accrued and whether or not they relate to the benefits of occupancy.

In *Montgomery Ward*, the third circuit's decision imposes an extra obligation of almost $1 million on the trustee merely because the landlord held up an invoice by a few days!

Congress was trying to solve a problem for landlords with the 1984 amendment. Before that, rent could be an administrative expense only to the extent that the occupancy benefited the bankrupt estate. This placed a burden on the landlord to prove that the rent and other required payments under the lease were reasonable, and the debtor received full use of the occupied property during the period of possession.

This "unsatisfactory arrangement" was described in the majority opinion:

> The "reasonable value-actual use" standard meant that (i) if a DIP physically occupied only a portion of the premises, it would, in turn, only be liable for the pro rata rent corresponding to the percentage of space actually occupied, and (ii) the court could limit a landlord's recovery to a fair market rate where the contract rate in the lease appeared clearly unreasonable.

Under the *Montgomery Ward* decision, some would say that the pendulum has swung too far. Now, a few days' occupancy can burden the debtor's other creditors with advance rent applicable to periods beyond the occupancy, and for accrued pass-through obligations and other required payments running into millions of

223

dollars. Bankruptcy trustees and debtors-in-possession will now have to tread cautiously before continuing to operate for even one day. Theoretically, that day could now obligate them for obligations beyond their wildest dreams.

41 CAN SHOPPING CENTERS CONTROL BANKRUPT TENANTS' LEASE TRANSFERS? (WITH MODEL CLAUSES)

Most real estate professionals know that when tenants become bankrupt, landlords may lose the benefit of their leases—and their income. What many of them do not know is that landlords may suffer a worse fate. They may be stuck with a substitute tenant that they have not chosen or approved, and who does not have to comply with standards set forth in the existing lease. That could include restrictions on use, alterations, and limits on competition within a radius of the site of the property.

How could this happen in America, under a legal system that prides itself on the rights of owners to choose whom they want to deal with and on what terms?

Shopping Center Protection

According to *In re Rickel Home Centers, Inc.*, 240 B.R. 826 (Bankr. Del. 1998), *aff'd on grounds of mootness*, 209 F.3d 291 (3d Cir. 2000), the answer lies in the Bankruptcy Code. A superficial reading of the code might lead one to the conclusion that, even in bankruptcy, certain terms in a shopping center lease are inviolate. Congress obviously provided special protections for landlords of shopping centers that are not available to other owners. Section 365(b)(3) of the code provides that when there has been a default in a shopping center lease, before the lease may be assigned, adequate assurance of future performance must be provided. That includes assurance:

(A) of the source of rent and other consideration due under such lease, and in the case of an assignment, that the financial condition and operating performance of the proposed assignee and its guarantors, if any, shall be similar

225

to the financial condition and operating performance of the debtor and its guarantors, if any, *as of the time the debtor became the lessee under the lease*;

(B) that any percentage rent due under such lease will not decline substantially;

(C) that assumption or assignment of such lease is subject to all the provisions thereof, including (but not limited to) provisions such as a radius, location, *use*, or exclusivity provision, and will not breach any such provision contained in any other lease, financing agreement, or master agreement relating to the shopping center; and

(D) that assumption or assignment of such lease *will not disrupt any tenant mix* or balance in such shopping center.

11 U.S.C. § 365(b)(3)(A)–(D) (emphasis added).

In *Rickel*, Chief Judge Joseph J. Farnan, Jr. of the U.S. District Court for the District of Delaware ruled for the debtor, which had sold 41 leases formerly occupied by it as a home improvement center to Staples for the sum of $35.5 million. Three of the affected landlords had raised objections to the sale based on arguments that the sale would violate various lease restrictions. The landlords objected that the sale would cause the stores to be closed while the lease was being sold, would violate use restrictions in the leases, would require subdividing the leases, and would disrupt the tenant mix and cause loss of percentage rent.

De Facto Anti-assignment Provisions

While the court acknowledged that Section 365(b)(3) was adopted to protect shopping center landlords, it supported its decision by relying on another code section that permits a trustee in bankruptcy to assign leases. Section 365(f)(1) provides: "notwithstanding a provision in an ... unexpired lease ... that prohibits, restricts, or conditions the assignment of such ... lease, the trustee may assign ...." The court adopted the view that this assignment section not only bans lease provisions that specifically prohibit assignments, but also those lease provisions that are so restrictive that they constitute "de facto anti-assignment provisions." It then concluded that under the circumstances the applicable lease provisions were "de facto anti-assignment provisions."

With several leases, Staples sought to operate only a portion of the larger store and to sublet the remaining space to other tenants. For example, in one case, Staples intended to operate only 24,000 square feet and to divide the remaining space of 14,000 square feet into a series of smaller stores. The landlords objected that this would be a violation of the use restrictions for several reasons. First, Staples' use was a change from the Rickel Home Improvement Center operation. Secondly, the store would have to "go dark" during the proposed alterations, and the percentage rent would be affected at least during that time.

In response to that, the court accepted the debtor's testimony that the type of home improvement center operated by Rickel would either become obsolete or was struggling to remain in existence as a result of competition from other types of home improvement stores like Home Depot. In light of that, there was no demand for warehouse-style home center stores. Judge Farnan concluded that since there was no market for home improvement centers, enforcement of the use restrictions would make it impossible either for the debtor to assign leases to any entity or for Staples to assign or sublet the remaining unused space. Therefore, under the circumstances, the use restriction was a "de facto anti-assignment" provision.

The court then dealt with the objections based on the lease provisions that limited alterations. It held that the restrictions on painting and division of the space were merely "nuisance" provisions and should not be used to prohibit an assignment of a lease. Also, that it was reasonable for the store to go dark for the limited period of time necessary to complete the alterations. In a case of one of the landlords, Vornado, Inc., a debtor presented testimony that Vornado already had eight Staples stores in various other locations and based on that, it found that Vornado's concerns about the alterations were disingenuous.

Sales and Percentage Rent

Staples had offered evidence of sales figures that impressively showed that Staples generated a profitable business. This obviously influenced the court in its conclusion that provisions preventing subdivision would constitute "de facto anti-assignment" provisions and that the payment of percentage rent would not be adversely affected by the proposed alterations.

The court also discussed the landlord's objection to changing the tenant mix. One of the landlords objected that during the changeover to the new tenancy, the store would have to close. Testimony indicated that it would take approximately six months for a Staples store to become operational. The court did not find this period of time so unreasonable that it would adversely affect the use or tenant mix within the meaning of the Bankruptcy Code; and in considering the plan to sublease the portion Staples would not use, the court agreed with Staples' argument that subleasing was the best way to lease that space as quickly as possible.

In addition, the court rejected the landlords' arguments about the loss of percentage rent. It emphasized that Rickel had not been paying any percentage rent because it had been liquidated and, therefore, there could not be any decline in that rent when Staples came in, particularly in light of the evidence of Staples' profitable operations.

The court assured Staples that if the landlord attempted to enforce any lease provision in an unreasonable manner, Staples would be free to return to the court for appropriate relief. It also gave the same rights to the landlord if Staples acted to "unreasonably disregard" lease provisions in attempting to sublet the properties or in violating provisions of Section 365 of the code.

Landlord's Perspective

The court did not give all of the victories to the debtor. While the landlord lost on practically every front, it did win some small battles. For example, the court made it clear that while it was going to permit the partitioning into smaller stores and subleasing, it was not supporting further partitioning or subleasing for future tenants. Also, the court accepted the landlord's arguments that the lessees' requirements for a minimum achievement of gross sales should be enforced against Staples. In addition, language in the decision indicated that if the use restrictions were needed to protect other shopping center tenants that had been granted exclusive uses, the court might have decided against the debtor and supported those restrictions.

It is noteworthy that even when tenants, other than the bankrupt tenant, are protected by exclusive use restrictions, those restrictions may fall to the bankruptcy axe, particularly when the courts are not dealing with a shopping center. For example, in one case, a tenant had a store at the street level of a three-story commercial building under a lease that prohibited the land-lord from renting space in the building to any other tenant who would sell only ladies' clothing. Martin Paint Stores, which went bankrupt, had operated a paint store in the same building under a lease that limited its use to selling hardware, paint, and related items. *In re Martin Paint Stores*, 199 B.R. 258 (Bankr. S.D.N.Y. 1996), *aff'd, Southern Boulevard, Inc. v. Martin Paint Stores*, 207 B.R. 57 (S.D.N.Y. 1997).

When the paint store filed for bankruptcy under Chapter 11, it auctioned off its leases and to the ladies' store's chagrin, the paint store lease was purchased and assigned to a competitor of the ladies' store that sold only ladies' clothing. The court concluded that the "congressional policy favoring assumption and assign-ment" outweighed the purported concerns of the objecting tenant and the landlord. In addition, it held that the objecting tenant did not even have legal "standing" to object to the assignment in a Chapter 11 proceeding. It is noteworthy that in *Martin Paint Stores* the court was not dealing with a "shopping center" within the protections of Section 365 of the Bankruptcy Code. If it were dealing with a shopping center, it is possible that the court would have reached the opposite conclusion. See Harris Ominsky, "Leases: Exclusive Use Clauses Shot Down in Bankruptcy," 30 *Mortgage and Real Estate Executives Report* 4 (March 1, 1997).

The *Rickel* case stands as a dramatic example of how the Bankruptcy Code can shift potential assets from one class of credi-tors to another. In that case, the $35.5 million paid for the lease assignments will benefit the general creditors. If the assignments had not been permitted, that value would have apparently been available to one category of creditors—the landlords. Without bankruptcy, presumably the restrictions would have thwarted the assignments and the landlords would have been able to receive the benefits of their leases by making their own deals with Staples or some other new tenant or tenants of their choice.

Tracking *Trak*

The U.S. Fourth Circuit Court of Appeals in contrast with the *Rickel* case, has taken a different position on a landlord's rights to enforce lease restrictions on use, alterations, and other operating issues in shopping center leases. The case of *In re Trak Auto Corp. v. West Town Center L.L.C.*, 367 F.3d 237 (4th Cir.

2004), will go down in legal history as a major victory for shopping center owners.

The circuit court, in what may be the first circuit court to decide these issues in favor of a landlord, reversed the district court decision, which had relied heavily on the *Rickel* case in rejecting a lease provision that restricted the tenant's use to a retail auto parts store. The lower court had permitted the debtor to assign the lease to a discount clothing store. In coming to that conclusion, the lower court had rejected the landlord's arguments that the change in use violated "tenant-mix" considerations under Bankruptcy Code Section 365(b)(3). In that case, the landlord's expert had testified that the percentage of clothing stores in the landlord's center already exceeded an optimal mix, and that committing the large floor space of the former auto parts store to clothing would harm the viability of the center. Specifically, the national average for clothing stores in retail centers was 10 percent, while the percentage following the assignment in this case would increase the clothing stores in the center to more than 20 percent.

In order to avoid the impact of Section 365(b)(3), the tenant argued that for various reasons the applicable property should not be considered part of a "shopping center," and therefore the special protections in that section should not apply. The tenant maintained that the "center" property is merely a cluster of buildings located next to or near each other owned by different property owners. The court sidestepped that issue by assuming for purposes of the decision that the store was located in a shopping center.

Instead, the lower court based its decision, as had *Rickel,* on Section 365(f)(1). While the use of restrictions does not specifically prohibit assignment, the court found that this particular use restriction was so narrow that it constituted a "de facto anti-assignment provision" prohibited by Section 365(f)(1). The court struck the offending use provisions of the lease and gave effect to the remaining non-offending provisions.

The lower court noted that the shopping center area was already saturated with auto stores and, therefore, no prospective assignee would be interested in the space for that use. Also, the court held that this particular restrictive use provision permitted only auto stores named "Trak Auto," effectively prohibiting assignment to anyone but the original, non-bankrupt tenant.

According to the lower court, even a more general restriction to an auto parts store was unenforceable because most of the arguable objectives could be achieved without that restriction. The protection of a controlled tenant mix was not very significant, given that the landlord did not control many other stores in the immediate area.

The court also rejected the argument that the center needed an auto parts store to draw male shoppers, because other stores in the center sold auto parts, and other tenants drew male shoppers without Trak Auto in that space. In addition, many leases in the center did not restrict space devoted to those in clothing sales, thus undercutting the landlord's claim that its overall plan relied on limiting the total amount of space or clothing stores in the center. Essentially, the landlord was not able to show that the "alleged tenant mix was part of the bargained-for-exchange of its lease and the leases of the other tenants."

In reversing the lower court, the circuit court of appeals effectively killed the debtor's deal to sell the lease for $80,000 to the apparel-store owner. The opinion emphasized the intent of Section 365(b)(3), which required "adequate assurance" that the assignment "is subject to all the provisions [of the lease], including (but not limited to) provisions such as a radius, location, use or exclusivity provision," and that it "will not disrupt any tenant mix or balance in such shopping center."

In reaching this conclusion, Judge Michael, speaking for the three-judge circuit court, analyzed the legislative history and concluded that the more specific provision that was intended to protect shopping center owners trumped the more general legislative provision intended to prohibit anti-assignment clauses.

Congressional Intent

In reviewing the legislative history, Judge Michael pointed out that the House Judiciary Committee was concerned about a shopping center being a "carefully planned enterprise" where "the tenant mix in a shopping center may be as important to the lessor as the actual promised rental payments, because certain mixes will attract higher patronage of the stores in the center."

Pursuant to congressional hearings in 1984, Congress concluded that the practice of avoiding use restrictions in bankruptcy was creating problems with tenant mix and adversely affecting shopping centers. This was being done to facilitate assignments by debtor-tenants. "These locations were losing their balance-of-merchandise drawing card which was a threat to overall sales revenues in the shopping center sector of the economy." Therefore,

Congress responded in 1984 by amending the shopping center provisions in the Bankruptcy Code.

As stated by the circuit court: "Among other things, Section 365(b)(3)(C) was amended to delete the word 'substantially' from the provision previously requiring that assignment of a shopping center lease must not 'breach substantially' certain restrictions. This section was also amended to provide that any assigned shopping center lease would remain subject to all of the provisions of the lease and not just the provisions of 'any other lease' relating to the center. Again, the amended provision that we interpret today provides: 'adequate assurance of future performance of a lease of real property in a shopping center includes adequate assurance ... that assumption or assignment of such lease is subject to all the provisions thereof, including (but not limited to) provisions such as a radius, location, use, or exclusivity provision.'"

It is noteworthy that on appeal the landlord sought only to enforce the use provision concerning the sale of automobile parts and accessories. It wisely did not attempt to enforce the restriction that the store could be used only as a "Trak Auto Store." That provision would have presented a more difficult issue for the landlord because it would have forbidden assignments even to other companies in the auto supply business. As Judge Michael pointed out, Senator Hatch, in explaining the 1984 amendment to Section 365(b)(3)(C), said that it was not intended to enforce requirements to operate under a specified trade name.

Leading Case

In criticizing the bankruptcy court's decision, the circuit court held: "This analysis overlooks the fact that West Town, the shopping center landlord, made the judgment that an auto parts retailer is important to a successful mix of stores in the center. And, in its lease with Trak Auto, West Town successfully negotiated to have the leased space dedicated to the sale of auto parts. West Town insists that this use restriction be honored by any assignee of Trak Auto and that is West Town's right under Section 365(b)(3)(C), regardless of market conditions. Section 365(b)(3)(C) simply does not allow the bankruptcy court or us to modify West Town's '*original* bargain with the debtor.'"

The *Trak Auto* case will undoubtedly become a leading case and will frequently be cited in future battles between bankrupt tenants and shopping center owners. Look at the earlier major bankruptcies involving such companies as Rickel Home Centers, Bradley Stores, Montgomery Ward, Service Merchandise, and K-mart. Many of the issues in those cases would have been decided differently by the Fourth Circuit Court of Appeals.

The message of *Trak* is clear. Bankruptcy courts cannot invalidate use restrictions merely because another use will be more valuable, or even if the court determines that the tenant has not been able to find anyone interested in occupying the space for the required use. It seems that the landlord's choice of tenant mix in a shopping center lease must be honored, whether or not it is a wise choice by the owner, or even whether it is presently feasible because of changes in market conditions.

Earlier Cases

In the past, courts have relied on the congressional intent of Section 365(b)(3) to give shopping center landlords protection from unwanted changes in an assigned lease. For example, the *Rickel* case distinguished *In re Joshua Slocum*, 922 F.2d 1081 (3d Cir. 1990), which sustained a minimum sales requirement that was averaged over a six-year period. Although the bankrupt tenant, Joshua Slocum, was not currently meeting the minimum sales requirement, the court of appeals held that the landlord had the right to hold future tenants to that provision even though the track record of Slocum showed that it was unlikely to ever meet the requirements, and it would be unlikely for any new store to be able to meet that average in the short period of time left to the six-year period. The court emphasized that Congress intended for courts to be very sensitive to the contractual rights of nondebtors when applying Section 365(b)(3).

Also, in *In re Federated Department Stores, Inc.*, 135 B.R. 941 (Bankr. S.D. Ohio 1991), the court refused to allow the assignment of a lease from a retail department store to a "specialty" department store marketed toward the cost-conscious customer. The court found that the assignment would disrupt the tenant mix by changing the image of the shopping center. The assignment would have also required subdivison of the space and left part of the space dark until another tenant was found. Lastly, the court stressed that it was especially reluctant to approve the assignment over the landlord's objections since the lease involved an anchor store, which necessarily has a major impact on the entire shopping center.

This case may be distinguishable from *Rickel* because in *Federated* the landlord provided very specific reasons why the opening of a "specialty" department store would frustrate the long-term goals of the shopping center to appeal to a more upscale clientele. Conversely, in the *Rickel* case, the court found that the new tenant would not hurt the tenant mix, and that the landlords' objections appeared "disingenuous." The court stated that in one Rickel's lease, rent payments were $2.22 per square foot, compared to a fair market value of $10.00 per square foot. So, the landlord stood to make a large profit if it could prevent the assignment of the lease.

On the other hand, some cases have approved assignments and rejected landlords' objections based on percentage rent, use restrictions, tenant mix, and average sales clauses. For example, in *In re Paul Harris Stores*, No. 91-2100-RLB-11 (Bankr. S.D. Ind. February 14, 1992), the court allowed the assignment of a women's apparel store to a maternity apparel store. The court found that the provision requiring the tenant to operate under the name "Paul Harris" was a de facto anti-assignment clause, and that the other lease restrictions would not be violated by the proposed assignment.

In light of the *Rickel* case, it appears that at least some of the anticipated protection for shopping center use clauses under Section 365(b)(3) has not been realized. See Bruce H. Roswick and Stephanie McEvily, *Use Clauses in Shopping Center Leases: The Effect of the Tenant's Bankruptcy*, 14 REAL ESTATE L.J., 3, 5, 20, 25 (1985). That article discusses how the Bankruptcy Act amendment in 1984 eliminated the requirement that an assignee would only have to conform substantially to the tenant mix.

"The most relevant provision requires that the terms of the lease, *especially the use clause*, be fully honored, so that the tenant mix is not disrupted at all. The unamended code, as noted herein, required only substantial compliance and, as discussed, some judges interpreted this language as permitting them to modify or disregard the provision entirely." Roswick and McEvily, above, at 25–26 (emphasis added).

Special Landlords' Lease Clauses

In evaluating the standard of "adequate assurance of future performance" under the code, the *Rickel* court compared the financial and business prospects of the liquidated Rickel Home Improvement Center to the successful Staples operation. In that context, a new prospect for a failed store will frequently appear to be a better alternative than the failed operation and the bankrupt company that was running it. But, suppose the lease specifically required an assignee to compare favorably to the financial status and prospects of the original tenant (Rickel) *at the start of the original tenant's lease.* Would such a provision have helped the landlord in the *Rickel* case?

While the court did not discuss this issue, one of the code's standards for adequate assurance in a shopping center is that the financial condition and operating performance of the proposed assignee (and its guarantors) must compare favorably with that of the debtor "as of the time the debtor became the lessee under the lease." 11 U.S.C. § 365(b)(3)(A).

See Joseph Chervin and Paul L. Bindler, "What Rights Does the Commercial Landlord Have When the Tenant Goes Bankrupt?" 2 *Practical Real Estate Lawyer* 51, 56, 61 (March 1986). As discussed above, when the court discusses issues of percentage rent, use restrictions, and tenant mix, it compares Staples to the status of Rickel at the time of bankruptcy. It does not mention this section of the code nor do any analysis comparing financial conditions and operating performances of Staples to Rickel at the time Rickel started its lease.

For years, attorneys have debated whether landlords could help themselves by spelling out in their leases what "adequate assurance of future performance" means. For example, the lease could require that certain standards must be met before permitting an assignment. These might require evidence of sufficient liquid assets to meet rent obligations, and evidence that the new tenant compares favorably in various ways to the original tenant at the start of the lease and has experience in running the type of store it is taking over in a comparable type shopping center. See Edward P. Tewkesbury & Joseph Vann, "Get Post-Bankruptcy Protection from Shopping Center Tenant," *Commercial Lease Law Insider* 1–5 (August 1992).

What Can Landlords Do?

Is there anything that landlords can do to help themselves?

Perhaps the landlord in *LaSalle* would have been helped had other store tenants negotiated for limitations on the number or total square footage of clothing store tenants in the center in the leases. Also, the landlords in these cases may have fared better if they had established a "master plan" for the anticipated tenant mix and the plan had been given to tenants before any leases were signed.

Another possibility is that landlords could require tenants to share "profits" with them if tenants assign or sublease. For example, if a tenant makes a net profit of $10 per square foot after accounting for all allowances, fix-up costs, and other expenses, the landlord and tenant will each receive $5 of that "profit." If the tenant receives a lump sum for the assignment, that will similarly be split.

While such a clause is not easy to draft, it is sometimes used in leases and may apply whether tenants are bankrupt or not. That kind of clause will give landlords some benefits from assigned leases where agreed rates are lower than the market rate. It is not clear whether those provisions will be enforceable in bankruptcy, but it will be more difficult for a debtor to argue that such a sharing clause is a "de facto anti-assignment provision." For example, if that provision had been part of the Rickel's leases, that would not have inhibited the assignment to Staples. It would just have resulted in less money for Rickel creditors.

Despite that logic, several courts have held that similar profit-sharing clauses were unenforceable in bankruptcy. *In re Jamesway Corp.*, 201 B.R. 73 (Bankr. S.D.N.Y. 1996) (50 percent to 60 percent of "profits" to landlord); *Robb v. Schindler*, 142 B.R. 589 (D. Mass. 1992) (80 percent of assignment proceeds to landlord); *In re Standor Jewelers West, Inc.*, 129 B.R. 200 (B.A.P. 9th Cir. Cal. 1991) (75 percent of the appreciation in value of the lease was to be paid to landlord).

In re Jamesway took the position that Section 365(f)(1) gave the court a right to invalidate lease provisions "restricting, conditioning or prohibiting debtor's right to assign. . . ." 201 B.R. at 78. That court stated: "The Landlords cannot, by artful drafting, thwart the fundamental bankruptcy policy allowing a debtor to realize maximum value from its assigned leases for the benefit of its estate and creditors." *Id.* at 79.

Some cases contain language leaving open the possibility that the courts might have ruled differently had the amounts payable by the debtor upon assignment been less. See, e.g., *Robb v. Schindler*, 142 B.R. 589 at 592 (D. Mass 1992); *In re Office Prods. of Am., Inc.*, 140 B.R. 407 at 412 (Bankr. W.D. Tex. 1992); *In re Howe*, 78 B.R. 226 at 230 (Bankr. D.S.D. 1987). None of these courts ruled that the contract provisions in question would be enforced if the debtors had to pay a "reasonable" percentage of the assignment proceeds. Nothing in Section 365(f)(1) supports the landlord's position.

In light of the *Rickel* and other cited cases, there can be no assurance to landlords that bankruptcy courts will protect any clause that may appear to provide additional income to the landlord upon assignment. However, the cited cases above involved leases that gave the lion's share of profits to the landlord and used formulas that could be interpreted as being unfair to the tenants.

It is possible that a clause such as the one at the end of this article (Model Lease Clause—Base Rent Increase) with a percentage sharing of less than 50 percent might have helped the landlord in these cases and may help landlords in future bankruptcy cases. It is also noteworthy that none of the above cases that bar profit sharing are appellate decisions.

In addition, while future courts may not heed the attempts of the parties to define the conditions for acceptable assignments, it is possible that spelling out those conditions may give courts some guidance in disputes when they are trying to determine what the parties intended at the time they entered the original leases. For example, it may help landlords to provide a clause such as the one at the end of this article (Model Lease Clause—Consent to Assignment). Since there can be no assurance that either of the attached clauses will be enforceable in bankruptcy, and it may be difficult to obtain tenants' agreement to these provisions, the author invites readers to comment on whether they have any additional solutions to propose to landlords in the face of the *Rickels* rule. These model lease clauses should be used only as checklists of provisions to consider where the landlord has a strong negotiating position with the tenant, and the desired provisions may vary significantly from deal to deal and from state to state. For example, in states that follow the "majority view" (see Howard E. Kane, "Dealing with Assignment, Use, and Operating Covenant Lease Clauses," 2 *The Practical Real Estate Lawyer* 45–54 (May 1986), courts may support a negotiated right of a landlord to withhold consent arbitrarily. In those states, the landlord may not want to use a clause requiring "reasonable" consent.

The *Rickel* and *Trak* decisions can be considered a primer on which lease restrictions will be enforced in bankruptcy. A conflict still exists in the courts between balancing the rights of a landlord to enforce negotiated lease provisions and the bankruptcy goals of maximizing the debtor's assets for all creditors.

Unless tenants in bankruptcy are able to inform prospective bidders for their leases that restrictions on activities such as use, alterations, and subleasing will not inhibit their plans for the space, they will be unlikely to offer maximum prices to the tenants.

Recent Bankruptcy Code Changes

A recent change in the Bankruptcy Code will affect shopping center lease assignments. This may be viewed as a chapter in the historic clash between legislative and judicial power. The amendment to Section 365(b)(3) of the Bankruptcy Code was included in the new bankruptcy reform act, which was signed into law on April 20, 2005, and was intended to become effective October 18, 2005 (the Bankruptcy Abuse Prevention and Consumer Protection Act of 2005, S.256).

The short amendment modifies subsection 365(f)(1), which invalidates so-called "anti-assignment provisions." It attempts to clarify that the shopping center protective provisions in Section 365(b) are exceptions to the anti-assignment section. Based on the *Trak Auto* case and earlier legislative history, many will agree that this is exactly what Congress intended with the shopping center protective provision passed in 1984. However, in attempts to help creditors of bankruptcy estates, bankruptcy judges generally eroded that congressional intent.

Now Congress has spoken again and seems to say, in effect, "This time we really mean it." It remains to be seen whether the courts will now follow the reasoning of *Trak Auto*, and interpret these recent congressional changes in that way. For example, one issue that is still not clear is whether requiring a tenant to use a specific trade name in a shopping center store will now be enforced on assignees. If that happens, a use restriction that requires a landlord's consent to change the store's identification would effectively give landlords control over most attempted assignments of those type leases, even in bankruptcy.

MODEL LEASE CLAUSE

Consent to Assignment[1]

1. **Conditions.** After opening of the Premises for business with the public, Landlord agrees not to withhold its consent unreasonably to an assignment of this Lease or a subletting of the entire Premises by Tenant provided that:

    (a) **Information on Assignee or Subtenant.** At least thirty (30) days before the proposed effective date of the assignment or subletting Landlord receives for approval a copy of a fully executed assignment or sublease together with (1) reasonably detailed information as to the character, reputation, and business experience of the proposed assignee or subtenant, including but not limited to experience in retail shopping centers of comparable size to the Center and in the sale of merchandise and services permitted under the Lease; and (2) financial information and bank references on the proposed assignee or subtenant (including, at Tenant's expense, a current Dun & Bradstreet report and a financial statement certified as being true and correct by the chief financial executive of the proposed assignee or subtenant);

    (b) **Tenant Not in Breach or Default.** No breach or default on Tenant's part exists at the time of the consent request and at the effective assignment or subletting date;

    (c) **Terms of Lease Govern.** Any assignment or subletting will be upon and subject to all terms and conditions of this Lease, including those regarding the permitted use of the Premises as specified in Article ___ hereof;

    (d) **Assumption; Attornment.** Any assignment must specifically state that the assignee assumes and agrees to be bound by all terms and conditions of this Lease,

---

1.   This provision is adapted with permission by Brownstone Publishers, Inc. (1-800-643-8095; http://www.brownstone.com) from Vol. 2, *The Commercial Law Lease Insider's Best Commercial Lease Clauses*, Sublet/Assignment, 46–47 (2000).

and any sublease must specifically state that at Landlord's election the subtenant will attorn to Landlord and recognize Landlord as Tenant's successor under the sublease for the balance of the sublease term if this Lease is surrendered by Tenant or terminated by reason of Tenant's default;

(e) Processing Fee. Upon request and as additional rent Tenant will pay to Landlord a processing fee of $1,000, or such greater amount as may be reasonable under the circumstances, for document review and/or preparation in connection with the proposed transaction;

(f) Center's Existing Tenants, Occupants, and Agreements. No assignment or subletting will be to a then-existing tenant or occupant of the Center or its subtenant or assignee or an Affiliate of any of those parties; nor violate or conflict with the rights of any such party, or any other party who has rights under an agreement with Owner;

(g) Rental Rate. No assignment or subletting will be for a lesser rental rate than is being charged by Landlord for comparable space in the Center;

(h) Additional Security. Upon request the assignee (in the case of a proposed assignment) or Tenant (in the case of a proposed subletting) will increase the original security deposit hereunder to such amount as Landlord may require (or if no security was initially deposited hereunder, will post with Landlord such security as Landlord may require);

(i) Approval by Mortgagee. The assignment or subletting must first be approved in writing by any mortgagee of Landlord having the right of approval thereof;

(j) Affiliate. For purposes hereof, an Affiliate means a corporation or other business entity that directly or indirectly controls, is controlled by, or is under common control with such occupant; and

(k) Alterations. Such subtenant or assignee must occupy the space of the demised premises in full and shall not divide the premises into separate spaces or separate uses or permit any alterations that will cause structural changes, exterior changes, partitioning, changes in customers' pedestrian-traffic patterns, or any exits or entrances other than shown on the original approved plans.

2. **Denial of Consent Not Unreasonable**. Without limiting Landlord's rights, it is agreed that Landlord will not be unreasonable if it does not approve any assignee or sub-tenant that is likely to:

(a) perform governmental or quasi-governmental functions; or

(b) operate any business that in Landlord's opinion is unsuitable for the then tenant mix of the Center and will not benefit all Tenants of the Center and enhance the image, reputation, and profitability of the Center, or will not generate satisfactory Percentage Rent.

MODEL LEASE CLAUSE

Base Rent Increase[2]

1. **Limited Base Rent Adjustment.** Without limitation on the restrictions on transfers contained herein, in the event of a Transfer, the monthly Base Rent (as such term is defined in Paragraph [*Insert # of lease paragraph defining Base Rent*] under this lease) shall be subject to a limited increase computed in the following manner:
   (i) Owner shall determine the "Adjusted Rate" for the Subject Space;
   (ii) Owner shall determine the "Lease Rate" for the initial or extension or renewal term of this Lease then in effect;
   (iii) Owner shall subtract the Lease Rate from the Adjusted Rate (the difference herein referred to as the "Rate Difference");
   (iv) Owner shall multiply the Rate Difference by [*Insert negotiated percentage*] % (the product of such computation herein referred to as the "Rate Adjustment Factor"); and
   (v) The monthly Base Rent under this lease shall be increased by an amount equal to the Rate Adjustment Factor multiplied by the number of square feet contained in the Premises (or in the Subject Space), if the transfer involves a sublease of less than the whole Premises) (the "Base Rent Adjustment").

2. **Term of Base Rent Adjustment.** The Base Rent Adjustment shall commence on the effective date of the Transfer and continue for the term of the Lease (and any extensions and renewals thereof).

3. **"Adjusted Rate."** "Adjusted Rate" shall mean the average effective rate of rent on a per square foot per month basis received by Tenant as a result of any subletting, assignment, or license except for the following: (a) payments

---

2. This provision is adapted with permission by Brownstone Publishers, Inc. (1-800-643-8095; http://www.brownstone.com) from the monthly newsletter, *The Commercial Lease Law Insider,* 4–5 (March 1991).

attributable to the Amortization of the Tenant Work paid for by Tenant; (b) payments attributable to the Amortization of leasehold improvements made to the sublet or assigned portion of the premises by Tenant for Sub-tenant or Assignee; and (c) other reasonable expenses incident to the subletting or assignment, including standard leasing commissions.

For this purpose, "Rent" shall include any sums or other economic consideration received by Tenant, directly or indirectly, as a result of the subletting, assignment, or license, whether designated as rentals under the sublease or otherwise (prorated to reflect obligations allocable to that portion of the premises subject to such sublease or assignment); including but not limited to any payments made for, or attributable to, the sale or assignment of the leasehold improvements and fixtures, and the value of any other property rights or other consideration received in lieu of such payments. Payments or other consideration received in connection with a transfer shall be deemed to be rent when recovered.

4. **"Lease Rate."** Means the average effective rate of Base Rent on a per square foot per month basis for the initial or extension or renewal term of this Lease then in effect (with any free rent, fixed increases, tenant improvement costs, or other economic concessions provided by the Owner with respect to such initial or extension or renewal term averaged over such term).

5. **"Amortization."** For purposes of Paragraph 3, "Amortization" shall be calculated by dividing (a) the cost of the applicable Tenant Work and leasehold improvements by (b) the number of months in the term of the sublessee's sublease (without options), or the number of months remaining in the lease assumed by the assignee. Such costs shall be certified by owner by Tenant's independent certified public accountant (at Tenant's expense).

42 BANKRUPT LANDLORD'S SALE TERMINATES LEASES

We frequently see cases involving bankrupt tenants and their rights to terminate leases. Cases that involve the effect of a landlord's bankruptcy on tenants' rights are less common.

Section 365(h) of the Bankruptcy Code, 11 U.S.C. § 365(h), deals with that issue by limiting the landlord's power to reject the lease, thus protecting the tenant against eviction. The section provides that "the lessee may retain its rights under such lease . . . that are in or appurtenant to the real property for the balance of the term of such lease and for any renewal or extension of such rights to the extent that such rights are enforceable under applicable non-bankruptcy law." Section 365(h)(1)(A)(ii). This provision attempts to strike a balance between the rights of the debtor-landlord and its tenant. The tenant retains the right to possess the property for the remainder of the bargained-for term, while the debtor-landlord is free to reject other burdensome lease obligations, for example, the duty to provide services to the tenant.

First Impression

The case of *Precision Industries v. Qualitech,* 327 F.3d 537 (7th Cir. 2003), dealt with whether a bankrupt landlord can overcome tenant protection against lease rejection by selling the property free and clear of the tenant's lease interest. Seventh Circuit Court of Appeals' Judge Rovner decided that issue in what she called a case of "first impression" at the circuit court level.

In reaching the decision, Judge Rovner attempted to reconcile Bankruptcy Code Section 365(h) tenant-protection provisions with another code section that permits the sale of the landlord's real estate "free and clear of any interest." Section 363(f).

244

The court pointed out that the property may be sold free and clear only if one of the following conditions applies:

(1) applicable nonbankruptcy law permits the sale of such property free and clear of such interest;

(2) such entity consents;

(3) such interest is a lien and the price at which such property is to be sold is greater than the aggregate value of all liens on such property;

(4) such interest is in bona fide dispute; or

(5) such entity could be compelled, in a legal or equitable proceeding, to accept a money satisfaction of such interest.

11 U.S.C. § 363(f). Section 363 also provides that "on request of an entity that has an interest in property ... proposed to be ... sold ... by the trustee, the court, with or without a hearing, shall prohibit or condition such ... sale ... as is necessary to provide adequate protection of such interest." 11 U.S.C. § 363(e).

Sale Order

In *Precision Industries,* the debtor (Qualitech) owned and operated a steel mill in Indiana. The tenant (Precision) constructed a supply warehouse at the property for the sole purpose of providing supply services for Qualitech. In 1998 Precision entered into a 10-year supply agreement with Qualitech. If a termination or default occurred under either agreement prior to expiration, Precision had the right to remove all improvements and fixtures. Otherwise, Qualitech could buy the improvements and fixtures for $1.00 at the end of the term.

Qualitech filed its Chapter 11 bankruptcy petition on March 22, 1999, and on June 30, 1999, sold substantially all of its assets at auction pursuant to the sale order "free and clear of all liens, claims, encumbrances and interest" under the above-quoted Section 363(f) of the Bankruptcy Code. The sale order approved the sale to a group of pre-petition secured lenders for $180 million.

Precision, which had proper notice of the sale, did not object. The purchasers then transferred their interests in the property to a new entity that assumed the rights of the purchaser under the sale order and took title to the property. The sale order also provided that the purchaser retained the debtors' right to assume and assign executory contracts pursuant to Section 365 of the Bankruptcy Code.

Negotiations for assumption of the lease proved to be unsuccessful. The result, according to the Seventh Circuit, was that "Precision's lease and supply agreement were de facto rejected." By December 3, 1999, Precision had vacated and padlocked the warehouse on the property and shortly thereafter, the purchaser changed the locks on the building without Precision's knowledge or approval.

Reversals

That's when Precision filed suit, claiming that its possessory interest in the leased property, protected under Section 365(h), survived the bankruptcy sale. The bankruptcy court disagreed, and held that because Precision's lease was an "interest" under the sale order, the purchaser had obtained title to the property "free and clear" of the lease under Section 363(f).

The district court reversed, ruling that the terms of Section 365(h) prevailed over those of Section 363(f). It reasoned that no statutory basis existed for allowing the debtor-landlord to sell its property and terminate the underlying lease. That would limit the tenant's post-rejection rights solely to cases where the debtor-landlord retained title and possession of the property.

The Seventh Circuit court reversed the holding of the district court. It stated that sale orders are final, appealable orders, and Precision never objected to the sale order. Once the appeal period expired, res judicata precluded a subsequent lawsuit to contest the order. The court then examined the meaning of "interest" in Section 363(f). Although the term is not defined in the Bankruptcy Code, the court cited supporting case law that a tenant's leasehold estate was an "interest" under that section.

The court also noted that the parties never disputed whether the landlord had met one of the five statutory conditions (listed above) required to sell free and clear of an interest. Therefore, the court assumed that a sale of the property free and clear of Precision's leasehold interest was permissible under Section 363(f).

Bankruptcy Bombshell

The court's analyses on these threshold issues is revealing. But the decision's most significant part is the holding that Section 365(h), which protects the rights of a tenant when a landlord rejects a lease, did not trump the sale of the real estate "free and clear" of the lease. In reaching this conclusion, the court reversed the district court and confirmed the ability of bankrupt landlords to terminate property leases. The decision can be viewed as a bankruptcy bombshell that will reverberate in legal circles around the country. Tenants may now be left with only a claim for damages that may or may not have priority against the sale proceeds, potentially frustrating tenants' lease expectations. Also, while the case did not involve a leasehold lender, the decision will cause anxiety among leasehold lenders who normally rely on the security of leases as collateral for their loans.

Judge Rovner began her decision by pointing out that the court was asked to reconcile two distinct provisions of the Bankruptcy Code in apparent conflict. She decided the case in favor of the "free-and-clear" provision for three reasons.

First, the code provides no cross-reference from one section to the other indicating that the broad right to sell real estate free of any interest is subordinate to the protections that Section 365(h) accords to tenants. "The omission suggests that Congress did not intend for the latter section to limit the former."

Second, the court stated that "the plain language in Section 365(h)(1)(A) suggests that it has limited scope. By its own terms, that subsection applies 'if the trustee [or debtor-in-possession] *rejects* an unexpired lease of real property.'" (Emphasis added.)

Judge Rovner pointed out that what initially occurred was a sale of the property that Precision was leasing rather than a "rejection" of its lease. However, the judge granted that if the sale order operated to extinguish Precision's right to possess the property, as the court concluded, then the effect of the sale might be understood as the "equivalent of a repudiation of Precision's lease."

Despite this "repudiation," the court found that "nothing in the express terms of Section 365(h) suggests that it applies to any and all events that threaten the lessee's possessory rights. Section 365(h) instead focuses on a specific type of event—the rejection of an executory contract by the trustee or a debtor-in-possession—and spells out the rights of parties affected by that event. It says nothing at all about sales of estate property that are the province of Section 363. The two statutory provisions thus apply to distinct sets of circumstances."

Third, she pointed out that Section 363 provides for a mechanism to protect the rights of parties whose interests may be adversely affected by the sale of estate property. Section 363(e)(3) directs the bankruptcy court, on the request of an entity that has an interest in the property to be sold, "to prohibit or condition such ... sale ... as is necessary to provide adequate protection of such interest." Therefore, a tenant of a property being sold has the right to insist that its interest be protected. This does not guarantee that tenants can continue in possession of the property, but it does in the alternative require that the tenant be compensated for the leasehold value "typically from the proceeds of the sale."

In summary, the court noted that "the two statutory provisions can be construed in a way that does not disable Section 363(f) vis a vis leasehold interests." Where estate property under lease is to be sold, Section 363(f) permits the sale to occur free of a tenant's possessory interest, provided that the tenant "upon request" is granted adequate protection for its interest. Where the property is not sold and the debtor remains in possession, but chooses to reject the lease, Section 365(h) comes into play and the tenant retains the right to possess the property.

Problems for Tenants

One of the problems with the circuit court's conclusion that the two statutory provisions apply to "distinct sets of circumstances" is that once you decide that Section 363(f) applies over Section 365(h) and the tenant's lease is terminated, a sale has the same effect on the lease as a rejection. The termination by sale is just not labeled a "rejection," and therefore the tenant's remedies will differ.

One of the questions raised by the case, but not answered in the decision, is how the tenant will be compensated for the loss of its lease. Liens and claims that are cut off in a Section 363(f) sale attach to the proceeds of a sale. But it is not clear whether the tenant will receive any of the proceeds because other secured creditors may be trying to reach the same proceeds. Also, in a multi-parcel sale, the tenant will find segregating that portion of the whole purchase price applicable to the parcel it leased difficult.

In addition, calculating damages on a terminated lease will not be easy. The American Land Title Association has struggled with this problem in trying to define the damages recoverable under leasehold title insurance. What are the damages suffered by a tenant who loses a 20-year lease at a "bargain rental" that an expert determines is at a dollar a square foot less than a fair market rental rate? Will the lost value of improvements be calculated on a depreciated basis? Will moving and relocation damages be included? How will various renewal rights and lease options be evaluated? Will "goodwill" be included? How about lost subleases? Also, the tenant may have to compete with a leasehold-mortgage holder whose claims may include future interest and prepayment premiums.

Major office buildings and shopping centers throughout the country have been built by tenants on leasehold interests. Think of all of the long-term leases that spawned high-rise buildings developed along New York's Park Avenue and Lexington Avenue over former Penn Central Railroad tracks. The master tenants in these transactions have subleased building space to large companies, which in some cases have sub-subleased space to many other occupants. What will happen to all of these leases and subleases if a bankrupt landowner goes into bankruptcy and sells free and clear of the leases?

Many mortgage lenders now demand better protection against borrowers' bankruptcies by requiring borrowers to establish so-called "bankruptcy-remote" entities. These entities will own only the secured property, and by their structure theoretically will be unable to incur outside debt. This is one way to ward off the likelihood of bankruptcy.

In light of the *Precision* decision, perhaps prospective long-term tenants will want to require bankruptcy-remote landlords.

Lessons

A couple of lessons emerge from the *Precision Industries* case on possible ways to avoid these "free-and-clear" sales under Section 363(f). First, when a tenant receives notice that "interests" in the property are going to be terminated at the proposed sale, the tenant should not wait to assert its rights to "prohibit or condition" the sale "as is necessary to provide adequate protection" of its interest. The tenant should immediately assert these rights even if the proposed sale order only refers to "liens, claims, encumbrances, and interests" in a general way and does not specifically mention the tenant's lease. Possibly Precision didn't comprehend the full significance of the free-and-clear notice.

Also, a tenant should consider challenging whether Section 363(f) applies to its lease under any of the five statutory conditions. In *Precision Industries* the court didn't have to analyze those conditions because the tenant did not object on those grounds. But based on the facts set forth in the opinion, whether any of those conditions would have applied to the Precision lease is not clear. If Precision had challenged, would the court have found that criterion one was met—applicable non-bankruptcy law would have permitted a sale free and clear of the lease? Could the debtors have argued that under state law either a senior lien creditor, or a municipality owed real estate taxes, could have foreclosed against the property and sold it free and clear of the lease? Or would condition five have been met—that the tenant could have been compelled in a legal or equitable proceeding to accept a money satisfaction for its lease?

Precision Industries stands as an important case on what could happen to a tenant when its landlord goes belly-up. Lawyers and bankruptcy experts will probably cite it as a leading precedent in future cases, and undoubtedly its implications will stir debate and commentary in legal periodicals, seminars, and workshops.

43 BARRATRY AND CHAMPERTY BAR CONTINGENT FEE FOR COLLECTIONS

Since law school, you may have forgotten the exact meaning of "barratry" and "champerty." If so, *Accrued Financial Services, Inc. v. Prime Retail, Inc.*, 298 F.3d 291 (4th Cir. 2002), which invalidated tenant audit contracts between tenants and their consultant to help the tenants collect overcharges made under their leases, will refresh your memory.

Control Over Litigation

The two-judge majority of the court invalidated the audit contracts because they had authorized the auditor, Accrued Financial Services (AFS), to retain 40 or 50 percent of any discrepancy discovered and collected, and because the auditor had taken an assignment of all legal claims that the tenant had against the landlords and had taken "control over any litigation that might ensue."

The auditor contended that it had performed audits and discovered that the landlords had overbilled the tenants over a period of time for what would likely result in an aggregate of "millions of dollars." In addition, it contended that these overcharges could not be explained as mere errors or even aggressive billing practices. The errors were systematic and pervasive. As a result, the auditor persuaded additional tenants to enter into similar contractual arrangements and thereby launched a larger attack against the landlord than it originally contemplated.

Rather than negotiate with the plaintiff, the landlord filed an action seeking a declaratory judgment that the plaintiff lacked standing to assert the claims, and also moved to dismiss them because the assignments were champertous and void as a matter of public policy under Maryland law. The assignments provided that California law should govern, but the opinion stated that it would have that choice only to the extent that the chosen law did not violate a fundamental public policy of the forum state, which was Maryland.

The court supported the landlord's defense because the auditor's interest in the litigation was "solely to collect fees that its audits and [their] litigation would generate." The provisions of the agreement that disturbed the court were the contingent fee percentage, the requirement that if the tenant should want to withdraw, the auditor could proceed without the tenant, and the provision stating that if the tenant refused to cooperate, it would still be obligated to pay the fee that would otherwise have been earned if litigation had been successful.

In light of this type of a contract, the court held: "Because we see these broad assignments as nothing more than arrangements through which to intermeddle and stir up litigation for the purpose of making a profit, we conclude that they violate Maryland's strong public policy against stirring up litigation and are therefore void and unenforceable in Maryland." *Id.* at 298.

Common Law

The court tracked the history of barratry, maintenance, and champerty by explaining that at first the courts recognized these concepts that were part of the early common law. Over time, the early definitions proved too broad and interfered with emerging commercial conditions, the recognition of assignments in general, and the rise of attorney representation under contingent fee contracts. But despite the narrowing of definitions, Maryland continues to reserve a policy against some of the originally prohibited conduct. In fact, the court cited the Maryland criminal statute that outlaws barratry as follows: "Without an existing relationship or interest in an issue[,] a person may not, for personal gain, solicit another person to sue or to retain a lawyer to represent the other person in a lawsuit." *Id.* at 299.

The court concluded that the applicable contracts were violations of the law and public policy because the tenants' rights were assigned not in exchange for an existing value, but for future fees to be determined by decisions and value judgments controlled by the consultant, who had no interest in the underlying claims. "As such, AFS was given the power to mine lawsuits, promote them, and profit off of them without regard to the interests and desires of the injured party." *Id.*

The court rejected AFS's position that the real purpose of the contract was to provide consulting services within its expertise. In response, the court stated that it did not intend by this decision to undermine or devalue the claims that AFS had discovered and that the tenants may have. Rather, the decision stated that if those claims are viable, AFS can continue that business without the objectionable assignments, and there should be no barrier for the tenants to prosecute claims with the assistance of AFS.

Dissent

Judge Michael wrote a 12-page dissent that took the position that the California law provision in the contract should have been applied, and that these types of assignments are legal in California, and should not be against Maryland public policy. He pointed out that for Maryland to reject another state's law, Maryland must have a strong public policy against enforcing that state's law. He raised the question about how there could be a strong Maryland public policy when barratry and champerty are rules that are "tending to become obsolete." He pointed out that Maryland has not used these common-law doctrines to invalidate any contract in the last 100 years. He stated:

> ... Accordingly, no strong public policy against the California law allowing the assignments in this case can be gleaned from whatever, if anything, might remain of the common law doctrines of maintenance, champerty, and barratry in Maryland.

Id. at 303.

He disagreed with the majority interpretation that AFS's actions violated the criminal code section quoted earlier, because AFS was not pushing or soliciting litigation here. Its first and most important task under the agreements and assignments was to conduct audits, audits that the tenants had the right to pursue under their leases. Litigation was only available as a last resort and AFS had to pursue litigation in only less than 10 percent of the cases it handled.

The dissent pointed out that even 150 years ago the law of champerty did not outlaw every effort by a person to encourage or assist another in pursuing litigation. That concept was recognized by a Chief Baron of the Court of Exchequer who said in an 1843 case, "[I]f a man were to seek a poor person in the street oppressed and abused, and without the means of obtaining redress, and furnished him with money and employed an attorney to obtain redress for his wrongs, it would require a very strong argument to convince me that [that] man could be said to be stirring up litigation and strife." *Id.* at 306. In addition, Judge Michael pointed out that today, "For example, contingent fees are legal ... lawyers are allowed to advertise ... choses-in-action may be assigned ... and class actions are permitted ... ." *Id.* (citations omitted). To the extent that the common law is still viable, it would be aimed only at the stirring up of a certain kind of litigation, specifically, litigation that is groundless, vexatious, or multitudinous. In this case, AFS was making a serious claim, based on a partial audit, that the landlord overcharged its tenants by aggressive billing or fraud in amounts that could total millions of dollars. He further stated, "The majority's decision thus hurts the tenants, not just AFS. The decision benefits the mall owners and managers, who could be getting away with the overcharging and fraud." *Id.* at 307.

Contingent Fees

It is clear that even in Maryland and states that still have laws barring barratry and champerty, contingent fee arrangements are not in themselves improper. The issues that seem to have led to the majority's decision in *Accrued Financial Services, Inc.* were the complete assignment of the tenants' rights to AFS and the strong language in those assignments that required the tenants to give up control over their cases. Also, while this does not appear to be stated as a reason for the decision, the court may have been bothered by the fact that after discovering the discrepancies for one tenant, AFS then solicited and signed up an additional 16 tenants to enter into similar contingent fee arrangements.

While barratry and champerty may still be alive in certain states, a reading of the Fourth Circuit decision leads to the conclusion that contingent fee arrangements that don't overreach should be enforceable even in those states.

PART III

Buying and Selling

Can parties enforce an agreement of sale that does not set a purchase price, but rather provides for the sale at fair-market value?

The prevailing view is that "fair market" is a sufficiently objective standard to enforce. (See *Northup v. Hushard*, 514 N.Y.S.2d 304 (N.Y. App. Div. 1987).) But sellers, buyers, and attorneys who rely on a fair-market determination may be asking for trouble.

In *Latour v. Davis*, PICS No. 00-0500-23-00 (CP Columbia County, PA, March 10, 2000), a buyer sought to appoint an appraiser and enforce a real estate agreement of sale. The reluctant seller filed for summary judgment on the pleadings, charging that the agreement was not enforceable because there was no specified purchase price.

The court quoted the disputed language of the agreement:

> Latour and/or Davis will retain *TBA* (sic) [named appraiser] to appraise the real property to determine its then fair market value, specifically, including goodwill associated with the operation of a bed and breakfast business on the real property, using the same methodology used to determine the purchase price when Latour and Davis purchased the property. If *TBA* (sic) [appraiser], is unable to appraise the real property for any reason, Latour and Davis will reasonably agree on a substitute appraiser to appraise the property using the same methodology. Latour and Davis will each pay 50% of the appraisal fee.

The expressed concept is simple: merely engage an appraiser to tell the parties what the bed-and-breakfast business is worth, including its goodwill. The legal issues this generated are a little more complex.

The seller argues that the contract is "indefinite, uncertain and incomplete" since the parties never agreed on a price or an appraiser. The buyer argues that designating the appraiser was not essential to the creation of an enforceable contract and that fair-market value is sufficiently certain to bind parties under Pennsylvania law.

Reasonable Certainty

In holding that the contract was enforceable, the court relies on what might be characterized as two slightly different formulations of the law. One group of appellate cases emphasizes the concept that equity will not decree specific performance of a contract unless its terms are "clear and capable of ascertainment from the instrument." *Kelly v. Rhodes*, 421 A.2d 299, 301 (Pa. Super. 1980); *Schmidt v. Steinacker*, 67 A.2d 664, 665 (Pa. Super. 1949); citing *Hammer & Dauler v. McEldowney*, 46 Pa. 334 (1863).

The other line of cited cases specifies that the intention of the parties must be determined with a "reasonable degree of certainty." See *Seiss v. McClintic-Marshall Corp.*, 188 A. 109 (Pa. 1936); *Kirk v. Brentwood Manor Homes, Inc.*, 159 A.2d 48 (Pa. Super. 1960).

While these standards are close, there could be a difference between something that must be "clear," and something that must be determined with only a "reasonable degree of certainty."

The court said that where a price is to be measured by the "fair market" or "reasonable" value of the property, courts have generally held that the price is sufficiently certain to make a real estate agreement enforceable. *Zvonik v. Zvonik*, 435 A.2d 1236, 1243 (Pa. Super. 1981). The court points out that courts will, if possible, construe a contract to carry out the reasonable intention of the parties.

Also, even though no appraiser was named in the agreement, it is still valid. While the court declined to designate an appraiser, it was willing to set the purchase price and enforce specific performance of the agreement."

Market Rental Rate

In some states an option to renew a lease at the "then existing market rental rate for comparable shopping centers" is too vague to be enforceable. Even when that formula is used as part of the stated standard for calculating rent, the vagueness may taint the whole option so that the tenant loses its right to renew the lease. In the case of *AMB Property, L.P. v. MTS, Inc.,* 551 S.E.2d 102 (Ga. App. 2001), *recon. denied* (July 11, 2001), a Georgia court of appeals ruled that when one part of an "either-or" formula is too vague, the entire provision is void.

MTS, Inc. had leased space for 10 years and 5 months, with a five-year renewal option. The option provided that the rent for the renewal period "shall be the greater of (a) base rent for the last year of the original term; or (b) the then existing market rental rate for comparable shopping centers." When the tenant exercised the renewal option, the landlord set the rent at $29.50 per square foot, claiming that the amount was comparable to rent charged in other shopping centers. The tenant objected and requested a declaratory judgment to have the "market-rental-rate" language severed, thus setting the renewal rent on the rent for the last year of the original term as set forth in the first part of the rental formula.

The trial court supported the tenant's argument that the second part of the renewal option was unenforceable because it was too vague. Therefore, the court concluded that the alternative basis for the rent would apply—the rent at the end of the initial term.

The landlord appealed. The court of appeals reversed, holding that although alternative (b) of the renewal option was unenforceable, it was an integral part of the lease agreement and a formula for determining the rent. The words "the greater of" in the renewal option provision shows an intent that the pricing be used as an integrated formula requiring that two components be compared. The court held that removing one of the two components results in a pricing provision radically different from the language agreed to by the parties and, therefore, no renewal was available to the tenant.

The court stated:

> ... Rather than being assured that the renewal rental rate would not be less than the current market rental rate, the landlords under the modified provision are required to accept a rate applicable to the original term. Although they originally negotiated that the last year's rental rate would be the floor or minimum rent for the renewal, under the trial court's order, that has now suddenly become the ceiling also.

AMB Property at 104.

Unintended Consequences

The *AMB Property* decision emphasizes the rule of unintended consequences. From the landlord's perspective, by insisting on a renewal option with a market-rent-rate formula alternative, the landlord inadvertently provided the tenant with a renewal option that was not even enforceable.

One could test the implications of the decision by looking at it from the perspective of a devious landlord who wants to avoid being stuck with renewal options. The devious landlord simply could negotiate an option with a vague formula. By that strategy, the landlord could sign up a 10-year tenant without the burden of an unwanted option. In effect, the formula gives the landlord a veto over the renewal option.

From the tenant's perspective, the tenant who desires to renew based on the rent for the last year of the original term, as set forth in the (a) section of the formula, literally could be "betting the store" by not accepting the landlord's computation of "market rental" under the (b) portion of the formula. By that tactic, the tenant in *AMB Property* lost the right to renew on any terms.

Suppose a tenant negotiates an alternative renewal rent in its favor. For example, a tenant negotiates a renewal rate for a set rental amount or, in the alternative, the "then existing market rental rate, if that is less." Unlike the landlord's formula in *AMB Property,* this formula would be to the tenant's advantage because the rent would be based on the lower of two alternatives, rather than on the "greater of" those alternatives. But based on the reasoning of the *AMB Property* case, the formula still would be considered vague and unenforceable. Therefore, by pushing for a better renewal rent, the tenant would have negotiated itself out of any enforceable renewal option.

That only goes to illustrate the old expression, "Be careful about what you wish for, because your wish may come true."

Practical Issues

Even a superficial reading of these cases leads to the conclusion that parties are asking for trouble when they fail to agree on a specific purchase price and instead, must rely on others to set the price at "fair market value" or some similar standard. That's particularly true where, as in *Latour,* the parties somehow neglected to designate the appraiser they wanted.

Even when the agreement provides a clear method of choosing an appraiser, that is not the best way to establish a purchase price. Books are written about sometimes conflicting appraisal theories, particularly when the goodwill of a going business must be determined.

The *Latour* case involved the sale of a bed-and-breakfast business. Much of the value in these businesses depends on how well the specific owners serve their guests over a period of time. In determining the value of goodwill, should an appraiser assume that the present operators will continue in the business? Will the chef remain, and for how long? How much personality and business experience do the new owners possess, and should that be taken into account?

Despite these issues, the *Latour* case seems to be in accord with the prevailing view throughout the country that "fair market" is a sufficiently objective standard to enforce. (See *Northup v. Hushard,* 514 N.Y.S.2d 304 (N.Y. App. Div. 1987).) However, if those types of clauses must be used, it is recommended that the drafter flesh in the rules to guide the appraisers or courts who will later have to set the price. At a minimum, these clauses should set standards for the choice of the appraiser, the timing issues, notices, penalties for failure to cooperate in designating the appraiser, and methods of appraisal that should be used. Also, they should specify rules for arbitrating the issues if the parties wind up in a dispute, as they frequently do.

45   LETTERS OF INTENT

. . . the known certaintie of the law is the saftie of all.
—*Sir Edward Cooke*

Preliminary Agreements

Letters of interest or letters of intent may be defined as preliminary agreements, usually arrived at during complex negotiations, that state proposed terms for a final contract. Depending on the circumstances, the parties may or may not intend such terms to be binding.

Letters of intent serve various purposes. Sometimes a client will need a document to present to a potential creditor or investor, or board of directors, even though no final agreement has been reached. Letters of intent also help facilitate complex transactions by spelling out preliminary agreements and allowing negotiators to focus on key open terms. They may assure a property is taken off the market while the parties investigate the condition of the property, income, expenses, applicable documents, and other facts.

Courts have found letters of intent to be binding in certain cases. Specifically, cases have used three theories to find letters binding:

- a binding contractual obligation to carry out the established terms of the agreement;
- an obligation to bargain in good faith on open terms; and
- an obligation based on detrimental reliance or "promissory estoppel."

Binding Contractual Obligations.   Courts have long held that parties are bound by a preliminary agreement if they intend to be bound by the agreement and viewed the signing of a later formal contract as merely a "convenient memorial." Arthur L. Corbin, *Corbin on Contracts* § 30 (1963). *Restatement (Second) of Contracts*

§ 27 (1981); *Mississippi & Dominion S.S. Co. v. Swift*, 29 A. 1063 (Me. 1894).

A Massachusetts case required the seller to go through with a sale even though the form was labeled an "Offer" and had a typewritten insertion that stated it was "Subject to a Purchase and Sale Agreement satisfactory to Buyer and Seller," *McCarthy v. Tobin*, 706 N.E.2d 629 (Mass. 1999). The Supreme Judicial Court of Massachusetts emphasized a provision that stated, "This is a legal document that creates binding obligations." It was persuaded by that language and its analysis that the "material" terms of the agreement, as contrasted with "ministerial" and "non essential" terms, had been included in the document.

Traditionally, however, courts have been reluctant to find that preliminary agreements create binding contractual obligations. In particular, courts have required these agreements to be complete for all essential terms. If the parties have not agreed to all those terms, or have conditioned their obligations on a future agreement, many courts have held the agreement unenforceable as a mere "agreement to agree." *Corbin,* cited above, § 29. But, as will be discussed later, the parties may still be liable on other theories.

Intent of the Parties. Today, courts seem less concerned about the missing terms, and are far more willing to find an agreement complete and binding. The most important factor in determining whether a given agreement is binding is the apparent intent of the parties. If the parties "intend" to be bound by a preliminary agreement, they are held bound.

The relevant inquiry is not what the parties subjectively believe they have done; rather it is based on what the outward, objective manifestations of their subjective states are. Courts consider the following factors in determining the intent of the parties:

- the terms of the letter;
- the context of the negotiations;
- the existence of open terms;
- partial performance; and
- trade custom.

Teachers Ins. and Annuity Ass'n v. Tribune Co., 670 F. Supp. 491 (S.D.N.Y. 1987). The following cases provide some insights into the applications of these factors.

The *Texaco* Case. A much-publicized case involving a preliminary agreement was *Texaco, Inc. v. Pennzoil Co.*, 729 S.W.2d 768 (Tex. App. 1987), *cert. dismissed*, 485 U.S. 994 (1988). In this case, Pennzoil and Getty Oil had been involved in negotiations for the acquisition of Getty. The parties reached a tentative agreement and issued identical press releases announcing their planned merger. The documents stated that the parties had reached an "agreement in principle" but that the agreement was *"subject to execution of a definitive merger agreement, approval by the stockholders of Getty Oil and completion of various governmental filing and waiting period requirements." Id.* at 789 (emphasis added).

Despite the agreement, there was evidence that Getty's investment banker continued to look for higher bids, and three days later, Getty entered into a merger agreement with Texaco for $15 per share more than the Pennzoil bid. *Id.* at 787. Pennzoil sued Texaco on the theory of tortious interference with contract.

The jury returned a $10.5 billion verdict for Pennzoil (roughly $7.5 billion in contract damages and $3 billion in punitive damages). On appeal, the court upheld the contract damages, holding that there was ample evidence that the parties intended to be bound by the preliminary agreement. The court noted that the parties used strong, indicative language in the letter, instead of hypothetical or subjunctive language. The fact that the parties made the agreement "subject to" various conditions was held not dispositive. *Id.* at 790. The court did reduce the punitive damage award from $3 billion to $2 billion. See also *Field v. Golden Triangle Broadcasting*, 305 A.2d 689 (Pa. 1973), in which a letter of intent was held binding despite the parties' failure to agree on all terms, and even though a later formal contract was anticipated, and *Newport, Ltd. v. Sears Roebuck & Co.*, 6 F.3d 1058 (5th Cir. 1993), in which a letter of intent to sign a lease stated that it "will form the basis of a much more detailed document, the terms and conditions of which are subject to the mutual agreement of the parties."

The *Arcadian* Case. Another case on preliminary agreements is *Arcadian Phosphates, Inc. v. Arcadian Corp.*, 884 F.2d 69 (2d Cir. 1989). Here, the crucial memo was held *not* to establish a contractual obligation because it referred not only to the "possibility" that negotiations might fail after the letter of intent was signed, but also to a future binding agreement. Some observers say that if the *Arcadian* decision had come down before *Texaco* was settled, it might have influenced the outcome of *Texaco*. *Wall Street Journal*, Sept.

8, 1989, at B1. See also *Reprosystem B.V. v. SCM Corp.*, 727 F.2d 257 (2d Cir. 1984), *cert. denied*, 469 U.S. 828 (1984).

No General Rule. *Tamir v. Greenberg*, 501 N.Y.S.2d 103 (N.Y. App. Div. 1986), is another case where the court held that the letter of intent was not binding. The court cited conditional language in the letter that said the parties planned to draw up a formal contract within 10 days, and concluded that the parties did not intend to be bound by the letter.

As these sample cases indicate, courts seem to be erratic in their treatment of letters of intent. Commentators try to distinguish among jurisdictions and differentiate cases on factual specifics, but basically the decisions are found "all over the place." See Stephen R. Volk, *The Letter of Intent*, 16 INST. ON SEC. REG. 143 (1985). Each individual case turns on an idiosyncratic fact pattern, making it very difficult to come up with "general rules" in this area. An apparent ambivalence in the courts should sound the alarm for negotiators to be cautious and circumspect before entering into preliminary agreements.

Obligations to Bargain in Good Faith. Even when a letter of intent fails to establish an actual contract because it is conditioned on a final agreement or because "essential" terms are left open, courts may still find that the parties entered into a binding "contract to bargain" on these open terms. This commitment obligates the parties to make a "good faith" and "best efforts" attempt to close the deal. See generally, Charles L. Knapp, *Enforcing the Contract to Bargain*, 44 N.Y.U. L. REV. 673 (1969).

But what is the character of this good faith obligation and how far does it extend? In *Teachers Insurance Annuity Ass'n of America v. Tribune*, 670 F. Supp. 491 (S.D.N.Y. 1987), the court noted that:

> This [good faith] obligation does not guarantee that the final contract will be concluded if both parties comport with their obligation, as good faith differences in the negotiation of the open issues may prevent a reaching of final contract. . . . *The obligation does, however, bar a party from renouncing the deal, abandoning the negotiations, or insisting on conditions that do not conform to the preliminary agreement.*

Teachers Insurance, 670 F. Supp. at 498 (emphasis added). The following cases have applied these principles.

Recent cases in New York and the state of Washington have dealt with obligations to bargain in good faith. The case of *180 Water Street Associates v. Lehman Bros. Holdings, Inc.,* 776 N.Y.S.2d 278 (N.Y. A.D. 1st Dept. 2004), held that a letter between the parties obligated them to negotiate in good faith, even though the letter expressly disclaimed any binding effect and did not constitute a lease. The plaintiff's allegation that Lehman Brothers was negotiating with other landlords from the beginning was held to be sufficient to state a cause of action for breach of an agreement to negotiate.

In *Keystone Land & Dev. Co. v. Xerox,* 94 P.3d 945 (Wash. 2004), the Supreme Court of Washington ruled that it was unnecessary to decide whether Washington will enforce a contract to negotiate, because the court found that the circumstances of the case presented only an "implied agreement to agree," and agreements to agree are not enforceable in the state of Washington.

"Negotiate to Completion." *Channel Home Centers, Division of Grace Retail Corp. v. Grossman,* 795 F.2d 291 (3d Cir. 1986), dealt with a preliminary agreement for the lease of a shopping center. The Grossmans owned the shopping center and were trying to procure an anchor tenant. They negotiated with Channel and in December 1984 drew up a controversial letter that outlined all the terms. Grossman had requested the letter of intent so he could present it to lenders to show he had a deal with Channel. The letter provided:

> . . .To induce the Tenant [Channel] to proceed with the leasing of this Store, you [Grossman] will withdraw the Store from the rental market, and only negotiate the above described leasing transaction to completion.
>
> Please acknowledge your intent to proceed with the leasing of the captioned store under the above terms, conditions and understanding by signing. . . ."

Channel, 795 F.2d at 293.

Grossman contended this letter was given on the condition that the lease agreement would be completed within 30 days, and that Channel, which was to prepare the lease, did not conform to this schedule. After entering into the letter of intent, Channel carried out some planning, prepared a survey, and even claimed to have procured certain construction materials. Grossman applied to the township for zoning approval. In January 1985, more than 30 days after the letter of intent, Channel sent a 41-page lease to Grossman, who sent it back with proposed changes. Channel and Grossman went back and forth with negotiations on the lease and never signed it.

Meanwhile, Grossman received an offer from Mr. Goodbuys for the same space for more than double the Channel rent. The negotiations with Channel were terminated, and Grossman made a deal with Mr. Goodbuys in February 1985.

Channel sued to enforce the letter of intent, but the U.S. District Court rejected Channel's arguments on the grounds that the letter did not recite the mutual obligations essential to a contract and that it also clearly contemplated further negotiations. Channel appealed to the circuit court, which reversed and found in favor of Channel, holding that the letter imposed an obligation on Grossman to negotiate in good faith. The court also held that Grossman did not bargain in good faith with Channel when he terminated negotiations and accepted a higher offer from Mr. Goodbuys.

"Make Every Reasonable Effort to Agree." Another leading case on the obligation to bargain is *Itek Corp. v. Chicago Aerial Industries*, 248 A.2d 625 (Del. 1968). In 1964, Chicago Aerial Industries (CAI) had accepted an offer by Itek to purchase all CAI's assets based on $12 per share and a 1/20 share of Itek stock, which amounted to a total of approximately $13 per share. Itek drafted a letter of intent to CAI, spelling out all the terms of the deal, and both parties signed it. The key language stated that:

> Itek and CAI shall *make every reasonable effort* to agree upon and have prepared as quickly as possible a contract providing for the foregoing purchase . . . *subject to the approval of CAI stockholders*, embodying the above terms and such other terms and conditions as the parties shall agree upon. If the parties fail to agree upon and execute such a contract they shall be under no further obligation to one another.

Itek, 248 A.2d at 627 (emphasis added).

Afterwards, CAI negotiated a floor on the value of the credit it would give for Itek's stock and required an escrow arrangement by Itek to assure CAI's liabilities would be paid. Itek agreed to these demands and the parties started working on a formal contract. Meanwhile, the same day, a CAI committee revived an earlier interest shown by another suitor (Bourns). The committee met with Bourns, told him they had reached an impasse in negotiations with Itek, and closed the deal at $16 per share, which was approximately $3 more than the Itek offer.

Itek attempted to hold CAI to the letter of intent. CAI responded that the letter clearly disclaimed any contractual intent, since the document stated that "If the parties fail to agree upon and execute such contract they shall be under no obligation to one another." *Id.* at 627. However, the court held that the letter obligated each side to attempt in "good faith" to reach a final and formal agreement. Furthermore, the court stated CAI's agreement with Bourns at a higher price provided evidence that CAI failed to negotiate in "good faith" and to make "every reasonable effort" to agree on a formal contract.

In both the *Channel Home Centers* and *Itek* cases, the parties had specifically agreed to "negotiate." In *Channel Home Centers,* the owner had agreed to "withdraw the Store from the rental market, and only negotiate the above described leasing transaction to completion." 795 F.2d at 292. In *Itek*, the parties agreed to "make every reasonable effort to agree upon and have prepared as quickly as possible a contract." 248 A.2d at 627.

It is not clear what those courts would have done with slightly different language. For example, a Pennsylvania Superior Court letter-of-intent case distinguished *Channel Home Centers* because the letter of intent in the Pennsylvania case did not provide for any duty to negotiate. *Philmar Mid-Atlantic, Inc. v. York Street Assocs. II*, 566 A.2d 1253 (Pa. Super. 1989).

The *GMH* Case

Finding that the owner had breached an oral contract with the buyer when it accepted a higher price from the competing buyer, a trial court awarded a prospective buyer of a group of office buildings approximately $30 million in compensatory and punitive damages. The case, involving a property known as "Bala Plaza," was later reversed. *GMH Assocs., Inc. v. Prudential Realty Group,* 752 A.2d 889 (Pa. Super. 2000). However, a review of the trial court decision is illustrative.

Trial Court

The lower court had agreed with the buyer's claims on all of the following counts:

- breach of contract
- fraudulent misrepresentation
- fraudulent nondisclosure
- promissory estoppel
- breach of duty to negotiate in good faith

Judge Cavanaugh, speaking for the majority of the three-judge panel in the Superior Court of Pennsylvania, reversed the lower court's decision on every one of those counts. The facts are complex and raise difficult legal issues. The sheer weight of the opinions (110 pages in the lower court, and 32 pages in the Superior Court) may discourage detailed analysis by the casual reader. However, the case is replete with lessons in contract and tort law, and both decisions are well worth reading for both business and litigation attorneys.

Letter of Interest

Among other issues, the *GMII* case involved a signed letter of interest (LOI) to negotiate for the sale of the Bala Plaza. Although the LOI allowed either party to terminate negotiations with notice at any time, the owner, Prudential, advised GMH that the properties were "off the market" during the negotiations and promised GMH an "exclusive look." Despite that, Prudential, while the deal was still under discussion with GMH, started actively negotiating with a competing buyer. At one point Prudential denied, and actively "concealed," the negotiations from GMH "in order to use the suitors for the property as pawns against one another in a scheme to drive up the purchase price of the property." (See trial court decision.)

Of all of the issues in the case, the one that seems to have stirred up the most attention in legal circles is the issue of a seller's duty to "negotiate in good faith." The lower court had found that Prudential had breached its duty to negotiate in good faith and cited two federal circuit cases purporting to predict what the Pennsylvania Supreme Court would do on this issue. See *Flight Sys., Inc. v. Electronic Data Sys. Corp.*, 112 F.3d 124 (3d Cir. 1997), and *Channel Home Ctrs. v. Grossman*, 795 F.2d 291 (3d Cir. 1986).

On this issue, Judge Cavanaugh was less willing than the Third Circuit Court of Appeals to predict what the Pennsylvania Supreme Court would do. He stated "[o]ur courts have not determined whether a cause of action for breach of duty to negotiate in good faith exists in Pennsylvania." However, he cited a principle that an earlier Superior Court decision had quoted "with approval":

> ... The full extent of a party's duty to negotiate in good faith can only be determined, however, from the terms of the letter of intent itself.

GMH Assocs., Inc., 752 A.2d at 903.

Judge Cavanaugh concluded that the LOI expressly provided that either party could terminate negotiations at any time for any reason without incurring liability to the other before it signed a written contract. The LOI did not contain any provision requiring a duty to negotiate in good faith, or one requiring the property to be taken "off the market." He stated:

> ... Thus, we conclude, if our courts were to recognize the existence of such a cause of action, that the duty to negotiate in good faith was not breached in this case by Prudential's failure to keep the property "off the market" or to reveal that it was entering negotiations with GSIC.

Id. at 904.

Good Faith and Fair Dealing

The concept of an implied duty of good faith and fair dealing in commercial contracts is one that courts around the country have been struggling with for many years. Some commercial lawyers worry that this concept can open a Pandora's box of rights that are difficult to recognize, and even more difficult to apply. Should a party have a duty to negotiate "in good faith," even if the agreement is not otherwise binding, provides conditions that have not been met, and fails to tie down all of the material terms?

How many judges would look forward to deciding whether a party should be held liable for failure to negotiate "long enough"—or even "hard enough"? When the parties to a transaction run into a snag in negotiations, how will they be able to withdraw from these discussions without exposing themselves to liability?

If the courts hold parties to standards of good faith and fair dealing, there will be few safe-harbor rules because courts cannot measure good faith by dollars, scales, or minutes on a dial. Also, standards for what is "good" and "fair" may vary from Wall Street to Walla Walla, and from rabbis to real estate developers.

Practical Guidelines

Based on *GMH* and other letters-of-intent cases, the following principles emerge. First, if you can avoid using ambivalent and ambiguous preliminary agreements, do so. As one commentator noted, letters of intent are "an invention of the devil and should be avoided at all costs." Stephen R. Volk, *The Letter of Intent*, 16 INST. ON SEC. REG. at 145.

However, sometimes avoiding preliminary agreements is impossible. For example, letters of intent are often helpful in facilitating complicated negotiations. They may be required so that negotiators can take the next step in a deal, such as obtaining board approval or financing.

Some negotiators, using what might be called "planned ambiguity," may even prefer the vagueness often created by assurance letters and letters of intent. Such obfuscation may prevent the opposition from focusing on sensitive issues that may precipitate a dispute, such as the party's right to withdraw before signing a formal agreement.

Preliminary Agreements Generally Favor Buyers

Who gains the advantage from using a preliminary agreement or letter of intent instead of going right into the final agreement? It depends on the circumstances, but generally the buyer of a company or real estate will benefit more than the seller. If it is unclear whether the letter of intent is binding, the letter may provide the buyer with enough ammunition to tie the project up in litigation (or threaten to do so) until the parties resolve that issue. Meanwhile, the letter will not necessarily deter the buyer from pursuing other acquisitions.

On the other hand, if the buyer wants to terminate a preliminary purchase agreement, it probably will be able to withdraw with impunity. The seller may have little incentive to enforce the agreement. If it attempts to do so, the ambiguity may be enough to discourage other prospective buyers from engaging in serious negotiations until a court has decided whether the letter is binding. In light of that, the seller will be likely to let the buyer off the hook and try to sell to someone else. This is particularly true if the seller does not hold an adequate deposit and the buyer is not creditworthy.

However, while negotiators may sometimes gain an advantage from confused agreements, the risks of such planned ambiguity are high, as the cited cases illustrate. An irate adversary may call your bluff.

Key Language to Use in Letters of Intent

Good faith and good sense call for a different approach. If you use a letter of intent that is not intended to be binding, specifically disclaim any contractual intent and try to discourage any detrimental reliance. For example:

> UNTIL THE DEFINITIVE AGREEMENT IS FINALIZED, APPROVED BY THE RESPECTIVE BOARDS OF DIRECTORS (WHICH APPROVAL SHALL BE IN THE SOLE SUBJECTIVE DISCRETION OF THE RESPECTIVE BOARDS OF DIRECTORS), AND PROPERLY EXECUTED, NEITHER PARTY SHALL HAVE ANY LEGALLY BINDING OBLIGATION TO THE OTHER (WHETHER UNDER THIS LETTER OF INTENT OR OTHERWISE), INCLUDING, BUT NOT LIMITED TO, A LEGAL DUTY TO CONTINUE NEGOTIATIONS TO REACH SUCH A DEFINITIVE AGREEMENT, AND EITHER PARTY MAY DISCONTINUE NEGOTIATIONS AT ANY TIME FOR ANY REASON WHATSOEVER.

The recipient of this letter may not be too happy, but it should clarify the positions of the parties.

Sometimes the parties intend the letter to be binding in a very limited way. They may agree to indemnify each other against certain conduct during a designated due-diligence period, to pay specified costs or brokers' commissions, or to take the property off the market for a few months. If so, the lawyers can carve these exceptions out of the general disclaimer.

Similarly, when drafting assurance or comfort letters, use the disclaimer of contractual intent suggested above. While this express disavowal of contractual obligations may impede negotiations, it should help prevent damaging litigation in the future.

Guidelines for Using Letters of Intent

Based on the applicable cases, the parties might consider the following guidelines when using letters of intent (adapted from

272

unpublished outline by Laura B. Bartell, *Liability Under Commitment Letters and Other Preliminary Indicia of Agreement*):

- If you do not intend to be bound, do not use the language "agreement in principle" or "memorandum of intent." If possible, go right to the formal agreement stage.
- Avoid what might appear as inconsistent representations of intent in oral statements, side letters, or file memoranda.
- Do not charge nonrefundable fees. They tend to make a writing binding. And don't impose any other obligations before the final formal agreement is signed.
- Don't act as if the letter is binding: no press releases, no disclosure to lenders or other investors, no partial performances until the parties reach a final formal agreement.
- Specifically list any open terms and state that they are still not resolved.
- Try to obtain a confidentiality requirement in the letter of intent to discourage third parties from relying on it.
- Specifically disclaim any liability against either party if the negotiations terminate.
- Negate any intent to negotiate or bargain in good faith, and specifically agree that you may cut off and terminate negotiations without obligation unless a final binding agreement is signed by a designated date.
- Avoid carrying out negotiations with other parties for the same asset during the applicable period of the letter of intent; and after terminating negotiations, permit a respectful period of "mourning" to pass before making a more favorable deal with another party.
- If you break off negotiations, try to affirm that your decision was made in "good faith." For example, in *Philmar Mid-Atlantic, Inc. v. York Street Assocs. II*, 566 A.2d 1253 (Pa. Super. 1989), the owner terminated negotiations when the zoning board objections to the proposed construction became apparent.

SIDE LETTER
(Standard Form)

The following letter was acquired from the confidential files of Karl Holtzschue, a colleague in the American College of Real Estate Attorneys. We have reviewed it and edited it, but have assumed and relied on its completeness as to matters of fact and law. We have not made any independent investigation of it, and we make no representation as to the sufficiency of our investigation for your purposes.

It is not intended to be relied upon by any individual or entity.

20__

To: Messrs.

Re: Contract of Even Date

Sirs:

In reference to the Contract of Even Date (hereinafter called the "Apparent Deal"), this letter sets forth the further understanding of the parties (hereinafter called the "Real Deal"). This Real Deal is, of course, sincerely meant by the parties, but shall be enforceable in the manner indicated below (check one):

Not at all.

By the same legal means as the Apparent Deal.

By the withholding of future business.

By strong, swarthy youths with sticks.

By notification to defaulting party's spouse of events occurring after signing ceremony.

By unspecified means too hideous to mention.

Considering that the parties have entered into the Apparent Deal without realizing the implications of the Worst Case, the parties now declare the Real Deal as follows (check one or more, as appropriate):

The Apparent Deal is off.

Only the Apparent Deal will be publicly disclosed.

All monetary amounts express in the Apparent Deal hereby are increased/decreased by a factor of _____.

Expressions of mandatory commitments in the Apparent Deal hereby are declared to be only Best Efforts.

Clauses _____ through _____ of the Apparent Deal are in there only to show the Board of Directors of the parties, but form no part of the Real Deal.

Undisclosed personal fees and commissions are payable to negotiators of the Apparent Deal as follows: _____.

Only the seller in the Apparent Deal shall be bound.

Only the buyer in the Apparent Deal shall be bound.

The terms "Buyer" and "Seller" in the Apparent Deal hereby are reversed.

Very truly yours,

Firm

By:

Title:

(Check one)

Agreed and accepted
Read but not understood
Yes, but if asked will deny
Signed under duress

Firm   By:

By: Title:

Title:

46   BUYERS NEED PROPER MORTGAGE CONTINGENCY CLAUSES

When a buyer of real estate needs a mortgage to close on the purchase, it is customary for the agreement to be made contingent on obtaining a mortgage commitment. These subject-to commitment provisions are frequently found in form agreements and permit buyers to obtain refunds of their deposits if they do not obtain a commitment in a minimum sum at a maximum interest rate. If they do not notify the seller of their failure to obtain that commitment by a certain date, they may have waived that condition and be required to close—even without financing!

Buyers' Trouble

A New Jersey Superior Court decision indicates how a buyer may get into trouble with this type of clause. In the case of *Malus v. Hager*, 712 A.2d 238 (N.J. Super. Ct. App. Div. 1998), a residential real estate contract contained such a clause and the buyers obtained the expected commitment within the specified time. A closing was scheduled, and four days before the closing date, the employment of one of the buyers was terminated. The next day, the sellers, unaware of this development and expecting to close a few days later, moved out of their home and placed their belongings in storage until they were able to complete their own relocation.

Unfortunately under the terms of the mortgage commitment, the lender reserved the right to cancel the commitment "if prior to funding, your financial condition or employment status adversely changes...." 712 A.2d at 239. Based on the buyer's loss of employment, the lender exercised its right and declined to fund the mortgage.

When the buyers sought the return of their deposit, the sellers refused to do so, the buyer sued, and the trial court required the return of the deposit. However, the appellate division disagreed with the trial court and with an earlier appellate division case, and permitted the seller to retain the deposit as liquidated damages. The earlier case had held that the mortgage contingency clause conditions the buyers' obligations not only on the mortgage commitment, but also "on the availability at closing of the mortgage proceeds."

According to the *Malus* court, any other construction of that contingency clause would place the parties in an intolerable state of limbo until the closing is finally consummated. The court believed that, after a certain point, a contract of sale for a home should be an enforceable agreement. It concluded that only further confusion and uncertainty can result from extending the mortgage contingency clause to the date of closing, as a matter of law. The court observed "[i]f the parties wish to provide in their contract for an eventuality such as this, they are free to do so. We decline, however, to impose the risk of an otherwise firm deal unravelling upon an unknowing and blameless seller, leaving him with no ability to recoup his increased expenses." *Id.* at 240.

The buyer in *Malus* was out of luck and out of a job. The buyer forfeited a deposit and did not have recourse against the lender that had conditioned the mortgage commitment on the change of status.

Rosen Case

In *Rosen v. Empire Valve & Fitting, Inc.*, 553 A.2d 1004 (Pa. Super. 1989), a sale was contingent on mortgage financing with the Philadelphia Authority for Industrial Development and the Philadelphia Industrial Development Corp. (PIDC). The buyer obtained the requested mortgage commitment by the required date in the agreement, but after that and before settlement had taken place, PIDC withdrew its commitment because of a perceived change in the financial circumstances of a corporation that was to guarantee the payment of the mortgage.

The buyer asked for his money back, and when the seller refused, the buyer sued for it. The seller argued that the buyer had not notified the seller of his inability to obtain mortgage financing before an agreed mortgage commitment date. The reason the buyer could not meet the cutoff date was obvious: He received the commitment on time and even notified the seller that he had, but the commitment was later withdrawn by PIDC after the deadline.

However, the trial court agreed with the seller and therefore would have required the buyer to forfeit his deposit.

On appeal, the Superior Court read the contingency clause differently. It made a distinction between the "mortgage commitment" and the actual "mortgage loan," holding that the obligation to purchase was not absolute "immediately upon the issuance of a *mortgage commitment.*" 553 A.2d at 1006. Instead, the court held that the agreement unequivocally provided that "if said *mortgage loan* cannot be obtained, this agreement shall be null and void and all deposit monies shall be returned to the buyer on or before date for settlement." *Id.*

"Firm" Commitment

Suppose the buyers' obligations to purchase are conditioned upon receipt of a "firm" mortgage commitment. If the mortgage application has been approved subject to the sale of the buyer's present home, does the buyer have a firm commitment?

In *Potts v. Epler*, 84 BERKS L.J. 219 (1992), the Court of Common Pleas of Berks County, Pennsylvania, held that buyers, who had not sold their home before settlement, could terminate a purchase agreement and require their deposit to be returned to them. The court, which could find no other case defining the terms "firm commitment," decided that "firm" means "unconditional." Since the buyers were unable to sell their home to satisfy the mortgage contingency, the commitment was not "firm."

Risk of Non-funding

The lesson to be learned is that the parties must spell out what they mean by a mortgage contingency. What happens when the commitment comes through but not the mortgage? Obviously, if the mortgage doesn't close because the buyers act in bad faith, they should be in default even if they do not get the mortgage funds.

However, if the lender defaults under the commitment and at the last minute does not advance the committed money, or if the buyer is unable to meet some condition in the commitment, who should take that risk?

These are issues that should be resolved in the agreement of sale. What we are talking about may be designated as "who takes the risk of non-funding?"

Obviously, buyers would like sellers to take the risk. Buyers do not have enough money to close without the actual mortgage and therefore will argue that they never intended to take that risk. They have done everything they can, and the lender has not provided the money needed to close.

Seller's Needs

On the other hand, sellers will argue that buyers have selected the lender and that risk of non-funding by their lender should fall on the buyers. Normally, the mortgage contingency will designate a cutoff date. If the buyer has not obtained a mortgage commitment by that date, the buyer can cancel the agreement and obtain a refund of the deposit. However, the seller will want to know that if the buyer does not cancel by that date, the buyer is hooked into the agreement. Sellers do not want to wait for the actual day of closing to find out that the deal is not going through. Often, they have good reasons for that.

Suppose you are selling your old house so that you can move into your fresh new condominium. You may want to have a closing the same day so you can move right out of your old home into your new one. But to do this, you may need to buy the new home with the money you receive from the sale. If you do not close on the old home, you may forfeit a deposit under your agreement to buy the new one.

One of the ways you can settle this problem is to make it clear that your buyer is committed irrevocably as of the date the buyers receive their mortgage commitment. Let the buyers take the risk of non-funding. Then you can commit to buy your new home and accept the reasonable risk of forfeiting your deposit there.

It is not a foolproof system because even if the buyers' commitment binds them to settle with you, they may not close. Therefore, you still may not be able to complete your purchase of the new home. However, it is comforting to know that at some point, long before the scheduled settlement on the sale of your old home, your buyers are irrevocably committed. That is the way you will want to write your mortgage contingency clause.

In addition, you may have other buyers out there who are willing to pay the same price, or more. If buyers are not committed until they actually meet all of the mortgage conditions in the commitment, you may lose several opportunities that would otherwise have been available to you if you had established an earlier cutoff date.

The *Rosen* case was decided on a rather narrow issue of interpretation, but the implications are profound.

Buyers' Needs

A corollary to the *Rosen* case involves buyers who may be able to close but who are caught with the wrong type of mortgage contingency clause. Those buyers can lose a favorable purchase even when they have received a timely mortgage commitment and would like to close.

Buyers' problems occur when they receive a common type of mortgage commitment within the designated deadline in the agreement of sale, but that commitment contains customary conditions such as verification of income or receipt of a satisfactory inspection report or appraisal. Mortgage companies customarily issue a form letter approving the mortgage loan application in a designated dollar amount for a specified term, sometimes even providing that a formal commitment letter will be issued setting forth additional details later. The seller may argue that such a letter does not satisfy the mortgage contingency as defined in one of the commonly used form agreements.

Backing Out

Why would a seller want to terminate an agreement even though it appears that the buyer has received the anticipated financing? For one thing, as set forth above, the seller may be concerned that the buyer will not be able to meet the conditions to close. But there may be other less legitimate motives. For example, the seller may have a higher offer from another buyer and may be looking for a way out of what is perceived as a bad bargain, or the seller may simply have decided not to sell.

Some sellers have attempted to terminate agreements by invoking subject-to-financing clauses when buyers were a little late in producing a mortgage commitment or when the stated mortgage terms were inadequate. (See *Kalina v. Eckert*, 497 A.2d 1384 (Pa. Super. 1985), and *Brown v. Morris Real Estate Consultants Inc.*, 347 S.E.2d 563 (Ga. 1986).) But courts have been reluctant to permit sellers to accomplish that.

In the *Kalina* case, the Pennsylvania Superior Court held the seller to the contract even though the written commitment was not issued until two days after the designated financing deadline, because the buyer had received a lender's timely oral assurance that the buyer's application would be approved. The court was reluctant to declare a "forfeiture" of the buyer's rights based upon such a flimsy flaw. Even though the buyers won some of these cases, they had to resort to litigation with all of its attendant delay and expense.

Sellers' Clause

Unfortunately for buyers, many standard agreements commonly used help the seller who is trying to break the contract. For example, the printed form of agreement for residential real estate by the Pennsylvania Association of Realtors sets forth the mortgage contingency as follows:

(B)   Within ten (10) days of Seller's approval of this Agreement, Buyer shall make a completed mortgage application to a responsible mortgage lending institution ...

(C)(2)   Mortgage commitment date _____ 20___. If a written commitment is not received by the above date, Buyer and Seller agree to extend the commitment date until seller terminates this Agreement in writing.

(3)   Seller has the option to terminate this Agreement in writing, on or after the mortgage commitment date, if the mortgage commitment: (a) Is not valid until the date of settlement, OR (b) Is conditioned upon the **sale and settlement of any other property,** OR (c) *Contains any other conditions not specified in this Agreement.* [Emphasis added.]

The Problem

The contingency specifies that if the seller elects to terminate, the buyer shall not be required to purchase the property, and the buyer's deposit money shall be returned. Ironically, the buyer may terminate only if the seller does not extend the commitment date! See paragraph (C)(2) above.

What is wrong with that provision?

For one thing, as described earlier, just about every commitment contains conditions of some sort. If buyers follow normal procedure and obtain what they think is a commitment by the specified date, the seller may have an out because of customary, standard conditions. To make it worse, the form agreement provides that time is "of the essence" in the agreement. Essentially, this means that specified dates, including the mortgage commitment date, are inviolate and enforceable even though the other party may not be damaged by a slight delay. The date becomes crucial regardless of materiality, and the buyer may have no time to satisfy the condition or obtain a revised commitment.

Also, this provision does not even give the buyer a chance to waive the contingency by notifying the seller that the mortgage contingency has been met. The buyer may be unwilling to do that when the commitment's conditions are problematical, but should have the right to make that decision.

Generally, an agreement of sale will require a down payment in the form of a deposit equal to 10 percent of the purchase price. When the buyer waives the mortgage contingency clause, the seller should derive some comfort from knowing that the buyer is then required to close on penalty of default, including forfeiture of a deposit of that magnitude.

Common Language

Another mortgage contingency provision used by the Main Line (Pennsylvania) Board of Realtors does not give the seller a right to terminate the agreement upon the buyer's failure to obtain the mortgage commitment.

Essentially, it provides that if the buyer has not obtained a mortgage commitment by the designated date, the buyer may either cancel the agreement or proceed to settlement in the same way as if there were no mortgage contingency. The buyer is required to notify the seller by a certain date that the mortgage commitment was not obtained; and if the buyer fails to do so within the time limit, the buyer is obligated to proceed with the settlement.

There is another more subtle issue in the PAR contingency clause. As quoted above, it treats a commitment as flawed if it contains "any other condition not specified in this agreement." In a later provision of the same form that sets forth the buyer's right to terminate (as contrasted with the seller's), it permits the buyer to terminate if the commitment contains a condition "which the buyer is unable to satisfy by the date of settlement."

That additional language is omitted from the section that gives the seller the right to terminate. Does that mean that the seller can terminate even if the condition is one that the buyer is able to "satisfy by the date of settlement"?

The reason for that distinction is not clear. It seems, however, that the seller should not have a right to terminate because of a condition that the buyer is not only able to satisfy by the date of settlement, but is also willing to commit to satisfy, particularly when backed by the potential of a forfeiture of deposit money if the buyer fails to do so.

Careful Review Needed

This analysis is based on one commonly used mortgage contingency clause, but other clauses may precipitate similar or other problems. If the normal expectations of sellers and buyers are to be realized, these clauses must be carefully reviewed and revised where needed.

Many brokers and buyers will be surprised to find that a reluctant seller may be able to avoid an agreement of sale because of a technicality involving the mortgage contingency provision in the PAR form agreement.

In addition, buyers, mortgage companies, and brokers should focus on language in the standard mortgage commitment to make sure the commitment is issued promptly and that it is a firm commitment. While the commitment must contain certain standard conditions that must be met by closing, such as marketable title and a termite certification, it should be written so that it does not include any unusual conditions. The buyer will then be in a better position to meet a seller's argument that the commitment does not conform to the mortgage contingency provision.

47 AGREEMENTS OF SALE: LIQUIDATED DAMAGES WITHSTAND CHALLENGE

Generally, a seller may recover liquidated damages from a defaulting buyer even when the seller resells the property at a better price—but that is not always true. In the case of *Sheehan v. Wargo*, 635 A.2d 215 (Pa. Super. 1993), a buyer agreed to forfeit $40,000 upon default under a real estate agreement. That was 10 percent of a $400,000 purchase price. While other issues were raised in the case, the most significant was the buyer's claim that forfeiture of $40,000 is an unenforceable penalty and a "windfall to the seller" in light of the fact that the property was later sold for $450,000. According to the buyer, after subtracting commissions, the seller realized $418,500—$48,500 more than the seller could have received if the buyer had gone through with its sale.

10 Percent Is "Fair"

Despite this, the court held that a liquidated damage provision is enforceable "where the parties reasonably preestimate their probable damages." The court quoted an earlier case that held that a forfeiture is not enforceable if intended to be a "penalty" or "a punishment, the threat of which is designed to prevent the breach," and not a pre-estimate of probable actual damages. In *Sheehan*, the liquidated damage clause was not intended "*in terrorem* to secure compliance with the terms of the agreement."

A modification of the agreement had provided that the seller acknowledged that the agreed liquidated damages were full and sufficient compensation for breach. Since both sides apparently believed the $40,000 to be fair and reasonable compensation, that added significantly to the court's rationale that this sum was not a penalty. It also found that the special treatment accorded liquidated damage provisions in real estate agreements seems to be due to the belief that such damages are uncertain and difficult to ascertain. The court reasoned that a forecast by the parties of a 10 percent liquidated damage loss is not excessive in view of the fact that the settlement under the agreement could have been six months after signing, and the agreement took the property off the market for at least that period. In addition, the court noted that taxes and other expenses of the property remained the responsibility of the seller during that period.

The relevant inquiry is what were reasonable liquidated damages for that period of time, not whether, at some time in the future, the seller might sell the property for a good price. Liquidated damage clauses are enforceable. *Hooper v. Breneman*, 417 So.2d 315 (Fla. Dist. Ct. App. 1982) (13.3 percent of purchase price is not unconscionable liquidated damages), and *Wilfong v. W.A. Schickedanz Agency, Inc.*, 406 N.E.2d 828 (Ill. App. Ct. 1980) (10 percent liquidated damage clause is enforceable).

In *Kelly v. Marx*, 705 N.E.2d 1114 (Mass. 1999), the Massachusetts Supreme Court held that a 5 percent liquidated damage provision in the agreement of sale was collectible by the seller when the buyer defaulted, even though the seller was able to sell the property for $5,000 more than the original price. In that case the court held that the test should be whether the liquidated damages are "grossly disproportionate" to a reasonable estimate of actual damages made at the time the agreement was signed. The court refuted the so-called "second look" doctrine that would argue that the parties should look at what really happened after the buyer defaulted.

No Loss

While the *Kelly* court did not cite other cases on this issue, decisions in some states would prohibit sellers from retaining the full down payment when the seller has resold the property without loss. (See *Kutzin v. Pirnie*, 591 A.2d 932 (N.J. 1991); *Stabenau v. Cairelli*, 577 A.2d 1130 (Conn. App. 1990); and *Bensinger v. Davidson*, 147 F. Supp. 240 (S.D. Cal. 1956).) The treatment of forfeiture of deposits throughout the country in an agreement of sale is discussed at length in Milton R. Friedman, *Contracts and Conveyances of Real Property* 1043–73, § 12.1(c) (5th ed. 1991).

California law has attempted to protect buyers with a statute that makes an earnest money deposit of 3 percent "presumptively valid and reasonable," while a greater forfeiture is valid only if the seller can demonstrate that it is based on a reasonable liquidated damages provision. In *Allen v. Smith,* No. D036608 (Cal. App. 4th Dist. January 2, 2002), modified January 23, 2002, the parties entered into a residential agreement of sale for $1,750,000, and in an apparent attempt to circumvent the 3 percent threshold, the parties agreed on a deposit of $100,000 "as a non-refundable purchase option."

The California Court of Appeals did not accept that characterization and permitted the seller to recover only 3 percent of the purchase price after the buyer defaulted. The court based its conclusion on an interpretation of the agreement of sale that obligated both parties to close. The court alluded to contract language that committed the buyer to perform upon satisfaction of designated contingencies.

In contrast with that, the court indicated that a traditional option binds only the seller, and that the buyer has no obligation to perform. For example, the buyer who has a real option could not be sued for specific performance.

Also, since the parties had used a printed form, despite the fact that they tried to use option language they had initialed a liquidated damages box in the contract that seemed to show an intent to treat the deposit as non-refundable liquidated damages, this was inconsistent with the option language.

A recent New York case upheld a forfeiture of a 25 percent down payment on the purchase of four luxury condominiums in New York City. *Cem Uzan v. 845 UN Limited P'ship,* 778 N.Y.S.2d 171 (N.Y. App. Div. 2004). The case involved the purchase of luxury condominiums on the top floors of Trump World Tower in New York City, and the forfeited amount totaled approximately $8 million! The court ruled that Trump Towers could retain the full 25 percent down payment because that had been negotiated between sophisticated businesspeople, represented by counsel; and if the buyers were dissatisfied with the non-refundable sum, they should have objected "at the bargaining table."

To insure recovery of liquidated damages, some suggest that the buyer pay the agreed sum as a nonforfeitable price for the option, as with stock or commodity options. While it is not clear that courts will approve a large liquidated damage sum, such as 15 or 30 percent, courts may not be willing to distinguish between the enforceability of a deposit forfeiture based on whether the deal is structured as an option or an agreement of sale.

The *Sheehan* and *Cem Uzan* cases should give comfort to Pennsylvania and New York sellers who have been concerned about the enforceability of liquidated damage clauses in real estate contracts.

48   PURCHASE MONEY AND WRAPAROUND
MORTGAGES

When low interest rates evaporate, or traditional loans become inadequate to meet borrowers' needs, lenders and borrowers find more creative ways to structure real estate mortgages.

Purchase Money Mortgages

As traditional mortgage financing becomes more costly, and more scarce, buyers are often able to convince sellers to wait for payment of part of the purchase price and take back purchase money mortgages (PMMs). Usually a seller agrees to take back a second mortgage in order to induce the buyer to pay the seller's price. Frequently, the buyer invests some of its own funds, and also either assumes the existing mortgage or obtains a new first mortgage from a bank or other lender to cover a substantial portion of the purchase price, and the seller's PMM "fills the gap."

PMMs come in many forms. Often the PMM is structured with a below-market interest rate and either no amortization or with a lengthy (15- to 20-year) amortization schedule, although a "balloon" payment (that fully pays the mortgage) may be due after three or five years. Some PMM interest rates are variable, fluctuating with the prime lending rate or with some other index. In these cases, maximum and minimum levels may be set for the floating rate.

A PMM usually means that buyers pay a higher price than they would otherwise have paid for an all-cash deal (or a price higher than they could afford, absent the PMM). The incentives sellers give to buyers to pay the negotiated price include relatively low mortgage payments and a much smaller down payment than the buyer could achieve with more traditional financing. In addition, the higher purchase price in the PMM deal may give the buyer a higher tax basis for depreciation. On the other hand, it could also precipitate an enlarged real estate tax assessment and higher real estate transfer taxes.

Sellers are usually satisfied because they have, ostensibly, received their asking price. However, they should carefully consider the disadvantages of this type of alternative financing.

Seller's Disadvantages

If the seller is a taxable entity, an unrealistically high price may trigger an unnecessarily high capital gains tax (which may be deferred under installment sale reporting rules, but only for cash-method taxpayers). Also, if the PMM is a second mortgage, the sellers expose themselves to all the traditional risks of a junior creditor.

Excessive Risk

If a senior lender forecloses, the seller's PMM may be wiped out. Suppose a balloon payment becomes due under the first mortgage and the buyer does not meet this payment. The seller may be forced to pay off the first mortgage to protect its PMM. Even if the first mortgage has favorable terms and no balloon, the buyer may nevertheless default, and the senior lender may accelerate the first mortgage. If this occurs at a time when interest rates are high, the original owner holding the PMM may be forced to refinance at an inopportune time. The owner may encounter substantial delays and costs as it attempts to collect on the PMM, especially if the buyer is in bankruptcy. In the worst case, the seller may never collect its full sale price.

Sellers who agree to take back subordinated PMMs should protect themselves as far as possible by structuring the terms and conditions of the loan. The sales agreement should include controls on the first mortgage that the buyer may obtain. The amount of the first mortgage should be limited to a sum that assures that the buyer has sufficient equity in the property so that it will not easily walk away from it. The first mortgage's interest rate, debt service, and prepayment penalties should be controlled or "capped." Sellers should attempt to insert clauses in sales agreements that prohibit balloon payments in the first mortgage. The contract and PMM should require the first mortgagee to give the seller notice and an opportunity to correct any default before the first mortgage may be foreclosed, and provide that such default will trigger a default under the PMM.

One strategy for minimizing defaults on the first mortgage is to take back a wraparound mortgage (described below) instead of a more traditional second mortgage.

Phantom Interest

If a seller should unexpectedly need cash and try to sell a low-interest-rate junior PMM (or borrow by pledging it), it will probably yield a surprisingly low cash value.

This reality check highlights the phenomenon of "phantom" interest. When the buyer pays a premium price for a property because the seller is willing to take back a low-interest-rate second mortgage, the true cost of that loan may not be fully appreciated by either party. In reality, part of the true interest cost is incorporated into the price of the property.

Tax Implications of PMMs

If the seller has the choice of receiving a series of payments, as either principal or interest, from a tax standpoint it usually prefers to receive them as principal rather than interest. Interest, generally, is taxable as ordinary income, whereas PMM principal payments represent payments of the purchase price and will be taxed only to the extent that they represent the seller's profit, and then usually at lower capital gains rates. The buyer, on the other hand, usually would rather pay interest than principal, because it may, subject to various limitations, deduct interest from taxable income on a current basis. On the other hand, a higher cost for the property merely increases depreciation, which produces significantly slower deductions.

Sellers may try to disguise interest receipts as capital receipts by structuring a deal that inflates the purchase price and reduces interest payments. To prevent this, the Internal Revenue Code permits the IRS to "impute" interest if the loan does not call for at least a minimum interest rate that is published by the IRS each month (known as the "applicable federal rate"). When the IRS imputes interest, the effective sale price is reduced for tax purposes, and the seller must recognize additional interest as taxable income allowing the buyer to benefit from additional interest deductions.

Accrued Interest and PMMs

Sellers may permit some of the interest on the PMM to accrue (rather than be paid currently), as a device that allows them to obtain a high purchase price and still charge high interest rates. This will permit the buyer to maintain a higher cash flow. In these transactions, the buyer may pay only a portion of the designated interest in any year. For example, the required interest payment may be based on or capped by the buyer's net earnings. The buyer accrues the balance of the interest and defers payment either until earnings are sufficient or the mortgage matures. Since the accrued interest will often exceed the principal reduction, the effect of this structure produces negative amortization, i.e., the debt actually increases.

Regardless of which accounting method the parties use, the interest will have to be accrued for tax purposes as "original issue discount."

Wraparound Mortgages

Wraparound mortgages have become less popular than they were in the 1980s, but when interest rates rise some more, wrap loans may once again become revived as a form of alternative financing. A wraparound mortgage is essentially a second mortgage that, instead of being a separate instrument, "wraps around" an existing first mortgage to create a single loan. The face amount of the wrap loan consists of the outstanding balance of an existing mortgage plus the amount of cash (or credit) that the junior lender agrees to advance to the owner. Then, for each installment the borrower makes a single payment of debt service to the wrap lender, who in turn pays the debt service on the senior mortgage.

When the interest rate on the wrap mortgage exceeds the rate on the first mortgage, the return to the wrap lender will exceed the stated rate of the wrap mortgage (the overall rate). Also, since the wrap lender collects the funds required to pay both mortgages, it derives more protection against a default on the first mortgage than if it had merely held a second mortgage.

Uses

The wraparound mortgage can be used to preserve the benefits of an existing mortgage with interest rates that are lower than present rates. Therefore, wraps are more likely to be used at a time when interest rates are rising. A wrap can be used for construction financing or to draw cash equity out of an existing property. It is also frequently used as a technique to sell a property. Unfortunately, many low-interest-rate mortgages contain clauses that prohibit secondary financing and, in those cases, the alternative of using a wraparound mortgage may not be available.

When they are not prohibited, wraps can also be used to deal with existing mortgages that either impose burdensome prepayment penalties or prohibit prepayment. However, wrap lenders should be aware of the pitfalls in using this device.

Many wraparound agreements will magnify the proportion of the debt service on a loan that qualifies as interest deductions. This occurs whenever the debt service on the wrap consists of interest only, while the debt service on the underlying loan includes an amortization component.

Consider the implications when the wrap lender receives its interest payment on the wrap and then makes a payment from this sum to the first mortgage holder. Since the latter payment includes principal, the wrap lender has received more interest than it paid out, and it therefore must pay income tax on an amount equal to the amortization component of the first mortgage. This spread is often referred to as "phantom" income, i.e., income without a corresponding cash flow. This explains why the principal wrap lenders are often either tax-exempt institutions, like pension funds, or lenders who can effectively minimize taxable income. On the other hand, the economic benefit of the amortization is enjoyed by the wrap lender rather than the borrowers.

Tax Savings

In addition to preserving the advantage of a low-interest-rate mortgage, which can induce a buyer to pay more for the property, the wrap technique may be used to save income taxes. It may be used to help alleviate the plague that many sellers have with what is known as "negative tax basis." That could occur where a seller has depreciated its tax basis below the amount of the remaining balance of the mortgage. For example, if the tax basis has been reduced to $500,000 and the existing mortgage is $800,000, when the seller sells the property for $1,000,000, it will have a gain of $500,000 even though it may receive only $200,000 in cash. If the property is sold subject to the existing mortgage and the buyer persuades the seller to take back a $200,000 purchase money second mortgage, the seller will have to recognize gain in the year of sale equal to the excess of the existing mortgage debt over the seller's cost basis (on the theory that the purchaser has assumed responsibility for the existing mortgage). Therefore, in this example, the seller will have to pay a tax on $300,000 of gain even though no cash is received, and the remaining $200,000 of gain will be deferred until the seller receives it.

The wrap provides a vehicle for cash-basis taxpayers to alleviate that problem. If the seller can take back a wraparound $1 million mortgage instead of a $200,000 second mortgage (with the same economic effect), the gain can be postponed until cash is received. In effect, the wrap loan consists of the combined first and second mortgages totaling $1 million. The seller, in effect, is saying it will remain liable to the first lender for payment of the debt service on the $800,000 loan and the purchaser is liable to it on the $1 million wrap loan. Therefore, the entire purchase price is in the form of a purchase money mortgage, and the seller does not have to recognize gain in the year of sale. Instead, the $500,000 gain ($1 million purchase price less $500,000 tax basis) is recognized pro rata as installment payments are made. While the IRS initially rejected this position, the Tax Court has upheld it (and the IRS has subsequently agreed). See *Professional Equities, Inc. v Commissioner*, 89 T.C. 165 (1987), Acq. 1988-2 C.B.1.

49 THE PROS AND CONS OF INSTALLMENT SALE AGREEMENTS

When a seller offers purchase money financing in a real estate transaction, it has the alternative of either transferring title to the buyer and taking back a purchase money mortgage or retaining title and giving the buyer an installment sale agreement (ISA). Like a mortgage, the ISA may be recorded. With either device, possession is turned over to the buyer and financial terms are described in the documents. The buyer can be required to make the identical down payment and identical monthly payments at the same interest rate, whether the parties use a mortgage or an ISA.

Advantages of an Installment Sale Agreement

There are several reasons why parties would want to use an ISA. Sometimes a seller has an existing low-interest mortgage that is not assumable by a purchaser. If the due-on-sale provision in the mortgage only prohibits deed transfers, the parties may be able to avoid triggering the provision by the use of the ISA (under which the seller retains title). When the final payment of the purchase price is made by the buyer, title will have to be transferred and the mortgage paid off. But this may be years away; and meanwhile, the buyer benefits from the existing low-interest loan.

A second possible advantage of an ISA is postponement of real estate transfer taxes until title is transferred. Under most transfer tax schemes (e.g., Pennsylvania's), agreements of sale are not taxable. This cost can be a major factor. For example, the Philadelphia transfer tax is 3 percent, and the Pennsylvania state transfer tax is 1 percent. If the parties take the route of an immediate deed and purchase money mortgage, they will pay $40,000 on a $1 million transfer.

Disadvantages to the Buyer

Unfortunately, buyers may pay a price for using an ISA. For one thing, when they eventually complete the required payments, they may have a problem obtaining the sellers' signatures on the deed. The seller may be an individual who disappears or dies after the agreement is signed, or it may be a corporation that has been liquidated.

Also, judgments may have been filed against the seller that become a lien against the real estate. Even when the buyer's interest is superior because the ISA was recorded first, the buyer may have to sue to clear title. There may be substantial legal costs involved, and the title transfer could be delayed for months or years.

It is possible the seller will go bankrupt. This could create difficult legal issues. The bankruptcy code protects buyers if they are in "possession" of the property, but what does this mean? For example, when property is being rented to tenants and the buyer has leased the property to other parties, is this "possession" for purposes of the Bankruptcy Code?

Another disadvantage of an ISA is that a buyer of nonresidential real estate has less protection in the event of a default than one who took title. Upon default and foreclosure under a mortgage, a buyer can pay the balance of the mortgage before the sheriff's sale and retain title to the property. However, in a nonresidential transaction using an ISA, a seller may attempt to forfeit the buyer's interest without formal action. Then the buyer may have difficulty establishing its right to take over the property after forfeiture, even if it is willing to pay off the balance of the purchase price. (By contrast, many states give a home buyer under an ISA the same right of redemption as under a purchase money mortgage.)

These potential problems can be alleviated somewhat by various legal devices such as protective provisions in the agreement, deeds in escrow, and special title insurance.

Disadvantages to the Seller

Sellers also should beware potential problems with ISAs. Because a seller retains title, the seller may be exposed to liability for personal injury claims long after possession is delivered to the buyer. The seller must make sure of continuous liability insurance coverage. Also, because the seller is still the recorded owner, the seller may be cited for code violations.

Sellers should also anticipate possible mechanic's liens resulting from a buyer's failure to pay contractors for property improvements. If the buyer has the right to make such improvements and if the seller is aware of them, the seller may have difficulty terminating mechanic's liens in the event the buyer defaults under the ISA. Although there is a strong argument that the liens should fall when the buyer's interest is terminated because of default, the law is not clear on this in many states.

This same problem would not exist if the seller were merely a lender. As a holder of a mortgage, the seller could foreclose in the event of the buyer's default and thereby wipe out any mechanic's liens against the buyer.

The seller's protection against fire damage under an ISA may not be as good as if it held a purchase money mortgage. A mortgagee is protected under fire policies even though the purchaser may have committed arson or fraud against the insurance company. However, an installment seller is not in the same position; the insurance company may not be willing to pay the seller under these circumstances. Therefore, a seller must be careful to obtain the same insurance protection as it would have had if it were a mortgage holder.

Uncertain Remedies

A more subtle issue involves the seller's default remedies. If a seller wants to take back title, it will notify the buyer that its rights are terminated, but then what? The remedies of a seller under a purchase money mortgage are clear. It follows the required procedural steps in foreclosure.

In many states, a seller's rights under an ISA are not as certain. If it attempts to sue for "ejectment" or "to quiet title," the buyer might defend by arguing that the installment seller is in substance a mortgage lender, and therefore its only remedy is foreclosure. See Grant S. Nelson and Dale A. Whitman, *Real Estate Finance Law* 104–08 (2d Ed. 1985).

On the other hand, if the seller attempts to foreclose under the ISA, the buyer may defend on the ground that the seller cannot foreclose unless it holds a mortgage. This uncertainty whether the agreement is a duck or a swan could lead to a substantial delay in the seller's exercise of its rights.

Conclusion

In summary, the ISA may sometimes be used to the advantage of the parties in avoiding due-on-sale provisions and transfer taxes. However, upon default the ISA may not provide the seller with greater protection than a mortgage. And worse, it may provide both parties with problems that would not arise with a purchase money mortgage.

50   TAX-FREE EXCHANGES: IRS PROVIDES GUIDANCE TO EXCHANGE OF PARTNERSHIP INTERESTS

The IRS has issued guidelines that will help taxpayers to determine whether a transfer of an undivided fractional interest in rented real estate will be eligible for a tax-free exchange under Section 1031 of the Internal Revenue Code.

What does all of this mean, and how will it help real estate owners? To understand the significance of these guidelines, one must be aware of the background of the tax-free exchange rules under which the IRS operates. Section 1031 permits taxpayers to avoid recognition of income when property used in a trade or business or held for investment is transferred in exchange for "like kind" property. It is one of the few big breaks in the tax code for owners of real estate. Essentially, it permits an owner to exchange the business or investment real estate it owns for business or investment real estate it acquires, and thereby avoid gain on the property sold. To receive that treatment, the taxpayers must follow a set of deadlines and technical rules listed under the Internal Revenue Code. Those who are able to comply may save millions of dollars in taxes.

Partnerships

One of the limitations on the use of tax-free exchanges has been a provision in the 1984 Tax Act that amended Section 1031 to provide that a partnership interest does not qualify for like-kind exchange treatment. Therefore, interests in real estate partnerships are denied that special treatment, even though for most other purposes the IRS considers partnerships merely as "pass-through" entities, that is, it ignores the partnership as a separate entity from the partners, and taxes income at the partners level, rather than the partnership level.

It is not exactly clear what tax policy drove this provision, but real estate owners and tax lawyers have been struggling with this rule ever since it was instituted. The IRS reiterated that rule in April 1991 by issuing regulations that made the advantages of Section 1031 inapplicable to any exchange of partnership interest "regardless of whether the interests exchanged are general or limited partnership interests or are interests in the same partnership or in different partnerships." 26 C.F.R. § 1.1031(a)-1.

A partnership can still take advantage of Section 1031 if it is willing to transfer the real estate in exchange for other real estate that will be transferred to the partnership. But, what if some partners want to sell the real estate for cash rather than participate in a like-kind exchange? The partners who would like to sell may be able to sell their partnership interests, but under the Internal Revenue Code and applicable IRS regulations, they will not qualify for nonrecognition of gain. That's because they would be transferring their partnership interests for cash and not participating in a like-kind exchange of the real estate itself. This becomes particularly important in some states because under realty transfer-tax laws, there could be an advantage to selling the partnership interest rather than the real estate itself.

Tenancies in Common

One major issue in determining the treatment of the transfer of fractionalized interests in real estate is the effect of these rules on the transfer of interests of what are known as "tenants in common." These interests are the sisters of partnership interests but are treated differently under both real estate law and Section 1031. The central characteristic of a tenancy in common is that each owner is deemed to individually own a physically undivided part of the entire parcel of property. Each tenant in common is entitled to share with the other tenants the possession of the whole parcel and enjoys the associated rights to a proportionate share of rents or profits from the property, to transfer the interests, and to demand a partition of the property. Richard R. Powell, *Powell On Real Property,* §§ 50.01–50.07 (Michael Allan Wolf ed. 2000).

If owners could transfer their real estate interests from a partnership to a tenancy in common and retain the same proportionate interests, the partners who want to participate in a like-kind exchange could then do an exchange of partial interests in the real estate for other real estate, and avoid the IRS limits on transfers of partnership interests. The partners who want to sell could transfer their partial interests in the real estate for cash in a taxable transaction without adversely affecting the tax treatment of the other partners. However, a tenancy in common that is converted from a partnership may not qualify for this special treatment unless it holds title as a tenancy in common for a period of time.

For obvious reasons, it became important to determine whether the IRS would disqualify tenancies in common from Section 1031 treatment by recharacterizing them as partnerships, because if a tenancy in common interest is treated as a partnership interest, the owner of the interest cannot participate in a like-kind exchange. Unfortunately, the IRS had taken the position that it would not issue advance rulings on whether the undivided tenant in common interest in real estate was eligible for this special treatment. The IRS was concerned that certain tenant-in-common interests might constitute an interest in an entity classified as a partnership for federal income tax purposes; and this made it very difficult for taxpayers to predict the outcome of exchanges of these interests.

Guidelines

That is where the revenue procedure comes in. On March 19, 2002, the IRS announced the conditions under which it will consider a request for a ruling on these issues, and it repealed the earlier ban on advance rulings. Rev. Proc. 2002-22; 2002-14 IRB 1(19 Mar. 2002).

This revenue procedure provides little guidance for what constitutes a qualifying tenant-in-common interest. It also states that the IRS may still decline to issue an advance ruling "whenever warranted by the facts and circumstances of a particular case and whenever appropriate in the interest of sound tax administration." However, it may lead to guidance in future rulings, and possibly announcements.

For those interested in tax-free exchanges, it is important to read the actual guidelines. One of the significant sections (section 6) provides "conditions for obtaining rulings." This section sets forth, among other things, the following conditions that will lead toward a ruling that a real estate interest is a tenancy in common, as contrasted with a partnership:

- Title must be a tenancy in common recognized under state law;
- There must be no more than 35 co-owners;
- Co-ownership may not file a partnership return, or conduct business under a common name or hold itself out as a partnership;
- Certain major management decisions must be unanimous, and other actions must be made by at least 50 percent of the interests;
- There must be proportionate sharing of revenues and costs.

These are only a few of the listed factors, but it will give the reader a sense of some of the distinctions that the IRS intends to make.

The new guidelines have now opened the door a little and shed some light on a dark and murky area of tax law. However, until further clarifications are issued, taxpayers and their lawyers and consultants will still be stumbling around in the dark when trying to distinguish between partnerships and tenancies in common.

51   LAWYERS AS ESCROW AGENTS

Should lawyers act as escrow agents when one of their clients is involved in the transaction?

Duty of Loyalty

Acting as an escrow agent in your clients' transactions may be customary in some states, but that could be risky. In the case of *Galvanek v. Skibitcky,* 738 A.2d 1150 (Conn. App. 1999), a lawyer acted as an escrow agent and also represented one of the parties to the escrow arrangement. The court held that that arrangement was void because the lawyer's duty of loyalty to his client barred serving as an escrow holder.

Connecticut lawyers objected that it was necessary for them to serve as escrow agents because Connecticut provided little opportunity for independent escrow agents to do business. The legislature then passed a law that validated lawyer escrows, which was upheld in the case of *Rockwell v. Klein,* No. CV990174980 (Conn. Super. Ct. December 12, 2000), *rev'd on other grounds, remanded sub nom., Collard & Roe, P.C. v. Klein,* 806 A.2d 580 (Conn. App. Ct. 2002). See also *Young v. Young,* 781 A.2d 342 (Conn. App. Ct. 2001).

These cases have been the focus of comments around the country in a national Internet listserv called "DIRT." Participating lawyers have pointed out that the standard practice in the state of Washington and in other western states is that if an attorney served as an escrow agent, that attorney could not represent any party to the escrow arrangement. One exception is that lawyers can act as escrow agents where there is no other choice of a proper escrow holder, and only after the parties have been given proper disclosures and warnings.

Although there are many title companies and other institutions that may act as escrow holders, lawyers will sometimes act in that capacity, even when they represent one of the parties. They may even do it without a detailed written agreement. That could be risky, because lawyers may find themselves right in the middle of a dispute over the escrow fund.

Escrow Agreements

If lawyers act as escrow holders, they should at least insist on an escrow agreement and explain the agreement to their client. That agreement should spell out the precise event for the release of the escrow—and that event should not be subjective. For example, instead of the attorney having to make a decision about whether certain repairs have been made, the triggering event should be the receipt of a letter from a designated party certifying the repairs have been made.

In addition, if there is a dispute, attorneys should be able to continue to represent their clients, and should be able to either deposit the escrowed item into court in an interpleader, or hold it until a court order is received. Also, the attorney should be indemnified against any costs or expenses by the parties to the escrow.

Title companies that occasionally act as escrow holders have devised specific forms of escrow agreements that are designed to protect them. These types of agreements could be used as a basis for drafting an attorney's escrow agreement.

Disputes

Despite all of those protections, attorneys who are optimistic enough to think that they can accommodate their clients by acting as escrow agents with impunity may be in for a rude awakening. Take a simple case where a sum is to be held in escrow after a home purchase in order to assure that the seller repairs the roof. Even with an escrow agreement, a dispute could arise about whether the repair has been fully completed.

Suppose the attorney, acting as an escrow holder, had represented the seller in the transaction and, because of a dispute, simply decides to hold the escrowed sum until the dispute is resolved. The angry seller thinks that she has done everything she was supposed to do and now needs the money to pay the roofer. She then decides to sue the buyer, who disagrees with her, and also to join the escrow holder, who is her attorney. She may claim that her attorney owes a duty of loyalty to represent her, and that her attorney has violated that duty. Even if that argument doesn't stand up in court under the agreement, she will have to go out and find another attorney to represent her.

Unfortunately, the accommodating attorney has been placed in an uncomfortable position. In addition, that example involves a relatively simple triggering event for the release from escrow. Imagine what nightmares may be stirred up if the release raises more complex issues, such as confirming that the required document meets certain standards or involves other parties than just the buyer and the seller.

Loss of Escrow Fund

An additional nightmare materialized in the recent case of *Bazinet v. Kluge*, 788 N.Y.S.2d 77 (N.Y. App. Div. 2005), in which a client sued a lawyer for loss of escrow funds when the depository bank tanked. In that case, the trial court had refused to grant summary judgment for the lawyer until it heard expert testimony of whether a lawyer should have a duty to be more careful in its selection of the depository bank. The lawyer had deposited down payments of over $2.7 million in the Connecticut Bank of Commerce, which to his dismay had closed two days before he attempted to draw the funds. Only a portion of the deposit will be recoverable from the FDIC insurance of $100,000 per account and the sale of the bank's assets. The claim was made against the lawyer for malpractice because he did not deposit the escrow funds "in some form of interest-bearing account or instrument that would have been covered by FDIC insurance or taking some other steps to ensure preservation of those funds." 764 N.Y.S.2d 320 at 322.

The New York Appellate Division has now given some comfort to lawyers who act as escrow agents. It reversed the trial court and held that there is no requirement imposed by law on an attorney-escrow agent to place escrow funds in an account fully insured by the FDIC, and that the "proximate cause" of the client's loss was the bank's unforeseen demise. An attorney should only be held liable if it can be proved that his or her conduct fell below the ordinary and reasonable skill and knowledge commonly possessed by other lawyers.

Even though the lawyer may have escaped liability in this case, he may not have escaped embarrassment, a loss of stature—and a loss of a client. The *Bazinet* case sends a message to all lawyers to be careful about whether they should act as escrow agents, and even if they graciously accept these assignments to accommodate clients, they should not carry out their responsibilities casually.

52 SUCCESSOR LIABILITY: PURCHASERS AT FORECLOSURE MAY INADVERTENTLY ASSUME LIABILITIES OF BORROWER

The purchaser of a property subject to timeshare owners' rights may be required to honor its predecessor's commitment to provide parking, restaurants, and recreation facilities on an adjacent hotel property. That issue arose in a case decided in the Eighth U.S. Circuit Court pursuant to the Arkansas Time-Share Act, where the separately owned hotel had terminated the amenities despite what purported to be an "irrevocable" license agreement. *Kessler v. National Enters., Inc.,* 238 F.3d 1006 (8th Cir. 2001).

In that case a developer had constructed a hotel and an adjacent 20-unit condominium resort. Before completion of the construction, the developer sold the property to the Lakeshore Resort and Yacht Club Partnership. Lakeshore began a time-share project at the resort pursuant to the Arkansas Time-Share Act. Lakeshore obtained a license agreement from the developer that allowed time-share purchasers to use hotel parking as well as the recreational amenities at the hotel. The Arkansas Real Estate Commission approved the time-share proposal only after a license agreement was made irrevocable.

Foreclosure

Lakeshore marketed the time-share units with a sales brochure stating that "as a Lakeshore owner, all of the facilities at the [hotel] are yours to use and enjoy." When Lakeshore defaulted on its loan, National Enterprises, Inc. (NEI) purchased the property at a foreclosure sale. Thereafter, the hotel continued to honor the license agreement for seven or eight years (of the 35-year time-share term).

After a series of changes in financing and ownership of both the resort and the hotel, the hotel took the position that it was not legally required to honor the license agreement. The time-share owners then began a suit against NEI alleging that the denial of access to the hotel facilities and parking breached the time-share owners' contracts with the developer, which NEI had assumed pursuant to the state time-share act. The time-share owners demanded equitable rescission of the remaining portion of the time-share units and a partial refund on the purchase prices.

Circuit Court Reverses

The U.S. District Court ruled in favor of NEI and held it was not liable as a successor, and also the developer was not liable for breach of contract or misrepresentation. That decision was reversed on appeal by the Eighth Circuit Court of Appeals, which ruled that under the Arkansas Time-Share Act a successor owner is liable for all obligations of the initial owner. According to the court, that statute does not limit the obligations transferred, but instead includes all of the original developer's obligations related to the original time-share owners.

The court noted that the Arkansas provision is derived from a model act adopted by several other states. Tennessee, faced with the precise issue in this case, held that a new owner purchasing at a foreclosure sale took subject to all of the obligations of the earlier owner. The court stated that the overriding purpose of the act was to protect consumers. To limit those obligations to a developer forced into foreclosure would be meaningless. A similar decision had also been reached in Florida, although that statutory language was somewhat different.

In summary, the court held that the new owner was bound by the original developers' promises concerning continued access to the hotel facilities and parking. Therefore, the time-share owners were entitled to equitable relief in the form of partial rescission, and the case was remanded to the district court for the calculation of damages.

In this case the time-share owners were helped by specific language in the time-share act that mandated that a developer's successor "shall be subject to the obligations of the developer." If a similar issue had arisen in a different context, such as a development of a conventional residential community of separate homes, the homeowners may not have been successful.

In *Kessler* the plaintiffs made an alternative argument that NEI had assumed the developer's obligation under common-law principles of corporate successor liability. In a footnote, the court expressed its doubts that these common-law principles would apply, or that NEI would have been liable absent the requirements of the time-share act.

Hotel Amenities

In this case, NEI was saddled with an obligation to supply hotel amenities, even though it was legally incapable of actually furnishing the described services. While the court does not get into the substantive reasons for it, NEI had attempted to enforce the licensing agreement against the hotel and had not succeeded in the district court. The case at hand was not about enforcing the licensing agreement against the hotel. Rather, it was about the time-share owner's rights against NEI to refunds and rescission.

From the perspective of the condo owners, the loss of hotel rights was crucial. Apparently the condos had no parking without that, and did not have access to any other property for parking. In addition, the utilities were furnished by the hotel and could have been disconnected. Also, evidence indicated that without access to the hotel's recreation amenities, such as swimming pools and the marina, there would be little reason for owners to stay in the condos.

On the other hand, from the hotel's perspective, the successor liability that might have applied to future hotel owners could have been disastrous. A lender that secured its loan by a mortgage on the hotel might find itself stuck with a very significant liability. If the obligations were evidenced only by a licensing agreement, it might not even show up in a title search against the hotel property.

Suppose years later the hotel started losing money and a better use of the property compelled closing the hotel and the parking lot to develop it in another way. Then the hotel owners might be barred from doing that because they were committed to the licensing agreement with the residential community. Under those circumstances, would the successor be required to continue to operate the losing restaurant, the lakefront activities, and the golf and tennis facilities without limit into the future, even though it was losing substantial amounts every year? Also, would courts place any limits on the losses that the owners must sustain, or capital expenditures that may be needed to keep it operating; and would they be willing to monitor the level of continuing services that such a successor must maintain?

53   USA PATRIOT ACT AFFECTS REAL ESTATE CLOSINGS

In 2001 the federal government enacted the "Uniting and Strengthening America by Providing Appropriate Tools Required to Intercept and Obstruct Terrorism," commonly known as the USA Patriot Act (Pub. L. No. 107-56). Title III of the Patriot Act, also known as the International Monetary Laundering Abatement and Financial Anti-Terrorism Act of 2001, made numerous amendments to the anti–money laundering provisions of the Bank Secrecy Act, 31 U.S.C. § 5311 *et seq.* The amendments are intended to make it easier to prevent, detect, and prosecute international money laundering and financing terrorism.

Comments Invited

Section 352 of the Patriot Act amended 31 U.S.C. § 5318(h) of the Bank Secrecy Act to require financial institutions to institute anti–money laundering compliance programs. Under the act, the Financial Crimes Enforcement Network of the Treasury Department (FinCEN) temporarily exempted certain financial institutions including those involved in real estate closings and settlements from the act's anti–money laundering requirements. The stated purpose of the exemption was to enable the Treasury Department to study the affected industries and to consider the extent to which anti–money laundering requirements should be applied to them.

FinCEN issued an advance notice of proposed rulemaking with respect to real estate closings and settlements. FinCEN posed a wide range of questions, including how to define "persons involved in real estate closings and settlements," the money laundering risks posed by such persons, and whether they should be exempted from this requirement. Anti-Money Laundering Program Requirements for "Persons Involved in Real Estate Closings and Settlements," 68 Fed.Reg. 17569 (proposed April 10, 2003; no final rule as of January 2006).

Based on the public comments received from affected groups, including lenders, title companies, and lawyers, a cynic might conclude that this Anti-Terrorism Act has visited a form of terror on some of those parties.

Let's look at the act's proposed requirements of particular concern to these parties.

The act would require every "financial institution," including "persons involved in real estate settlements and closings" to establish an anti–money laundering compliance program that includes at a minimum:

(i)   the development of internal policies, procedures, and controls;

(ii) the designation of a compliance officer;

(iii) an ongoing employee training program; and

(iv) an independent audit function to test programs.

While the independent audit may prove to be the most intrusive and expensive requirement, the other requirements impose more fundamental concerns.

Money Laundering Risks

Let's look at the money laundering risks that Congress perceived in real estate closings and settlements. The request for comments stated that money launderers have used real estate transactions to attempt to disguise the illegal source of their proceeds. For example, narcotics traffickers have purchased property with monetary instruments that they purchased in structured amounts, that is, multiple purchases each below the Bank Secrecy Act reporting thresholds ($10,000) that in aggregate exceeded the thresholds.

Also, traffickers have tried to launder cash proceeds by exchanging them for checks from a real estate company. According to FinCEN, the funds from illegal activities or funds intended to support illegal activities could be introduced into the financial system through the payment for real estate with a large cash down payment. In addition, multiple pieces of real estate could be bought and resold, exchanged, swapped, or syndicated, making identification of the true origin of the funds even more difficult.

Some examples provided by FinCEN of how the real estate industry is vulnerable to money laundering were apparently identified by the American Land Title Association. They include the following:

- A prospective buyer pays for real estate with funds from a high-risk country, or one that has been designated as a "primary money-laundering concern."
- A seller requests that the proceeds of the sale of real estate be sent to a high-risk country.
- A person seeks to purchase real estate in the name of a nominee without providing a legitimate explanation for the use of a nominee.
- A person acts as an agent for an undisclosed party and is reluctant to provide information about the party or the reason for the agency relationship.
- A person does not appear to be sufficiently knowledgeable about the use or the purpose of the real estate being purchased.
- A person appears to be buying or selling the same piece of real estate within a short period of time or is buying multiple pieces for no apparent, legitimate purpose.
- A prospective purchaser or seller seeks to have documents reflect something other than the true nature of the transaction.
- A person provides suspicious documentation to verify his or her identity.

Obviously, this list of red-flag situations could include some in which brokers, lawyers, title companies, or lenders routinely find themselves. If so, then the statutory duties imposed under the act may be visited upon them.

Persons Involved in Real Estate Closings and Settlements

FinCEN points out that neither the Patriot Act nor the earlier Bank Secrecy Act defines "persons involved in a real estate closing or settlement as a financial institution." Also, according to FinCEN, the legislative history offers no insight into how Congress intended to define the term.

Therefore, a reasonable interpretation could apply the section even to participants other than those who actually conduct real estate settlements. Among those potential participants are real estate brokers, attorneys, banks, mortgage brokers, other financial entities, title insurance companies, and even appraisers and inspectors. The guiding principle, according to FinCEN, is to apply the statute to those whose services can be abused by money launderers, including those positioned to identify the purpose and nature of the transaction.

Of primary concern for diligent lawyers is that FinCEN found that attorneys often play a key role in real estate closings and "thus merit consideration along with all the other professionals involved in the closing" process. The advance notice of proposed rulemaking specifically states that FinCEN does not believe that the application of the act's requirements to attorneys poses any obligations inconsistent with the attorney-client privilege. It states:

> In fact, attorneys already must exercise due diligence when they receive funds from clients where there is an indication that the funds may be tainted, and cannot simply accept funds without the risk that their fees will be subject to forfeiture. When engaging in conduct subject to anti-money laundering regulations, attorneys, like other professionals, should take the basic steps contemplated by Section 352 to ensure that their services are not being abused by money launderers.

The proposal should be considered in conjunction with the broader range of recommendations issued by the Financial Action Task Force (FATF), providing that attorneys should be "gatekeepers" not only subject to the due diligence FinCEN currently proposes but also to whistleblowing requirements, that is, the reporting of suspicious client activities. In fact, FATF issued a revised version of its "The Forty Recommendations" in June 2003, which requires not only client investigation but the reporting of suspicious client activities by attorneys who act in the purchase and sale of real estate as well as in the management of client money, securities, or assets; the organization or creation of companies; and the purchase or sale of business entities. FATF, "The Forty Recommendations" (June 2003).

Critical Comments

As expected, the proposed rules have spurred those groups that deal with real estate closings to provide critical analyses on the proposed rules. For example, a spokesperson of the American Land Title Association has responded that property transactions are not a very good way to launder money because many cash-reporting requirements already exist. While this point is questionable, the underlying concerns are well taken.

The American Bar Association House of Delegates passed a resolution in February 2003 opposing any anti–money laundering law that would force lawyers to disclose confidential client information or compromise the lawyer/client relationship. The resolution noted that the ABA would continue to review its Model Rules to determine whether they should be modified in order to permit some disclosure if it is clear that clients intend to violate money-laundering laws. The ABA Task Force on Gatekeeper Regulation and the Profession has stated that any requirement that attorneys must report the activities of their clients to the federal (or any) government "would undermine the independence of the Bar from the government, erode the essential trust relationship between the attorney and the client which is a bedrock of the U.S. administration of justice and rule of law, and compromise the principle of confidentiality in communications between the lawyer and the client."

Currently, the ABA Model Rules of Professional Conduct prohibit attorneys from revealing information related to their representation of clients without client consent. This assures the client that full and frank communication can occur without fear of disclosure. The single exception to the rule has been a modification to some state bar rules that requires attorneys to divulge information disclosed by clients when that disclosure may be necessary to prevent the commission of a crime, or death or bodily harm to others. However, even under this very limited exception, attorneys have no obligation to conduct investigations of clients.

It should be noted, however, that the ABA, under pressure because of the Sarbanes-Oxley legislation, proposed modification of the Model Rules to permit disclosure to prevent, mitigate, or rectify substantial injury to the financial interests of another where the client used the attorney's services. While not specifically directed at money laundering, the proposed amendments would open the door to whistleblowing rules.

The American College of Mortgage Attorneys (ACMA) has submitted comments that argue that mortgage and real estate attorneys should not be subject to any requirements under the Act—that they should be exempt from being considered "financial institutions" or "involved in real estate closings and settlements."

ACMA emphasized the effect that the proposed rule would have on sole practitioners and smaller firms not able, on a cost-effective basis, to perform the proposed required tasks:

> They will not have the time, financial means or ability to develop the requisite internal policies, higher compliance officers or provide training programs—and certainly will not be able to establish and carry out independent audit functions involving the client's intentions and the source of its funds, which additionally would place attorneys in the awkward, and perhaps unethical, position of informing on their clients to federal authorities with their clients' knowledge or consent. To impose such requirements on attorneys would significantly increase the cost of legal services and may even cause some attorneys to abandon this area of the practice of law.

ACMA also has pointed out that many closings are conducted without the physical presence of the parties who sign documents in advance, and that many involve individuals or the use of ownership entities often created for the specific purpose of holding title to the real estate. It further stated:

> The institution of the proposed rule would likely require attorneys for both lenders and borrowers to be present at the closing, along with all of their clients in order to properly and completely investigate the individuals and/or entities receiving or providing funds at the closing. Such a requirement would often add a significant closing expense to clients ... Further, it would seem impractical—if not impossible—for attorneys representing borrowers to effectively investigate the source of funding of loans from financial institutions making the loan in question or to check the background of the principals of the parties to the transaction. The attorney, who may be acting only as local counsel in the transaction or may not even have met the client before the closing (or who very often will never meet the client at any stage of the transaction), often will have

314

no knowledge of the identity of all the shareholders or constituent members or partners of a corporate, limited liability company or partnership client that is purchasing property or obtaining a loan especially at "second-tier" or non-management levels. At the very least, an attorney involved in a real estate closing should be able to rely on a FIRPTA-type affidavit or certification from another participant at the closing as to the source and nature of the funds and/or the fact that such other participant has performed appropriate due-diligence regarding the parties to the transaction and their business purpose and constituent members for the purpose of complying with applicable anti-laundering and terrorism statutes and regulations.

The American College of Real Estate Lawyers (ACREL) also has drafted a detailed response to the proposed rulemaking. ACREL has proposed what might be characterized as certain compromise positions for FinCEN to consider. One such position is that a protocol be set up that would require only one participant in a real estate closing to have primary responsibility for performing due diligence investigations and confirming to the other participants the results of those investigations. Depending on the nature of the transaction, that "confirming party" may be the lender, the escrow agent, the title company, or the broker; and the other participants would be entitled to rely on the confirming party's certification (with certain limited exceptions).

Also, ACREL suggested that certain real estate closings should be exempt from the act's requirements. The suggested exemption would include transactions below a significant amount (say $10 million), where an institutional lender finances the transaction. This amount is substantially higher than other whistle-blowing rules that currently set a threshold of $5,000. The exemption also would apply to certain transactions where the due diligence investigation has been performed previously, and those where real estate is not the principal asset. ACREL is most concerned with any requirements that would obligate a lawyer to perform due diligence investigations on the lawyer's own client because such activities may violate the attorney-client privilege and the duty of client confidentiality. The investigation requirement also forces the lawyer to assume an adversarial relationship with the client. ACREL's full comments are well worth reading and are available at its Web site (www.acrel.org, click on "Public Documents").

In light of all the critical and incisive comments submitted, FinCEN will have its work cut out in trying to devise reasonable regulations to implement the Patriot Act that will accommodate both the needs of the government to combat terrorism and the needs of the real estate industry. All lawyers involved in real estate closings should follow the progress of the rules very carefully so that they and their clients do not find themselves targeted as law-breakers in the new federal environment. (Note: The June 28, 2004, Department of the Treasury's Semiannual Agenda report states: "Abstract: FinCEN will issue a series of regulations regarding anti-money laundering program requirements for persons involved in real estate closings and settlements, as defined in the Bank Secrecy Act." Semiannual Agenda, 69 Fed.Reg. 37965.)

Real estate options are peculiar. They are not interests in real estate and yet they have some of the characteristics of real estate ownership. They can be used like agreements of sale, but they are very different.

This chapter explores many of those characteristics and the problems that arise in the use of real estate options, including how option holders can sometimes lose them. It covers:

- how tenants can negotiate renewal options
- some common errors that landlords make in granting options of first refusal
- when a seller may benefit from giving real estate options
- issues in using options as security for loans
- losing an option

Negotiating Tenants' Renewal Options

Successful tenants may take a leaf out of Franklin Delano Roosevelt's book and seek several renewal terms. But tenants have an advantage over U.S. presidents. They can assure their extensions without having to face someone who's trying to throw them out.

Despite this, many firms negotiate their office leases without any options to extend. At the time they sign their leases, the end of their term seems too far away to worry about. In fact, when a tenant's original term expires, it usually has no problem working out a desired extension, even without an option.

Options to Extend.   However, without that option, tenants leave too much to chance. They may have built up a successful practice during a 5- or 10-year period, have a beautiful reception area

317

and be completely satisfied with the installation and location of their telephone equipment, word processing center, and library. Then, at the end of their term, the landlord may want the space back or may have another firm willing to pay more rent. Tenants may then wake up to the fact that they have not taken care of themselves as well as they would have done with any one of their clients.

One way to prevent this is to negotiate options to extend as part of the original lease. Perhaps the landlord will agree to a set rental for the option periods. It may want a high increase because it is trying to cover itself against higher market rental rates and inflation; but that's better than nothing.

Assume the option calls for a 25 percent increase in rent during a five-year extension. If the fair-market rental is lower than that when the time comes, tenants do not have to exercise the option. Before their lease expires, they can try to negotiate an extension at the then-market rate. On the other hand, if the market rate is more than the agreed option rate, they can exercise the option and have the best of all possible worlds.

Frequently, a landlord will not set an extension rate. After all, it does not have a crystal ball to see what the future will hold for this site. But, it may be willing to base the rent extension upon percentage increases in the Consumer Price Index (CPI).

CPI Increases. The CPI measures the average change in prices over time in a fixed market basket of goods and services. The Bureau of Labor Statistics publishes CPIs for two population groups: (1) a CPI for All Urban Consumers (CPI-U), which covers approximately 80 percent of the total population, and (2) a revised CPI for Urban Wage Earners and Clerical Workers (CPI-W), which represents about half the population covered by the CPI-U.

The index measures price changes from a designated reference date that equals 100.0. An increase of 22 percent, for example, is shown as 122.0.

There is no clear-cut advantage for a tenant to select one of these indexes over the other. Frequently, they have increased at an identical rate.

The tenant has another important choice to make: whether to use the "all items" or the "rent" figure. Most rent adjustment clauses in leases use the "all items" figure in the CPI rather than the figure for rental costs, which actually is for residential rather than for commercial rents. (There is also a separate figure for home ownership costs.) In general, residential rent increases have not kept pace with the overall CPI increase; consequently, use of the all-items measure as the standard for rent escalation generally works in favor of landlords.

A lease should also provide for an alternative calculation if the publication of the CPI index is discontinued or its composition materially altered. One alternative would specify another nationally recognized publisher of similar statistical information, preferably to be designated by the tenant, if the need arises.

The parties may structure these CPI increases in various ways. A tenant would like the CPI percentage to apply only to that portion of the rent that represents the landlord's "net cash flow." If the landlord agrees to that, it will probably also want the tenant to pay a pro rata share of increases in operating costs and real estate taxes over a specified base year. These are sometimes called "pass-through costs."

Tenants may be able to convince landlords to charge these pass-through costs, and to apply only a 15 to 20 percent portion of the CPI increases to the basic rent. After all, that should cover landlords for the decreasing cost of the dollar based on their anticipated spendable cash flow after expenses.

Why is that fair? Tenants can point out that since they pay for increases in costs, the portion of the gross rent that goes to pay costs is covered, and a large portion of the rent generally goes to pay mortgage servicing charges that don't increase with inflation. On the other hand, landlords may want tenants to pay 100 percent of the CPI increases. They may demand this, not only on the basic rent, but also on the pass-through costs that tenants pay each year. Tenants should point out to landlords that this gives them what might be designated as a "double increase." That approach will require tenants to pay for increases of operating expenses, and also for CPI increases on those increased expenses. Even this may not satisfy some landlords, because they are still not protected against the possibility that values and rents at that location may increase at a much faster rate than the CPI.

What is left to negotiate? Those landlords who are unwilling to establish set rental figures or CPI standards may agree to an extension at the reasonable or fair market rental value at the time of the extension. That shouldn't be difficult to sell. If leases expire and landlords want to rent the property to someone else, presumably, they'd only be able to rent at the fair-market rental value anyway. Why shouldn't they give the present tenant a first chance at it?

319

What Is "Reasonable?"

One problem with this type of option is that a "reasonable" or "fair" market rental may not always be so easy to determine. Hundreds of thousands of dollars of rent may be at stake when parties cannot agree. Many landlords and tenants will not want to use this standard because they fear they are buying into litigation.

It may even be argued that a renewal option at a reasonable market value is unenforceable because the rent is too indefinite. Is such a provision merely an "agreement to make an agreement," binding only if the parties can negotiate a rental figure at some future time? A New York appellate court has ruled that the questioned language was enforceable and upheld a tenant's renewal term. According to the court, the rent was reasonably certain, and "market value" established an objective enough standard to determine the rent by a number of methods, including judicial resolution. *Northup v. Hushard*, 514 N.Y.S.2d 304 (N.Y. App. Div. 1987). This seems to be the prevailing view.

One issue that will be more prevalent in this age of increasingly significant telecommunications issues is how you evaluate a fair-market value for what might be considered a more valuable and improved potential use for the space. If the space is fit up with high-speed communications connections and fiber-optic connections, it may be rented at several times the existing rental rate.

Cases on Renewal Options

One case held that rent to be fixed by the landlord's then "scheduled rent" did not mean that fair-market rent had to be charged. In that case the landlord was allowed to charge rent for the option period that was substantially higher than the then fair-market rent, and even higher than rent that was then charged on other floors of the building. *CH2M Hill Northwest v. Parktel I, Inc.*, 812 P.2d 840 (Or. Ct. App. 1991).

Other courts have struggled with setting their own standard when the parties did not do a good job of setting one. In *Brown's Shoe Fit Co. v. Olch*, 955 P.2d 357 (Utah Ct. App. 1998), the parties set a minimum rent plus a percentage override on sales above a certain gross volume threshold. However, the parties were to agree "on the gross volume figure" for the calculation of the override. "Gross volume" was never defined.

The Utah appellate court held that there was no duty to negotiate fairly or in "good faith" to reach a fair-market rent for an extension term where the lease did not specify a standard for setting the rent. Therefore, the terms of the option were too vague to be enforceable.

In contrast, another court held that the landlord is required to set rent at a fair market rental even when the lease clearly gave the landlord the right to raise the rent "in its sole discretion" and permitted the tenant to terminate if the tenant did not want to renew its lease at the higher rate offered by the landlord. *Amoco Oil Co. v. Ervin*, 908 P.2d 493 (Colo. 1995). That case involved the renewal rent for a gas station, and the court required the landlord to follow a standard of "good faith and fair dealing."

Option: Tenant's Lease May Affect Prevailing Market Value

Another case raised the question about whether rent paid by a tenant is relevant in determining the fair-market value to be paid under that tenant's purchase option. *Petula Assocs. v. Dolco Packaging Corp.*, 240 F.3d 499 (5th Cir. 2001).

In this case, Petula had a 15-year lease starting in 1985 on a commercial building. The lease contained three options:

- a lease renewal option;
- a fixed-price purchase option during the first five years; and
- a "fair-market-value" purchase option during the next five years.

In 1990, one month before the expiration of the first five years, the parties amended the lease to provide that the tenant's rent would be lowered during the next five years, and this reduction would be offset by a higher rental in the last five years. Also, the parties then extended the fixed-price purchase option, and agreed that the fair-market-value purchase option would be available at the end of that option. The tenant later gave timely notice of its election to purchase under the fair-market-value option.

Fair-Market Value.   Then the parties couldn't agree on the value, they started the process of appointing appraisers under the lease. However, the parties disputed whether the appraisers were to take into account the actual lease in estimating fair-market value. Since the current rent had been pushed to a higher level to

321

offset the lower earlier rents, there was evidence that the fair-market value would be much higher if the current rental were taken into account in the calculation of value. The value of the property with the lease was appraised at $5.15 million by the seller's appraiser. Without the lease, the buyer's appraiser valued it at $2.75 million.

The lease defines "fair-market value" as follows:

> In determining the "prevailing fair market rate" or "fair market value" for the purposes of a provision in the lease, such rate or value shall be the rate or value, as the case may be, which Landlord and Tenant shall mutually agree upon, considering *like premises in the Dallas, Texas area, of the same quality and age of the building* and also considering the length of the renewal term then under consideration (as to fair market rate), *and the quality, utility and location of the space involved.*

(Emphasis added.)

Petula filed an action for declaratory relief to settle the question of the meaning of this clause, and the trial court found that the definition did not require the appraisers to take into account the existing lease, as the lease was not mentioned as one of the factors that the appraisers were to take into account. In case you think that the reference to "the renewal term then under consideration" should help answer the question of the parties' intent, it was established that this language only related to the determination of "fair rental value" for the lease-renewal provision, which was not an issue in the case.

Count the Lease. On appeal to the Fifth Circuit court, the landlord won, and the court of appeals ruled that the lease should be taken into account. To support its decision, the court explained that the lease should be taken into account because no one in the market could buy the property free of the lease, and consequently, the lease is a necessary characteristic of the property that would be offered in a hypothetical market transaction. It cited an Arizona court of appeals case that decided the same way on very similar facts.

The court rejected the trial court's analysis that the term "fair-market value" ought to be determined only in accordance with the factors listed in the lease clause that defined that phrase. It noted that the list was not stated to be exclusive, and that there was no reason to read it in that way. Further, it stated that the appraiser was to determine the value of "like premises," and "like premises" would have a similar lease or else it wouldn't be "like."

Criticism. The circuit court's decision has been generally criticized by the commentators. It has been stated that virtually all of the court's reasoning assumes its conclusion. For example, if the lease is intended to be taken into account, other leased premises are "like premises." If the lease is not intended to be taken into account, then they are not.

Also, while the list of terms to be considered in determining fair-market value is not stated to be exclusive, neither is it stated to be non-exclusive. As indicated by the trial court, a strong argument can be made that the parties set forth a list of factors for the appraiser to consider and did not intend the appraiser to look at other factors, such as the rent under the lease itself.

In addition, it seems reasonable to believe that the tenant intended that the option gave it the opportunity to terminate the lease by paying the fair-market value of the building without taking into account the jacked-up rent. In one sense, the approach taken by the court would require the tenant to pay the fair-market value for its lease, as well as for the building.

It is noteworthy that if the tenant purchases the building, the tenant's lease will terminate by merger and then there would be no more lease. Therefore, if the option is exercised, the terms of the existing lease would be irrelevant, except that those terms may be some evidence of the fair-rental value that would normally go into the evaluation of the building. An appraiser should be able to look at rental and determine whether it is unreasonably high or unreasonably low, depending on the background of the negotiations and on comparable rentals.

The circuit court disagreed with the trial court on this interpretation. It is possible that future decisions dealing with similar provisions could go either way. The lesson here is that when you're drafting an option for a tenant to buy a property at the "prevailing fair-market value," you'd better specify whether or not you intend the rent under the lease itself to be included as a factor.

Tips on Definitions. Uncertainty can be alleviated somewhat if the parties flesh in some standards in case they can't agree. They might designate the rate paid on "comparable rental space in the property for a comparable period."

However, this definition works best for a large building in which tenants frequently come and go, and new tenants help establish a market rate for comparable space. Even then, issues may arise about whether the other deals are comparable. For one thing, no two spaces are exactly the same. Also, tenants often negotiate different arrangements for renovation allowances, expansion options, and other terms difficult to equate to rent.

A tenant will want to set the rate without accounting for any leasehold improvements made during the initial term by or for the tenant. Obviously, space is more valuable to an existing tenant than to other prospects. Because other tenants will probably have to demolish existing partitions and rebuild, they will demand a renovation allowance. Otherwise, they will pay less rent.

The definition of "market rate" should be keyed in with what this hypothetical third party would pay at arm's length, not what the space is worth to the existing tenant. In addition, even if the space may be converted to more valuable uses, the rate should reflect only the property's current use.

If tenants occupy a large block of space, they should try to clarify the definition in another important and frequently overlooked aspect. They will want to base the rate on "comparably sized" space in comparable buildings. Since large, multi-floor users frequently command a discount, tenants will then have a strong argument that they are not bound by higher comparables for partial floors. In fact, with that kind of language, a multi-floored tenant may be able to argue that even the rental rate of a single-floor comparable should be discounted.

The issue of market rate also raises the issue of whether a landlord will pay for any improvements, refurbishing, repainting, or renewal. For example, a tenant will want to negotiate an allowance that requires the landlord to pay for these costs, at least up to a specified sum. The landlord may resist an allowance even though the tenant points out that the landlord may only receive comparable rent from another tenant if the landlord willingly spends a certain amount to fix up the space for that tenant.

Tips on Arbitration.   Even with clear definitions, parties will sometimes disagree, and a system for dispute resolution should be set. Parties commonly use arbitration to resolve fair-market-value disputes, but that can be time-consuming and expensive. Sometimes, each party chooses an arbitrator, and then each arbitrator chooses a neutral arbitrator. The three arbitrators then determine fair-market rent.

Additional provisions should be made for conflict resolution at each step of the arbitration process. For example, if the first two arbitrators are unable or fail within a designated time period to choose a third, then provisions may be made for the appointment of a third arbitrator by a local court or an independent agency such as the American Arbitration Association.

Usually tenants will want to specify the minimum qualifications of the arbitrators. For example, they ought to have at least a designated number of years' experience with leasing office space in that vicinity.

The parties should also resolve what happens when the arbitrators can't agree. One solution would average out the findings of all three. This, however, will favor the party whose selected arbitrator comes in with a biased figure. One common way to discourage that is to eliminate the most extreme of the three appraisals from any averaging.

Options and Bankruptcy.   Many options condition the tenant's right to exercise the option on not being in default under the lease. A bankruptcy case gave a tenant a break, and permitted the exercise of the option even though the bankrupt tenant was in default under the lease. In *Coleman Oil Co. v. Circle K Corp.*, 127 F.3d 904 (9th Cir. 1997), *cert. denied*, 522 U.S. 1148 (1998), the Ninth Circuit Court of Appeals gave the debtor the right to exercise an option to renew a lease even though the lease prohibited that renewal when there was an existing default. In that case, the tenant had an option to renew for five years and the court of appeals stated that "the purpose behind § 365 is to balance the state law contract right of the creditor to receive the benefit of his bargain with the federal law equitable right of the debtor to have an opportunity to reorganize." *Id.* at 909.

It held that Section 365 of the Bankruptcy Code provides that once the bankruptcy petition is filed, Section 365 suspends the termination of the lease that is in default, and it also extends a tenant's opportunity to cure any defaults until that debtor/tenant has the chance to decide whether to assume the lease. The court reasoned that if the bankruptcy court could not allow a debtor/lessee to renew a lease without first curing defaults, Section 365's basic purpose would be frustrated. The debtor would be denied the benefit of Section 365's "suspension of time," which is necessary in order to determine whether to assume or reject the lease. The dissent in *Coleman Oil Co.* concluded that the bankruptcy code does not extend a debtor's time to exercise an option, nor to extend the time to meet conditions precedent to the exercise of that option.

In another bankruptcy case, the court granted the tenant an extension to close on the purchase pursuant to an option in the lease, but the tenant lost its option anyway. In the case of *In re Schrock Family Corp.*, De FAX. Case No. D90354 (Bankr. Del. March 5, 1999) (unpublished), the debtor/tenant failed to produce sufficient evidence of its financial ability to perform under the terms of the option to purchase the leased property, and therefore was barred from assuming the contract post-petition.

In that case the tenant leased an inn from the shareholders of the tenant, and pursuant to an option to purchase it notified the shareholders of its intent to purchase the inn. However, the tenant did not close the sale as of the deadline contained in the lease, by which time the tenant had filed a Chapter 11 petition in bankruptcy. The tenant filed a motion with the bankruptcy court for permission to assume the purchase option as an executory contract and argued that it had given timely notice of its intent to exercise the option; and that its petition for bankruptcy automatically extended the deadline to close the sale.

The landlord argued that because the term of the lease had expired by the date of the tenant's bankruptcy petition, and because the tenant had failed to close the sale before the purchase-option deadline, the tenant had no post-petition rights in the inn.

The court found that under the terms of the lease, the tenant had given timely notice of its intent to exercise the purchase option, and therefore, as of the date of its bankruptcy petition, the tenant had an interest in the inn. Moreover, the court observed that although the tenant had not closed the sale within the time limits set forth in the lease, the tenant did file a motion before that date for permission to assume the option as an executory contract.

Tips on Renewal Notices. The landlord will want as much lead time as possible for renewal notices. It will undoubtedly ask for a year or more so that it has time to seek another tenant. Tenants will want short notice periods so they can fully explore their needs and the rental market. For a long-term lease, six months' notice may be as short a period as they can expect.

In many states, if tenants miss that notice date, they are out of luck because courts imply "time of the essence." To avoid any misunderstanding, the landlord will probably want to spell out that time *is* of the essence.

One way tenants can protect themselves against missing this crucial deadline is to negotiate a "renewal reminder provision." They can shift the burden of remembering to the landlord.

Landlords' Rights to Cancel.   Tenants may not realize it, but their options to renew a lease may be canceled by traditional lease language used to deal with fires. In the case of *11382 Beach Partnership v. Libaw*, 70 Cal. App.4th 212 (Cal. Ct. App. 1999), a tenant lost its rights to six five-year option periods because of a fire.

In that case the fire clause provided that "If, during the last twenty-four (24) months of this term there shall be a total destruction or partial destruction which cannot be rebuilt within thirty (30) working days, either party shall have the right to cancel and terminate this Lease within thirty (30) days of the happening thereof, by serving written notice upon the other." *Id.* at 215. Unfortunately, during the final two years of the original term a fire destroyed the property.

The tenant immediately exercised its first five-year option. Two weeks later, the owner canceled the lease and claimed he was entitled to all of the fire insurance proceeds. The tenant argued that once it exercised its option, the lease immediately extended for an additional five years, so that the cancellation clause became inoperative. Also, it argued that the exercise of the option related back to the day of the original lease and gave it priority over the cancellation clause. The tenant pointed out that the cancellation clause should be subordinated because it is repugnant to the lease's general intent, which was that the tenant would be permitted the use of the property for up to 50 years, if the tenant so desired. He argued that the lease should be construed to avoid a forfeiture.

The court rejected all of these arguments and held that a renewal option like this, which was exercised after the fire, did not extend the time of the lease for purposes of the cancellation clause. It agreed that a lease should be construed to avoid a forfeiture.

However, it also held that since the lease clause provided for a termination of the lease under certain contingencies not related to any act or default of the parties, no forfeiture had occurred.

In addition, the landlord could recover the value of the use of the property for any period during which the tenant unlawfully occupied it after the cancellation. This case serves as an important warning to lawyers who are drafting fire-cancellation clauses in leases where the tenant has been given options to renew.

Tips on Drafting. Extension provisions must be drafted carefully. If parties can't agree on a fair-market value and the renewal term has begun, the landlord will want the tenant to pay the requested rent until the issue is finally resolved. Then, if the tenant is entitled to a refund, it will be reimbursed for the overage.

Frequently parties will set a deadline for resolution of the market rental. What happens when parties do not agree by that deadline? Tenants should avoid provisions that might terminate their option if they cannot agree on the renewal rent.

What happens if the tenant cannot reach an agreement because the landlord has an inflated idea of what the property is worth? The courts will probably rule that the lease is not terminated unless the landlord acts in good faith in trying to resolve the renewal rent. But tenants should be sure to deal with this issue in drafting the lease.

When tenants want to enter into a new lease, they will undoubtedly read the landlord's form and attempt to negotiate changes triggered by the stated provisions. However, unless tenants have made a point of it in advance, one of the most important issues they should deal with will not even appear in the lease form. As discussed earlier, that issue is the tenant's right to extend the term of the lease after the initial term expires. If tenants can properly resolve this, they may never have to face the anxiety and uncertainty of competing for a second term.

Right of First Refusal

A right of first refusal means that a recipient has the right to meet an outsider's offer when the seller puts the property up for sale. These rights sound simple and do not seem much of a sacrifice by a landlord but often things go wrong.

Gifts. If a landlord gives a tenant the right of first refusal on a sale or transfer of the property, the landlord should exclude gifts from such transfers. The landlord generally does not intend to give the option holder the advantage of a "sweetheart deal."

If the gift does not trigger the option, should the option survive so that the outsider who buys the property must honor it when the outsider later decides to sell? A dispute can be avoided with proper drafting.

The owner can specifically exclude from the option of first refusal certain transfers that are not at arm's length. An owner will also want to except a sale to affiliated corporations. See *Cottrell v. Beard*, 9 S.W.3d 568 (Ark. Ct. App. 2000), in which a gift without consideration did not trigger a right of first refusal because it was not a "bona fide offer" as described in the grant of option.

One example of troublesome language was in *Tiger Inc. v. Time Warner Entertainment Co.*, 26 F. Supp.2d 1011 (N.D. Ohio 1998), where the right of refusal was triggered by "any offer to purchase" the applicable lot. In that case the option was applied even though the defendant assigned rights in the lot to what it claimed was a "related party," and even though it did not record any transfer of title. Despite the fact that only the "economic benefits" of the lot were transferred in exchange for a partnership interest, the district court held that a "purchase" had occurred.

Package Deals.   Suppose the owner who is burdened by an option of first refusal decides to sell not only the real estate that is the subject of the option, but also property in a package deal. For example, the owner may want to sell the real estate, equipment, and goodwill of the going business. Or the owner might want to sell the property that is subject to option plus other buildings that are not. Also, it may want to sell only part of the property.

What happens if the optioned real estate is owned by a corporation, and the shareholders want to sell all or part of the corporate stock? Should the option of first refusal extend to the stock sale?

The simple right of first refusal for real estate will not provide answers to these questions. The parties should recognize that these issues could arise and attempt to resolve them when the option is written.

For example, they could provide that the option does not apply to a package sale; or in the alternative, they could provide that the option is extended to the whole package.

If the parties do not extend the option to the whole package, a landlord might be able to manipulate the tenant out of the option by never offering the option parcel alone. In *Raymond v. Steen*, 882 P.2d 852 (Wyo. 1994), the court protected the option holder who had negotiated a right of first refusal in a real estate purchase contract. It held that the owner could not sell the property that was subject to the option, as part of a larger sale, but could only offer it for sale as a separate unit.

Similarly, in *Hahalyak v. A. Frost, Inc.*, 664 A.2d 545 (Pa. Super. 1995), the court protected a tenant that had been given a right of first refusal to lease other space in its building. The court held that the landlord could not defeat that right by offering a package deal to another tenant.

In this case, the landlord offered the other tenant a lease for new space, conditioned on the other tenant's obligation to surrender its occupied space. The landlord claimed that the surrendered space was a key component to the transaction because he counted on leasing that surrendered space at a much higher rental. Since the holder of the right of first refusal could not possibly surrender that other space that he didn't occupy, he could not meet that part of the offer.

The Pennsylvania Superior Court held that "A right of first refusal . . . cannot be defeated by including that property in a multi-property or multi-asset transaction." *Hahalyak*, 664 A.2d at 549. The landlord could have drafted a more limited first refusal provision, but because he didn't, he was stymied in this attempt to complete a deal with the other tenant.

"Same or Comparable." First refusal rights for additional space that the tenant needs, generally are to be offered to the tenant on the "same or comparable terms" as those offered by a third party. This language often creates difficulties because it requires that the tenant meet the exact terms of a third-party offer.

For example, the tenant will usually need different tenant improvements than the third party. That can probably be handled by using language that requires the offer to include the same dollar value of tenant improvements as offered to the third party.

However, the existing tenant may want the lease term on the first-refusal space to coincide with the remaining term of its lease. This could create a problem for the landlord because if the landlord concedes to this tenant's request, the landlord may lose a potential long-term lease with a third party in order to honor the first-refusal obligation, which may be for a much shorter term.

The *Chevron* Case. A leading Pennsylvania case highlights the problems of an owner who gives a right of first refusal in a real estate transaction but does not cover the possibility that the property might be offered in a package deal. In *Boyd & Mahoney v. Chevron U.S.A.*, 614 A.2d 1191 (Pa. Super. 1992), Chevron purchased a gasoline station, subject to a simple right of first refusal benefitting the grantor. Chevron then sold the station to Cumberland Farms in a sale that included real estate throughout the United States with terminals, warehouses, offices, gasoline stations, inventories, accounts receivables, and other assets. The total purchase price for the sale exceeded $310 million, and Chevron did not offer the optioned gas station to the beneficiary of the option. The court held that the right of first refusal was triggered and that the applicable price should be the estimated fair market value of $158,000. In addition, the court awarded the option holder over $500,000 as lost rents and profits, plus interest.

The result of this was that the beneficiary of the option was awarded not only the property, but also over $300,000 in excess of the purchase price. This is a good example of how an owner would have benefitted if it anticipated a multi-asset sale and excluded that from the option language.

Similarly, in a case of first impression in Wisconsin, the court of appeals held that the sale of a 180-acre farm triggered a right of refusal by a third party as to 25 acres. *Wilber Lime Products, Inc. v. Sonentag Family Limited P'ship*, 673 N.W.2d 339 (Wis. App. 2003). The court held that the price for the smaller parcel should be established at its fair market value.

In reaching its conclusion, the Wisconsin court concluded that there was a split among the various jurisdictions, with most holding that a right of first refusal cannot be defeated by the sale of a larger parcel that includes the portion covered by the right of first refusal. The Wisconsin Court of Appeals has now joined the majority on that issue.

Corporate Merger. Parties sometimes dispute whether first refusal rights were intended to apply not only to a sale of the asset (or stock), but also to a merger, dissolution, or other more subtle type of transfer. That issue was highlighted by a decision that found that shareholders were not bound by first-refusal rights held by other shareholders, when they tendered their shares for cash under a cash-out merger of the corporation. *Seven Springs Farm, Inc. v. Croker*, 748 A.2d 740 (Pa. Super. 2000). In that case, which involved disputing shareholders of the Seven Springs Resort, two-thirds of the shareholders voted to sell the resort through a merger agreement that would give cash to all of the shareholders in exchange for their shares.

First Refusal Rights. An earlier buy/sell agreement governed the rights of shareholders to dispose of their stock, and required a selling shareholder to give the other shareholders rights of first refusal. Despite that, the pro-merger group refused to honor the dissenting group's first-refusal rights, and the Superior Court agreed with them on the theory that the merger was a corporate act and the right of first refusal governed only a shareholder's act. The court emphasized that the agreement did not specifically address a merger, and therefore did not prohibit "Seven Springs, as an entity, ... from engaging in conduct that is fundamental to the existence of the Corporation." *Seven Springs Farm, Inc. v. Croker*, 748 A.2d 740, 746 (Pa. Super. 2000).

The buy/sell agreement had previously been amended to make clear that in a transaction of the contemplated size, a sale of shares would be exempt from rights of first refusal if it were approved by at least 75 percent of the shareholders. Since only 66 percent of the shareholders had approved the sale, the dissenting shareholders argued that their rights of first refusal were being circumvented by the sale of substantially all of the corporation's assets through the device of a corporate merger, which required only majority shareholder approval.

The dissenters posed the question as follows: "Should a court in equity allow some shareholders to avoid a right of first refusal, applicable to any direct sale or other disposition of stock, by their selling their stock to a third party through a cash-out merger requiring shareholder approval?" 748 A.2d at 744.

Conspicuous Silence. In rejecting their arguments, the court held: "The most we can say is the parties either intended to exclude mergers, or did not anticipate or consider such an event." *Id.* In other words, if the parties wanted to provide that mergers would trigger rights of first refusal, they should have said that in the agreement. According to the court, the parties were not unsophisticated. They were familiar with corporate formalities and had the benefit of legal advice in drafting the agreement and its amendments. Therefore, the silence about a fundamental corporate act such as a merger is conspicuous. The court stated: "The Agreement expressly speaks to specific stockholder events such as voluntary and involuntary petitions in bankruptcy, and assignments for the benefit of creditors, but not to a single corporate act such as merger. We cannot conclude this distinction was an oversight." *Id.* at 745.

The court acknowledged that the shareholding families were "embroiled in bitter infighting" and that it could even conclude the majority had cloaked a sale in the accoutrements of merger "to circumvent appellant and the block of shares she represents; however, one may as easily conclude appellant's block is objecting to the merger for obstructive personal reasons as well. Both conclusions may be true, but this is immaterial to our inquiry. We are interpreting a contract, not the reasons for the positions of the parties." *Id.* at 746.

Dissent. Judge Johnson filed a dissenting opinion, which was joined by two other justices. He criticized the majority's "flawed" analysis in three respects: misinterpreting the plain language of the buy/sell agreement, concluding that the proposed merger did not constitute "shareholder action," and not properly considering the intent of the parties. He stated:

> In my view, a cash-out merger clearly falls within the parameters of the Buy/Sell Agreement, even when strictly construed. The proposed transaction is called a "cash-out merger," but this Court cannot, as the Majority has done, rely on this label alone in determining whether such a transaction is contemplated in the Buy/Sell Agreement; rather, we must look at the substance of the transaction, including its consequences.

Id. at 749.

He argues that by "surrendering" their shares, the shareholders will have "disposed of" their shares in a cash-out merger transaction. He was persuaded that the buy/sell agreement was intended to embrace situations such as this, where the shareholders were disposing of their shares.

Judge Johnson concluded that the plan of merger should have triggered the right of first refusal.

He concluded:

> Finally, adoption of the Majority's conclusion that the cash-out merger is not subject to the terms of the Buy/Sell Agreement would place in jeopardy the validity and effect of restrictive shareholder agreements in closely held corporations throughout the Commonwealth. Board members of such corporations will be on notice that they may use the device of the cash-out merger to circumvent shareholders' agreements heretofore understood to be binding. I find this to be a troubling precedent, if permitted to be established.

Id. at 756.

Restrictions on sale of real estate or stock interests appear in many business contexts. In addition to stock agreements, they appear in restrictive covenants on property, in leases, or in due-on-sale provisions in loan documents. The *Seven Springs* case should alert lawyers and businesspeople to the possibility that these agreements may be subject to strict scrutiny in the event of a dispute. In light of that, prudent drafters will anticipate not only the possibility of the outright sale of stock (or real estate, if that is the asset being sold), but also mergers, dissolutions, gifts, and involuntary transfers, such as petitions in bankruptcy and foreclosures.

Disguised Sales. Another subtle issue is whether an option of first refusal is intended to apply to a foreclosure sale under a mortgage given by the owner to secure a loan. The option holder does not want to lose its rights if the owner defaults on the mortgage and the lender forecloses. Unless the option rights are protected, the devious owner might try to avoid an unwanted option by giving a mortgage to an affiliated party and then defaulting, resulting in a "disguised sale" free of the option.

The owner could make a good case for excluding even disguised sales from the scope of the option because foreclosure sales are generally public, and anyone may bid. Even if the optionee does not have any special rights under the option to deal with foreclosures, that holder still would have the right to buy the property by simply matching the other bidders and adding one dollar to its bid.

Method of Acceptance. A less subtle issue involves how the option holder must respond to an offer. The owner will want to require acceptance or rejection of the outsider's offer within a short period of time to minimize the possibility of losing the prospective buyer because of delay. In addition, the owner will want more than just an acceptance from the holder. The owner will want the holder to sign a binding agreement of sale with a cash deposit so that the owner does not lose the "bird in the hand."

From the owner's perspective, an option of first offer is better than an option of first refusal. In that way the owner can test the market with an offer to the option holder before the owner tries to get an offer from an outsider. The seller can ask its price and either obtain a refusal or an acceptance from the holder before going public. See the first and third provisions set forth in the appendix to this chapter.

In addition, the option of first refusal is more of an obstacle to making a sale. Some prospective purchasers will not want to make an offer when they know they are only being used as a "stalking horse" and an insider may "trump" them. That is particularly true when the prospect, before making an offer, must spend money and time with an architect or engineer and a lawyer to check the land use code, plan for alterations, take preliminary bids, and arrange for financing. These issues highlight the significance of requiring a quick response to any offer.

Financing Terms.   In the current business climate, the prospective purchaser may offer an acceptable price on the condition that the seller take back purchase money financing at a low interest rate. The outsider might also try to exact other conditions from the seller in the offer, such as requiring income or environmental warranties.

Should the option holder be required to meet the price with cash, or should the holder be given the benefit of all of the offered terms? This should be addressed in the option agreement.

However, a provision requiring the same financing terms for an option holder as for outsiders may not be acceptable to the seller. The outsider may be Chase Manhattan Bank, and the insider may not even have enough to pay its rent. The owner will argue that the option of first refusal is not intended to place the owner at a disadvantage.

Drafting Rights.   Cases have indicated how the parties could have been clearer in drafting rights of first refusal. In the case of *Peter-Michael, Inc. v. Sea Shell Assocs.*, 709 A.2d 558 (Conn. 1998), the court had to interpret what the landlord meant where it gave an option to purchase the property during the "term of the lease." The court held that the language meant that the option survived during the month-to-month holdover of the tenant.

In that case, the lease had provided that the landlord could treat the tenant holding over as a month-to-month tenant "subject to all the terms and conditions of this lease, except as to duration thereof." *Id.* at 560. The holdover arrangement continued on that basis for five years, and the dispute arose when the landlord sold the property without notifying the tenant. The court concluded that sufficient ambiguity existed in the written documents to permit the parties to produce evidence about what they really intended.

In the case of *Briggs v. Sylvestri*, 714 A.2d 56 (Conn. App. Ct. 1998), the court was asked to interpret a first-refusal option to determine whether the owner had to provide the option holder with proof of a third party's offer. In that case the option required the owner, before selling the property to a third party, to offer it to the holder of the right on the same terms it was willing to accept from the third party.

The court found that there is no implied requirement that the competing offer be documented. The owner was only required to offer the opportunity to meet the competing terms within the option period.

Lawyers should remember that if their tenant/client expects to see the specific offer to confirm that it is bona fide, that should be specifically set forth in the option language.

Alternative Forms.   The appendix to this chapter contains sample forms of first-refusal and first-offer options that illustrate many of the issues raised in the text.

A common way to handle a rejection of a right of first offer is to provide that a landlord may then accept another offer that is on terms that are "not substantially less favorable" than the rejected offer. See the appendix form titled "Right of First Offer." If terms like "substantially" or "materially" are used, there is obviously a potential question of interpretation of these words when the landlord would like to accept different terms.

In addition, although it is not obvious on the surface, there could be a big difference between the phrase "not substantially less favorable to the seller" and the phrase "not substantially more favorable to the buyer." Where the offer the tenant is attempting to match would involve a brokerage commission payable by the landlord and the offer of the tenant would not involve a brokerage commission, the optionee may seek to reduce the price by the amount of the commission. The tenant could then take the position that the decreased offer provides a net return to the landlord, which is just as favorable as the higher offer less the required commission, which the landlord will have to pay. See the discussion in Milton R. Friedman, 2 *Friedman on Leases* 1049, § 16.1 (4th ed. 1997).

It's More Blessed to Give than to Receive

Conventional wisdom tells us that it never hurts to receive an option, and there are no benefits from giving one. Generally, this maxim is correct, but developments have shown how these statements are not always valid when they relate to real estate options. The following three exceptions are subtle:

- If a seller gives a buyer an option to purchase instead of an agreement of sale, the seller bolsters its rights to retain the buyer's deposit if the buyer defaults.

- Giving an option of first refusal may undercut an option holder's right to implement an alternate option. For example, what happens to the buyer's fixed-price option after the owner receives a higher offer from a third party?

- A seller can save income taxes if it gives a potential buyer an option to purchase instead of arranging an installment sale.

Let's take a look at each one of these aberrations.

Seller Wishes to Terminate the Agreement. When a buyer defaults, it's generally easier for the seller to terminate an option contract than an agreement of sale. When they consider option contracts, courts acknowledge that the buyer's down payment merely purchased time to tie up the property. As illustrated below, if the same payment is labeled a deposit under an agreement of sale, the courts tend to view it differently.

Although these two types of agreements are sometimes thought to be interchangeable, the seller has an edge against a defaulting buyer who holds an option to purchase rather than an agreement of sale. However, this edge could be reduced if the agreement of sale provides for clear remedies and that "time is of the essence."

The Connecticut case of *Cutter Development Corp. v. Peluso*, 561 A.2d 926 (Conn. 1989), illustrates this issue. Cutter agreed to pay a million dollars for a property by making deposits of $7,500, $42,500, and successive monthly deposits of $25,000 over the next nine months. The agreement was labeled an option agreement, but many of its provisions indicated that it was an agreement of sale. After a dispute, the sellers refused to deliver. Cutter sued for specific performance, and the sellers defended by arguing that the agreement should be treated as an option to purchase that Cutter had not exercised within the allotted time. The sellers contended that the agreement was an option because it imposed no binding obligation on Cutter to purchase.

The court rejected that argument and granted specific performance to Cutter. However, the decision emphasizes that if the sellers had clearly given Cutter an option agreement instead of an agreement of sale, they would have been in a better position to cut off his rights when he defaulted.

In addition, in many states, courts will not permit sellers to retain a deposit under an agreement of sale if the seller, after default, has sold the property to another buyer at a higher price and therefore has not suffered any loss. In some jurisdictions, the deposit is treated as an unenforceable penalty even when the agreement labels it as "liquidated damages." See Milton R. Friedman, *Contracts and Conveyances of Real Property* 923–47, § 12.1(c) (4th ed. and 1990 Cum. Supp.) But see *Kelly v. Marx*, 705 N.E.2d 1114 (Mass. 1999), where the Massachusetts Supreme Court upheld a 5 percent liquidated damage clause on default by the buyer, even though the seller resold the house at a profit. Generally, option payments cannot be so treated.

An Option of First Refusal Poisons a Fixed-Price Option. Sometimes an owner gives away two options in the same document. For example, a landlord might give a tenant a fixed-price option to purchase a leased property for $100,000 and also an option of first refusal that is triggered when the landlord decides to sell to a third party. Tenants with a strong negotiating position may demand and receive both kinds of options.

Like the greedy fisherman's wife in the fable, they may lose everything because they have demanded fulfillment of one wish too many. What if another buyer then offers to buy the property for $175,000? Obviously, the over-optioned initial buyer would rather exercise the fixed-price option at $100,000, but that option may have been "poisoned" by the second option. Courts in several states have held that once an option of first refusal is triggered, the fixed-price option is extinguished, unless the agreement contains clear language to the contrary. See *Moon v. Haeussler*, 545 N.Y.S.2d 623 (N.Y. App. Div. 1989); contra, *McDonald's Corp. v. Lebow Realty Trust*, 710 F. Supp. 385 (D. Mass. 1989), *aff'd*, 888 F.2d 912 (1st Cir. 1989); *M & M Oil Co. v. Finch*, 640 P.2d 317 (Kan. Ct. App. 1982); *Tarrant v. Self*, 387 N.E.2d 1349 (Ind. Ct. App. 1979); *Shell Oil Co. v. Jolley*, 296 A.2d 236 (Vt. 1972); and *Adams v. Helburn*, 249 S.W. 543 (Ky. 1923). Contra, *Amoco Oil Co. v. Snyder*, 478 A.2d 795 (Pa. 1984).

A Texas appellate court case confirmed that concept. In *Markert v. Williams*, 874 S.W.2d 353 (Tex. Ct. App. 1994), a service station lease contained a fixed-price option and a right of first refusal. When the owner presented a bona fide purchase offer to the tenant, the tenant chose not to exercise its right of first refusal, and the owner sold the property. Two years later, the tenant attempted to exercise the fixed-price option, and the court held that by refusing to exercise its right of refusal earlier, the tenant's other option had lapsed. In arriving at that decision, the court cited with favor earlier cases that expressed concern that a contrary result would deprive an owner of the ability to sell the property to a good-faith purchaser.

First-refusal option clauses sometimes provide that if the seller has an offer from a third party, it must put the offer to the tenant, who has the right to meet that offered price. If that tenant does not meet it within a designated period of time, the owner can sell to the third party at the offered price.

It is not hard to see how the courts could hold that this provision overrides a fixed-price option in the same lease. Some courts reason that the fixed-price purchase option applies only until there is a purchase offer by a third party, and at that point, the fixed-price option is extinguished. If the tenant could invoke the fixed-price option after the landlord has received a better offer, the right of first refusal would be meaningless because the tenant would never have to meet a higher price offered by a third party. And a potential buyer would never make a higher offer if the tenant's fixed-price option survived so it could be later invoked to force a sale at a loss.

Giving an Option to Purchase May Save Taxes.   Frequently, an owner has the choice of structuring a sale as either an installment sale or as an option to purchase.

- *Unwinding the transaction.* There is one type of installment sale in which the seller transfers title to the buyer and takes back a purchase money mortgage payable over several years. The obligation of the mortgage can be nonrecourse so that should the buyer default, the seller (a) retains the payments that it has received to date, and (b) forecloses the mortgage and recovers the real estate—but nothing else. An installment sale involving a series of option payments equivalent to the mortgage payments in a sale can give the parties similar rights and remedies, but the option makes it easier for the seller to unwind the transaction should the buyer default.
- *Different Tax Treatment of Periodic Cash Receipts.* When the seller is retaining possession until final closing, anoth-

er major consequence of choosing an option to purchase rather than an installment sale is the favorable tax treatment to the optionor. The installment seller, who is a cash-basis taxpayer, must treat a portion of each installment that it receives as taxable income (as profit on the sale). (An accrual-basis taxpayer must report the entire profit as taxable income in the year of sale.)

On the other hand, the owner-optionor may not have to treat the payments that it will credit towards the purchase price as "income" until the option is exercised or has lapsed, regardless of its method of accounting. (Sometimes transactions are structured so the seller receives payments to keep the option alive that are not credited against the price. These are taxable as ordinary income when received.)

Also, with certain limited exceptions, the installment buyer has an immediate deduction for interest attributable to each payment, but the optionee-buyer must treat the option payments as a nondeductible capital investment until the option is exercised or lapsed.

When courts are asked to decide whether a contract is an option or an installment sale, they treat labels as less important than the facts and circumstances. The IRS may recharacterize an option as a sale if the up-front option payment is so large a percentage of the sale price as to suggest that the "optionee" is economically committed to purchase. See *Koch v. Commissioner,* 67 T.C. 71 (1976), acq. 1980-2 C.B. 1.

Options and Estates

The tax regulations result in substantially different tax effects for transactions when one of the parties dies before a pending transaction is completed (i.e., before all payments are made under the installment sale or before the option is exercised). When an installment seller dies before receiving all the payments, the profits portion of all unpaid installments is considered "income in respect of a decedent." That means that the unpaid portion of the installment note does not receive an increase ("step-up") in basis to fair-market value as do most other items that are included in the decedent's estate. As a result, the estate or the heirs ultimately must pay an income tax on the deferred profit when it is collected (subject to a deduction for its related estate taxes, if any). On the other hand, if the decedent had given an option, the heirs would have received a step-up in basis and a reduction in taxable gain. This phenomenon illustrates another blessing of giving.

- *Example: Option permits estate to benefit from increased basis.* Assume that real estate with a tax basis of $50,000 has a fair-market value of $1 million. The owner's other assets are such that if the real estate is in the owner's estate when the owner dies, the federal estate tax on the value of the real estate will be $500,000, assuming a 50 percent effective estate tax rate. Upon the owner's death, the estate may increase its basis up to $1 million so that when it subsequently sells the property for $1 million, the estate need not recognize any gain.

  If the owner had given the buyer a $1 million option to purchase the real estate, the demise of the seller would have had no effect on the transaction—the federal estate tax of $500,000 would still be payable; the property's tax basis would be stepped up to $1 million; and if the option were then exercised, the estate or heirs would realize no taxable gain.

- *Example: Option saves seller's estate $112,500.* Now, assume the owner had sold the real estate for $1 million under an installment sale and died before receiving the first payment. Under Section 691 of the Internal Revenue Code, the untaxed gain under the installment note would be considered "income in respect of a decedent." Since the seller did not use an option agreement, the value of the installment obligation is included in the estate for estate tax purposes as of the time of the seller's death without the benefit of an increase in tax basis. As shown in Exhibit 1, the estate must pay an estate tax of $500,000 and, upon receipt of the purchase price, the seller (now the estate) must pay income tax on the gain. (The seller would be allowed a deduction for the estate taxes so that, assuming a $1 million sale price, the net gain would be only $450,000, and the federal income tax would be $112,500, assuming a 25 percent tax rate.)

EXHIBIT 1: Tax Treatment of Installment Note	
Face amount of note	$1,000,000
Less tax basis cost of real estate	50,000
Taxable income	950,000
Deduction for estate tax paid	500,000
Net taxable income	450,000
Income tax (at 25%)	112,500

Conclusion. Owners give away options in a variety of real estate documents, including leases, deeds, or reciprocal easement agreements. While options generally benefit only the recipient, real estate professionals should be aware that in some cases, it may be "more blessed to give than to receive."

Transferring or Financing an Option

Suppose an option holder grants its creditor a security interest in the option. Does that option have value to the creditor? What must the creditor do to maintain a priority claim against future purchasers of the property, creditors of the borrower, and lienholders? This issue has been discussed by John C. Murray of the First American Financial Corporation in seminars and on the Internet (First American's Web site is at http://www.firstam.com).

UCC Provisions

A "naked" option is one that is unrelated to any recorded interest, such as a mortgage, that the holder may otherwise have in the applicable real estate. Normally, if someone acquires a naked option it does not obtain an interest in the property that is the subject of the option. That occurs because the purchaser of the option can only receive an interest in the real estate if the option is exercised according to its terms.

Any security interest given in such an option would be considered "personalty" rather than realty, and that interest will be considered a "general intangible" under Section 9-106 of the Uniform Commercial Code (UCC).

"General intangibles" are any "personal property ... other than goods, accounts, chattel paper, documents, instruments, investment property, rights to proceeds of written letters of credit, and money." UCC § 9-106. Such an interest would normally be perfected by filing a UCC financing statement with the Secretary of State's Office in the jurisdiction in which the debtor is located under Section 9-103(3)(b).

If the owner of that option right sells the right to a third party, the secured creditors' perfected security interest would attach to the proceeds of that sale under Section 9-306(1) because proceeds under that section are defined as "whatever is received upon the sale, exchange, collection or other disposition of collateral or proceeds." However, if the option should expire by its terms or is otherwise terminated, the security interest would become valueless because the holder of the option would no longer have any legal or property rights to which the interest could attach.

Bankruptcy and Naked Options

Bankruptcy of the holder can complicate matters. In one case the bankruptcy court addressed an option problem where the debtors who were husband and wife held two options to purchase from different landlords (one option agreement was separate from the lease agreement; the other was contained in the lease). *In re Merten*, 164 B.R. 641 (Bankr. S.D. Cal 1994).

The debtors then exercised the options after filing a Chapter 11 bankruptcy petition. Earlier the debtors had granted a creditor a pre-petition security interest in all of their contract rights and general intangibles, which had been perfected pre-petition when the creditor filed a UCC financing statement with the California Secretary of State. The court found that under applicable California law, a security interest in an unexercised option by the debtor to acquire real estate is a general intangible subject to the UCC, and that a security interest in an unexercised option is personalty, rather than realty. Therefore the creditor had properly filed a pre-petition financing statement on its interest in the option and had obtained a perfected security interest in the unexercised option right. However, the court permitted the debtors to exercise their option to purchase the two properties and held that the option exercise divested any security interest it had in the collateral under the UCC because the option rights no longer existed. According to the court, at that time the option ceased being a "mere option."

The court also held that upon the exercise of an option to purchase real estate, the transaction is converted to a "sale or bilateral executory contract of purchase and sale, whereby the optionee acquires an equitable interest in the land." Therefore, because the sale had occurred and the holder of the options acquired the real property, whatever security interest the creditor may have had in the option rights was abrogated and transferred to the real estate.

In light of that, the creditor's transferred interest became converted to an interest in real estate. That interest was not properly recorded and perfected in the county recorder's office, and therefore was not enforceable under the "strong arm" provisions of Section 544 of the Bankruptcy Code against the debtor in possession or against subsequent purchasers or creditors without notice.

To make the matter worse for the creditor, the court, having authorized the debtors to exercise the options, also authorized the debtor to resell the properties to a third party, free and clear of the creditor's security interest. The court rejected the creditor's motion to compel turnover of the proceeds from the debtors' sale of the properties and rejected the creditor's argument that its security interest in the option contract rights should have survived the sale and attached to the proceeds.

This case illustrates the importance to a creditor that obtains a security interest in a "naked option" to perfect that interest, not only by filing a UCC financing statement with the Secretary of State's Office, but also by recording an instrument with the county recorder's office evidencing its interest in the real estate to which the option relates. See, e.g., Steven O. Weise, *U.C.C. Article 9: Personal Property Secured Transactions*, 50 BUS. LAW 1935 (1999) (which states that the option to acquire the property should have been secured by recording the option and a mortgage against that option).

One wonders whether if the option were set forth in a lease, that same security could have been perfected by recording the lease and the assignment of the lease from the tenant to the secured party. In any event it is obvious that purchasing an option or lending money based on an option to purchase real estate can be a dangerous pitfall and that such transactions would be an appropriate subject for legislation to clarify the issues raised in this article.

Losing an Option

Courts are sometimes reluctant to enforce options of first refusal, even when they have been negotiated at arm's length.

Are Successors of Owner Bound?   A Georgia case focused on whether a right of first refusal to buy an owner's remaining property ran with the land so that it would be enforceable against the seller's successors. In *Ricketson v. Bankers First Savings Bank*, 503 S.E.2d 297 (Ga. Ct. App. 1998), the buyer purchased part of a property from the seller and the seller covenanted that if it sold any remaining portion of the acreage, the seller would give a right of first refusal to the purchasers. It recorded a security deed (sometimes called a "mortgage") on the remaining property, in favor of the bank that said that it was "subject to the Right of First Refusal" as described in an affidavit.

Upon foreclosure the property was transferred to the bank by a deed-in-lieu-of-foreclosure and the bank then transferred title to the seller's father. After the father defaulted on the mortgage, the bank foreclosed and sold the foreclosed property to a third party without giving the original buyer an opportunity to exercise its option of first refusal. When the buyer sued for violation of that option, the court held that the option was personal to the original seller and that it was not enforceable against the bank or the new third-party purchaser. According to the court, that option did not constitute a servitude on the remaining land. Even though the bank took the security deed subject to the right of first refusal, the language in the covenant did not indicate that it ran with the land or that it applied to the original seller's successors or assigns. Since that intention was not expressed by the parties and the covenant was not recorded, the option did not bind the successors.

The logic of *Ricketson* would probably be followed in most states. The lesson is that if these options are intended to be enforced against successors of the optionors, the parties should clearly state their intention and the options should be recorded.

Restraint on Alienation.   The option holder also lost its right of first refusal in another case. In the case of *Urquhart v. Teller*, 958 P.2d 714 (Mont. 1998), the seller had sold a 270-acre tract under a contract for deed that gave the buyers a right of first refusal for the seller's adjacent 10-acre tract at a purchase price of $10,000. Twenty-two years later the seller conveyed the 10-acre tract, then worth $375,000 to $400,000, to a nonprofit conservation corporation and ignored the first-refusal right. In an action to enforce the right of first refusal, the court held the right was an unreasonable restraint on alienation and void. The court noted, among other things, the great disparity between the right-of-first-refusal price and the market value of the land 22 years later.

Under the applicable agreement the right of first refusal was triggered by the seller's sale or other disposal of the applicable 10-acre tract.

The court apparently was reaching to help the seller extricate itself from what appeared to be a bad bargain because the property was now worth nearly 35 times the option price. Therefore, the court reasoned that since the parties had entered the agreement, the buyer had transferred its property to several different owners. Thus the buyer's "legitimate purpose of obtaining ownership to neighboring property can no longer be served by enforcing the option. Enforcing the right of first refusal at this point would simply restrain Teller from transferring the property or give the Urquharts the bargain purchase of the century." *Id.* at 718.

To support its position, the court cited two other cases that held that much smaller variances between the option prices and the market prices were unreasonable. See *Ross v. Ponemon*, 263 A.2d 195 (N.J. Super. Ct. Ch. Div. 1970) ($10,000 fixed option to purchase property valued at $40,000 was unreasonable restraint); and *Procter v. Foxmeyer Drug Co.*, 884 S.W.2d 853 (Tex. Ct. App. 1994) (option price of $79,955 unreasonable where property value had risen to $550,000).

In the *Urquhart* case, the option holder lost his option because of the court's perception that the bargain made by the parties was essentially unfair.

APPENDIX

The following are alternative forms of first-refusal options. The first is a simple commercial lease provision. It is an "option of first offer."

Provision One

Lessee Given "First Right to Purchase" or "Right of First Offer":

> It is further agreed that if, during the term of this lease, the lessor desires to sell the demised premises, then the lessee shall have the privilege of purchasing the same for the same price for which the lessor would be willing to sell to any other person; but if the lessee does not exercise the option of purchase within ten days after notice in writing from the lessor of such desire to sell, then this lease shall be and become void upon a conveyance of the demised premises by the lessor.

Provision Two

The following clauses appear in Milton R. Friedman's highly regarded *Friedman on Leases*, published by Practising Law Institute, pp. 946–49 (3d ed. 1990). They provide a "right of first refusal."

> Tenant shall have the right of first refusal of the demised premises as hereinafter in this Article set forth. If at any time during the term, Landlord shall receive a bona fide offer, *other than at public auction*[1] from a third person (which does not have the power of eminent domain) for the purchase of the demised premises, which offer Landlord shall desire to accept, Landlord shall promptly *deliver to Tenant a copy of such offer,*[2] and Tenant may, within ____ days thereafter, elect to purchase the demised premises *on the same terms as those set forth in such offer.*[3] If Tenant shall not accept such offer *within the time herein specified therefor, said right of refusal shall cease to exist,*[4] but this

---

1.   See "Disguised Sales" discussion on page 334.
2.   See *Briggs v. Sylvestri*, page 335.
3.   See "Financing Terms" discussion, page 335.
4.   See "Method of Acceptance" discussion, page 334. The procrastinating tenant loses the option.

lease shall continue otherwise on all the other terms, covenants, and conditions in this lease set forth. This right of refusal shall be inapplicable to a transfer, *by way of sale, gift,* or devise, including a trust, to or for *a party related to a Landlord,*[5] or to any transfer, in whole or in part, from one such related party to another, but shall apply to any subsequent transfer to a third person. For the purpose of this Article, if the then owner of the demised premises shall be an individual, a related party shall include a spouse, lineal descendant or spouse of such descendant, ancestor or sibling (whether by the whole or half blood), a partnership of which such owner is a member, a joint ownership or ownership in common, which includes the then owner of the demised premises, or a corporation, the majority of whose securities is owned by the owner of the demised premises, or any one or more of the foregoing parties. If the then owner of the demised premises shall be a corporation, a related party shall include an affiliate, subsidiary or parent corporation, a successor by merger or consolidation, or the holder or holders of the majority of the securities of such corporation.

An offer made by Landlord for the sale or other transfer of the demised premises to a third person, other than in lieu of condemnation, shall give Tenant the same rights under this Article as if such offer were an acceptable offer made to Landlord by a third person.

If the premises shall be conveyed to the Tenant under this right of first refusal, any prepaid rent shall be apportioned and applied on account of the purchase price.

(Emphasis added.)

In part of an alternative clause intended to aid the tenant, Friedman provides:

If any acceptable third party offer to Landlord for the demised premises shall include other property,[6] Tenant's

---

5. See "Gifts" discussion, page 328. This provision exempts the sale to a related party but does not deal with the bargain price "favor" to an unrelated party.

6. See discussion of package deals and the *Chevron* case, pages 330–31.

right of first refusal shall [, at Tenant's election,] be [either: (a)] applicable to the entire property covered by such offer [; or (b) applicable to the demised premises alone, at a purchase price which shall be that part of the price, offered by the third person, which the value of the demised premises shall bear to the value of all the property included in such third-party offer].

(Footnotes omitted.)

The bracketed provisions are intended to be alternative suggestions to the drafter for a tenant-oriented solution to the issues raised in the article. Clause (b) requires an allocation of "value" to the optioned parcel, and that could easily be the subject of dispute.

Provision Three

The following "Right of First Offer" has been drafted by the author pursuant to negotiations between a landlord and tenant. It covers many of the issues omitted in the first clause of this appendix.

Right of First Offer. Any provision of the Lease to the contrary notwithstanding, Tenant shall have the right of first offer of the Premises as hereinafter set forth.

(A) If at any time during the term, Landlord decides to sell the Premises to a third person, Landlord shall deliver to Tenant the terms on which Tenant intends to sell ("Proposed Offer"), and Tenant may, within fifteen (15) days thereafter, elect to purchase the Premises on the same terms as those set forth in such Proposed Offer. If Tenant shall not accept such Proposed Offer within the time herein specified therefor, subject to the limitations described below, said right of refusal shall cease to exist, but the Lease, as amended, shall continue otherwise on all of the other terms, covenants, and conditions set forth in the Lease.

(B) If Landlord should desire to sell the Premises for a purchase price that is more than 5% less than the purchase price set forth in the Proposed Offer or on other terms and conditions that are materially more favorable to the buyer than those set forth in the Proposed Offer, Landlord shall provide Tenant with a right of First offer on the revised terms and Tenant may within fifteen (15) days thereafter, elect to purchase the Premises on the same terms as those set forth in such revised offer.

(C) Any revised subsequent offer shall be treated as a new Proposed Offer and shall have the same force and effect.

(D) This right of first offer shall apply to a sale of the Premises or any portion thereof, including but not limited to any sale, deed, conveyance, or grant of easement.

(E) Landlord shall have no obligation to give Tenant a right of first offer, as provided above, unless the Lease at the time of Landlord's proposed offer to sell is in full force and effect, without default beyond any applicable grace period, provided that this right of first offer shall be inapplicable to a transfer, by way of sale, gift or devise, including a trust, to or for a party related to Landlord, or to any transfer, in whole or in part, from one such related party to another, but shall apply to any subsequent transfer to a third person. For this purpose, if the then owner of the Premises shall be an individual, a "related party" shall include a spouse, lineal descendant or spouse of such descendant, ancestor or sibling (whether by the whole or half blood), a partnership of which such owner is a member, a joint ownership or ownership in common, which includes the then owner of the Premises, or a corporation, the majority of whose securities is owned by the owner of the Premises, or any one or more of the foregoing parties. If the then owner of the Premises shall be a corporation, a related party shall include an affiliate, subsidiary or parent corporation, a successor by merger or consolidation, or the holder or holders of the majority of the securities of such corporation.

(F) If the Premises shall be conveyed to the Tenant under this right of first offer, rent and other charges shall be apportioned and adjusted as provided in the Proposed Offer.

PART IV

Real Estate Brokers

55 EVERYTHING YOU WANTED TO KNOW ABOUT REAL ESTATE BROKERAGE AGREEMENTS

A real estate brokerage agreement could be compared to a new suit for a special occasion. You may want to have it custom-made rather than pick it off the rack.

Although a brokerage contract is an important document in a real estate transaction, it is amazing how many sellers of real estate in significant transactions will sign a broker's printed form without analyzing it. Most owners are aware of the importance of setting the amount of the commission and the asking price. Some will negotiate the commission in a major real estate deal to less than the customary 6 percent. However, some of the following more subtle issues may escape the unwary seller.

Proper Price

Once you establish a sales price in a brokerage agreement, you may be stuck with that price (or a real estate commission) even though you would like to hold out for a higher price. If your broker produces a willing and able buyer at the designated price, and you change your mind about selling for that price, you are obligated to pay a commission, even though you don't sell the property.

Therefore, it is crucial to set a proper price in the brokerage agreement. Make sure it is not too low, because you may not be able to adjust it. If it is too high, you may discourage enthusiastic interest by the broker and potential buyers.

Purchase Money Financing

Printed form contracts generally do not distinguish between cash purchases and those that involve a payout of some sort. The commission is based on the total purchase price, even though a relatively small amount of cash may be paid to the seller. Under the standard contract, sellers may find they do not receive enough cash at the closing to pay their broker's commission.

Here's how that could happen. If a seller has agreed on a 6 percent real estate commission on a $1 million sale that is subject to an existing mortgage, the buyer will pay only the difference between the purchase price and the mortgage balance. If the mortgage balance is $930,000, the buyer will pay $70,000 cash and, after payment of real estate transfer taxes, there may not be enough left over to pay the broker the full commission.

This also could happen if the seller takes back purchase money financing. Moreover, if the buyer defaults on the mortgage, the broker will have been fully paid, but the seller may never receive the balance of the purchase price. The seller may have to take back the property after an expensive and time-consuming foreclosure—and pay another commission when the property is sold again.

One way to avoid this problem is to arrange with the broker to pay the commission as cash is received on the purchase money financing. The broker also may ask for a pro rata share of the interest payable on the mortgage, and this is not an unreasonable request.

The advantage of spreading out the commission is that the broker has a stake in the full recovery of the purchase price, and the broker's interest in structuring favorable low-risk financing is similar to the seller's.

Defaulting Buyers

The standard contract provides that a broker has earned its commission when it has produced a buyer at the listed price. But suppose the buyer signs an agreement of sale and defaults before closing. Should the broker get a commission? If the buyer forfeits a deposit, who is entitled to this?

Unless you change the printed form, you will probably find that the broker gets its full commission from the deposit and you get the leftovers, if any. One way to handle this is to provide that the broker gets its commission "if, as and when closing is consummated and the purchase price is distributed to the seller."

Despite popular belief, it is not enough to provide that the commission is payable "at closing." This has been interpreted to mean that the broker is entitled to a commission at the time of closing, even if the buyer defaults. Many brokers will not want to change their standard form, but they will negotiate some arrangement to accept less than the full commission when a buyer defaults and a deposit is forfeited.

Promotion and Advertising

One of the most frequently neglected issues is spelling out what brokers are to do for their commissions. Of course, brokers must find buyers for the listed price. But how will they go about it?

Standards should be set. Although most brokers do not need much prodding to do these things, the broker should be required to list the property with appropriate multiple listing organizations, to promote and advertise the property on a continuous basis, and to place adequate signs on the property. In some cases, brokers should be required to advertise in specified newspapers and journals and to print and distribute a minimum number of certain quality promotional brochures to real estate developers, brokers, and others.

With a difficult or unusual property, such as a vacant school or church, a broker may insist that the seller pay for the cost of the brochures or special advertising. The seller should negotiate a limit on this and urge that the costs be reimbursed out of the commission if the property is eventually sold. When dealing with an unusual estate, new homes, or condominiums, a seller may want to spell out such details as how many salespeople will be at the property on Saturdays and Sundays.

Existing Prospects

Like a giant fine-meshed net, the printed form is designed to catch fish of every species, whenever they arrive. If before signing you have negotiated with prospects that may be interested in the property, or if other brokers have been out casting their lines for you, the agreement will give an exclusive broker a full commission if any of these prospects finally commit themselves.

If you intend to exclude earlier prospects from the agreement, you should do this before you sign. The broker may resist this or may want some arrangement to reduce the commission for these prospects. If you intend to sell to your son, your daughter, or your Uncle Louie, make sure you tell the broker in advance—or you could wind up paying a commission on a family transfer.

Like a net entangled with seaweed at the bottom of the ocean, the commission net may continue to catch fish long after it is discarded by the fisherman. Brokers may be entitled to commissions even after they are discharged if a deal is closed with one of their prospects. If another broker closes the deal, you may have to pay a double commission. To avoid this, the agreement should require the broker to name all prospects at termination and to agree that a commission will be payable only if a sale to one of the listed prospects occurs within two or three months after the termination.

Although a real estate brokerage agreement can involve millions of dollars and major legal implications, sellers frequently do not consult their attorneys until after the agreement is negotiated, or even signed. Like the bride who wants her wedding dress altered, a seller may find that if she visits the seamstress on the eve of her wedding, it may be too late.

56   BUYER'S AGENT MUST TELL ALL TO SELLER

An Arizona Supreme Court case raises issues that may make life more difficult for buyers' agents and possibly their lawyers. In the case of *Lombardo v. Albu,* 14 P.3d 288 (Ariz. 2000), the Arizona Supreme Court held that both a buyer and a buyer's broker have a common-law duty to disclose adverse, financial information about the buyer's ability to perform, even if such information is publicly available. The court refused to permit the broker to hide behind a duty of loyalty to the buyer, because nondisclosure is a tort, and agents cannot facilitate torts.

The case arose at a time when both the sellers and the buyer were not in sterling financial shape. The sellers were behind on their home mortgage payments and one of their lienholders had extended the payment period to give them an opportunity to sell the house.

The buyer had presented an offer to the sellers through her broker, and then signed an agreement of sale. Before the agreement was signed, the buyer had told her agent that her husband had filed for bankruptcy and had been hit with IRS tax liens. She had also told the agent that she was making the offer to purchase in her own name in the hope that the "lenders would not make the connection or would extend credit to her only." She told the broker that she and her husband expected to be a special financing case.

The court concluded that the broker did not reveal any of this to the seller and if he had, the seller would have sought other conditions in the agreement—for example, the right to keep the property on the market pending closing. The buyer was never able to close and, eventually, the sellers lost their equity in the property at a trustee's sale.

Because the case arose on the buyer's motion for summary judgment, the facts set forth above, which were pleaded by the sellers, were construed in the light most favorable to the sellers. Even in that light the sellers' case is not an easy one.

Lower Courts

Two lower courts, the trial court and the court of appeals, had concluded that as a matter of law, a buyer's agent owes a seller no legal duty to disclose these kinds of facts about his principal. In addition, the court of appeals that affirmed the trial court had stated that the information in question was available to the seller through a credit check, a demand for loan pre-approval, or other devices and, therefore, is not "latent" information. Also, that court stated that the broker has a duty of loyalty to the broker's own client—the buyer—that precludes the disclosure when the seller could have obtained the information in other ways.

On balance, it had concluded that the buyer had no duty to disclose that information. The court expressed concern that if it imposed a duty to disclose this type of information, it would make it difficult for a broker to know what is relevant and what is not, perhaps causing brokers to compromise their interests and their clients.

Common-Law Disclosures

In reversing these courts, the Arizona Supreme Court found that there is a general duty at common law for both the buyer and the agent to disclose adverse financial information about the buyer's ability to purchase even when that information is available to the seller in some other way. It compared this to the duty of the seller to disclose defects in a property, citing a case involving termite damage. It reasoned that this is not a "one-way street," and that a buyer has a similar duty as significant to the seller as the buyer's ability to perform. It stated:

> ... The buyer cannot present himself as a ready, willing, and able buyer if he knows that there is a significant risk that the deal will never close because of his inability to perform. This would violate the buyer's duty to deal fairly under the contract and the legal duties imposed by Restatement (Second) of Contracts § 161 and Restatement (Second) of Torts § 551.

The court then concluded that where the buyer had duties, the buyer's agent cannot argue that the duty of loyalty to the buyer precludes a duty by the agent to disclose, since nondisclosure is a tort, and the agent does not have a right to facilitate a tort.

High Bar

The sellers had also argued that the broker was liable under a regulation of the Department of Real Estate that supported a private cause of action based directly on the regulation. That regulation required licensee/brokers to disclose any material information that the buyer "may be unable to perform."

The court stopped short of finding that such a regulation could create a private cause of action, but it held that an administrative regulation could prescribe an appropriate standard of conduct under the Restatement of Torts, even where the regulation doesn't specifically provide that it may be used in private litigation.

This decision sets a high bar for agents to reach. On one hand, agents owe a duty of loyalty to their principals. On the other hand, this court seems to be imposing a duty on them to inform the seller of anything that might be material; and that obligation supersedes the duty of confidentiality to the buyer.

Aside from the rules of confidentiality and issues of loyalty to one's client, how will agents be able to determine what's material? In the *Lombardo* case, for example, the buyer told the broker that she was going to purchase the property in her own name and with her own credit. At the time she said this, it may not have been clear how her husband's bankruptcy would affect financing.

How much should the husband's financial troubles tar the wife's ability to buy a house? Was the agent's decision not to disclose based on her judgment that the deal might still be made, or on trying to hang on to her commission? If brokers mistakenly disclose information that turns out to be immaterial, they will not have happy clients.

If agents are required to disclose everything that may seem relevant, buyers will be reluctant to confide in their agents, and as a matter of policy, that could thwart transactions more than a rule that honored loyalty and confidentiality. Also, if the *Lombardo* doctrine can impose tort liability on a buyer's broker, can liability of buyers' attorneys be far behind?

PART V

Land Use and Title Issues

Courts around the country have been struggling to define
the limits of governmental power to condemn private property for
a so-called "public use." Recent cases that have stirred the debate
are *Kelo v. City of New London*, 2005 U.S. LEXIS 5011 (2005);
Southwestern Illinois Dev. Auth. v. National City Envtl., L.L.C.,
768 N.E.2d 1 (Ill. 2002); and *County of Wayne v. Hathcock*, 684
N.W.2d 765 (Mich. 2004). ABA's *Probate & Property* journal
(March/April 2005, pages 11–19), published a series of five articles
analyzing this area of the law and offering suggestions for striking
the proper balance between private property rights and the government's authority to take property.

The *Kelo* case, in which Connecticut homeowners challenged the right of the state to condemn their homes to make way
for commercial development, was decided by the U.S. Supreme
Court on June 23, 2005. The majority of the sharply divided court
deferred to the local government's right to condemn those properties to make them available to private developers for a hotel and
conference center, housing, and office space under an economic
development plan that could increase tax revenues and improve
the local economy.

Justice Stevens wrote:

For more than a century, our public use jurisprudence has
wisely eschewed rigid formulas and intrusive scrutiny in
favor of affording legislatures broad latitude in determining what public needs justify the use of the takings power.

Also:

Given the comprehensive character of the plan, the thor-
ough deliberation that preceded its adoption, and the limited scope of our review, it is appropriate for us, as it was

in *Berman*, to resolve the challenges of the individual own-ers, not on a piecemeal basis, but rather in light of the en-tire plan. Because that plan unquestionably serves a public purpose, the takings challenged here satisfy the public use requirement of the Fifth Amendment.

The majority also emphasized that it would defer to states that impose stricter public-use requirements.

We emphasize that nothing in our opinion precludes any State from placing further restrictions on its exercise of the takings power. Indeed, many States already impose "public use" requirements that are stricter than the federal base-line. Some of these requirements have been established as a matter of state constitutional law, while others are ex-pressed in state eminent domain statutes that carefully limit the grounds upon which takings may be exercised.

In her dissent, Justice O'Connor raised serious concerns about private property rights. She stated: "The specter of condem-nation hangs over all property. Nothing is to prevent the State from replacing any Motel 6 with a Ritz-Carlton, any home with a shop-ping mall, or any farm with a factory."

Also, she was concerned about the unfairness that might result from the majority's policy:

Any property may now be taken for the benefit of another private party, but the fallout from this decision will not be random. The beneficiaries are likely to be those citizens with disproportionate influence and power in the political process, including large corporations and development firms. As for the victims, the government now has license to transfer property from those with fewer resources to those with more. The Founders cannot have intended this perverse result. "That alone is a just government," wrote James Madison, "which impartially secures to every man, whatever is his own."

In another case that attracted national attention, the Illi-nois Supreme Court set limits on the use of condemnation to permit a privately owned racetrack to expand its parking lot. *Southwest-ern Illinois Dev. Auth. v. National City Envtl., L.L.C.,* 768 N.E.2d 1 (Ill. 2002). The Southwestern Illinois Development Authority had been created by the Illinois legislature to assist in the construction and acquisition of commercial projects, including racetracks and parking facilities. When the authority exercised its power to condemn property so that a privately owned automobile racetrack could expand its parking facilities, the court ruled that the authority's action violated the takings clause of the U.S. Constitution because the taking was not for a public purpose.

The authority had earlier issued revenue bonds and lent the proceeds to a motor sports corporation to build a racetrack. When the track became successful, the corporation wanted to expand its parking onto an adjoining property owned by National City Environmental (NCE), which was in the business of shredding cars and appliances, and recycling metal. NCE intended to use the condemned land as a landfill when its current landfill reached capacity, and it had rejected the attempts of the racetrack to buy the site. At the urging of the racetrack, the authority then condemned the site in order to transfer it to the track.

Private Use

NCE challenged the proposed taking because it was for an unconstitutional "private use." The Illinois circuit court disagreed, and ruled that the taking was for a public purpose because serious public safety issues were involved. Because of limited parking, patrons of the racetrack were forced to cross a highway, causing congestion and the risk of accidents. In addition, traffic created congestion on the nearby interstate highway, and evidence indicated that converting NCE's tract to a parking lot would eliminate these problems. Also, the increased attendance at the racetrack would benefit the area economically.

The history of the case shows how the courts have struggled with this issue. The appellate court reversed the circuit court and held that the authority had exceeded its rights to condemn. The Supreme Court of Illinois then reversed the appellate court, but after granting a rehearing, it reversed itself, affirmed the decision of the appellate court, and finally struck down the taking. The U.S. Supreme Court denied certiorari on October 7, 2002.

The high court framed the controlling issue as whether the development authority had exceeded its authority by transferring property to a private party for a profit where the property was not put to a public use. The court agreed that additional parking could benefit members of the public using the racetrack and that a public purpose may be satisfied in light of public safety concerns. However, it emphasized that the racetrack is not for public use but for private profit, and therefore, the public use requirement was not satisfied, particularly because the racetrack could have built a parking garage on the existing property to serve its needs.

The court emphasized that the authority's true intentions "were not clothed in an independent, legitimate governmental decision to further a planned public use." *Id.* at 10. Instead, the authority had advertised that, for a fee, it would condemn land at the request of private developers for their private use. Some have viewed the authority's role as analogous to a broker seeking to be paid a fee for acquiring properties for private use. Therefore, unlike the process followed in the *Kelo* case, the taking was not rooted in an economic and planning process, but was undertaken solely in response to the racetrack's expansion goals and its inability to buy NCE's land at an acceptable price. The authority did not attempt to premise the taking on the theory that it was eliminating blight or slums.

U.S. Supreme Court

In support of its decision, the court cited earlier precedent, including U.S. Supreme Court cases. It stated:

> ... While, from time to time, the courts have attempted to define public use, there is much disagreement as to its meaning. ... Great deference should be afforded the legislature and its granting of eminent domain authority. ... However, the exercise of that power is not entirely beyond judicial scrutiny ..., and it is incumbent upon the judiciary to ensure that the power of eminent domain is used in a manner contemplated by the framers of the constitutions and by the legislature that granted the specific power in question.

Id. at 8 [citations omitted].

It found that the "true beneficiaries" of the taking were private businesses and not the public, and quoted from an earlier Illinois appellate case:

> If property ownership is to remain what our forefathers intended it to be, if it is to remain a part of the liberty we cherish, the economic by-products of a private capitalist's

ability to develop land cannot justify a surrender of ownership to eminent domain.

Id. at 10.

The court conceded that a highway toll authority may justify the use of eminent domain to ensure that motorists have reasonable access to gas stations. However, it questioned whether that
power includes the ability to use eminent domain to take additional
land for a car wash, and then a lube shop. Also, could it use its
power to facilitate additional expansions for a motel, small retail
shops, and entertainment centers? It stated that the initial, legitimate development of a public project does not justify condemnation
for "any and all related business expansions."

Dissent

In a vigorous dissent, Justice Freeman (joined by another
justice) accused the majority of being disingenuous in its citation of
earlier authorities and in seeking "to unravel the holdings of these
opinions." Freeman also stated that "the majority applies the
wrong standard of review and ignores the evidence adduced at
trial." *Id.* at 23.

In reaching that conclusion, he reviewed in great detail the
evidence that supported the public purpose of the additional parking. He took the position that the court should have an "extremely
narrow" role in reviewing a legislature's judgment of what constitutes a public use and that the court should defer to the legislature's determination. In addition, he emphasized "that a taking for
a public use is not transformed into a private taking through a subsequent transfer to a private party." *Id.* at 19. Also, he disagreed
with the majority about service stations and restaurants used in
connection with a toll road system. He concluded that those facilities should be considered a public use whether they are operated by
the Toll Highway Commission or leased to a private corporation
that may be better able to carry on the business.

In his dissent, he also emphasized that the majority cannot
dispute the public objective of alleviating certain economic and
other conditions in the southwestern part of Illinois, which is the
legislative purpose in setting up the authority. He stated that, "the
majority effectively interdicts any taking for the purpose of economic development." *Id.* at 22.

Death of Social Legislation

Freeman queried: "I must inquire of the majority what development project can satisfy the requirement that the public be 'entitled to use or enjoy the property, not as a mere favor or by permission of the owner, but by right'? Can a member of the general public enter a manufacturing plant as of right? What of a sports facility? Can a member of the general public enter a stadium, or for that matter the racetrack at issue, without paying a fee for the privilege? ... Again, I ask what project will survive the majority's requirement of use as of right by the general public?

... I suggest that, in its attempt to reach a particular result, the majority does great harm to the public use doctrine and to the interests of this state." *Id.* at 23.

In conclusion, Justice Freeman states: "Lastly, the majority commits great disservice to the State of Illinois and its citizens in engrafting upon the public use doctrine the requirement that property taken by eminent domain must be accessible to the general public as of right. This requirement is the death of social legislation in furtherance of economic development and revitalization." *Id.* at 25–26.

The limits of eminent domain will continue to be debated in future cases, and *Southwestern Illinois Development Authority* will undoubtedly be cited many times by proponents of the importance of protecting private property rights against excesses of states' police powers. It is somewhat ironic that this lofty issue has arisen in a case that may be viewed as a dispute over conflicting private automobile uses. The objecting owner wants to use its property for shredding and recycling old and damaged cars. The racetrack wants to park cars there to accommodate its business of racing other cars at high speeds. Unfortunately, when those cars lose control, they crash, and for all we know, in the long run they may wind up on the coveted site—even though the condemnation has crashed.

Courts around the country have been struggling to define the limits of the government's power to condemn private property for a public use. Recent cases that have stirred the debate are *County of Wayne v. Hathcock,* 684 N.W.2d 765 (Mich. 2004); and *Kelo v. City of New London,* 2005 U.S. LEXIS 5011 (2005). ABA's *Probate & Property* journal (March/April 2005, pages 11–19) published a series of five articles analyzing this area of the law, and offering suggestions for striking the proper balance between private property rights and the government's authority to take property.

The *Kelo* case, in which Connecticut homeowners challenged the right of the state to condemn their homes to make way for commercial development, was argued before the U.S. Supreme Court on February 22, 2005. Based on the questioning of some of the justices, observers have reported that the court seemed concerned about balancing the rights of private citizens to be secure in their unblighted homes against second-guessing the land-use decisions of city and state governments.

58 U.S. SUPREME COURT REJECTS COMPENSATION FOR GOVERNMENT'S TEMPORARY BAN ON DEVELOPMENT

Under the U.S. Constitution, the government must compensate landowners when it denies them all use of their land. But what if it stops use for only three—or six—years?

The U.S. Supreme Court has now ruled, in a six-to-three decision, that while such bans may be compensable "when they go too far," a 32-month moratorium on development did not cross that line. *Tahoe–Sierra Preservation Council, Inc. v. Tahoe Regional Planning Agency*, 122 S. Ct. 1465 (2002).

In that case, the Tahoe Regional Planning Agency (TRPA) had placed a moratorium on land development around Lake Tahoe. The affected owners sought compensation, and the case reached the Supreme Court, which refused to compensate them, concluding that temporary moratoria must be decided on a case-by-case basis. Justice Stevens, writing for the court, held that even a complete moratorium for a 32-month period did not automatically give the affected owners the right to compensation. He wrote that "[l]and-use regulations are ubiquitous and most of them impact property values in some tangential way—often in completely unanticipated ways." He said that treating all such curbs as per se takings "would transform government regulation into a luxury few governments could afford."

The Lake

The Lake Tahoe case goes back two decades. The TRPA, a bistate unit created by Congress in 1969, stopped all development for 32 months, from 1981 to 1984, to study environmental problems in the 500-square-mile Lake Tahoe Basin and devised a long-range land-use plan. Little development has been permitted since that

32-month ban, but for procedural reasons the Supreme Court addressed only that ban, not the continuing restrictions. In discussing the reasonableness of the ban, Justice Stevens wrote that Lake Tahoe is "uniquely beautiful," and noted that "Mark Twain aptly described the clarity of its waters as 'not merely transparent, but dazzlingly, brilliantly so.'" A federal district court had observed earlier that, if development were allowed to continue unabated, "the lake will lose its clarity and its trademark blue color, becoming green and opaque for eternity."

The Landowners

The Tahoe-Sierra Preservation Council represents about 2,000 owners of improved and unimproved parcels in the Lake Tahoe Basin. The plaintiffs in the case also included about 400 individual owners of vacant lots who bought their properties before the restrictions were enacted. Their plight has been the subject of several suits in lower courts, and their claims were eventually consolidated. A district court ruled for the plaintiffs, in part, but the U.S. Court of Appeals for the Ninth Circuit, in San Francisco, ruled for the TRPA.

The Supreme Court showed less sympathy for the landowners than for the lake. The opinion mentions testimony that the "average holding time of a lot in the Tahoe area between lot purchase and house construction is twenty-four years." It also speculates that a property will "recover value as soon as the prohibition is lifted." It goes even further by suggesting that the value may rise because "values throughout the Basin can be expected to reflect an added assurance that Lake Tahoe will remain in its pristine state."

The Dissenters

Chief Justice William H. Rehnquist, and Justices Antonin Scalia and Clarence Thomas disagreed with the majority, and opined that a ban on development as protracted as the one in the Lake Tahoe case "does not resemble any traditional land-use planning device." The chief justice stated that the majority ruling could encourage governments to skirt the Constitution's just compensation clause by labeling virtually any prohibition as "temporary," even if it lasts for years.

For procedural reasons, the majority concluded that the moratorium had lasted only 32 months, but the dissent assumed that it lasted almost six years. When viewing this discrepancy, one might use Justice O'Connor's "bundle-of-sticks" metaphor from *United States v. Craft* (a tenancy-by-entireties case). Under this analogy, the chief justice determined, in effect, that the government had taken more sticks from the owners' bundle of property rights than the majority will acknowledge.

Rehnquist accepts that the planning agency's efforts to preserve the lake "were made in good faith in furtherance of the public interest." But he stated that the distinction between "temporary" and "permanent" prohibitions is "tenuous." He quoted Justice Holmes' admonition of 80 years ago with approval. At that time, Chief Justice Holmes wrote: "We are in danger of forgetting that a strong public desire to improve the public condition is not enough to warrant achieving the desire by a shorter cut than the constitutional way of paying for the change."

The Precedents

The decision and the dissents, totaling 54 pages, provide a detailed analysis of the history of landmark cases related to owners' rights to recover for takings in the face of various land-use regulations. Among those cases are *Agins v. City of Tiburon*, 447 U.S. 255 (1980); *Lucas v. South Carolina Coastal Council*, 505 U.S. 1003 (1992); *First English Evangelical Lutheran Church v. County of Los Angeles*, 482 U.S. 304 (1987); *Palazzolo v. Rhode Island*, 533 U.S. 606 (2001); and *Penn Central Transportation Co. v. New York City*, 438 U.S. 104 (1978).

The decision is worth reading just to see the varying analyses of the majority and dissenters on these cases. One of the major differences of interpretation involves the *Lucas* case, which sets forth an important "per se takings" test. The majority seems to limit significantly the application of that case, and goes out of its way to show that "regulatory" takings are by nature different from "physical" takings. It also seems to reject the common impression that *Lucas* recognized an owner's "right to build" and that owners should be compensated when regulations deny all economically viable use, even where the land retains some value.

Stevens stated:

> The categorical rule that we applied in *Lucas* states that compensation is required when a regulation deprives an owner of *"all* economically beneficial uses" of his land. *Id.*

372

at 1019. Under that rule, a statute that "wholly eliminated the value" of Lucas' fee simple title clearly qualified as a taking. But our holding was limited to "the extraordinary circumstance when *no* productive or economically beneficial use of land is permitted." *Id.* at 1017. The emphasis on the word "no" in the text of the opinion was, in effect, reiterated in a footnote explaining that the categorical rule would not apply if the diminution in value were 95% instead of 100%. *Id.* at 1019, n. 8. Anything less than a "complete elimination of value," or a "total loss," the Court acknowledged, would require the kind of analysis applied in *Penn Central. Lucas,* 505 U.S. at 1019–1020, n. 8.

Certainly, our holding that the permanent "obliteration of the value" of a fee simple estate constitutes a categorical taking does not answer the question whether a regulation prohibiting any economic use of land for a 32-month period has the same legal effect. . . .

122 S. Ct. at 1483.

The Policy Issues

The majority clearly deferred to the "consensus of the planning community" on the importance of moratoria. It was concerned about "inefficient and ill-conceived growth" and it recognized that land-use restrictions may even enhance property values, rather than reduce them.

While the court does not dwell on the *in-terrorem* effect of unintended takings, there are difficult policy issues at stake. If local governmental regulations and moratoria could possibly result in condemnation payments to affected landowners, what townships are wealthy enough to risk that result? If there is any uncertainty, that is, any possibility that land regulations could result in takings, it is likely that municipalities will be reluctant to institute regulations. Uncertainty will tip the balance about this in favor of landowners and against land-use controls. The majority stated that concern in the following passage:

. . . A rule that required compensation for every delay in the use of property would render routine government processes prohibitively expensive or encourage hasty decisionmaking. Such an important change in the law should be the product of legislative rulemaking rather than adjudication.

122 S. Ct. at 1485.

While the majority opinion will give some comfort to municipalities, it still raises questions that municipalities will have to answer in order to predict when their regulations will "go too far." Take just two of the factors discussed in the *Lake Tahoe* case. If the majority were dealing with a six-year moratorium instead of one that was imposed for 32 months, would the decision have gone the other way? The dissent, which viewed the procedural issue differently, focused on a moratorium of almost six years. Also, the case dealt with unchallenged findings of fact that the TRPA was acting for good reasons and in good faith. With slightly different facts on those issues, the court could easily have gone the other way.

The issues that the court struggled with are difficult, and they will not go away. The conflict will go on between private property rights and the government's inherent right to regulate the use of property for the public good without paying for it.

The Rehnquist Twist

In his dissenting opinion, Rehnquist speculates that the majority would not view "even a ten-year moratorium as a taking under *Lucas,* because the moratorium is not 'permanent.'" To drive his point home about the impact of a six-year moratorium, he puts a little twist on the problem based on *Lucas.* He contends that a regulation that completely bans use for six years is, from the landowners' perspective, the equivalent of a physical appropriation. He points out that the "practical equivalence," of a temporary ban on all economic use is a forced leasehold:

> ... For example, assume the following situation: Respondent is contemplating the creation of a National Park around Lake Tahoe to preserve its scenic beauty. Respondent decides to take a 6-year leasehold over petitioners' property, during which any human activity on the land would be prohibited, in order to prevent any further destruction to the area while it was deciding whether to request that the area be designated a National Park.
>
> Surely that leasehold would require compensation. In a series of World War II–era cases in which the Government

had condemned leasehold interests in order to support the war effort, the Government conceded that it was required to pay compensation for the leasehold interest. ... From petitioners' standpoint, what happened in this case is no different than if the government had taken a 6-year lease of their property.

122 S. Ct. at 1493.

Suppose one of the *Tahoe* claimants did not have outright ownership, but, in fact, had only a 32-month leasehold interest in the property. Furthermore, suppose that tenant intended to build a small beach house or use the property in other ways that were barred by a moratorium instituted the day after it signed and paid for the lease. A 32-month moratorium would then function as a permanent bar of that tenant's property rights. As to that claimant, there would no longer be any issue about whether the "average holding time" before construction is 25 years, or whether the moratorium might increase the value of the claimant's property in the long run. It seems that if the tenant were not entitled to compensation, the government would be accomplishing by regulation what it could not accomplish through eminent domain—that is, taking property without paying for it.

This issue of whether owners should be compensated for "temporary" takings brings to mind the frequently quoted comment of economist John Maynard Keynes: "In the long run we are all dead."

59 ADVERSE POSSESSION: TENDING LAWN MAY GROW TO BE HOSTILE

You should be encouraged to know that working hard on your neighbor's lawn can give you more than good exercise and the civic association's good neighbor award. It may also constitute continual, hostile, and "adverse" possession, and give you the ownership of the lawn you are tending.

Lawns

That's what happened in the case of *Brennan v. Manchester Crossings, Inc.*, 708 A.2d 815 (Pa. Super. 1998). The Superior Court reversed a lower-court decision that held that the claimants' use of the property was not sufficiently hostile because the record owner had "implied" his consent to the claimant's use of the disputed tract. The Superior Court disagreed with the trial court because acquiescence in the claimant's use of that property did not indicate that the owner affirmatively granted permission to use it.

While the record owner may not have cared whether the claimant used his land, he had never expressly objected. In addition, the act of surveying the property, standing alone, was held not sufficient conduct by the record owner to break the continuity of the claimant's possession, especially when there was no evidence to suggest that the claimants were even aware that the survey was being performed.

In this case, the claimant had acted for a period of over 21 years in tending a portion of the lawn and that added up to adverse possession under Pennsylvania precedent. This case only goes to support the adage "beware of strangers bearing gifts." If your neighbor continually takes care of part of your lawn for over 21 years, you had better be alerted to the fact that you may wind up losing that part of it.

The courts throughout the country are split about whether simple lawn mowing can constitute adverse possession. In many cases, the courts, unlike *Brennan*, assume that the true owner is simply accommodating his or her neighbor where the next-door resident, as here, mows beyond his boundary on the property. See *Walker v. Murphree*, 722 So.2d 1277 (Miss. App. 1998). That may be more convenient and helpful to the next-door resident than to the true owner.

However, a South Dakota Supreme Court decision agreed with the reasoning in *Brennan*. In the case of *Jutting v. Hendrix*, 606 N.W.2d 140 (S.D. 2000), the court held that property owners are entitled to title by adverse possession of a strip they had planted, and on which they maintained the grass and trees. In that case, the winning party became the owner of a 10-foot strip adjoining his property because he had planted two trees on it, and for a period of 28 years had continuously watered and mowed the grass.

To understand *Brennan*, it helps to visualize the site. The true owner owned farmland and had no lawn other than the disputed lawn that was adjacent to the claimant's residence. That fact helped lead to the finding of adverse possession because of the way the continuous tending of the lawn appeared to observers.

The extended lawn was the same width as the claimant's residential lot and it extended 60 feet beyond that. That extended lawn was all of the land between the claimant's parcel and an overgrown gravel driveway. The claimants not only seeded, fertilized, and mowed the grass to the same height as their residence's lawn, but also used that tract for recreational activities, occasionally parking vehicles, and storing firewood. According to the court, the "land simply appeared to be an extension of appellant's own lawn, with farm fields surrounding the combined tracts."

Woodlands

Where the disputed property is undeveloped woodland, actual possession beyond mowing or general maintenance of the property may be required. *Bride v. Robwood Lodge*, 713 A.2d 109 (Pa. Super. 1998), held that in such a situation, sporadic hunting, hiking, planting timbers, and occasionally removing timber, may not establish adverse possession even if that conduct occurred continuously over a 21-year period. There the court overruled a contrary finding of fact by the trial court, which shows that the court was quite serious in requiring more significant evidence of possession.

It is noteworthy that other jurisdictions have permitted occasional hunting and similar activity to support adverse-possession claims where the equities tended to favor the adverse possessors more clearly. In *Bride*, the true owner claimed that he had been in actual possession of the property himself and that the adverse possessor at one time paid for an easement across the property from its true owners for purposes of building a road. Those facts mitigated against a finding of adverse possession.

Public Policy

Adverse-possession cases are fact-sensitive and obviously not easy to decide. In both of the cited Pennsylvania cases, the appellate court overruled the trial court's judgment. However, some observers feel that the court overreached in finding adverse possession in the lawn case.

One commentator said that where an owner observes his neighbor making a trespassing but inoffensive use of the owner's property, and that use does not exclude the owner from access or otherwise permanently alter the character of the property, we should not assume that the owner should view this as a "challenge to title." Where a neighbor crosses over a boundary but makes use of the crossover property for nothing more than landscape tending, the commentator questions what public policy is served by viewing this conduct as a "claim of ownership" that ripens into title after 21 years.

If you feel you will have the time and energy during the next 21 years, maybe you should get out there and start cultivating a part of your neighbor's lawn. They may even thank you and treat you to iced tea and brownies. Also, in light of current cases, you may wind up owning it by adverse possession.

60 TITLE POLICY PROTECTS AGAINST PURCHASER'S OWN TAX LIEN

A Michigan case held that a title policy can be read to protect a purchaser even against his own tax lien. In the case of *Archambo v. Lawyers Title Insurance Corp.*, No. 202289 (Mich. App. September 3, 2002) (unpublished opinion), Michigan's court of appeals interpreted a title insurance policy so that a standard exclusion against those liens "created or suffered" by the insured did not let the title company off the hook.

Missed Lien

In this case, Archambo had been a shareholder in a solar heating company, and the IRS filed a tax lien against the corporation and all of its shareholders, including Archambo. When he changed careers and became a home builder, he was forced to buy back a house he had built, and he took title in his own name. Lawyers Title Insurance Company missed the IRS lien when it did the search on the purchase of his property, so the liens did not appear as an exception in the title policy it issued to him. The lien was finally discovered when Archambo sold the house and was forced to borrow money to pay off the lien. He then sued Lawyers Title to get that money back.

The Michigan Supreme Court remanded the case to the court of appeals two times. In its last remand, the supreme court pointed out that Archambo knew about the tax lien, but he testified that he thought the lien had expired because an IRS agent told him that this lien would be valid for only five years.

Also, that court pointed out how the earlier lien became a lien against the purchased property. Some readers may not be aware that federal tax liens are afforded the special status of attaching to "after-acquired real estate."

379

"Created" or "Suffered"

The title company defended by arguing that the tax lien was excluded from policy coverage under section 3(a) of the listed exclusions as a matter "created" or "suffered" by the insured. The court of appeals ruled against the title company and noted that the policy does not define those words. Therefore, it based its decision on a summary of cases in an ALR article it cited on this exclusion. It summarized that ALR commentary this way:

> ... That annotation states that generally the provision has not barred coverage for liens that were brought about by the insured's negligence. ... Conversely, where the lien has resulted from the intentional misconduct of the insured, the clause will bar coverage. ... While none of these foreign cases deal with a federal tax lien, other states have consistently held that an insured must intentionally act in order to be deemed to have come within the terms of the exclusion. ... The word "suffered" within the exclusion has been deemed to be synonymous with the word "permit" and to imply power to prohibit or prevent. ... An insured is not barred from coverage if he was merely negligent.

Id. at 2–3 [citations omitted].

The court found that Archambo neither created nor suffered the lien because all the evidence "[established] that plaintiff had no responsibility for the payment of taxes in the corporation and in no way agreed to the placement of a lien." *Id.* at 5. That analysis was based on the evidence that he had not been in charge of the corporate books of the solar heating company, and had testified that he did not know that the company had failed to pay the federal taxes.

This case, which interprets a standard title policy exclusion used all over the country, will undoubtedly be used as a precedent for many claimants who seek to avoid the exclusion when they are responsible in some way for liens against properties that they purchase or finance. The "created, suffered, assumed and agreed to" exclusion is invoked by title insurers more than any other exclusion from coverage in the standard ALTA policy.

Section 3(a) excludes coverage for "[d]efects, liens, encumbrances, adverse claims or other matters" that are "created, suffered, assumed or agreed to by the insured claimant."

As discussed by the court in the *Archambo* case, several courts have construed the exclusion narrowly, and have interpreted the "created" and "suffered" language to require intentional, as contrasted with negligent, unintentional, or mistaken, conduct on the part of the insured.

Policy Issues

However, several commentators have suggested that the word "created" should be interpreted to include all acts of the insured that cause defects, including intentional and unintentional acts. Otherwise, title insurance companies will be insuring against those liens that are the insureds' own fault. Some commentators believe that it should be contrary to public policy to allow an insured to obtain insurance against its own tax obligations. In this case, the tax lien was Archambo's debt even though it stemmed from a corporate obligation, and he knew about the lien. If the lien had resulted from Archambo's failure to pay his own taxes, it seems that the court would not have held the title company liable under the policy.

One of the issues in the case is whether someone can "create" or "suffer" something without intending to do so. For example, if you do not pay your debts, or you are an officer in a company that does not pay its debts, can it be said that you did not have anything to do with creating a lien that resulted from your failure to pay? A reasonable argument can be made that the words "created" and "suffered" should be interpreted to include even unintended, but careless or negligent acts.

The drafters of the policy form could have done a better job in writing this exclusion. In its everyday use, the word "suffered" might include just about every encumbrance visited on an insured. For example, a desk version of *The Random House Dictionary* defines "suffer" as "1. to undergo or feel (pain or distress). 2. to undergo or experience (any action or condition). 3. to tolerate or endure. 4. to allow or permit."

None of these definitions require the recipient to intentionally create the pain, distress, action, or condition in order to suffer it.

The case does not discuss the related issue of what will happen if the title company is forced to pay the tax lien. Since it is paying Archambo's lien, shouldn't it be entitled to subrogation of the

IRS's lien against him, or against the solar heating company that owed the taxes in the first place?

Archambo paid the lien and made a claim under the title policy. Under those circumstances a title company would have to invoke a subrogation right for a payment made directly to its own insured. That would seem to be a more difficult claim to support than if the company paid the IRS lien and took an assignment of it.

Also, what about the customary title affidavit that is usually taken by an insured party? The affidavit provides that the insured has no other liens or encumbrances against him or her, other than those listed in the title report. Under those circumstances, when an unexpected lien later shows up, couldn't the insured be sued by the title company for damages suffered from a false affidavit?

In light of the *Archambo* case and other cases that have narrowed the scope of exclusion 3(a) of the ALTA policy, it would not be surprising if the title industry now adopted a clearer definition of that exclusion so that title companies will not be insuring buyers against their own debts.

61   TITLE COMPANY NOT LIABLE FOR FAILING TO INSURE TITLE

      Is a title company liable to an applicant for title insurance when it refuses to insure title?

      According to the New York Supreme Court, the answer may depend on whether the title work was "negligently performed." *Brackman v. Southern Tier Abstract Corp.*, 734 N.Y.S.2d 282 (N.Y. App. Div. 2001). In *Brackman,* the buyer offered to purchase New York real estate. No formal contract of sale was ever executed because one condition of the offer was not met, namely, a demonstration that the deed could include access rights to a nearby lake. When the parties contacted the abstract company through their common attorney, the company determined that no insurable lake rights existed in the property's chain of title.

      The seller then sued the title company for $3,000 in damages for a "loss of a sale" because the company had erroneously determined that his property did not have the legal access needed to close the sale. For purposes of the case, the court assumed that the seller was the one who had dealt with the abstract company, even though the record was not completely clear on this. Nevertheless, the New York Supreme Court affirmed the lower court's dismissal of the case because it determined that no competent proof was offered to establish that the company's conclusion about lack of access was erroneous. However, the court also stated that if the seller had contracted with the abstract company to do title work, and the company negligently performed the search, the seller would have a "cognizable cause of action" for damages.

Scope of Liability

      This case raises issues about the nature of a title company's obligations to a title applicant when it either erroneously issues a title report or merely turns down the application. A title company would be surprised to discover that it could be responsible to an applicant when it hasn't even entered into a contract to issue a policy or received a fee for the search. Title insurers generally limit their liability to the stated policy limits and they take the position that everything else they do is merely a preface to issuing the policy. Also, for a fee, sometimes title companies will obligate themselves to liability for accuracy of the search, but will place a limit on that obligation.

On the other hand, applicants have taken the position that title insurers are aware that others rely on them and on the accuracy of their searches, and therefore, even without a specific agreement, they attempt to impose an obligation on the companies to perform the search in a reasonably prudent manner. Those claimants will concede that a title company has no obligation to insure a title. For example, sometimes title companies will be particularly cautious about agreeing to insure questionable aspects of title, such as access to a body of water. The decision not to insure may not merely be based on the merits of the case, but only because certain types of insurance have become a large source of litigation. The *Brackman* case did not even decide whether or not there was a valid right of access to the lake. Even if there had been, however, the insurer would not be obligated to insure that access.

In some states, like Pennsylvania, the title company might have been helped by insurance regulations or industry standards. For example, Pennsylvania Title Insurance Rating Manual, Rule Rate Rule 2.2 states, "Insurer, upon notification to its applicant, may decline to search, examine, issue its commitment or insure any title, or to issue any endorsement to a policy. Insurer may, at any time in its sole discretion, refuse an application or cancel an unclosed application of the applicant, without liability on the part of insurer." However, the claimant is likely to argue that it is not bound by this rule, because while the rule regulates the insurance industry, it is not intended to set a standard for consumer-tort liability.

Business customs are likely to control the standards of liability. In many places, such as the Philadelphia area, the custom is for the title company to mark up and initial the title commitment at a closing. The buyer or borrower then pays a premium, and the "marked up commitment" binds the title company. It is then followed up by the actual title policy in which the title company must honor the commitment, and include those endorsements set forth in the commitment and insure title, subject only to those exceptions and caveats that are not stricken in the commitment. Of course, none of that even happened in the *Brackman* case.

Lessons

This leads to several lessons for real estate practitioners. For one thing, an applicant should never rely on a title search or title report unless it has a clear understanding that the title company is contractually obligated for accuracy of that information. An applicant should also determine the limits of the title company's obligations. On the other hand, title companies should be careful not to make any specific representations about the reliability of a preliminary commitment if they do not intend to be bound by it. It is not difficult to conceive of circumstances where courts could hold title companies liable for negligent searches or commitments if claimants prove that representations were made by the company and that buyers or lenders relied on those representations. Those representations may extend the obligation of a title company beyond the traditional title-policy obligations.

The *Brackman* case also highlights the importance of title clauses that are used to stipulate the buyer's obligation to purchase the property under an agreement of sale. Sometimes the buyer's obligations to purchase are conditioned on obtaining "good and marketable title, free and clear of liens and encumbrances and insurable as such by *any* title insurance company," or worse yet, "from *buyer's* title insurance company." With those provisions, the buyer may be able to wriggle out of liability under the agreement merely because it selects a title company similar to the defendant in the *Brackman* case. On the other hand, if the title may be so insured by "*a* title insurance company," the seller may be able to hold the buyer to the agreement of sale by finding another title company that would be willing to insure the title, including the lake access that the seller obviously thought that it had.

62   WHEN IS A PIG A PET?

"A pig is an animal with dirt on his face;
His shoes are a terrible disgrace."
—"Swinging on a Star"
Words by Johnny Burke
Music by Jimmy Van Huesen

Is a pig a "pet" or "livestock"? Your answer might very well depend on whether you associate pigs with your morning eggs or whether you're strictly kosher; whether you associate them with luaus or with the film *Babe*, which starred a sympathetic, resourceful pig.

Malvern Chickens

That question arose in an Alabama appeals court case involving a community restriction against keeping livestock in residences, but similar questions arise under various zoning laws. The *Philadelphia Inquirer* reported a zoning dispute in Malvern, Pennsylvania, involving two chickens, which the owners claimed as pets. A neighbor and the borough zoning officer squawked that the zoning ordinance requires at least three acres to "raise poultry," and the owners have requested a special exception from the Zoning Hearing Board. The decision may turn on the definition of a "pet."

In the case of *Gebauer v. Lake Forest Property Owners Ass'n, Inc.*, 723 So.2d 1288 (Ala. Civ. App. 1998), the courts were faced with the decision of whether a Vietnamese potbellied pig violated the neighborhood's restrictive covenant forbidding livestock. The applicable covenant provided:

No livestock of any description may be kept or permitted on the property with the exception of dogs, cats, and other animals which are qualified household pets, and which do not make objectionable noise or constitute a nuisance or inconvenience to owners of other lots nearby.

Gebauer, 723 So.2d at 1290.

Dickensian Tale

After a trial, the lower court found the pig, Taylor, was "livestock" and constituted a nuisance. The Alabama Supreme Court in a somewhat whimsical opinion reversed the lower court and held that Taylor was a domesticated pet who could continue to live at home.

You could get a little clue about which way the court was leaning from the beginning of its decision.

Taylor's is a sad, Dickensian tale in which a cold, hard-nosed triumvirate tries everything within its power to separate a woman from the potbellied porcine pet she loves.

Id. at 1288.

The triumvirate to which the court refers is the three member architectural review committee of the neighborhood association that, according to the court, "charged ahead like a wild boar in rutting season, single-mindedly pursuing its quest to have Taylor removed from her home." *Id.* at 1289.

For all you city folks, a potbellied pig is an animal far smaller than a regular farm pig, weighing between 75 to 100 pounds when fully grown. Its ears, tail, body hair, and other traits differ from its rural cousins. It cannot eat the same feed as a farm pig and, on doctor's orders, Taylor eats a brand of feed made especially for exotic pigs. Despite that, according to the court, the property owners' association gleefully wallows in the evidence that potbellied pigs and regular farm pigs are both, genetically, *swine*.

Pure, Pedigreed, Potbellied Pigs

Gebauer won the day by explaining that Vietnamese potbellied pigs are raised in the United States to be pets, not livestock. Their pedigrees are maintained, and purebred potbellies can be registered like thoroughbred dogs. Ms. Gebauer submitted a videotape, "A Day in the Life of Taylor," which shows the pig walking around the house, going up and down stairs, eating her treats, getting her belly scratched, and doing tricks like sitting on command and performing "some sort of pig dance." Taylor is even housebroken and has an igloo-shaped doghouse lined with handmade afghans, but apparently she sleeps indoors at night in her own bedroom.

In a triumph for visual aids, the court stated:

> ... Neighborhood dogs can be heard barking in the background of the tape, but with the exception of an oink, oink here and an oink, oink there, Taylor is quiet. There does not appear to be a rambunctious bone in her body.

Id. at 1289.

The court cited precedent that held that Vietnamese pot-bellied pigs are clearly not meant to be eaten like livestock, and all doubts and ambiguities in a restrictive covenant must be resolved against the party seeking enforcement. According to the court, this was not a case in which a family is treating a farm animal like a pet, such as Arnold, the pig of television's "Green Acres" fame. Gebauer had bought a breed of pig that is bred specifically as a pet.

In the case of the Malvern chickens, the owners would do well to study the *Gebauer* decision, and perhaps videotape these "pets" on a quiet day, when they're not laying eggs.

Pennsylvania Pig Case

In an earlier Pennsylvania case, the pig lost. Either the case or the pig was too big for the pig's lawyer to handle. In *Tirpak v. Summit Hill*, 515 A.2d 1018 (Pa. Cmwlth. 1986), the Commonwealth Court affirmed a common pleas court decision that barred a 1,000-pound pig from living in a residentially zoned area that prohibited "keeping of livestock or poultry."

The defendant had maintained the pig on a sunporch during the winter months, and in his backyard during the remainder of the year. He considered the pig as a pet, and had no intention of selling it for a profit. According to the court, he treated it "like a baby" and it was the object of his, and his grandchildren's, affection. The defendant argued that the dictionary definition of "livestock" is "domestic animals used or raised on a farm, especially for a profit." He argued that because profit was not his objective, the pig was not livestock.

The court rejected the idea that the owner's motivation for keeping the pig had to be investigated in order to determine whether he violated the ordinance.

It held:

> Further, Defendant's argument suggests that the owner's purpose in keeping an animal must be investigated to determine a violation. Motives for keeping animals are as many and as mysterious as man's tastes. This concept introduces an unacceptable vague subjective element into the ordinance. Beauty may lie in the beholder but zoning laws do not lie in the eye of the householder. The law simply does not permit the interpretation of language in a zoning ordinance to depend on the personal taste or motives of the citizenry. One man's pet may be another man's phobia. Zoning ordinances must serve the general public good and not a particular individual's whim or fancy.

> Finally, if we adopt Defendant's logic that his motivation or purpose precludes a violation of the livestock exclusion in the Ordinance, it would lead to absurd results. Carried to its logical conclusion, it would not be a violation for a hippo-loving neighbor to put a hippopotamus in his backyard and keep it as a pet. Nor would a citizen who installed a thirty-two foot long boa constrictor in his home because he believed it would protect his home from rodents violate the Ordinance. Defendant's position could well destroy the salutary purposes of the Zoning Ordinance in Summit Hill. We cannot and will not judicially countenance such an interpretation or result.

Borough of Summit Hill v. Tirpak, 9 CARBON CO. L.J. 286, 290 (1985).

In light of the success of the 100-pound pig in the *Gebauer* case, no one will ever know whether the Pennsylvania pig would have fared better if the owners could either have produced a videotape on the average day of the pig—or have put the pig on a strict diet so that it could have lost 900 pounds or so.

While *Gebauer* is certainly not the first case where an appellate court had to deal with piggish conduct, it is one of the few cases where the court seemed to have no trouble finding in favor of the pig.

63   TOWNS AND ASSOCIATIONS CAN'T STOP COMMUNICATIONS TOWERS

In the nursery tale *Jack and the Beanstalk*, the beanstalk sprouted until it reached the land of a giant up in the sky. That is a little bit like communications towers only the "pot of gold" is the communications network, and according to decisions, the "beanstalk" can't be cut down. Who knows who the "giant" is in the tower metaphor.

Decisions have applied federal telecommunications laws in a way that will make it difficult for townships or community associations to restrict the proliferation of communications towers. In one case, the U.S. Court of Appeals for the Third Circuit held that the Telecommunications Act of 1996 did not permit a township to deny the right to build a tower for transmission of wireless telephone signals. *Omnipoint Corp. v. Zoning Hearing Bd.*, 181 F.3d 403 (3d Cir. 1999).

Townships Can't Control

In that case, Omnipoint applied to Pine Grove Township, Pennsylvania, for a special exception under the Pennsylvania Municipalities Planning Code to build a 114-foot monopole to facilitate cellular telephone service. The Township Zoning Board denied the request for a special exception on the theories that no studies had been presented about the effect on neighborhood property values, and that Omnipoint had not carried the burden of proof about the effect on the general character of the neighborhood.

On appeal, the district court reversed the board because the record in the case did not establish the detrimental effect of the proposed tower with a "high degree of probability," and also because the board's decision was based on aesthetic considerations and a desire to preserve property values—factors that cannot justify denial of a special exception under Pennsylvania law. The district court ordered the board to issue the special exception for the tower.

On appeal to the U.S. circuit court, the court affirmed the district court and invoked the Telecommunications Act of 1996, P.L. 104, 110 Stat. 56, which was designed to accelerate private-sector deployment of telecommunications and information technologies and services. The court found that the zoning board's decision was not supported by substantial evidence as mandated by that act, and pointed out that case law from other circuits indicated that a few "generalized expressions of concern" with aesthetics and property values could not serve as substantial evidence to ban towers under the statutory standard.

"Eyesores" and Health

Among other things, the neighbors had complained that the tower's high-intensity radio transmissions would harm neighbors' health. The court pointed out that the Telecommunications Act was a deliberate compromise between competing aims—to facilitate nationally the growth of wireless telephone service, and to maintain substantial local control over siting of towers. However, the court cited with approval other cases that found that under the act, local zoning authorities were not permitted to make "zoning decisions based on concerns over the environmental or health effects of radio emissions associated with wireless telephone service." *Omnipoint Corp.*, 181 F.3d at 407.

The court did not say that zoning boards must permit these types of towers under all circumstances. The court distinguished an earlier case where two 135-foot wireless telephone transmission towers were denied after considerable community opposition. (*AT&T Wireless PCS v. City Council*, 155 F.3d 423 (4th Cir. 1998)). According to the court, the evidence in that case was less general and speculative than in *Omnipoint*. In *AT&T*, the protestors argued primarily that 235-foot towers would be "eyesores" if erected in the applicable neighborhood, which had no significant commercial development, no commercial antenna towers, and no above-ground power lines.

Township and Zoning Controls

A 1999 U.S. circuit court decision under the Telecommunications Act upheld the right of the townships to prohibit communications towers in certain areas. *APT Pittsburgh Ltd. Partnership v. Penn Twp. Butler County of Pennsylvania*, 196 F.3d 469 (3d Cir. 1999).

In that case, the circuit court of appeals sustained the township's right to limit the areas where towers could be built, and to refuse to grant a variance to construct a tower on land zoned for residential use.

The applicant had argued that the zoning ordinance was impermissibly exclusionary because it had the effect of prohibiting the applicant from closing a significant gap in its ability to provide remote users with access to its national telephone network.

The U.S. circuit court reversed the district court and held that since the zoning permitted towers on more than 600 acres of township land located in three different light-industrial districts, the zoning ordinance was proper. The applicant was unable to present sufficient evidence that the ordinance effectively foreclosed not only the applicant's use, but also all use of such towers. Therefore, the township's decision did not conflict with the prohibition of the Telecommunications Act.

Community Associations Can't Control

In a related matter, towers were the subject of a Federal Communications Commission (FCC) ruling that barred an association from requiring prior review of plans for television receivers on a property in a restricted subdivision (*In re Holliday*, 14 F.C.C.R. 17167 (CSR 5399-0, DA 99-2132) (October 8, 1999)). In that matter, lot owners in a restricted single-family subdivision constructed in their backyard five masts approximately 30 feet high (about the same height as their house). They installed five television antennas and three satellite dish receivers on these masts, which provided reception for 10 television sets, nine videocassette recorders, and seven satellite receivers. (The decision does not mention how many beer coolers were installed.)

When the association tried to enforce the architectural-control covenant that prohibits structures without advance architectural approval, the owners petitioned the FCC for a declaratory ruling. The FCC trumped the association by invoking a rule that prohibits any restriction that impairs installation, maintenance, or use of TV antennas that are designed to receive video programming services. The FCC supported the owners' arguments that there was no safety or historical-preservation justification for restricting their antennas and that the association's prohibitions could not be justified on aesthetic grounds.

The decision did allow for the possibility that an association can impose proper regulations where antennas are not necessary to provide the video programming available in a viewing area. But the record did not contain any evidence to demonstrate that the applicable antennas were not necessary to carry out that function, and according to the decision, the association has the burden of proof in order to bar these structures.

Some critics of this case have pointed out that the burden of proof might have been placed on the wrong party. Why shouldn't the lot owner have the burden of proof to establish that its forest of antennas was necessary to achieve TV reception? Why was the burden placed on the association?

These cases demonstrate the ongoing tensions between federal and local control on the fast growth of communications structures throughout the country. If it had been left to the government in *Jack and the Beanstalk,* then Jack, his mother, and the giant would all still be arguing over who had to prove what in order to plant and chop down the beanstalk—and who could make the final decision.

While federal courts are reluctant to sit as zoning appeal boards, cases have acknowledged that landowners have due-process rights to be free from arbitrary and irrational zoning actions.

Irrational Request for Easement

In the U.S. Supreme Court case of *Village of Willowbrook v. Olech,* 528 U.S. 562 (2000), the court criticized a municipality for acting in an irrational and arbitrary manner, when it turned down an owner's request to connect her property to its municipal water supply. Initially, Willowbrook had conditioned the approval on receiving a 33-foot easement from Olech. Ms. Olech objected, claiming that the village required only a 15-foot easement from other property owners. After a three-month delay, the village relented and agreed to the smaller easement. But Olech then sued the village, claiming a violation of her equal protection rights. Olech alleged that the village's original demand for the larger easement was irrational and arbitrary, and resulted from an earlier lawsuit she had brought against the village on an unrelated matter.

The court held that the purpose of the equal protection clause of the Fourteenth Amendment is to secure every person against intentional and arbitrary discrimination by a state whether occasioned by express terms of a statute or by the state's improper execution of its laws through its agents. Objections could be exercised by an individual person, and need not necessarily be brought by any class or group. Justice Breyer, concurring in the result, noted that a mere faulty zoning decision would not normally raise a constitutional issue. However, in *Village of Willowbrook,* Olech had alleged that the village was acting with a vindictive motive, enough to transform the case from a run-of-the-mill zoning case into a constitutional one.

Affordable Housing Denied

In a case involving 75 acres in Stroud Township, Pennsylvania, the township stymied an affordable housing project for what were alleged to be "improper motives." See *Woodwind Estates Ltd. v. Gretkowski,* 205 F.3d 118 (3d Cir. 2000). In that case, the Pennsylvania Housing Finance Agency gave Woodwind about $1.1 million in federal low-income-housing tax credits for the purpose of building affordable housing.

In March 1996, Woodwind then sought subdivision approval in order to meet a December 1, 1997, deadline for financing. The planning commission then held a series of meetings, ultimately denying approval on grounds that the project would have to meet the more onerous and time-consuming requirements of a planned unit development. However, until a local citizens' group opposed the project, the township had taken the legal position that the plan had satisfied the less onerous criteria for approval as a subdivision. It was not until after the local citizens' group had voiced objection to the project because of its low-income character that the planning commission, following about six months of inaction, finally recommended that the board of supervisors deny approval. The board of supervisors then denied approval without any stated reason.

When the attorney for the citizens' Improper Motives group advised the board that it had to state a reason for the denial, the board issued a second denial letter based on that attorney's suggested draft. The developer then brought a civil rights action against the township and its individual officers. The Federal district court dismissed the action, but the Third Circuit Court of Appeals reversed and remanded the case for trial.

The appeals court held that a jury could reasonably find that the denial of the permit was made in bad faith or for improper motives. According to the court, those requirements were satisfied by evidence that: (1) the township had no legitimate basis for seeking information about the socioeconomic background and income levels of the prospective tenants; (2) the planning commission denied approval by adopting significant portions of a letter drafted by the attorney for the opposing citizens group; and (3) the planning commission blocked or delayed the issuance of a permit while aware that this would prevent the developer from meeting the deadline for financing the project.

The court concluded that the citizens group opposed the project because they did not want low-income residents living in their neighborhood. The court criticized the planning commission's concerns about the income level and socioeconomic background of prospective tenants, and the potential adverse economic effects the project would have on local property values. It pointed out that, "None of these concerns, however, are conditions for subdivision approval under the township's ordinance," and that developers have a due process right to be free from "arbitrary and irrational zoning actions."

To make matters worse for the township zoning officials, the court denied them personal immunity simply because they relied on the planning commission's and township solicitor's recommendation. The court held that considering the evidence in the light most favorable to the developer, the defendants could not reasonably believe that their conduct did not violate the developer's rights.

In a somewhat different approach, the Supreme Court of Texas recently supported the zoning board members' defense of official immunity. It reversed the court of appeals and held that the jury should not have considered evidence of subjective bad faith. *Ballantyne v. Champion Builders, Inc.*, 144 S.W.3d 417 (Tex. 2004).

In that case, the board had voted to revoke a permit for a small apartment building and during deliberations, some board members argued that the apartments might attract "undesirable residents" who may be loud and disruptive and commit crimes. The developer sued to recover losses suffered as a result of the delay caused by the board on the theory that individual board members should be responsible for their negligence and tortious interference with contract.

The Texas Supreme Court applied an objective standard and held that the officials' subjective intent, or possible malice, is irrelevant. According to the court, immunity should apply if a reasonably prudent official could have believed that the decision was justified.

Conclusion

These cases enforce the position that township officials cannot act as little dictators. Any indication that land use decisions are being made in bad faith or for improper motives will result in careful judicial scrutiny. If officials base decisions on unrelated matters or because neighbors simply don't like proposed projects, they may have to face the wrath of the federal courts.

PART VI

Operations and Ownership

65   LIMITED PARTNERS MAY HAVE TO REFUND DISTRIBUTIONS

Generally, limited partners in a limited partnership are insulated against liability from the partnership's creditors. In this sense they consider themselves like shareholders in a corporation. As long as they don't overreach in taking control of the business, they should be safe from the grasp of creditors when the deal goes bad.

Contractors' Claims

Limited partners who receive distributions of partnership funds, however, may become liable to the partnership's creditors. In *Henkels & McCoy, Inc. v. Adochio,* 138 F.3d 491 (3d Cir. 1998), Judge Rosenn of the U.S. Court of Appeals for the Third Circuit held that under New Jersey law, 19 limited partners were proportionately liable to an unpaid contractor of the partnership who had installed sewer systems. That case involved an "interrelated maze of corporations and partnerships devised by the limited partners and the general partner in their efforts to develop two separate real estate projects." *Id.* at 493. One of those projects was "aborted shortly after conception" and the other became the subject of the litigation by the unpaid contractor.

While some of the facts were disputed, the limited partners became liable to the extent of the distributions to them. That occurred even though they had only retrieved funds that had been invested for the abandoned project (and not for the project for which the sewers had been installed). Also, the refunds were made before the contractor's work was completed or billed; and one of the refund installments had been made even before the contractor's work was started.

The case focused on two sections of New Jersey's Uniform Limited Partnership Law (ULPL) entitled "Liability upon return of contribution." One of those sections makes limited partners liable to creditors even when those partners don't violate the partnership agreement. That liability benefits creditors who extended credit during the period the partners' contributions were held by the partnership.

The other section makes limited partners liable for partnership contributions returned to them "in violation of the partnership agreement." That liability continues for a period of six years after the partners' contributions have been wrongfully distributed to them. New Jersey ULPL § 42:2A-46(b).

After analyzing the partnership agreement at some length, Judge Rosenn concluded that the partnership had distributed the partners' investments to them in violation of the partnership agreement. He interpreted the agreement in a way that required the partnership to establish reasonable reserve funds from the partnership in order to meet partnership debts; and failure to do that triggered the liability of the limited partners. In effect, the court decided that partners should not receive back their invested funds with impunity when there was a *possibility* that a creditor would not be paid out of the remaining assets of the partnership.

In his dissenting opinion, Judge Stapleton disagreed with this interpretation. Although he acknowledged that the partnership agreement permitted the general partner to establish reasonable reserve funds from partnership income in order to provide for debt service or other payments, he concluded that there was no *requirement* under the partnership agreement to reserve these funds. He emphasized that the payments to the limited partners represented a return of their capital contribution in connection with the abandoned project in contrast with the project benefitting from the contractor's work. In addition, he pointed out that during the period when payments were made to the limited partners, the partnership had no significant liabilities of any kind and had a significant net worth over and above the potential liabilities of the partnership. Furthermore, all invoices that had been submitted by the contractor during this period had been paid in full.

Judge Stapleton concluded that the reasonable-reserve section of the partnership agreement was intended for the protection of the limited partners and not for creditors. Also, he found that even if the partnership agreement could reasonably be read to *require* a general partner to set aside funds for the creditors whenever a reasonable general partner would do so, under the actual circumstances of the case there was no basis to conclude that the general partners' reasonable business judgment would require setting aside that reserve.

While the majority opinion applied New Jersey law, the applicable sections of the ULPL have been adopted throughout the United States in one form or another. For example, Pennsylvania has the same statutory sections on limited partners' liability, except that the statute of limitations for distributions that violate the partnership agreement has been reduced from six years to four.

This rule may be compared to rules governing shareholders' liability for unlawful dividends. In Pennsylvania, shareholders may be liable to return unlawful dividends to the corporation, but the statute of limitations is only two years. See 8A P.L.E. Corporations § 224 (Suppl. 1998-1999).

Buyer's Claim

In *Hullett v. Cousin,* 32 P.3d 44 (Ariz. Ct. App. 2001), remanded on issue of statute of limitations, 63 P.3d 1029 (Ariz. 2003), a creditor of a limited partnership was able to recover distributions from the partnership to its limited partners in order to satisfy a claim against the partnership that was not even known to the limited partners at the time of the distribution.

In this case, the limited partnership had sold its only asset, an apartment project, and took back a purchase money note. It accepted a discounted payoff of the note, dissolved the partnership, and then made liquidating distributions to the limited partners. More than six years after the sale, and 14 months after the dissolution, the buyer sued the partnership and the general partner for a misrepresentation in connection with the sale. A default judgment was entered, but it proved uncollectible because both the partnership and the general partner were insolvent.

No Warning—No Day in Court

Then, almost four years after the dissolution, the buyer sued the limited partners under the state's fraudulent transfer act, arguing that the liquidating distributions were voidable as fraudulent transfers; that is, the buyer maintained that the partnership made the distributions without receiving reasonably equivalent value for them, and the partnership was insolvent at the time of, or as a result of, those distributions. The trial court granted summary judgment to the limited partners, but the appellate court reversed the decision, with directions to grant summary judgment to the buyer.

From the limited partners' perspective, one of the most disturbing aspects of the case was that the claimant had not asserted its claim at the time of the distributions, and none of the partners had knowledge of the claim at that time! Despite that, the claim was taken into account as a partnership debt for purposes of determining the insolvency.

What seems even more draconian is that the buyer's claim was never put to the test of proof, or for that matter, the test of whether the statute of limitations had expired. Under the circumstances, no one ever contested the validity of the claim in court. The limited partners were not named as defendants in that suit, so they were not even served. The general partner was insolvent at the time the partnership was sued, so it didn't answer the complaint, and therefore the claimant was granted a $500,000 default judgment. It appears that the limited partners never had their day in court to argue the merits of the claim.

Clawing Back Distributions

The decision to claw back the distributions from the limited partners is not surprising in light of the Arizona Fraudulent Transfer Act and the Arizona Limited Partnership Act. The court cited the Arizona version of RULPA, Section 607, which essentially states that a distribution of partnership assets can't be made to the extent that, as a result of, or at the time of the distribution, the partnership remains or becomes insolvent.

Other states, in applying their statutes, may not have been so harsh on the limited partners. For example, unlike RULPA and many other states' limited partnership acts, the Delaware Limited Partnership Act not only takes into account the knowledge of the limited partners, but also expressly states that there is no liability for a wrongful distribution if the limited partner did not know that the distribution was wrongful. This seems to be contrary to the applicable Delaware Fraudulent Transfer Act, and the Arizona court's interpretation of that act. It is not clear how a Delaware court would resolve that conflict.

The result is not surprising in light of provisions in many state statutes that have been passed by legislatures to protect unpaid creditors against liquidating distributions to limited partners and corporate shareholders. For example, when a corporation in Pennsylvania is liquidated, it must make provisions for payment of all creditors, and, if it does not, the shareholders who receive the distributions may be liable to the extent of those payments.

Preparing Limited Partners

Some lawyers have attempted to protect partners and shareholders against these types of claw-backs in liquidating distributions by using staggered or "step" transactions. They sometimes will attempt to avoid a "liquidating distribution" by having the entity distribute most of the assets as profits at the time the property is sold. They then hold some of the assets back and postpone liquidation until a later date, at which time they distribute the remaining cash. In that way, the third-party claim may be limited to the remaining assets that were distributed.

Too little thought is given to the way partnership distributions are handled. The *Hullett* case underlines the importance of properly planning for those types of distributions, as well as the importance of preparing the partners for the possibility that they may have to return some or all of the money they have received.

Conclusion

The cases discussed above should serve as a warning to limited partners who receive distributions from their partners that their liability may not be as limited as they think. Also, lenders and other creditors of a failed limited partnership should be alerted that they may reach out beyond partnership assets and proceed against the limited partners' assets to the extent of their distributions.